THE
SPY WHO
CHANGED
HISTORY

SVETLANA
LOKHOVA

The Untold Story of How the Soviet Union Won
the Race for America's Top Secrets

**WILLIAM
COLLINS**

William Collins
An imprint of HarperCollins*Publishers*
1 London Bridge Street
London SE1 9GF

WilliamCollinsBooks.com

First published in Great Britain in 2018 by William Collins
This William Collins paperback edition published in 2019

1

A catalogue record for this book is available from the British Library

ISBN 978-0-00-823814-8

Maps by Martin Brown

All photographs are from the author's private collection or are in the public domain, except for:
pp. 3, 59 and 378, RGASPI; p. 73, G. I. Kasabova, *O vremeni, o Noril'ske, o sebe* . . . [Of the Times,
Of Norilsk, Of Myself . . .], Moscow: PoliMedia, 2001; p. 114, Belorussian State Archive; p. 160,
Krasnaya kniga VChK [Red Book of the VChK]; p. 186, courtesy Bennett Family Archive; p. 229,
in N. S. Babayev and Yu. S. Ustinov, *Kavalery Zolotykh zvozd: Voyenachal'niki. Uchonyye. Konstruktory.
Lidery*, Moscow: Patriot, 2001; p. 275, mil.ru (CC BY 4.0); p. 422, Sputnik Images. While every
effort has been made to trace owners of copyright material reproduced herein, the publishers will
be glad to rectify any omissions in future editions.

Set in Bembo by Palimpsest Book Production Ltd, Falkirk, Stirlingshire

Printed and bound by CPI Group (UK) Ltd, Croydon CR0 4YY

MIX
Paper from
responsible sources
FSC™ C007454

To my father for his unending love, help and support.

Train up a child in the way he should go: and when he is old, he will not depart from it.

Proverbs 22:6

CONTENTS

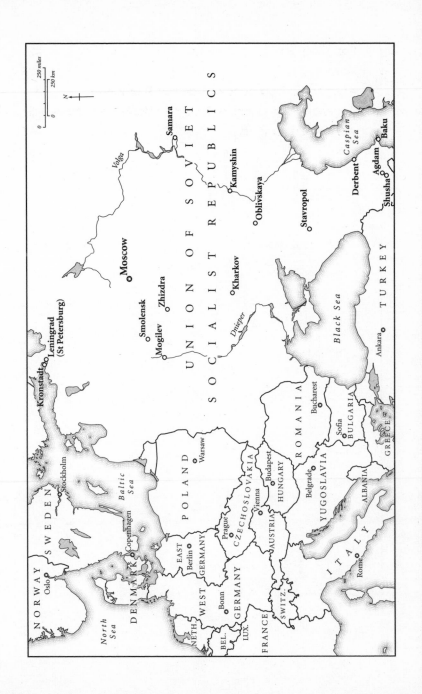

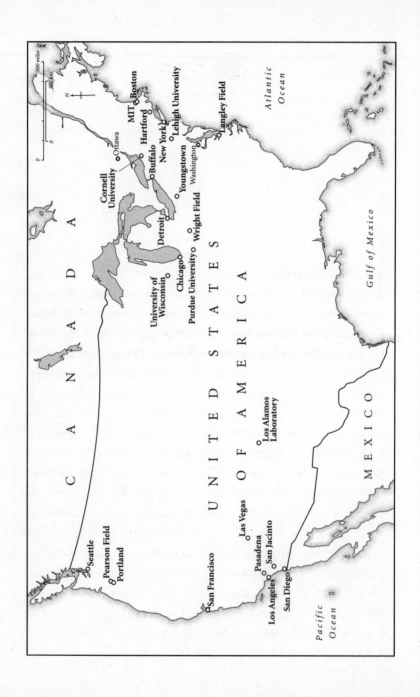

PREFACE

In 1931, Joseph Stalin announced, 'We are fifty or a hundred years behind the advanced countries. We must catch up in ten years. Either we do it, or they will crush us'.[1] These words began a race to close the yawning technology gap between the Soviet Union and the leading capitalist countries. The prize at stake was nothing less than the survival of the USSR. Believing that fleets of enemy bombers spraying poison gas would soon appear in the undefended skies over Russia's cities, and amid predictions that millions would die from inhaling the deadly toxins, Stalin sent two intelligence officers – an aviation expert and a chemical weapons specialist – on a mission to the Massachusetts Institute of Technology. He ordered them to gather the secrets of this centre of aeronautics and chemical weapon research and bring them back to the Soviet Union, along with the means to defend his population against the new terror weapons of modern warfare.

The results of this mission would change the tide of history and lead the KGB to acknowledge that after this first operation 'the West was a constant and irreplaceable source of acquiring new technologies' for the USSR.[2] After 1931, the Soviets would use scientific and technological intelligence, particularly in the field of aviation, to protect itself against its enemies, culminating in the defeat of Nazi Germany and, thanks to later espionage, helping tilt the global balance of power into an uneasy equilibrium. While both sides possessed weapons of equally massive destructive power, the Cold War did not become a hot war.

Ironically, America was the source of both sides' nuclear armouries. US agencies later termed the haemorrhage of sophisticated technology to the USSR as 'piracy' and tried unsuccessfully to staunch the flow of secrets. In the Soviet Union, the savings resulting from this technical espionage would eventually total hundreds of millions of dollars and be included in official state defence and economic planning.

The experts in the 1930s were half right in their predictions about the future of warfare. By 1945 a nation's power was determined by the strength of its strategic bombing capability. But the invulnerable high-altitude aircraft were not armed with poison gas. They carried a weapon of far greater destructive power: the atomic bomb. Undreamed of in 1931, this terrifying new device would prove devastatingly more potent a killer than poison gas. In 1945 a single bomb dropped from one plane killed over a hundred thousand people, and one country held a monopoly on this power: the United States.

Yet within four years the Soviets had built their own bomb, joining the US as one of the world's two superpowers. This pre-eminence would have been unimaginable a quarter of a century previously, when Stalin and Felix Dzerzhinsky sat down to plan the reconstruction of a fragile, illiterate nation reeling from war and successive revolutions. It would be achieved through the sacrifice of millions of lives, lost during the terrible famines that attended collectivisation and on the blood-soaked battlefields of the Eastern Front.

In 1931 a small number of Soviet secret agents infiltrated America to live their lives in the shadows. This is the story of how that long mission first began and how the prestigious Massachusetts Institute of Technology became the greatest, if unwitting, finishing school for Soviet spies – the alma mater of intelligence officers more talented and remarkable than the Cambridge Five traitors Philby, Burgess, Maclean et al. Without the fruits of the spies' work – the astounding number of technological and scientific secrets they smuggled out – it is hard to believe that the USSR would have prevailed against Nazi Germany or taken its place at the world's top table.

The stream of intelligence helped prepare the Soviet Union's armed forces and ready its industrial base for the trials of the Second World War and the Cold War. Across the battlefields of the Eastern Front and in its factories far behind the front lines, the USSR was able to grind Hitler's previously invincible legions into dust. Defying all expectations, the 'backward' Soviet Union mass-produced more planes, tanks and guns than the invading Germans. The secret to crushing the Nazis was stolen American know-how.

By 1942, Stalin was looking beyond the defeat of Hitler and planning for the future defence of the Soviet Union. He sought to overtake his erstwhile Western allies on their home ground, technology. Spreading his net across both sides of the Atlantic in the first coordinated intercontinental espionage gathering operation in history, Stalin's spies would break the US's monopoly on the atomic bomb and the high-altitude bomber. These two astonishing technical achievements were completed in four years, less than half the time expected by the Americans.

The US's global supremacy stemmed from its leadership in science and innovation. Its education system was the brain factory, at the centre of which lay its technical universities. Its economic success was founded on unrivalled techniques of quality mass production, the speed at which it transferred innovation from research centres to factory floors and on mass consumerism. In the 1940s, America's factories outproduced the world both in terms of quality and quantity. Yet US defence policy relied on the technological sophistication and superiority of the weapons in its armoury, not the number of boots the army could deploy on the ground. In the late 1930s that superior weapon was believed to be the unerringly accurate Norden bomb sight. By the mid 1940s it would be the A-bomb.

The start of the Soviets' long science and technology (S&T) mission to the US has remained unknown for over eighty years owing to the desire of Russian and US security services to keep their secrets. My sources include previously undiscovered Soviet-era documents that tell the story of the greatest triumph of Stalin's secret services. As well as how they did it, this book reveals that Soviet intelligence began penetrating the United States 'to catch up and overtake America' not to undermine its system of government. The Soviets sought to learn from scientists and entrepreneurs how to industrialise the American way. To surpass the US, they needed to 'combine American business quality with German attention to detail all on a Russian scale'.[3]

Over the next five decades the Soviet S&T mission would evolve in its goals, intensity, scale and success, but the main task would be the US, 'the most advanced country in S&T',[4] and the initial scientist-spies of the first operation would form the model. The mission's high points were the penetration of the Manhattan Project and the building of the Tu-4 bomber. The first spies would be followed in the 1980s by trained 'agents [who] were: Doctors of Science, qualified engineers specialising in atomic energy, radio electronics, aviation, chemistry, radars [focusing on] "brain centres": scientific research institutes, universities, scientific societies'.[5] These were the same targets that had been identified by the very first spy, Stanislav Shumovsky, in 1931. The skills that came naturally to him and those he learned on the job would form the basis of an entire KGB programme to train its brightest scientists for missions in the US.

This is the life story of the remarkable Stanislav Shumovsky, a man who changed history. As a young man, he served as a soldier. Against the odds he helped fight off the world's great powers who sought to strangle Communism in the cradle. When unfit to fight, he used science and technology to transform the Soviet Union from a land with a few imported aircraft to an aviation superpower and an unlikely victor in the Second World War.

Shumovsky was probably the most successful and audacious aviation spy in Soviet history. Appropriately codenamed BLÉRIOT after the legendary French aviator, he provided the USSR with the means to build a modern strategic bomber, which was commissioned to carry the atomic bomb. Among his other notable successes while operating in America during the 1930s, Shumovsky escorted one of the world's greatest aircraft designers, Andrey Tupolev, around dozens of key US aviation plants, research centres and universities. Along the way Shumovsky recruited as agents a generation of Americans working in the aviation industry (some from his own class at MIT) and filmed inside top-secret US defence plants. A master of public relations, he gave newspaper interviews and posed for photographs, hiding his activities in plain sight for years.

His model for the Soviet scientist-spy formed the key innovation in S&T espionage. Shumovsky would always consider himself an engineer capable of discussing aviation as an equal with the world's leading experts of the time. He persuaded the NKVD to finance the education of several American recruits by paying their fees at a top university. This is the first evidence of Soviet intelligence investing in young individuals who would prove useful sources in later life. Shumovsky also vouched for and mentored four NKVD officers who enrolled at MIT to learn the skills necessary to continue acquiring technological secrets. The training enabled his protégés to secure the greatest prize of all, the atomic bomb. By 1944, the best Soviet assets of Operation ENORMOZ (their penetration of the Manhattan Project) on both sides of the Atlantic had all been recruited or were run by Shumovsky's MIT alumni. Of the eighteen Soviet intelligence officers who worked on obtaining the secrets of the atomic bomb, the most senior were graduates of US universities.

Today, Shumovsky's photograph deservedly hangs in the SVR (Russian Foreign Intelligence Service) Hall of Fame. In Washington and Moscow, the details of his career are still officially classified. Another photograph, taken in 1982 (see page 422), shows Professor Shumovsky in old age at home. Behind him, on a shelf in a glass cabinet filled with books, is a second photo, evidently a precious memento. It is the picture of a younger Stanislav in his MIT graduation gown, taken in the summer of 1934 on the lawns outside the Institute's Building 10. The older, relaxed Professor Shumovsky can for the first time perhaps afford a broad smile in a photograph. He stares proudly at the camera, no doubt recalling how he achieved what Stalin had ordered of him all those years before: to provide the crucial information needed for his country's survival.

To catch up and overtake America is no longer a Russian goal. Others now follow the trail trodden by the Soviets in the 1930s. Today, selling American education abroad is big business. Over a million foreign students are currently enrolled at US universities, around 5 per cent of the total. Disproportionately around a third of those take courses in science, computer technology, engineering and mathematics (STEM). A third of foreign students are Chinese who, according to a 2017 report in the *New York Times*, contribute an estimated $11.4 billion to the US economy. The advantage to America is that foreign students generally pay full price for their education, subsidising domestic students. Graduates from STEM fields are projected to play a key role in future US economic growth. There is a concern that with so many places taken up by foreign students there may not be enough domestic STEM graduates to meet future job demand. Another is that Chinese and Indian graduates will use their new skills to erode America's treasured technological superiority. On 14 February 2018, Christopher Wray, head of the FBI, told Congress that 'Chinese intelligence operatives are littered across US universities, possibly to obtain information in fields like technology. Schools have little understanding of this major predicament.' Wray warned 'the level of naivety on the part of the academic sector about this creates its own issues . . . They're exploiting the very open research and development environment that we have, which we all revere. But they're taking advantage of it.' America remains trapped in a dilemma of fear and greed.

Books that focus on the history of Soviet espionage in the United States and its English-speaking allies often share a troubling Anglo-centric tradition characterised by a reluctance to embrace new non-English sources, in particular those that challenge established narratives. A dearth of Russian-speaking historians is only partly to blame for this continuing problem. The study of Soviet intelligence has been shaped predominantly by the reliance on a few Western primary sources or accounts by journalists and Soviet defectors. Little regard has been given to the inherent bias in this material. For example, the first-hand accounts from former Soviet collaborators-turned-informers such as Harry Gold, Elizabeth Bentley and Boris Morros were unreliable, self-serving and hence problematic. The National Security Agency's Venona Project that decoded intercepts of Soviet telegrams was considered unreliable as a sole source of identification as long ago as May 1950. The FBI itself recognised how hard it is to identify agents categorically. Even when Soviet sources became widely available after the collapse of the USSR the new material was used only to support established narratives, and documents that did not fit have been largely ignored.

How I found the new material is a story in itself. From the first clue in a declassified NKVD interrogation protocol of 1935, I followed a trail of evidence. That document suggested that in 1931 Soviet Military Intelligence was sending agents on espionage missions to MIT. By verifying this nugget of information through university records and public documents, I was able to uncover the whole story. This book first and foremost lets the new documents speak, and approaches the subject from the perspective of Soviet intelligence officers. This is not the traditional witch hunt to find long-dead traitors who betrayed their country for ideology or money in the 1930s or 1940s. On the contrary, this book looks at a few individuals whose lives were dedicated to the belief that they were making society better. History may have shown their vision of the world to be idealistic but nonetheless they strove hard to ensure that the Soviet Union and its hundreds of millions of people were at least somewhat prepared to fight off the scourge of the Nazis. For that, we should be grateful.

Among the many surprises and revelations in this book are the identification of a number of new Soviet spies on previously unknown operations. The findings establish that significant penetration of the US started a decade earlier than many previously believed. In addition, the involvement of major US figures in Soviet espionage began far sooner than has been made public before, with for example Earl Browder and Nathan Silvermaster active many years earlier than previously thought.

Women play a strong and full role in these early intelligence operations out in the field. In a profession dominated by men these women are not playing the traditional support roles of honey traps, such as Mata Hari. Ray (Raisa) Bennett and Gertrude Klivans are refreshingly modern young women who from an early age knew their own minds. We are privileged to hear their voices through their own words. Both were no shrinking violets but followed their own independent paths in life. Raisa Bennett had to juggle the responsibilities of being a Soviet Military Intelligence officer on a dangerous mission abroad while also mother to a young child. Gertrude Klivans had plenty of opinions and plenty of men, all the while training the future top spies how to be American.

Of historical significance is the story of Military Intelligence officer Mikhail Cherniavsky. At the time, his assassination plot attracted the close attention of the intelligence services and political elite. Only two pieces of intelligence were ever underlined by the NKVD and one was the revelation from a source in Boston of a growing Trotskyist opposition in Moscow linked to an international revolutionary movement. Cherniavsky was the ringleader of a plot to kill Stalin and replace him with Trotsky. It was Cherniavsky's bullets that Stalin referred to in his speech to the Graduates of the Red Army Academies delivered in the Kremlin on 4 May 1935:

> But these comrades did not always confine themselves to criticism and passive resistance. They threatened to raise a revolt in the Party against the Central Committee. More, they threatened some of us with bullets. Evidently, they reckoned on frightening us and compelling us to turn from the Leninist road.

Finally, through my research for this book I was delighted to lay to rest one ghost. I uncovered the life and intelligence career of Ray Bennett, the first American to serve as a Soviet Military Intelligence officer in the United States. Eighty years ago, Ray vanished from her young daughter's life. Joy Bennett ran into Ray's bedroom, as she did every morning, to discover her mother had disappeared. In 2017 I was able to explain to Joy her mother's career and the reason behind her arrest and eventual disappearance. Joy kindly described my work as 'sacred'.

During the period of history that this book covers the Russian secret services organisations changed their names many times, and for the sake of simplicity (and despite this being historically inaccurate), I have called them the NKVD or Military Intelligence throughout the book. To avoid confusing the reader further, Russian names are spelled using 'y' for 'i', so for example 'Andrey' not 'Andrei', and I have used 'Y' at the start of certain names, such as 'Yershov' not 'Ershov'.

INTRODUCTION

On the hot summer's day of Sunday, 3 August 1947, a large crowd of Muscovites gathered at Tushino airfield for Aviation Day.[1] From early morning they had made their way in their thousands to secure a grassy bank as a vantage point from which to watch the aerobatics and parachute jumps. They waited expectantly to cheer and applaud the heroic pilots, set to perform dizzying barrel rolls and stomach-turning loops.

The stars of the show were a new generation of military aircraft. The message that Soviet leader Joseph Stalin sent to his people and the watching world that day was clear: the Cold War had begun in earnest and his air force was equipped to respond to any threat. In the words of the rousing 'March of the Soviet Aviators',[2] which was constantly played:

> Our keen sight is piercing every atom,
> Our every nerve in determination dressed

And trust us, to all enemy ultimatums
Our Air Fleet will give a quick response.★

On the VIP balcony, to the left of the grey-haired Stalin in his generalissimo's uniform, stood a galaxy of Soviet aircraft designers – Alexander Yakovlev, Semyon Lavochkin, Sergey Ilyushin, Pavel Sukhoy, Artem Mikoyan, Mikhail Gurevich,† and the greatest of them all, Andrey Tupolev – who had given their names to a series of iconic military planes. As befitted a day dedicated to celebrating the country's air force, each man was resplendent in uniforms decorated by rows of gleaming medals.

Standing alongside the diminutive aircraft designer Tupolev was the far taller figure of Colonel Stanislav Shumovsky, a graduate of the Massachusetts Institute of Technology (MIT). The affable, bespectacled Shumovsky was Tupolev's friend and longterm collaborator; perhaps more significantly, he was also the most successful aviation spy in history. His latest intelligence coup, which he was still celebrating, had been to bring all of defeated Nazi Germany's advanced jet and rocket technology

---

★ The march was composed as a response to the Curzon Ultimatum. The British government threatened the Soviet Union with the end of their diplomatic and trade relationship. The Soviets anticipated that the next British step would be a resumption of military action. Despite being in no position to resist the demands, the Russians rejected them robustly.

† Yakovlev designed the YAK series of fighters. Lavochkin designed the La-5 and La-7 fighters; the top Allied ace of the Second World War, Ivan Kozhedub, shot down sixty-two German aircraft flying Lavs. Ilyushin was a bomber designer whose Il-2 ground attack aircraft, of which 36,183 were made, was the single most-produced combat aircraft design in history. Sukhoy was among the first Soviet designers of jet aircraft. Mikoyan and Gurevich were the brains behind the famous MiG design bureau.

back to the Soviet Union.[3] But he had enjoyed his most significant successes in the USA, where he had operated with impunity since his arrival at college in 1931.

Colonel Shumovsky in air force uniform

Shumovsky pointed out to the stocky Tupolev the faces of the foreign military attachés, who were standing in a separate enclosure. The observers expected to see a parade of prototype jet fighters scream across the sky. The Russians' plan was to enjoy watching the faces of the American military observers behind their gleaming sunglasses.[4] Little did the foreigners know that Tupolev had one major surprise up his sleeve. For the last two years, at the behest of Stalin, he had worked day and night on the Leader's pet secret project. Uncle Joe, with his flair for combining politics with a flamboyant brand of showmanship, wanted to send a clear message that would have military men in Washington, London, Paris and beyond choking on their tea, and reaching in panic for something far stronger. Thanks to Tupolev's unceasing, bone-shattering effort, that message was about to be delivered.

After the national anthem and a massive artillery salute, the crowd stood to watch the planes, shielding their eyes with their hands or using binoculars. From the distance, they could hear a faint hum that grew ever louder. Three dots emerged from the patchy clouds, becoming recognisable as giant planes. These were something new from Tupolev, his gift for the Red air force: a four-engined strategic bomber, the Tu-4. Despite the bright red stars on the planes' tails, the foreign military attachés thought at first this was a simple publicity stunt. Surely the three Tu-4s were just recycled US B-29 Superfortresses? In 1945, three B-29s had made emergency landings in the Soviet Far East while conducting bombing missions against imperial Japan. Perhaps the Soviets, who the military attachés assembled here knew were incapable of producing a high-altitude strategic bomber, had just patched up some American planes with a slick paint job?

Then another dot appeared. It was the Tu-70, a Tupolev-designed passenger version of the Tu-4, and its presence demonstrated that the Soviets were now somehow able to mass-produce their own strategic bomber fleet. Tupolev and Shumovsky glanced over at the American observers, who now looked aghast, deafened by the roar of the colossal aircraft flying above. For them, and indeed for every other Westerner present, it was manifestly clear that the global balance of power had shifted irrevocably to the Reds. Every inch of their territory – the capital cities and industrial heartlands which had long been considered safe from Soviet counter-attack – was now within reach of its modern heavy bomber fleet. This was a crisis. Now all the Soviets needed was the atomic bomb.

. . .

Two years later, on 29 August 1949, at Semipalatinsk in the Kazakh Soviet Republic, Russian scientists detonated 'First Lightning',★ their atomic bomb. The FBI started a massive, frantic investigation to find how out the 'backward' Soviet Union could possibly have accomplished this scientific feat.[5]

One line of enquiry led the Bureau to search for a shadowy figure they codenamed FRED, a Soviet espionage controller with links to the heart of the atomic programme. For a while, the FBI suspected that FRED was Stanislav Shumovsky.[6] Based on information from an informant named Harry Gold, they made the correct assumption that the linchpin in the atomic plot was an alumnus of one of the United States' finest universities, the Massachusetts Institute of Technology. But FRED was not Shumovsky. Stanislav had left the United States long before his aviation espionage exploits were exposed to the FBI. Despite turning over every stone, the Bureau never understood that Shumovsky was just one of many top Soviet spies, all alumni of

---

★ The plutonium device was a copy of 'Fat Man', the bomb dropped on the Japanese city of Nagasaki. It was detonated ahead of a Soviet-designed bomb as the model was reliable.

MIT, and part of an operation that had been up and running for nearly two decades. This is Shumovsky's story, which the FBI, with all their resources, failed to uncover.

• • •

The first leaders of the Soviet Union Vladimir Lenin and his successor Stalin had always felt threatened by the stronger and technologically superior forces that surrounded their new state. For its security, the Soviet government knew it needed to close the technology gap with those powers it considered potentially hostile, which was virtually everyone. Luckily for the Soviet Union, the nations they perceived as enemies had a flaw. Western countries never understood the value to the USSR of the knowledge and technology they were prepared to trade, teach or simply give away. In particular, Stalin took the decision as early as 1928 to rely on American manufacturers as the Soviet Union's main supplier of aviation technology.[7]

On Stalin's orders, seventy-five Soviet students, including Shumovsky (NKVD codename BLÉRIOT)[8] slipped almost unnoticed into the United States during the hot summer of 1931.[9] They did not tell the Americans welcoming them to their country that several of the students were also intelligence officers. Stanislav Shumovsky, the first super-spy, was in the vanguard of a mission that by its conclusion had achieved the systematic theft of a large quantity of the US's scientific and technological secrets – including its most prized of all, the Manhattan Project. But until now, the audacity of the scheme has not been understood or appreciated by the American public, the universities or even the FBI. The mission was distinguished by its daring – Shumovsky would openly film inside America's most secret sites while wearing his full Red Army uniform;[10] its scale – the volume of secrets plundered dwarfs the impact of Cambridge University's 'Magnificent Five' traitors;* and its success – with the fruits of the operation, Stalin was able to bridge the technological gap between the USSR and the USA, equip his air force with a strategic bomber capable of reaching Chicago or Los Angeles, and arm his country with its own nuclear weapons.

'Stan',[11] as Shumovsky styled himself during his years in the United States, never shot a man in cold blood, never jumped from a burning building (although he was not immune to moments of James Bond-like indiscretion with women).[12] Instead, the charismatic, charming and fearsomely clever Soviet intelligence officer cultivated an extrovert image that helped him obscure the cloak-and-dagger work he was conducting. The scheme was simplicity itself. While on campus, Stan's role was to spot American scientists working in areas of interest to the Soviet Union, approach them on a personal level for co-operation, and subsequently collect information from them. Shumovsky would eventually acquire US secrets on everything from strategic bombers to night fighters, radar guidance to jet engines.[13] Each acquisition saved decades' worth of research and millions of dollars of investment – he secured them for his country at almost no cost.

During his mission, Shumovsky would build a network of

---

* The five spies were Kim Philby, Guy Burgess, Donald Maclean, Anthony Blunt and John Cairncross, all of whom attended Cambridge University. 'Magnificent Five' is the Soviet term.

contacts and agents in factories and research institutes across the USA. Undiscovered for fifteen years,* he masterminded the systematic acquisition of every aviation secret US industry had to offer. Uniquely, he worked hand in hand with top aircraft designers and test pilots. Designer Andrey Tupolev, one of the world's greatest experts in 'reverse-engineering' (the dismantling and duplication of technology), would present Shumovsky with a 'shopping list' of information he needed to solve specific technical issues. What sets Shumovsky's career apart from those of other intelligence operatives is that he went further than merely gathering information. As talented a scientist as he was a spy, on his return to Russia he established a research institute to analyse and exploit the secrets his network gathered in America and elsewhere.[14]

•   •   •

If the trail-blazer Shumovsky had not discovered the usefulness of an MIT education, there would have been no Ethel and Julius Rosenberg, no Klaus Fuchs;† the world we know today would be a very different place. To an extent that has never been acknowledged before, the Soviet Union's survival during the

---

* There is one report that US Naval Intelligence made enquiries about his activities in 1940. However, it was not until July 1958 that the FBI tipped off the State Department that Shumovsky had operated as a spy in the US during the Second World War.

† The Rosenbergs were the only Americans executed for espionage in the Cold War; Klaus Fuchs, a naturalised British scientist who worked at Los Alamos, was a German-born Communist who spied for the Russians on both the US and later the British atomic projects.

Second World War was underpinned by the technological and manufacturing secrets, plundered from US universities and factories, that enabled the development and mass manufacture of the aircraft and tanks needed to defeat the Third Reich.

Yet Shumovsky is virtually unknown outside Russian intelligence circles. His service records remain classified. Paradoxically, it is his very obscurity that demonstrates most comprehensively his success: we inevitably know most about the spies who were caught or turned traitor. In 2002, on the centenary of his birth, Shumovsky's biography was published in Russia by MFTI (the Moscow Institute of Physics and Technology), the university that he helped found in 1946. It celebrated his life and achievements as a scientist and educator.[15] But there was a thorny problem to skate around: how to explain in an article that the founder of this prestigious place of learning was one of Russia's greatest spies. The Institute admitted they had few biographical details of Shumovsky's earlier career to rely on as he had worked there later in his life. Yet the *Journal of Applied Mathematics and Technical Physics* was able to publish a very warm but anonymously authored biographical sketch of him. Out of respect, and from a desire for completeness, the Institute turned to an unusual source for more information. As the *Journal* stated euphemistically, 'for reasons which, on the basis of the text, we can only guess at, the authors have concealed their names under the collective pseudonym "Colleagues and numerous scientific school pupils of S. A. Shumovsky".'[16] The contributors were in fact his friends and colleagues from the intelligence service, who had access to Shumovsky's still-classified personnel file. To remove all doubt as to their identity, the anonymous contributors added a footnote to the article that says: 'It is no coincidence that the portrait of

Stanislav Antonovich Shumovsky was placed in the "Hall of Fame" Memorial Museum of the SVR [Foreign Intelligence Service] at Yasenevo.'[17]

Only the employees of the Russian secret service are allowed inside the Hall of Fame. This is as close as Shumovsky has ever come to an official recognition by Moscow of his achievements as a spy.★

Stanislav Shumovsky is known rightly as one of the fathers of Russian aviation. This is the first full account of the unusual and surprising methods that he used to achieve his personal dreams and the goals of the Soviet Union.

★ The author approached the SVR, Russia's foreign intelligence service, and the FSB, its domestic security service, for information about Shumovsky's career; both declined to cooperate with the writing of this book.

1

'SON OF THE WORKING PEOPLE'*

Joining an exhilarated crowd heading back to Moscow from Tushino airfield and thrilled by the successful parade of new Soviet air power, Stanislav Shumovsky reflected on his extraordinary life. His mind drifted to the very first time he had seen a man fly, in his home city of Kharkov where he had stood as an eight-year-old in another large crowd, gripping his father's hand tightly with excitement. It was the summer of 1910 and, just like the rest of the vast Russian Empire, the young Shumovsky had caught aviation fever.

A year before, Shumovsky had clipped from the newspaper a picture of his lifetime hero, the French aviator Louis Blériot, taken after his epic flight across the English Channel.† The news announced an era of daring long-distance flight. For the sprawling Romanov domain, now covering over a sixth of the world's land

---

* Taken from the Red Army oath of loyalty, sworn by each new recruit.
† It was to the chagrin of the British *Daily Mail* that a Frenchman was the winner of the £1,000 prize offered by the newspaper to the first man to fly across the English Channel.

surface from the frontiers of Europe to the Far East, powered flight opened a world of new possibilities. Shumovsky also saved a newspaper clipping from the same year of the now-forgotten Dutchman who had been the first to pilot a flimsy plane from Russian soil. Unfortunately, he managed just a few hundred yards, but even this meagre feat enraptured the nation. The next summer, Shumovsky's clippings book bulged with articles showing, to the delight of vast crowds, intrepid Russians* climbing aboard imported aircraft to ascend a short, noisy distance into the sky. Everyone, but especially Shumovsky, wanted to see with their own eyes these miraculous machines and the heroes who flew them. Now, finally, it was Kharkov's turn. Determined not to miss the event, Shumovsky had made his father promise weeks before that they would go together.

The day was set to become a landmark event in his life. For the last week, the local newspapers had been posting on the boards outside their offices stories designed to whip up excitement to see the new triumph of science. A French-designed, but Russian-built Farman IV had finally come to town. The early plane with its many wings looked to the sceptical eyes of the crowd more like an oversized kite, yet somehow the wheezy engine of this ungainly, flimsy jumble of pine, fabric and wire was capable of propelling the pilot and his nervous passenger into the sky. The crowd held its breath and after an uneven and uncomfortable take-off, the plane lifted from the ground, then

---

* Mikhail Yefimov, on 21 March 1910 in Odessa, then the centre of Russian aviation, was the first Russian to fly. However, a Russian naval officer, Alexander Mozhaysky, had flown a monoplane powered by two steam engines 20–30 m near Krasnoye Selo in 1884. A ramp was needed for the take-off.

turned slowly to the left to circle the field before attempting an even bumpier landing. Shumovsky pulled at his father's hand to be allowed to join those chasing after the landing aircraft, eager to congratulate the pilot and his passenger, and to see up close this conqueror of gravity. The flight had lasted only a few minutes but its impact on Shumovsky was to last a lifetime. It fired a passion for aviation: he wanted to become a pilot.

Stanislav Shumovsky was born on 9 May 1902,[1] the eldest of four sons of Adam Vikentevich Shumovsky and his wife, Amalia Fominichna (*née* Kaminskaya). His parents were not ethnic Russians but Poles. The family treasured their traditions, practising Catholicism and speaking Polish at home.[2] Shumovsky belonged to an old noble family dedicated to public service. According to family legend, the Shumovskys had moved to Poland from Lithuania about six hundred years before with the conquering King Jagiello.[3] The Polish government commissioned a statue of this long-forgotten king for their display at the 1939 New York World's Fair.* (The prize-winning Soviet stand, adorned with statues of Lenin and Stalin, in contrast boasted a full-scale model of a Moscow metro station.)[4] Since the family move, successive generations of Shumovskys had valiantly served first the Commonwealth of Poland and Lithuania and now the twin-headed Russian eagle.[5]

Shumovsky's father was an accountant and bank official working for the Tsar's State Treasury in the thriving commercial city of Kharkov. His mother Amalia was born a noble. Her own father was the manager of the large estates of the noted Polish Prince Roman Damian Sanguszko in nearby Volyn

---

* The statue now resides in Central Park, New York City.

province. Amalia was a talented pianist[6] and ensured her boys spoke French and German.[7] As was expected among the tiny professional class of the time, family life revolved around musical and literary evenings where their mother would showcase her talent. The youngest of the Shumovsky boys, Theodore, recalled a vivid memory of their genteel, comfortable life. He described in his autobiography (appropriately, as events turned out, entitled *The Light from the East*) 'a large room with two windows; in the space between the windows stood a piano, that my mother plays. Her face, framed by her wavy black hair and her eyes focused far away, as always happens, when one surrenders to music.'[8] Theodore grew up to become a dissident academic and today is celebrated in Russia while his elder brother Stanislav, who devoted his entire life to building the Soviet Union, is almost forgotten.★

As a member of the gentry, Shumovsky's father Adam was entitled to patronage. For his four sons that privilege meant they could attend the *Gymnasium* in Kharkov.[9] Its curriculum encompassed a view of the world that included modern science, Shumovsky's passion. Less fortunate children growing up in the city at the same time managed, like the overwhelming majority of the Emperor's 125 million subjects, perhaps three brief years in a church charity school[10] where the priests reinforced the principles of autocracy, unquestioning loyalty to God and His representative on earth, the Tsar. At Shumovsky's school, the

---

★ Theodore was first imprisoned in 1938 for anti-Soviet activities along with the son of the legendary Russian poet Anna Akhmatova. He continued his protests throughout his life. Theodore was the first to translate the Qur'an into Russian.

teachers explaining the miracle of powered flight only increased his desire to see the sight for himself.

The annual International Trade Fair was the one time of year when the inventions and curiosities of the world were brought to the excited citizens of Kharkov. Like the country, the city was in the midst of massive social transformation. Kharkov was proud of its place at the forefront of developments and firmly part of a new Russia. Like its rival, the then capital city of St Petersburg, it was a window through which Russia looked to the West, to Europe. In contrast with provincial Moscow and Kiev, which were far more traditional, religious and backward, Kharkov embraced progressive thought and modern inventions. Blessed with a wealth of natural resources such as coal, iron ore and grain, the city was newly affluent. Sitting in the centre of the rich black soil of the Ukrainian plains and with an enormous new railway station, Kharkov was the leading transport hub and undisputed commercial centre of southern Russia. Shumovsky's father's job was to help regulate the numerous private sector banks that financed the ever-growing agricultural and mining enterprises. The city was a hive of steel-making and coal-mining, the epicentre of Russia's Industrial Revolution. Almost 300 automobiles jostled to drive along the few paved roads, past the horse-drawn taxis and slow-moving peasant carts.[11]

It should have been a wealthy and happy place. It wasn't; indeed, it was impossible to live in the sprawling city and remain unmoved by the inequality and social division which were the result of its rapid economic expansion. Shumovsky saw the evidence each day on his way to school as he passed the dispossessed peasants sleeping rough on the street. While Kharkov's grain found its way to the hungry cities of Western Europe, few enjoyed the profits that trickled back. The arrival of modern factories, steelworks and locomotive manufacturers had brought home to the city the issues and problems associated with Russia's rapid industrialisation. Government policy had been to finance this enormous investment through heavy taxes on peasants, forcing millions to work unwillingly in towns. Armed police, Cossacks and the army ruthlessly suppressed the many protests. Each spring thousands wandered hungrily into the city, vainly searching for a way to improve their lot and the lives of their families back in their home villages. These new peasant workers trailed miserably into the foreign-owned factories, exchanging one form of slavery for another. As Shumovsky would later remember, 'Most industrial enterprises, in fact, were under foreign control. In my home city, for example, the gas business was run by a Belgian company, the tramways by a French company, a big plant for producing agricultural machinery by a German company, and so on.'[12]

Russian industrial workers were not only the lowest paid in Europe but struggled under a burden of often unfair and inhumane practices. On his way to school, Shumovsky would pass children his own age heading to a long day at work.* Workers only had to be paid in cash once a month; the rest of their wages were returned to the factory owners' pockets by a voucher system, requiring the employees to pay their rent and buy overpriced goods in the company stores. Russian industrial labourers worked eleven-hour days, although shifts often exceeded this, in conditions that were unsafe and unhygienic. Kharkov's population had

---

* Officially children under twelve were banned from working; in practice foreign owners ignored the regulation.

increased and housing conditions were awful – it was no surprise that the city would soon become a hotbed of radicalism and politically motivated strikes. The official reaction to even mild protest was confrontational and violent.

Kharkov bore the vivid scars of the 1905 Revolution and the Tsar's broken promises. The large locomotive works where Ivan Trashutin (one of the students who would travel with Shumovsky to the US) was later employed had been extensively damaged by fierce artillery shelling at the climax of official efforts to dislodge its striking unarmed workers.[13] The revolution began after the army and police shot dead 4,000 peaceful protesters in St Petersburg who were taking a simple petition to the Russian Emperor asking for improved working conditions and universal suffrage.[14] The peaceful demonstration was organised and led by an agent of the Tsar's secret police, the feared Okhranka, in one of the *agent provocateur* missions for which it was renowned.★

In revulsion, the whole country rose in revolt at the lack of any reaction to or remorse for this bloodshed on the part of Tsar Nicholas II. Joseph Stalin's close friend Artyom (Stalin later adopted his son) set Kharkov alight with months of army mutinies and strikes. Barricades were set up on the main street, and there was armed insurrection. Large-scale street fighting broke out between the citizens demanding a voice and the paramilitary Cossacks. Across Russia's cities an alliance of radical students, workers and the peasants brought the autocracy almost to its knees. Shumovsky learned that secondary school children played their part by cooking up sulphur dioxide bombs in the chemistry

---

★ Tsarist secret agents would infiltrate a revolutionary organisation, arranging terrorist acts before betraying their fellow revolutionaries.

laboratory. The schools and the universities were proud to be the headquarters of revolutionaries. Tsar Nicholas eventually caved in to the people, offering great concessions and even promising a Duma, a parliament, but as soon as the strikes ended, he went back on his word. The people felt betrayed by their Tsar. Each year as Shumovsky was growing up, there were demonstrations in Kharkov under the slogan 'We no longer have a Tsar', commemorating the deaths of the 15,000 hanged for their part in the countrywide protests.

The Russian middle class, including the Shumovskys, became alienated from their government. They witnessed the shocking, violent crackdowns on peaceful protesters and the lamentable official failure to promote better social conditions. There was now a Duma for which men of property like Adam Shumovsky could vote, but in practice the Tsar was as autocratic as ever. The electoral laws were changed to exclude those considered to have been misled to vote for critical, radical parties and to promote and support conservatives, and the parliament was contemptuously referred to as a 'Duma of Lackeys'.[15] Although officially banned, discussions raged on in drawing rooms across the country about the latest scandals of the court faith healer Rasputin and the not-so-clandestine involvement of the Okhranka in terrorist activities, including assassinations and bombings.[16]

As Tsar Nicholas implacably set his face against change, opposition politics and debate moved ever further leftwards in search of radical alternatives. The certainty of change promised by the Marxist dialectic appealed to the methodical minds of Kharkov's citizens. In the face of an official policy of Russification, meanwhile, each of the empire's nationalities increasingly aspired to independence. Russian Jews were subject to harsher discrimination. Official quotas to limit the number of Jewish students were re-imposed at schools and universities, and violent anti-Semites formed savage gangs known as the 'Black Hundreds'.

Despite the holiday atmosphere of the International Trade Fair of 1910, new waves of strikes had begun. Kharkov contained a dangerously rich cocktail of workers seething with resentment at the failure of the 1905 Revolution, a free-thinking professional class reading socialist literature smuggled in from abroad and a rebellious, radical student body. All that was lacking was the spark. The province remained restive and occasionally erupted into violence. Peasants who stayed in their villages felt excluded from the economy. Their fathers had been virtual slaves; now their sons had no future on the land. Gangs of dispossessed peasants roamed the countryside, burning manor houses and murdering landowners. The army tried to keep order by shooting bands of miscreants. Meanwhile, the urban radicals had learned their lesson after the recent betrayals; there would be no half-measures next time. The revolutionaries were more determined than before. During Shumovsky's childhood, he would learn not just about flying, but of the tragic events in his country's recent history such as the 1905 Bloody Sunday killings of unarmed demonstrators marching to the Winter Palace to present their petition to the Tsar and the 1912 Lena Goldfields Massacre, when Tsarist troops shot dead dozens of striking workers protesting about high prices in the company shops.[17] Graphic postcards of dead bodies from the Lena massacre circulated, inflaming anti-government attitudes. In short, Russia was a country teetering on the brink of war with itself.

In a country devoid of hope, many gave up their dreams of

change and chose to emigrate in order to try their luck abroad, most often in America. The first wave of Russian emigration saw two and a half million former subjects of the Tsar settling in the United States between 1891 and 1914.[18] Many were economic migrants; others escaped anti-Semitic measures inflicted on them by the government; others still were frustrated firebrand revolutionaries. New York and other cities quickly developed large and thriving socialist undergrounds, eventually providing a refuge in the Bronx for Leon Trotsky before the 1917 Revolutions. Trotsky wrote for the radical Socialist Party's Yiddish newspaper *Forverts* (*Forward*), which had a daily circulation of 275,000. Russian emigrants came to dominate areas such as Brighton Beach, Brooklyn and Bergen County, New Jersey, keeping many of their 'old country' traditions alive. It was in these exile communities dotted around the US that many future spies found homes or were born. Arthur Adams★ escaped Tsarist torture to become a founder member of the North American Communist Party and later a successful Soviet Military Intelligence spy.[19] Like Gertrude Klivans[20] and Raisa Bennett,[21] Georgi Koval's[22] parents emigrated to the US to escape anti-Jewish measures. The families of Harry Gold,[23] Ben Smilg[24] and Ted Hall boarded boats to a new life.† Later Shumovsky would find a warm welcome in

---

★ A Military Intelligence officer who played a major role in the atomic espionage operation.

† Koval worked as a supervisor in the Oak Ridge Atomic facility. He was the only Russian spy to penetrate the Manhattan Project. Harry Gold was an American who acted as a courier for the Russians. He was turned by the FBI and became a key if unreliable witness. Theodore Hall, the youngest scientist to work at Los Alamos, provided the Russians with the design of the bomb trigger. He was not prosecuted by the FBI.

the Boston émigré circle.[25] Many maintained in secret their radical beliefs and links to international socialist organisations despite their outward embrace of all things American.

• • •

Tsar Nicholas II, Emperor of All Russia, was, like the young Shumovsky, a flying fanatic. For a man who devoted his life to resisting change, unusually Nicholas committed close to one million roubles of his money to the construction of an Imperial Russian Air Force.[26] The popular enthusiasm for aviation allowed the government to launch a successful voluntary subscription campaign, to which the Shumovskys contributed, for the design and purchase of new aircraft and the training of pilots. In 1914, to his delight, Russia arrived on the world stage as a leading aviation power. Its first major aviation pioneer, Igor Sikorsky, later famous for his helicopters, constructed a long-distance four-engined passenger plane, the *Ilya Muromets*.[27] The revolutionary aircraft featured innovations such as internal heating, electric lights, and even a bathroom; its floor, disconcertingly, was glazed to allow the twelve passengers to leave their wicker chairs to gaze at the world passing beneath their feet. As a sign of his confidence, Sikorsky flew members of his immediate family on long trips to demonstrate his invention. Until the First World War intervened, the first planned route for the airliner was from Moscow to Kharkov; sadly the monster *Ilya Muromets* was destined to be remembered not as the world's first passenger airliner but, with a few modifications, as the world's first heavy bomber. (In 1947 Tupolev would reverse the trick, turning a warplane into the first pressurised passenger aircraft.)

Russia created strategic bombing on 12 February 1915. Unchallenged, ten of Sikorsky's lumbering giants slowly took to the air, each powered by four engines. Turning to the west, the aircraft, laden with almost a half-ton of destruction apiece, headed for the German lines. The *Ilya Muromets* were truly fortresses of the sky. The aircrew even wore metal armour for personal protection. Despite the planes' low speed, with their large number of strategically placed machine guns no fighter of the age dared tackle even one of them, let alone a squadron. Today the *Ilya Muromets* remains the only bomber to have shot down more fighters than the casualties it suffered. It was only on 12 September 1916, after a full eighteen months of operations, that the Russians lost their first *Ilya Muromets* in a fierce dogfight with four German Albatros fighters, and even then it managed to shoot down three of its assailants. The wreck was taken to Germany and copied.[28]

Named after the only epic hero canonised by the Russian Orthodox Church, the aircraft became the stuff of legend. The medieval hero had been a giant blessed with outstanding physical and spiritual power. Like its namesake, *Ilya Muromets* protected the homeland and its people. Newspaper stories trumpeted the plane's achievements to flying fanatics and ordinary readers alike. Its propaganda value was inspirational to Russians, including the teenage Shumovsky, used now to a series of morale-sapping defeats inflicted by the Kaiser's armies.

• • •

The Tsar's decision in 1914 to mobilise against both Austria–Hungary and Germany had triggered world war, setting his country on the road to revolution. In August 1914, Russia initially appeared to unite behind his decision to fight. There were no more industrial strikes and for a short while the pressure for change subsided. A few months later, however, Shumovsky could feel the mood change in his city as, day by day, Russia's war stumbled from disaster to disaster and the human and financial cost mounted. Shumovsky distributed anti-war leaflets that proclaimed the real enemy to be capitalists, not fellow workers in uniform. Student discussion groups exchanged banned socialist literature and copies of the many underground newspapers. Students of the time treasured the writings of utopians, many moving rapidly from religious texts to find heroes among the French Revolutionaries. School reading clubs were the breeding ground for the future leaders of the revolution.

The Shumovsky family's comfortable lifestyle was steadily undermined by rampant inflation. Prices for increasingly scarce staples rocketed, and Shumovsky's father's state pay was no longer sufficient for his family's needs. They invested their savings in government war bonds that fell in value as the guns grew closer. His father complained bitterly at home about the irrational decision to secretly devalue the rouble by issuing worthless, limitless amounts of paper money. Savvy, distrustful citizens hoarded the real gold, silver, and the lowest denomination copper coins; the resulting shortage of small change compelled the government to print paper coupons as surrogates. Even the least financially aware, let alone a smart accountant, knew that the once strong rouble was fast becoming worthless. At the start of a financially ruinous war, the Tsar had done something remarkable, renouncing the principal source of his country's revenue. Having convinced himself that drunkenness was the reason for the disastrous defeat in the Russo-Japanese War and the 1905

Revolution that followed, he banned the sale of vodka for the duration of the war.[29]

While failing to curtail Russians' drinking, he thus created a major fiscal problem for the Treasury. Before the war, the Tsar's vodka monopoly had been the largest single source of government revenue, contributing 28 per cent of the entire state budget. It was the middle class that was hardest hit by the increased tax burden. Their resentment focused on the widespread corruption and prominent war profiteers, viewed as the Tsar's cronies. There were plentiful signs that Kharkov's workers were growing restive. The sharply rising food prices caused strikes, and these led to riots. The protesters first blamed their ills on greedy peasants who hoarded food and avaricious shopkeepers, but transferred their anger to treacherous ethnic Germans, Jews, police officers, bureaucrats, and ultimately to the monarch. Catastrophic defeats and vast retreats left Kharkov a critical staging post uncomfortably close to the front line. Day and night, trains pulled into the station with cargoes of fresh troops and munitions for the front. On their return, the same wagons carried away a tide of misery; the broken and dispirited remains of a defeated army. Kharkov became a city of despair, frustration and anger.

In 1915 Shumovsky's father moved the family 1,400 miles to the south-east corner of the empire, away from the war. He decided to settle in the seemingly idyllic 'little Paris of the Caucasus', Shusha.[30] It was an easy choice to make, despite the distance. The town was far away from the fighting, the cost of living low, there was ample food, and as a servant of the crown he held a position of respect. The Shumovskys packed up their possessions and made the arduous journey by rail and on foot to this remote region of Transcaucasia. Shusha resembled a picture-perfect Swiss mountain town with a few modern multi-storey European-style buildings nestled in wide boulevards. Justly famous for its intricate formal flower garden, as well as for its ice and roller-skating rinks, the town also boasted an Armenian theatre and two competing movie houses, The American and The Bioscope. Movies were shown inside in the winter, out of the cold, and outdoors in the hot summers. Shusha was the educational and cultural capital of the region, boasting excellent schools and assembly rooms that hosted cultural evenings of dances and concerts.[31]

The Caucasus had recently become part of the Russian Empire at the point of the bayonet. Oil had made the region one of the richest on the planet. The small Russian population of several hundred held all the top jobs, shoring up their position by favouring the Christian Armenians over the Muslim Azeris. Even at the best of times the Tsarist government had only just kept a lid on the simmering ethnic tension, but in November 1914 Russia went to war with the neighbouring Muslim Ottoman Empire, ratcheting up the tension several notches. Adam Shumovsky soon came to regret the decision to move to Shusha.

In September 1915, despite lacking the relevant military experience, Tsar Nicholas felt compelled to take personal charge of – and hence full responsibility for – the conduct of the war. He was blamed for the countless deaths of soldiers sent unarmed to the front lines and the decision to face sustained poison gas attacks without masks. Fifty times the number of Russian soldiers died from the effects of poison gas as American servicemen.[32] There was little food for the army, a catastrophic lack of artillery shells and, consequently, disastrous morale. The future White General Denikin wrote that the 'regiments, although completely exhausted, were beating off one attack after another by bayonet . . . Blood flowed unendingly, the ranks became thinner and thinner and thinner. The number of graves multiplied.'[33]

Until 1916 the Kaiser was more interested in fighting the British and French in the West. But as Russians died in their hundreds of thousands, their Western allies appeared to profit. The allies provided loans and paid extravagant bribes to keep Russia in the fight. There was nothing France, Britain and later America would not do to keep the war in the East going. If the Eastern Front collapsed, then German troops would be freed to move west to crush the remaining Entente powers.

Finally, in February 1917 the whole situation became too much. Paying for the government's mistakes had destroyed the very glue that had held the Russian Empire together for centuries. Inflation was making life in the cities miserable; peasants enjoyed good harvests but declined to sell their grain surpluses at the artificially low price fixed by the state. Food trickled into the markets, but at exorbitant prices which workers could not afford. The cities were starving. Autocracy had relied on the loyalty of its paramilitary gendarmes and the military to suppress the inevitable protests, but the defeated army now sided with the people. They would no longer obey orders to fire on the crowds of starving women.

By taking personal charge of the war Tsar Nicholas had gambled the future of the ancient system of autocracy, and lost. The Tsar had always been seen as appointed by God and omniscient. Faced with open mutinies, his own court now persuaded Nicholas to abdicate – a disastrous step. The linchpin that for so long had kept the Russian Empire going was gone. Just a few weeks after Lenin proclaimed that he would not see a revolution in his lifetime, the first uprising of 1917 toppled Tsar Nicholas and ended the Romanov dynasty. The nobles had sacrificed their monarchy to satisfy their greed; they wanted the allies' bribes, designed to keep the war going, so that they could have a share of war profits. They particularly wanted an end to the income tax that eroded the value of their landed estates. Their selfish agenda set Russia back a century. The common people wanted peace, bread and land, and only the Communists promised these. In the words of the great Soviet aviator Sigismund Levanevsky, 'I felt that the Communists would bring good. That's why I was for them.'[34] A second revolution in October 1917 (according to the old style calendar)* brought the Communists to power.

• • •

Russian society was shattered by the twin revolutions of 1917, and the effects of the cataclysm were felt most dramatically in the country's far-flung corners. In Shusha, government authority vanished overnight in February 1917 and with the October Revolution any semblance of law and order disappeared. In nearby Baku, the future capital of independent Azerbaijan, Communist oil workers and the Armenian minority joined forces to seize control, creating a short-lived commune and proclaiming Soviet power. Already a committed Communist, Shumovsky was keen to join the Soviet troops in Baku but was prevented from doing so by his parents. On 28 May 1918, Muslim Azerbaijan declared itself an independent state including, controversially, Shumovsky's home

---

* The Russian calendar was changed in 1918 to bring Russia into line with the rest of the world.

province of Karabakh. The Christian Armenian population there categorically refused to recognise the authority of the Muslim Azeris, and so on 22 July 1918, in his hometown of Shusha, the local Armenians proclaimed the independence of Nagorno-Karabakh and established their own people's government.

The new Armenian-dominated government restored order in the city by shooting 'robbers and spies'. There was a massacre. Murders were accompanied by looting, the theft of property and the burning of houses and mosques. In response, the Azerbaijanis subdued Nagorno-Karabakh with the overwhelming help of Turkish troops and headed on to Baku, now controlled by the British. For a while, Shusha was occupied by Azerbaijani and Turkish forces. They disarmed the Armenians and carried out mass arrests among the local intelligentsia.

Later, in November 1918, the tide would change after the capitulation of Turkey to the Entente. Turkish troops retreated from Karabakh, and British forces arrived. In the void, Karabakh returned to Armenian control. But the perfidious British, Armenia's ally, prevaricated on the controversial question of who should rule the territory until the wider Paris Peace Conference took place. The British supported those whom they considered the most likely to grant them oil concessions. However, they did approve a governor-general of Karabakh appointed by the government of Azerbaijan. The Armenians were shocked not only at the open support shown by their fellow Christian British for Muslim Azerbaijan but by the selection of the governor-general; he was one Khosrov Bey Sultanov, known for his Pan-Turkic views and his active participation in the bloody massacres of Armenians in Baku in September 1918.

Sultanov arrived in Shusha on 10 February 1919, but the

Armenians refused to submit to him. On 23 April, in Shusha, the fifth Congress of the Armenians of Karabakh declared 'inadmissible any administrative program having at least some relationship with Azerbaijan'.[35] In response, with the full connivance of the British and American officials now present in the region, Sultanov embargoed any trade with Nagorno-Karabakh, causing a famine. At the same time, irregular Kurdish-Tatar cavalry troops under the leadership of his brothers killed Armenian villagers at will. On 4 June 1919, the Azerbaijani army tried to occupy the positions of the Armenian militia and the Armenian sector of the city by force. After some fighting, the attackers were repulsed, until, under promises of British protection, the Azerbaijani army was allowed to garrison the city. According to the National Council of the Armenians of Karabakh, Sultanov gave direct orders for massacres and pogroms in the Armenian neighbourhoods, saying: 'you can do everything, but do not set fire to houses. Houses we need.'[36]

The foreigner's decisive intervention in local affairs added a new level of confusion to an already complicated situation. The local oil industry was too valuable a prize for anyone to ignore. The area around Baku was strategically precious. Since 1898, the Russian oil industry, with foreign investment, had been producing more oil than the entire United States: some 160,000 barrels of oil per day. By 1901, Baku alone produced more than half of the world's oil.[37] There were already millions of dollars of foreign capital sunk into the derricks, pipelines and oil refineries, and now it was all up for grabs. Every city, indeed seemingly the whole country, was the pawn of foreign powers. Shumovsky had seen the British arrive first, to be kicked out by the Turks, only to return later, while each time their local proxy allies set about massacring the innocent inhabitants who were unlucky enough to be born on the wrong side. He perceived this not just as a civil war of Reds versus Whites, but also as an embodiment of the worst excesses of imperialism and deep-seated ethnic hatred – precisely the cataclysm described in the leaflets he had distributed in Kharkov. Only the unity of the working people could fight off the massed forces of imperialism descending on Russia.

• • •

Within the wider tragedy was a family one. Despite the danger and vast distance involved, Shumovsky's mother Amalia overcame her fear of war each summer after the family's dramatic flight and went back to Volyn (today in the far west of Ukraine) to visit her father. He was still serving as an estate manager. In 1918 disaster struck when she failed to return to the family home by the expected date. Shumovsky's father sent a letter, care of his father-in-law, asking for information about the whereabouts of his wife. The letter came back, and written on the envelope were the stark words: 'not delivered owing to the death of the recipient'.[38]

By the summer of 1918, Shumovsky woke each day to see parts of his city burning and fresh bodies lying in the streets. Fear was in the air. Mobs attacked churches and mosques in turn, and random ethnic murders were commonplace as the city's population was divided down the middle. When Shumovsky arrived in the Caucasus, the army presence had kept an uneasy peace for the past fifty years. Now army deserters returned from the collapsed Turkish front, armed to the teeth, so the ethnic violence became organised and prolific. Shumovsky had played a role in the underground revolutionary movement in Kharkov with his classmates. Aged just sixteen, he decided to move on from distributing leaflets and reading underground newspapers quoting Lenin to fighting for his vision of a better future.

Shumovsky had completed his five years of secondary education. By his own account, he was already a gifted linguist, speaking Russian, Polish and Ukrainian as well as French and German, although not English. The anarchy now gripping Shusha led to the eventual closure of his prestigious technical school. Although the landmark building survived the violence, it was left abandoned, a shadow of its former glory, after the factional fighting subsided. One of the few non-Armenian pupils, Shumovsky had been a star student, studying mathematics and the sciences. Now he made his first life-changing decision, to join the Red Army to fight in the Civil War. He was one of a very small number of Communists, who were a tiny minority in the country at large. Shumovsky was turning his back decisively on his Polish and aristocratic roots, a fact clearly indicated when he changed his patronymic from the Polish-sounding Adam to the Russian Anton.[39] On volunteering for the Red Army, indeed, Shumovsky concealed much about his privileged upbringing, telling the recruiters he was the son of a Ukrainian peasant worker who somehow spoke French and German.[40]

• • •

The destruction and loss of life during the Russian Civil War was among the greatest catastrophes that Europe had seen. The conflict would rage with enormous bloodshed from November 1917 until October 1922. As many as 12 million died, mostly civilians who succumbed to disease and famine.[41] It was a time of anarchy. The armed factions lived off the land, extracting supplies and recruiting 'volunteers' at gunpoint while fighting to determine Russia's political future. The two largest combatant groups were the Red Army, fighting for the Bolshevik form of socialism, and the loosely allied forces known as the White Army. The divided White factions favoured a variety of causes, including a return to monarchism, capitalism and alternative forms of socialism. At the same time rival militant socialists, anarchists, nationalists, and even peasant armies fought against both the Communists and the Whites.

Shumovsky and his unit were stationed in southern Russia, at the centre of the bloodiest fighting. In all the carnage and suffering he was one of many teenagers given positions of responsibility in the army. There was nothing in his genteel background to prepare Shumovsky for the terrors he faced on the battlefield. In August 1918, he made a long, daunting and arduous journey of several hundred miles on foot to join a determined band of Communist partisans under their charismatic leader Pyotr Ipatov, based far behind the main battle lines.[42] On his arrival Shumovsky was given a red armband, a rifle and a cartridge belt. He was in action within two days. Ipatov's band supported the village militia units raised by local councils to fend off marauding armed bands of foragers from the White 'Volunteer' armies sent out by Generals Kornilov, Alekseyev and Denikin.[43] The White leader, General Kornilov, ruled by fear. His slogan was 'the greater the terror, the greater our victories'. In the face of the peasant resistance he was sticking to his vow to 'set fire to half the country and shed the blood of three-quarters of all Russians'.[44] In small towns and villages across the province Kornilov's death squads put up gallows in the square, hanged a few likely suspects and reinstalled the hated landlords by force. Rather than quell the unrest, such punitive action encouraged the Red partisan movement. Shumovsky's unit had grown strong enough to take the fight to the enemy, carrying out successful raids on White outposts to capture arms and ammunition. The fighters enjoyed the active support of Joseph Stalin and Kliment Voroshilov, who were leading the defence of the nearby city of Tsaritsyn.[45]

Shumovsky's band of partisans, 1918

By the time young Shumovsky joined the fight, the Whites' patience with the guerrilla attacks had reached breaking point. They decided to crush the partisan movement for good with an overwhelming force. Ahead of the harvest, the Whites unleashed a punitive expedition consisting of four elite regiments of troops supported by Czech mercenaries. When the partisans received the news of the approach of this powerful force, they prepared a last-ditch ambush at the village of Ternovsky.

Shumovsky helped to dig deep defensive trenches around the village. Eager to fight, two thousand volunteers streamed into the village responding to the desperate call for help. Ipatov's force had rifles, some machine guns and a captured field gun. The balance of defenders were enthusiastic but untrained farmers, armed only with homemade weapons.

The enemy approached in strength at dawn, expecting little resistance from the village militia. To the defenders' surprise, the Whites attacked head-on in a column, not even deploying properly for an attack. Maintaining uncharacteristic discipline, the partisans opened fire on the advancing enemy when they were just 150 yards away. The first volley stunned the Whites, who struggled to respond, not even returning fire. The partisan force, having quickly run out of ammunition, charged out of their trenches in pursuit of their broken enemy, waving pitchforks, shovels, axes, iron crowbars and homemade spears. No prisoners were taken. Shumovsky's first taste of action had been brief, bloody and chaotic. The defenders celebrated their decisive victory and the booty of arms and ammunition that had fallen into their laps.[46]

The disparate village guerrilla groups combined in September 1918 to form the 2nd Worker-Peasant Stavropol Division.[47] Despite the grand-sounding name, the Division could only stage raids at night due to an acute shortage of weapons and ammunition, their weakness concealed by the cover of darkness. Ipatov, a former gunsmith, built a mobile cartridge factory manufacturing 7,000 rounds per day. Even so, by the end of the month the guerrillas, cut off from any outside supplies, were almost out of ammunition. Often, the guerrillas went into battle with only three or four rounds each. Outnumbered and outgunned, under constant pressure from the advancing White Guard, the partisan units had to retreat into the interior of the province and then beyond. They were proud to record that even in this difficult period, the division was able to organise a massive transport of grain to Stalin, besieged in the nearby city of Tsaritsyn. In return, Stalin, commanding the desperate defence of the city that would later bear his name – Stalingrad – gave the partisans much-needed weapons and ammunition.[48]

In late November 1918, the band suffered its first defeat and serious casualties in a failed attack on a White base. They lost hundreds of men. Exhausted by four months of continual fighting and retreats, the survivors were forced further and further to the north-east, away from their homes and support. From December 1918, the partisans started fighting against a new and formidable enemy, the well-armed Cossacks. Their new opponent was highly mobile and well versed in guerrilla war techniques. It was bitter, unrelenting winter warfare, pushing Shumovsky's hungry unit onto the desolate Kalmyk steppe, a region known by Russians as 'the end of the world'. In the freezing winter conditions, Shumovsky's fighters suffered extreme hardship. For the hungry, poorly clothed and exhausted men, barely surviving on the bleak steppe, the final straw was a typhus epidemic. The disease was soon rampant not only in the army but in the rare settlements. By February, the steppe front was one large typhoid camp. It became necessary for the healthy to abandon the thousands of sick men, leaving them without protection from the advancing enemy. In early March, the 10th Red Army absorbed the remains of the partisans, and the survivors became the 32nd Infantry Division.[49] Now a member of the Red Army, Shumovsky swore the solemn oath he would keep for his whole life, that 'I, a son of the working people, citizen of the Soviet Republic, Stanislav

Shumovsky swear to spare no effort nor my very life in the battle for the Russian Soviet Republic.'

The Red Army was an army in name only. After a succession of defeats, it was on the point of collapse when Shumovsky joined. Only a quarter of the former Russian Empire remained under Communist control and the Reds were in full undisciplined retreat. The leadership had eschewed the services of professional military officers and logistics, a sure recipe for disaster. Their defeats were down to cowardice, treachery and panic. Even the senior commanders ran away at the sound of the first shot. It was not the use of superior tactics but a lack of ammunition that, often as not, determined the outcome of battles. In the circumstances, promotion through the ranks was rapid for a dedicated young Communist such as Shumovsky. He was made first a squad leader then a machine-gun commander, and even-tually a commissar. In the Civil War, fanatical teenagers, skinny boys in oversized uniforms, were regularly given command of large units made up of unreliable conscripts and recaptured deserters. The daily struggle for food took priority over military duties as the army lived off the land. Uniforms, including boots, were unavailable. The army provided its troops with no basic training, nor did it even teach its leaders rudimentary military tactics. With their inability to confront the Whites in a set-piece battle, the Red Army's military strategy depended on encouraging the feverish formation of local militia units to stand against Denikin's advancing volunteer army and supporting guerrilla attacks on the Whites' weak civil administration. In practice, none of the individual Red guerrilla units were sufficiently organised to be effective. However, there were so many groups that they became a veritable plague on the Whites.

After their run of bitter defeats, the Red Army finally introduced military discipline. The Soviet government established a Revolutionary Military Council of the Republic with a single commander-in-chief for all fronts. Unity of command would save the Red Army in the large-scale battles of 1919. The army developed the ability to transfer troops between fronts at times of pressing need. The establishment of an overall operational command and an insistence on the strict execution of combat orders led to an improvement in fighting ability over the lacklustre performance of the independent amateur partisan units. The reintroduction of the basic principles of a regular professional army – namely complete submission to orders, a strict hierarchy and rigid discipline – helped strengthen the combat capability of the Red Army to first confront, then overpower the Whites. The Red Army officers were now appointed according to military ability, not elected by the popular acclaim of their troops. Orders and plans were no longer put forward to the troops for debate. In extremis, Leon Trotsky introduced the infamous 'blocking troops'. He ordered the positioning of machine-gunners behind Red Army attacks to shoot waverers, deserters and shirkers.

The most important reform, however, was the introduction of a system of dual command. Professional military officers were paired with committed commissars, such as Shumovsky, to jointly command units. Commissars monitored not only the activities of military experts, but carried out the Communist Party's policy in the armed forces to 'provide class rallying, enlighten and educate personnel in the spirit of Communism'. This was a euphemism for removing the criminal elements in uniform that preyed on the civilian population.

The large-scale battles of 1919, stretched over southern and central Russia, involved hundreds of thousands of combatants on each side, and would determine the outcome of the Civil War. In the south of Russia, the Red Army faced its largest and most determined opponent, the well-equipped army of the fierce General Denikin. He was heavily supported both financially and militarily by the British and the Americans, while the Western powers turned a blind eye to the mounting evidence of an unpalatable genocide – known as the 'White Terror' – behind Denikin's front lines. There were large-scale massacres of suspected Communists and Jews, who were often seen as one and the same, in the territory that fell under Denikin's control. In their vast summer offensive, the Whites were able to deploy tanks, armoured cars and significant quantities of artillery, and advanced with the support of mercenary British pilots who bombed the retreating Reds. Denikin's goal was to deliver a coordinated knockout blow on Moscow. He believed its capture would ensure the complete destruction of Communism.

Denikin's army came close to achieving its goal, driving the enthusiastic but largely inept Red opponents before them. However, his army overran its supply lines and, lacking reserves, allowed the hard-pressed Red Army to bring up reinforcements first to halt the advance and then launch a large-scale counter-attack. In the midst of the renewed savage fighting in November 1919 for the critical Stavropol region, Shumovsky was wounded in the head by shrapnel near Kamyshin.[50]

By the end of the seesaw campaigning season of 1919, it was clear that the Communists would not only survive but were in the ascendancy. Winston Churchill, Britain's Minister of War and the architect of foreign intervention, was forced to bow to his public's war-weariness and pull his troops out of Russia, having failed to strangle Communism in the cradle as he had pledged.[51] Without British finance, arms, advisors and strong diplomatic hands to guide them, the White opposition movement squabbled among themselves and teetered on the brink of complete collapse. Their armies retreated on all fronts, a mere shadow of their former military power. By January 1920 the reformed Red Army had advanced to knock on the door of the Caucasus. Shumovsky was wounded for a second time, this time in the leg, during the rapid advance on the strategic town of Rostov-on-Don.[52] The defeated White General Denikin lost half his army in a disastrous retreat to Novorossiysk and was replaced as overall White commander by the more capable General Baron Wrangel, who is immortalised in the popular marching song of the Red Army:

> The White Army and the Black Baron
> Are preparing to restore to us the Tsar's throne,
> But from the taiga* to the British seas
> The Red Army is the strongest of all!

But the feared Baron Wrangel could only hole up with what remained of his beaten forces in Crimea to await his inevitable exile. Lenin decided the time was now right to seize Baku's oil wealth. The 11th Army – into which Shumovsky had been transferred – was given the task of supporting a planned workers' uprising. The tide of war had turned, bringing him home.

• • •

---

* The coniferous forests of Siberia.

Following the Turkish withdrawal, the British had returned in force, determined to stay in the region. They found Baku, a once beautiful town which had fallen into decay, much to their liking. When oil was discovered at the end of the nineteenth century, the city had become almost overnight one of the wealthiest on earth, with every famous European luxury store opening a branch on Baku's elegant tree-lined avenues. British naval officers requisitioned the oil barons' magnificent palaces and villas as they set about building a strong naval force to control the Caspian Sea. The ruthless British tactics involved first disarming their allies before moving out to attack the weak Red Navy. The Communist flotilla in the Caspian Sea was no match for the better-equipped British-backed forces. The British complained to London that the Reds refused to come out of port to fight them. But by March 1920, on Winston Churchill's orders, the British were long gone, and the region was a ripe plum ready to fall into Communist laps. The opposition, such as it remained, was deeply divided. The Whites refused to countenance any rapprochement with the Nationalists. Independent Armenia, Georgia and Azerbaijan dissipated their energies fighting territorial disputes between themselves. Each was in a state of financial and economic collapse. Epidemics of typhus raged unchecked, brought in by the hordes of refugees from the fighting. Just days after the campaign started, and without firing a shot, Shumovsky and the victorious 11th Army were marching down the streets of Baku. Soon Lenin was preparing a grander plan to establish Soviet power over the whole Caucasus region.

On his eighteenth birthday, 9 May 1920, his very first opportunity to do so, Stanislav Shumovsky became a full member of the Soviet Communist Party. He was to remain an active Party member for the rest of his life, earning the right to one of the first fifty-year anniversary membership medals awarded.*[53]

Although the government in Baku had no stomach for a fight with the Reds, many in Azerbaijan were not so eager to abandon their religion and embrace the ideals of Communism. Civilian revolts and mutinies centred on the old capital of Ganja. Shumovsky's army was tasked with suppressing the revolts in Azerbaijan and Dagestan, dangerous counter-guerrilla operations. On the hot summer's day of 3 July 1920, as he was slogging up the mountain roads at Agdam at the head of his unit, advancing towards his hometown of Shusha, Shumovsky suffered his third and most severe wound when he was shot through the neck.[54] During his recuperation, the 11th Army mopped up all remaining opposition to Communist rule in the Caucasus in Georgia, Armenia and Azerbaijan. The agonies of the Civil War were over.

• • •

As an able, committed soldier, Shumovsky would serve in the Red Army for a further six years,[55] taking on increasingly important administrative roles in major cities across the Soviet Union. He married Vera, and in 1922 they had a daughter, Maya.[56] In December 1924, he transferred to Smolensk to fulfil his childhood dream – for in the spring of 1925, Shumovsky climbed into the front pilot's seat of a two-man Polikarpov R-1 at an airfield of the newly formed Red air force at Smolensk.[57] The

---

* His Communist Party card records that he was rebuked for inflating the length of his military service by adding his partisan service to his military record.

mechanic spun the propeller and the engine coughed into life. Turning the aircraft into the wind, Shumovsky pointed its nose down the long grass runway, revving the motor. Opening the throttle close to maximum, he waited for sufficient speed to finally pull back on the stick to adjust the flaps, giving the plane enough lift to gently rise off the ground. With a broad grin spread across his face, Shumovsky had joined his boyhood band of heroes as a pilot. His observer reached forward to pat him on the head, congratulating him on his first successful take-off.

For nine months, Shumovsky would learn first to be the observer and then the pilot in the 2nd Independent Reconnaissance Squadron. He flew in the R-1, the first new aircraft built in the Soviet Union after the Revolution and the first Soviet plane ever sold for export.[58] The R-1 set the tone for future Soviet aircraft development. It was a copy of a captured de Havilland DH-9, but with substantial improvements on the original British plane. The Soviets lacked a design for a powerful aircraft engine and the ability to make them in large numbers. They had no access to the advanced aluminium moulding necessary to build powerful but lightweight engines. Old motors were bought abroad for the first aircraft and eventually copied in large numbers. The fuselage design was adapted to Russian conditions and materials, mahogany being replaced with local wood. The Russian plane was more robust and less powerful than its Western brother, but over 2,400 were built cheaply in a decade.[59]

Shumovsky clocked up many happy hours as a pilot in the skies over Smolensk and many more over a nine-month period as the rear-seat observer. But a crash brought an abrupt end to his flying career. He walked away, but the impact had damaged his left arm so seriously he was unfit to be a pilot. In the mid-1920s he sent his family a photograph of himself in uniform. His brother Theodore noticed 'the three rhombuses on the lapel collar'.[60] Aged just twenty-five, Stanislav was already an army commander. He had reached a rank equivalent to what we would understand today as a full general.* His final military posting was to the prestigious Kronstadt naval base at the electro-mining school of the Baltic fleet, alma mater of fellow spy Arthur Adams.[61] After the Kronstadt assignment, Shumovsky transferred into the military reserves and became the Ministry of Finance's head investigator for military affairs.[62]

Shumovsky's letter was not the only surprising communication sent to the Caucasus. In 1926, eight years after her apparent death a letter arrived from his mother saying that she was still alive in Warsaw and earning a livelihood giving music lessons in private homes. One of a vast number of refugees displaced by war and trapped outside the Soviet Union, she was unable to return home, as tension between the USSR and Poland was at an acute level. When the demand for music lessons dried up, Amalia moved to Łódź, where she had to work as a weaver. It was only in 1932 that she was able to return to the Soviet Union and finally live close to her family in Moscow. Broken by her experiences, she died soon afterwards; her only consolation was knowing that, in a time of blood, chaos and disaster, her eldest son had followed his beliefs and achieved great success.[63]

---

* The Red Army had scrapped ranks and adopted a system loosely based on job titles. Authority was displayed by lapel insignia. The author believes Shumovsky's brother's account is probably wrong because Shumovsky later came to the US as a colonel, which would have entailed a demotion from general.

2

'WE CATCH UP OR THEY WILL CRUSH US'

The Communist victors of the Russian Civil War inherited a ruined and backward land surrounded by enemies. By 1921, the level of the country's economic activity had plunged to less than a quarter of that in 1913. Agricultural production had tumbled to a point where it was insufficient for the country to feed itself. The Communists were big dreamers, but their initial grandiose projects to modernise the transport network at a stroke by buying thousands of railway locomotives abroad and carrying out a national electrification scheme were soon scaled back when no foreign nation would advance them credit. In frustration, the leadership turned once more to their political vanguard and gave them a new task. The country had to be rebuilt and modernised and the Party's elite was to bring to the factory floor the energy, drive and commitment responsible for the successes on the battlefield. Men like Shumovsky left the Red Army to lead the drive for industrialisation. The zealots were assigned to central roles in industry to replace the old, tired management teams.

In 1925, Shumovsky transferred to the military reserves and was assigned the pivotal role as head investigator of the armaments industry on behalf of the People's Commissariat (Ministry) of Finance.[1] War with the capitalists was expected to break out at any time and the armaments industry needed to be ready. Shumovsky brought his military experience and Party loyalty to the role. On his factory visits, he saw the dire state of Soviet industry, which after decades of neglect was suffering from an absence of training, underinvestment, and a lack of leadership. The plants he toured struggled under the burden of pre-war machinery that was worn out and outmoded. As a result, the end product was of poor quality and frequently obsolete. Across the armaments industry, productivity was unacceptably low, and this was not merely because of the quality of the machinery. Labour relations in the workers' state were a complicated and delicate issue. Factory directors, former Tsarist middle managers of questionable loyalty and motivation, lacked authority on the factory floor as workers did not respect their orders. Foreign consultant engineers brought in to advise on improvements despaired at Russian working practices. They noticed large numbers of Soviet workers disappearing on endless smoking breaks. Female workers often carried out heavy manual work in factories, while the men sat idly watching.

Early, piecemeal efforts to improve matters had failed. With their scant foreign exchange reserves, the Soviets had bought small amounts of expensive new manufacturing machinery abroad, which the unskilled Russian workers promptly ruined. Shumovsky noted that most of the new machinery sat unused in the factories, either uninstalled or broken. Spare parts were never on hand, nor were there engineers trained to conduct the regular maintenance required to service the machines. Faulty installation of new equipment was often to blame for the poor quality of the final output. In their current state, Soviet arms factories were incapable of making precisely engineered products even in small numbers. Above all, a chronic shortage of young engineers versed in the latest techniques and methods held the country back. Owing to a decade of war and strife, none had been trained. The armaments industry was in no state to support even a small-scale conflict. Shumovsky's reports to the Finance Commissariat detailed his dire conclusions. The reports matched similar ones written by the other inspectors, visiting factories across the whole of Soviet industry. The flow of bad news exacerbated a building sense of crisis.

The leadership was aware of the desperate issues and, under an ailing Lenin, a gradualist approach had been adopted. Lenin was a deep admirer of US invention, if not of its capitalist system. He spent considerable time in his office in Moscow's Kremlin flicking through his subscription copy of the magazine *Scientific American, the Advocate of Industry and Enterprise*. The US monthly showcased all the latest technological inventions and innovations. Lenin wanted to secure the technology to help build Communism. On the day before his death, 20 January 1924, the leader of the world's first proletarian state passed the day watching a film about the workings of a tractor assembly line in a Ford factory.[2] While Lenin believed that in the American factory, owners used machinery as a means of oppressing the working class, in the USSR the same US-made technology and modern production methods would help build Communism. Introducing modern machines together with efficiency measures in Soviet factories would eventually allow workers greater free time and higher living standards.

Lenin hoped that greedy American businessmen would sell

his government everything it wanted, even if the Soviets' ultimate goal was the destruction of capitalism. He was said to have joked that if he announced the execution of all capitalists, one would sell him the rope to hang the others. As he predicted, the US was intent on selling its technology and had the best on sale, but only for hard cash. Lenin's plans were expansive, but in the absence of credit he could buy only a limited number of US-built tractors, other advanced farm machinery and some factory equipment. In his business dealings, Lenin favoured market leaders, the likes of International Harvester and Ford, as his trusted partners. When the money ran out, which it soon did, he sold the nation's treasures. The Kremlin's famous bells had to be saved by the curator of its museum from being auctioned off abroad.[3] It was not only the crown jewels that were given away; in a sign of the Russians' commercial naivety, Trotsky negotiated to exchange the rights to exploit all Siberia's vast mineral resources for the next seventy years to one American company for a pittance.[4] The Communists had returned to the Tsar's method of offering long-term concessions to foreign investors. In desperation, the Soviets even resorted to barter; to its complete bemusement, the Douglas Aircraft Company was offered payment for an aircraft in oriental rugs and antiques. For US entrepreneurs venturing into the USSR, the experience of doing business under Lenin's New Economic Policy (NEP) was disappointing. Once profits began to flow from their Soviet concessions, the intrepid US investors complained that they were subject to unexpected taxes or the sequestration of assets. For the Russians, the results of the programme were all too slow and involved tolerating a wild free market, risking social chaos at the hands of a class of newly rich 'NEP men', Russian capitalists who thrived by exploiting others.

The exchange of American ideas for Soviet cash or concessions should have been mutually beneficial. But ideological issues sharply divided the two societies. There were those in the US who flatly opposed doing any business with the Russians. They believed that under direct orders from Moscow, the US Communist Party members were secretly working to destroy the whole American way of life. They argued that if Communism were to spread to the US, it would mean taking away religious freedom, private property and access to justice. To the Communist way of thinking, America was a society built entirely on unfairness and the institutionalised mass exploitation of the working class for the benefit and enrichment of a few. The greatest success of the US had been to mobilise mass consumer demand. The American working class was not political and aspired to a life of consumption that the Soviets viewed as a shallow, material existence. Every Soviet visitor to America would comment on the extraordinary proliferation of advertising hoardings cajoling consumers to purchase the latest model of automobile, Coca-Cola or cigarettes.

The key barrier to greater trade was the US government's implacable opposition to lending the Communists any money while Russia owed vast sums to US investors. Assets granted to American businessmen by the Tsar had after the revolution been expropriated by the Communists, who refused to pay any compensation. With the debt issue unresolved, the Soviets could not legitimately buy technology in the quantities they required. So they adopted a roundabout approach, which US manufacturers learned about the hard way: the unlicensed reproduction of foreign technology. Foreign cars, tractors, and other machinery exhibited at Soviet trade fairs were examined and copied. Henry Ford's deputy, Charles Sorensen, on a visit spotted near-perfect copies of Fordson tractors manufactured under the name Red Putilovets.[5] The Soviet design originated from technical drawings based on a dismantled American vehicle. Following the re-establishment of diplomatic relations, the first American ambassador to Moscow, William Bullitt, would be plagued by constant complaints from US firms about infringement of their patents.

It was not just mechanised harvesters and cotton pickers that Lenin imported to transform backward Russia, he adopted advanced US management techniques. The Soviet Union introduced the Taylor system of time and motion study – a technique to improve productivity – to encourage the scientific efficiency of labour in its factories. To much puzzlement, an army of officials armed with clipboards, stopwatches and tape measures appeared on factory floors. Russian workers were unimpressed and did not want to be timed, measured and subjected to flip charts. New technology from abroad, augmented with Gantt organisation charts – which broke down processes into their component stages – was supposed to lead to a rapid reduction in working hours and improvement in the quality of workers' lives. It didn't.

In a more successful step, the Soviets translated Henry Ford's works into Russian as essential reading for factory managers. There was an official government campaign to 'Do It the Ford Way'.[6] By such innovative manufacturing techniques of mass production, the United States had overtaken the British Empire as the world's number-one economy, helped in part by the Great War. Imported to the Soviet Union, these same techniques were expected to bring about the inevitable triumph of socialism. Capitalism was a smart, inventive beast. American business, as well as Marx, had much to teach those embarking on the sure road to socialism. The US had met and defeated the same challenges that confronted the newly formed Soviet Union, including how to industrialise with only untrained, unskilled workers and few managers. The US was the teacher, the model of mass production, an urbanised country boasting the highest living standards in the world. Copying US techniques and methods would turn Russia's army of uneducated, conservatively minded peasants, tied to their traditions and land, into a progressive communist urban proletariat.

From the 1920s, hundreds of Soviet engineers were sent abroad annually on short foreign trips for hands-on training with new technology. They were instructed to gather as much helpful information as they could on their visits. It was not a difficult task in the US. One engineer described his surprise at the openness of the Americans he met. While visiting a factory, he and his comrades would be given unhindered access to a broad range of technical data. They could make sketches and take copies back to the USSR free of charge. Their host company did not disclose its patented secrets, but everything else was considered advertising for the firm. From such early trips, the Soviet leaders gained the idea that America, more than any other country, was wide open to industrial espionage.

• • •

In October 1922, just a few weeks after the Reds' victory in the Russian Civil War, an ex-Russian Orthodox seminary student and his close friend, a former Jesuit student, set in motion a more radical long-term reconstruction of Russia. In their frequent correspondence, they planned a transformation of their backward land, now shattered and starved by three wars and revolutions in short order.[7] The lapsed Catholic, 'Iron Felix' Dzerzhinsky (his nickname arose on account of his ruthlessness and devotion to the Communist cause), was the founder of the Soviet security services. The former seminary pupil, Joseph Stalin, General Secretary of the Party, was on his path to become Lenin's heir. In 1925, Dzerzhinsky became the first and only known intelligence chief to be given simultaneously a major economic post as Chairman of the Supreme Economic Council. The two friends could discuss almost anything.

In their shared desire for rapid change, Dzerzhinsky and Stalin emphasised the use of intelligence as one tool to tackle the economic crisis. Both men had a fine appreciation of the value of espionage: Dzerzhinsky was a spymaster, and his friend the most spied-upon man in history. Dzerzhinsky had a pivotal role in identifying the potential contribution of both Western technology and scientific and technological (S&T) espionage to the modernisation of the Soviet economy. He identified America, the world's number-one technical innovator and leading industrial power, as a role model and target. Dzerzhinsky studied and grew to admire American industrial methods – most surprisingly those of the world's first billionaire, Henry Ford, the pioneer of the industrial practices from which Dzerzhinsky believed the backward Soviet economy needed to learn. Dzerzhinsky wrote in 1925: 'It is essential to engage in the study of Ford's methods and their adoption in practice . . . Perhaps it would be worth recruiting from abroad practitioners and organisers of Fordism.'[8]

Dzerzhinsky's ideas and recommendations were incorporated into the Five-Year Plans – Stalin's centrepiece programmes to industrialise the Soviet Union at breakneck pace. Ford's top architect, Albert Kahn, was recruited to design and build Stalin's giant dual military/civilian-use factories along Ford lines, and was responsible for establishing automotive, tractor and tank facilities in the Soviet Union.

On assuming control after the death of Lenin, the new leadership decided enough was enough and immediately galvanised the entire efforts of the state to build up heavy industry. Amid enormous publicity, Stalin announced the first Five-Year Plan in 1928. The first and second Five-Year Plans proposed the creation of new capital-intensive aviation, automobile, tractor and chemical industries. Stalin's plans were on a truly grand scale and required building over 1,500 modern factories between 1928 and 1933; yet he understood that the Soviet Union's early attempts at going it alone to develop industry without adequate foreign help had failed. The most notable example was the first project at the vast Magnitogorsk metallurgical plant. The inexperienced Soviets had tried to build the plant at breakneck speed, cutting corners; as a consequence, urgent and extensive repairs to the twin blast furnaces were needed just days after first starting them. The production of steel was pushed back years. The lesson of such failures was that the design and building of large, technically complex industrial facilities was beyond Soviet capabilities without significant long-term foreign expertise. The help of the West was required and was sought once more – this time in the new form of fee-based technical assistance programmes, not long-term concessions. Stalin's proposed commercial terms were attractive to foreign companies, as they were for a limited period and so did not require risky long-term investment. During the Great Depression of the 1930s Western companies desperately needed large orders, allowing the Soviet Union the opportunity to acquire advanced technology and technical skills quickly and cheaply.

Under the standard terms of the contract, a foreign firm would provide the Russians with a complete description of a project including specifications of equipment, machines and mechanisms. They transferred all the technological secrets, including patents, and sent representatives to the USSR to supervise the construction and start-up of the facility. The Russians had to compensate the foreign company for the cost of manufacturing drawings, business trips and the work of its employees in the USSR and provide the necessary living conditions. The international company would receive a fixed profit as a percentage of the estimated cost of the work. The contribution of US companies and engineers to the success of the first Five-Year Plan was enormous, yet it is generally forgotten, especially in America. Around 1,700 US engineers entered Russia in 1929 to work on major industrial projects.

The plan to work closely with the US had its genesis in September 1927, when Stalin set up a permanent commission of the Politburo of the Communist Party of the Soviet Union to manage technical and scientific relations with the United States. He stated: 'It is clear to me that the USA has more grounds for extensive business relations with the Soviet Union than any other country.'[9]

The vast new industrial capacity developed under supervision of US engineers boosted the economy. But most of them left in 1932–3 when hard currency ran out, sent home unless they would accept payment in roubles. From 1931 the USSR could only afford to import essential US technology. To survive on Stalin's route to the future, there was a need for elite engineers able to invent local solutions. The Soviet government had sought from its international partner an efficient balance of trade and a long-term supply of credit, but the US refused. On 25 August 1931, Stalin declared:

> Because of the foreign exchange difficulties and unacceptable conditions for loans in America, I demand an end to all business contracts with the United States. Instead we must seek every opportunity to break existing agreements. In the future all orders will be placed with European or Soviet factories, making no exceptions, even for the most important construction projects.[10]

The world's first Communist state had spent so heavily in the first stage of the investment plan that it had run out of money and credit. Turning the Soviet Union from a country of peasants with wooden ploughs into a modern industrial society was proving prohibitively expensive. Despite Stalin's exploitation to the full of American commercial terms, he now needed to rely on industrial espionage. The Soviets pressed on with their plans, but with no cash to pay engineers from abroad, they were required to use their own experts, helped by the information provided by their intelligence gathering abroad.

Until the money ran out, every large Soviet enterprise built in this period received most of its equipment from American or European engineering companies. As diplomatic relations between the US and the USSR improved, the floodgates had opened to facilitate the transfer of skills and technology to Russia. All Soviet commercial activities in the United States were overseen by its single agency, the American Trading Corporation or AMTORG, established in 1924 with offices on New York's Fifth Avenue, in Moscow and eventually in several other cities in the USSR and the USA. Although nominally independent of the state, which was a requirement if it were to obtain legal status to trade in the United States, it was the sole Soviet reseller as well as being tasked with providing information on all aspects of US business. All commercial deals and contracts with American firms, experts, and payment for their services went via AMTORG. It would develop a well-deserved reputation as a veritable nest of spies, its employees under constant US counter-intelligence surveillance.

• • •

The Five-Year Plans had three interrelated goals: to build an industrialised society, to create an educated population, and to ensure that the Soviet Union had the means to defend itself in the event of an attack. Stalin spoke of the imperative to modernise the Soviet economy as fast as possible to meet the imminent imperialist threat. A substantial challenge for Stalin's Russia was how to protect its vast land borders and natural resources. After invasions from the Polish King Stephen Báthory,* the Swedish

---

* Báthory was the nemesis of Ivan Grozny, known in English as Ivan the Terrible. The Polish king defeated Ivan's forces in the 1580s, securing an advantageous peace.

King Gustav Adolphus,★ the French Emperor Napoleon† and the German Kaiser, followed by the Allied intervention, the lesson of history was that the Soviet army must be equipped with the most up-to-date weapons to deter further invaders. Dzerzhinsky had analysed the Tsar's defeat. Iron Felix's assessment of Russia's performance in the Great War was strikingly similar to that of the current Russian foreign intelligence service, the SVR (Sluzhba Vneshney Razvedki), whose official history mocks the naivety of the Tsarist government in embarking on a modern war without the technical resources to equip its armed forces.[11] Dzerzhinsky's studies for the Supreme Economic Council in 1924–5 emphasised that the reason for defeat lay in the dependence of the Tsarist war effort on imports of arms and munitions from its Western allies. In 1914, Russia could not even manufacture sufficient rifles for its army. It was not until 1916, thanks largely to British finance and US industrial expertise, that Russia developed a somewhat more adequate munitions industry. The Western allies had rescued the wartime Tsarist arms industry for their own war aims but were unlikely to help Communist Russia. Like defeated Germany, the Soviet Union was treated as a pariah state.

The British Empire was seen as the likely enemy. Stalin was privately convinced, as Dzerzhinsky had been, that the modernisation of the Soviet defence industry also required S&T from

---

★ The war between Sweden and Russia lasted from 1610 to 1617. In Russia's Time of Troubles, a Swedish duke was put on the Russian throne. The war ended with a large Swedish territorial gain in the Treaty of Stolbovo which excluded Russia from the Baltic Sea.

† Napoleon's failed invasion of 1812 saw him capture Moscow, no longer the capital but the main population centre, but still lose the war.

the West – first and foremost from the United States. And, since Stalin believed that war with the imperialist powers was inevitable, S&T was therefore a top priority. As he was to declare in February 1931 in a speech to industrial managers: 'We are fifty or a hundred years behind the advanced countries. We must catch up in ten years. Either we do it, or they will crush us.'[12] Though he did not realise at the time who the most dangerous potential enemy would be, the forecast was to prove prophetic.

Given the urgency, Stalin turned to his intelligence service. His library gives an extraordinary glimpse into his thinking as he marked up the passages of his reading that he found most insightful. Stalin's deep interest in developing S&T operations in the United States grew from a fascination with US and British writing on espionage. Dzerzhinsky's death in 1926 seems to have slowed the development of S&T, but only for a short while. In 1929, the autodidactic Stalin devoured the informative book *Spy and Counterspy: The Development of Modern Espionage* by the US writer Richard Wilmer Rowan.[13] Stalin's copy survives in his archive, with notes scrawled in the margin. It was from this US book that he learned how to direct and organise intelligence-gathering operations. He was attracted to the idea of using spies, not least because, as Rowan argued, they were inexpensive and efficient. In Rowan he had found the solution to his problem of how to acquire the best technology without paying for it. But he needed extraordinary men and women to become his spies.

Shumovsky's reports had highlighted the extensive problems of the armaments industry. Given the perceived threat, the country had to develop its industrial capability to sustain a prolonged fight. Without modern factories to manufacture arms, Russia

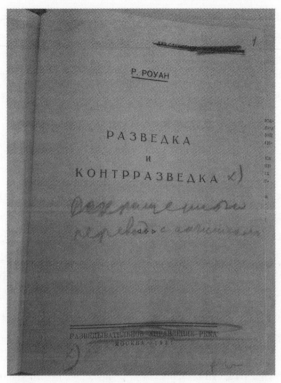

Stalin's copy of the Russian translation of Rowan's *Spy and Counterspy* – special edition for Soviet Military Intelligence. Stalin's note says 'Abridged translation from English'

remained vulnerable to a foreign invasion. Some modernisation of the armed forces was achieved thanks to secret Soviet-German military cooperation* during the 1920s, but not enough. Both

---

* Secret clauses in the Treaty of Rapallo established cooperation in air, mechanised and chemical warfare. The Germans additionally trained much of the Red Army High Command.

Germany and Russia believed, correctly, that the other was spying on them. Their shared distrust of the well-armed buffer state of Poland did not provide enough common ground to make them real allies. Moreover, the Germans were concerned that the Moscow-based Comintern (Communist International) interfered, sometimes violently, in their domestic politics. The Soviets, on the other hand, were convinced by the evidence that they were only gaining access to obsolete German military equipment, not the latest and best.[14] The issues were greatest in aviation. Dzerzhinsky highlighted to Stalin a joint venture to design and build aircraft with the German manufacturers Junkers in Moscow as a particular failure. The Soviet Union urgently needed a modern air force and Germany could not provide one. The United States, not Germany, Dzerzhinsky convinced Stalin, held the key to the future of the Soviet aircraft industry. But they also knew that only some American industrial expertise could be openly obtained through commercial contracts. In 1925, the Foreign Department (INO) of the NKVD adopted S&T operations as one of its objectives for the first time.[15] The US aviation industry was one of the key targets. Shumovsky and his cohort were the men that Stalin would come to rely on to help fulfil his dreams to industrialise and defend his country.

• • •

Stalin's Russia was the first country in the world to try to identify each year its ablest, most loyal workers to train as scientists and engineers. Some of these elite scientists and engineers would later become spies. As part of the Five-Year Plan launched in 1928, a thousand of the best and brightest young

Communist Party members (the *parttysiachniki*) were selected to receive the finest higher education on offer in Moscow and Leningrad. The Party had identified Shumovsky during his three years' work at the Ministry of Finance as a potential future leader, a Party cadre. Already a qualified pilot, he was one of a very few selected to study aeronautics at the elite Bauman Institute, where his Professor of Aerodynamics was none other than Andrey Tupolev, Russia's most famous aircraft designer. Teacher and pupil became fast friends. Towards the end of his course at the Bauman, Shumovsky was invited by the local Committee of the Communist Party to a meeting at the Lubyanka, the headquarters of the NKVD, that would once again change the course of his life. At this meeting, he met Stanislav Messing, the head of INO, and the legendary Artur Artuzov, then the deputy head.

As the foreign intelligence arm of the NKVD, INO was in 1930 tiny and poorly funded by the modern standards of espionage agencies. It deployed only ninety-four agents abroad to cover vast areas of responsibility and geography. The proposed addition of seventy-five new intelligence assets in the United States, working for up to three years, was a massive coup.[16] It was the largest and most expensive operation ever attempted by INO and required close cooperation with Military Intelligence, called at the time the Fourth Department of the Red Army. The members of the NKVD's American desk in Moscow Centre – the name given to the headquarters of the Foreign Intelligence department – that directed the highly successful campaign in the USA all sat in a small room and were perhaps at most five strong.[17] It was a small team to take on the FBI. Artuzov, by 1931 the head of INO, was the architect of some of the greatest

Soviet intelligence coups. He was responsible for the capture and execution of 'Ace of Spies' Sidney Reilly in the elaborate 'Trust' sting,* one of the greatest counter-intelligence operations of all time, earning a deservedly prominent place in espionage history. Artuzov was also responsible for setting in train the recruitment as agents of Communist students at universities across Europe who later in their careers might hold significant positions of influence in their governments. The programme's best-known products were the Cambridge Five.

It was the prickly aircraft designer Andrey Tupolev who insisted on the recruitment of Shumovsky for intelligence work. Since 1925 INO had been tasked with gathering S&T on top of political intelligence. There was a significant overlap with the work of Military Intelligence. Under the Five-Year Plan, the demand for S&T ramped up, creating the need for a fresh approach. A new type of intelligence officer with a unique set of skills was required. Besides the ability to speak languages and operate in a foreign country, this new breed of spies had to be at the top of their field in their chosen technical specialisation. Tupolev needed an aeronautics specialist on the ground in the US to bring TsAGI – the Moscow-based Central Aero and Hydrodynamics Institute, the country's leading centre of aircraft design – answers to thorny questions, not just blueprints. Above all, the agents needed to be unquestionably loyal.

Shumovsky's interview at the NKVD was a mixture of back-

---

* The CHEKA created and ran a fake White opposition movement between 1921 and 1926, trapping and turning agents sent into the Soviet Union. The White General Kutepov believed for years that there was an underground movement just waiting for an opportunity to revolt.

ground checks and ideological questioning. Given his record as a Russian Civil War hero, endorsements from the local Committee of the Communist Party and Tupolev, he passed. Accepting the job without a moment's hesitation, for he was a Party loyalist prepared to do anything for his proletarian motherland, he began a year of intense training, starting in Leningrad. Artuzov was responsible for developing the Soviet spy training programme using veteran practitioners as teachers. Later he industrialised spy training by building a dedicated school in the woods outside Moscow. Some previous operations had proceeded with no training at all, even in basic foreign languages; intelligence operatives used the cover of being a foreigner to explain away their accents and lack of language proficiency. One Soviet agent deployed to England had to get blind drunk to avoid exposure when he discovered the ambassador of Hungary, the country he claimed to be from, while speaking not a word of the language, was arriving to join the house party. Luckily, his English aristocratic hosts were used to such eccentric behaviour.[18]

Later, KGB defector General Oleg Kalugin would describe attending large classes in the 1950s that trained hundreds of newly minted agents to operate both domestically and abroad.[19] An heir of Shumovsky, Kalugin was to attend Columbia University to complete his assimilation into American life. By then, espionage training was conducted with military–style discipline, befitting those entrusted with protecting the Revolution. Shumovsky had no such formal training, but he received instruction from experienced officers in the skills of intelligence gathering, agent recruitment and how to avoid being followed. He also learned radio operations, working with codes and had a refresher on shooting a pistol. He was taught how to micro-film documents for ease of storage, concealment and transport.

Shumovsky was to operate as an intelligence officer without the benefit of diplomatic cover. As the USA was always his intended destination, he undertook a six-month intensive course in the English language, American customs and way of life. Intelligence officers, even novices, were well paid and, more important in a land of shortages, fed three hot meals a day. For recruits joining the NKVD, the experience was life-changing. One of them, Alexander Feklisov, described sleeping in a real bed for the first time in his life at the training school. The intelligence code included a vow of silence, which included never admitting to working for the organisation, even to one's parents. A new recruit would need to develop a good cover story, for his friends and family.[20]

Shumovsky's mission to enrol at MIT as a science student evolved into the perfect cover for a Soviet intelligence officer on a long-term S&T assignment in the USA. The plan was that he would enter the US concealed among a large party of students, thus attracting little attention. In 1930, the best of the 'Party Thousand', the *crème de la crème*, were chosen to study abroad. The Soviets used scarce foreign currency and gold reserves to give their elite the best education money could buy. With his exemplary academic record and political background, Shumovsky made the list with the help of the secret service. He resembled his fellow travellers in every respect. His background was iden-tical to that of his companions, as he was a recent graduate of Moscow's premier technical university. Crucially, as a student studying at a leading academic institution Shumovsky was granted a long-term visa by the US government without being asked probing questions, unlike an AMTORG employee.

As part of the plan, the Party Central Committee appointed a 'plenipotentiary' official to monitor the progress of the students abroad and send six-monthly reports back to Moscow.[21] This official had the power to order back to the Soviet Union any student making unsatisfactory progress or proving to be politically unreliable. However, their main job was to coordinate the information gathering. Raisa (Ray) Bennett, a Military Intelligence officer, was appointed to this important role.

• • •

Stalin's final priority within the Five-Year Plans was improving worker education. Among the greatest achievements of the Revolution had been universal literacy and access to education. The Tsarist government had feared education; successive rulers took active measures to limit literacy levels in their subjects by taxing village schools. They came to believe that if they allowed their people to read, they would become revolutionaries. The prohibitive measures ensured precisely the outcome the government feared.

Ministers shook at the thought of what might happen if the fate of the reforming Tsar Alexander II, who had promised a modicum of universal education, was repeated. Alexander's short-lived experiment with liberalisation had resulted in his assassination by anarchists. Lenin's beloved older brother was hanged for his part in the plot. After that unhappy episode, the autocracy did everything it could to stifle education for the untrusted masses, from whom they demanded devotion. It was no surprise that adult literacy rates in Tsarist Russia were less than 30 per cent, while literacy among males was roughly double that of females. My own great-grandfather, a leading Communist in the Crimea, was unable to sign his name until he learned to read after the Revolution. (Today's Russia has 99.7 per cent literacy.) As Professor Shumovsky, as he became, later told UNESCO, in 1917 only 9,656,000 students were in school out of a total population of around 175 million.[22]

The unenlightened policy held back the economic development of the country, as there was only a shallow pool of educated workers. Hundreds of thousands of Russia's most literate individuals emigrated, primarily to the United States, taking their talent with them in a dramatic brain drain. With less than half the Tsar's army able to read and write, the country was vulnerable to military attack. After the October Revolution, the idealist journalist John Reed (the only American to be interred after his death in the Kremlin Wall) wrote:

All Russia was learning to read, and reading – politics, economics, history because the people wanted to know . . . In every city, in most towns, along with the Front, each political faction had its newspaper – sometimes several. Hundreds of thousands of pamphlets were distributed by thousands of organizations and poured into the armies, the villages, the factories, the streets. The thirst for education, so long thwarted, burst with the Revolution into a frenzy of expression. From Smolny Institute alone, the first six months, went out every day tons, car-loads, train-loads of literature, saturating the land. Russia absorbed reading matter like hot sand drinks water, insatiable. And it was not fables, falsified history, diluted religion, and the cheap fiction that corrupts – but social and economic theories, philosophy, the works of Tolstoy, Gogol and Gorky.[23]

In the immediate aftermath of the October Revolution, education policy was overhauled with a tenfold increase in the expenditure on mass education. Lenin argued: 'As long as there is such a thing in the country as illiteracy it is hard to talk about political education.' Despite the utterly grim conditions, he launched national literacy campaigns. Victor Serge, a first-hand witness of the Communist Revolution, saw the tremendous odds facing educators and the miserable conditions that existed in the wake of the Russian Civil War. A typical school would have classes of hungry children in rags huddled in winter around a small stove planted in the middle of the classroom. The pupils shared one pencil between four of them, and their schoolmistress was hungry. In spite of this grotesque misery, such a thirst for knowledge sprang up all over the country that new schools, adult courses, universities and Workers' Faculties were formed everywhere.[24] In its first year of existence, the Communist literacy campaign reached an incredible five million people, of whom about half learned to read and write. In the Red Army, where literacy and education were deemed crucial, illiteracy was eradicated within seven years.

The Five-Year Plans and the Stalinist project to transform the Soviet economy were born of idealism as well as insecurity. The prospect of a great leap forward into a fully socialist economy kindled among a new generation of Party militants much the same messianic fervour as had inspired Lenin's followers in the heady aftermath of the October Revolution and victory in the Civil War.

The young Communist idealists of the early 1930s, among them Soviet intelligence officers and other Russian students at MIT, believed in Stalin as well as in the coming 'Triumph of Socialism'. Hailing from a generation who believed that the end justified the means, they would certainly not have recognised the prevailing view of Stalin among contemporary historians. The first group of elite Soviet students under the Politburo order was to be sent abroad in 1931. Individual Soviet specialists were already at many foreign universities, including a few in the US. The renowned Soviet atomic scientist Pyotr Kapitsa was number two in Ernest Rutherford's team at the Cavendish Laboratory at Cambridge University,[*] while Dr Yakov Fishman learned about the chemistry of poison gases at the Italian university at Naples.

As Shumovsky and his party prepared to depart for the United States, US legal firm Simpson Thacher began the process of arranging the visas.[25] (According to the 1948 FBI investigation,[†] Shumovsky was a late addition to the roster. It is unclear if that was a decision taken in Moscow or one determined by the availability of places on courses.) Like Shumovsky, the students in his party were not fresh-faced teenagers just out of high school, but married ex-military men who had not been able to begin formal education until the end of the Russian Civil War in 1922 and had since been fast-tracked towards greatness. Many were from humble backgrounds and acutely aware that, but for the Communist Revolution, they would never have had any prospect of an education. Central to their motivation was the desire to enable Soviet industry and military technology to catch up with the West. The offices of the Rockefeller and Carnegie Foundations

---

[*] Kapitsa was the first director of the Royal Society's Mond Laboratory and a fellow of Trinity College.

[†] After the Soviet atomic explosion the FBI belatedly began an investigation into Soviet espionage.

facilitated finding places at appropriate universities to help foster better international relations.[26] Back in Moscow, the finance was organised. As with every decision in the Soviet system, the budget was decided centrally at a Politburo meeting in 1930. Several thousand gold roubles was allocated for the trip, amounting to a total fund of $1 million. Each student was assigned from a key industry and that industry's management had the responsibility of paying.

The one tricky condition imposed by the American universities was that the students must demonstrate a high competence in English. Typically, the exam followed a two-year course, but this talented group was given just six months to reach the required standard.[27] There was a desperate need for teachers to give the Soviet students English lessons in Moscow before they went off to study at MIT and other US universities. Among those selected for the task was Military Intelligence officer, American Ray Bennett. Another was Gertrude Klivans, a young Radcliffe College-educated teacher from a family of Russian-Jewish jewellers in Ohio.

• • •

Klivans had become bored with life as a high school teacher in the Midwest and started travelling adventurously around the world. She was first talent-spotted by General Vitaly Markovich Primakov while both were journeying from Japan to Vladivostok aboard a cargo vessel, described by Klivans as 'an ancient hulk', which forced its small group of passengers to cling together 'as we pitched and tossed'.[28] Klivans's letters to her family reveal that during the voyage she became quite friendly with Primakov.[29] They clearly began an affair on board. Primakov, Klivans gushed

Gertrude Klivans, Radcliffe College, Harvard – yearbook.
The picture is captioned: 'Her eyes were stars of twilight fair/Like twilight, too, her dusky hair'

to her family, was 'the youngest full general in the Red Army', a man whose travels (in fact they were spying missions) had taken him as far afield as Afghanistan, China and Japan: he 'fought throughout the Revolution and on every battlefront during the Civil War – wears three medals, is always armed to the teeth – an expert swordsman and a cavalryman from a Cossack family that have been horsemen for generations, and withal, his head is shaven. But his eyes, the real gray blue, Russian eyes and fair skin make you forget that military custom.'

Klivans reported to her family that, during the long trans-Siberian train journey from Vladivostok to Moscow, 'I spent most of every day in Primakov's compartment, so I enjoyed all the privileges of first class, even accepting the offer of taking a bath.' She fell deeply in love. Although the train arrived a day late, 'I didn't care – I didn't want it ever to end.' She had intended to return to New York, but Primakov promised to help her find a teaching job in Moscow. Remarkably, she admitted to her family that he had suggested she work for Soviet intelligence: 'Imagine – I was offered a job in the [O.] G. P. U.★ as soon as I learned the [Russian] language.'

Primakov had enjoyed a glittering career in the Red Army and the intelligence service. He cut his teeth leading a squadron of troops in the attack on the Petrograd Winter Palace in 1917. The highlight of his espionage career came in 1929 when, disguised as a Turkish officer named Ragib-bey, he led a special operation of Soviet troops to try to reinstate Amanullah Khan as ruler of Afghanistan. He was arrested in 1936 and executed in the following year's Great Purge.[30]

Although in letters to her family Klivans complained that living conditions in Moscow had left her with 'a few bedbug bites', she declared herself 'very happy with my work'. She worked diligently to teach her charges all about America:

You can't imagine how well I know these boys, all of whom are at least five years older [than me] . . . They will do anything for me and believe me I do plenty for them, besides keeping them in cigarettes and informing them of certain Americanisms. I mean

---

★ An earlier name for the NKVD.

as far as deportment is concerned, I try to make each of them letter perfect in the President's English and if you think it isn't hard work you are mistaken. But there are always three at least who are making love to me outside of school hours so that I can never keep a straight face for at least five minutes going in class. If you would see them, all in their fur hats, high felt boots, and a week's beard for nobody shaves more than once in five days you would laugh. But they are fun, and I certainly will always have 15 fast friends in Russia. Probably someday one of them will be another Stalin – they are all party men, active and so understanding of my distorted view of life as they can understand the limitations of my bourgeois environment, the only thing they can't understand is why I haven't already embraced Communism without any reservations.[31]

To celebrate the end of the examinations after her language course, Klivans threw a party for the students on 15 April 1931, for which she prepared the closest approximation she could manage to American sandwiches and salads. The only woman at the party, she wore a 'Chinese suit' acquired on her travels. It was an emotional occasion with many hours of dancing and singing. Klivans travelled to the United States ahead of her Russian students, describing them in her letter home:

Let me tell you who the boys are. They are all 27 or 28. One [Alexander Gramp] is half Georgian and half Armenian – speaks both of these languages and knows every place on the map of Russia with his eyes shut – has a disposition that even Russian conditions cannot spoil. Another is a White Russian [MIT-bound

72

Eugene Bukley] – as clever as any three people I've met and had a sense of humor that works equally well in any language – the third [Peter Ivanov, a future student at Harvard] is a serious electrical engineer who served as a sort of lever in our hilarious spirits. Of the first two, one is a railway engineer, in fact, that got us tickets everywhere – something almost unheard of in Russia today. The other one is also an electrical engineer.[32]

Alexander Gramp's graduation, Purdue University, 1933

Klivans's closest relationship was with the railway engineer, Gramp, one of the five students with a place at Purdue University. He married her after his graduation, returning with her to Moscow following his appointment as Dean of the College of Railway Engineering.

Eager to ensure that her students made a good impression on their arrival at MIT and other US universities, Klivans pressed successfully for scarce foreign currency reserves. When they landed in New York, she wanted to buy them smart, well-cut suits.

3

'WHAT THE COUNTRY NEEDS IS A REAL BIG LAUGH'

To the disappointment and astonishment of Communists, the American working people did not rise up en masse during the Great Depression to demand even the overhaul – much less the overthrow – of their system of democratic capitalism, despite the failure to relieve their sufferings for more than a decade. Arriving at the height of the economic misery, a confident Gertrude Klivans held court in her stateroom on SS *Bremen* at the New York docks. She was back at long last in the United States, a returning political pilgrim and a secret convert to Communism. While she was already an agent of INO, Klivans did not consider herself a traitor to the US, but rather a contributor to helping the peoples of the Soviet Union.

Her courtiers were a small crowd of journalists, fans of the small-town socialite-turned-adventurer. She was a Youngstown, Ohio celebrity. Local magazines had serialised parts of the letters she had written to her family from the mysterious, godless USSR describing most of her adventures. Exposure to the socialist experiment had transformed her in just a year from a frustrated English Literature teacher at the local high school into a confident woman, delighted to be sought out for her views on the world. She was secretly engaged, if not already married, to her fellow agent Alexander Gramp. She adroitly ducked answering questions from the wire services on international politics, but was more than happy to announce that the first Soviet Five-Year Plan was a resounding success. Joseph Stalin must have been pleased. The journalists asked her if it was possible to teach the Soviet leaders anything. She replied, 'Indeed yes, in fact, they are the most teachable people to be found.'[1]

Amid America's worst ever socio-economic crisis, Klivans delivered the message that a socialist future was the answer to her society's ills. Before October 1929 the United States had believed that it would enjoy an uninterrupted period of increasing prosperity. This mirage was not an invention of the people but was what they had been told by their leaders. In his last State of the Union address in 1928, President Calvin Coolidge had said: 'No Congress of the United States ever assembled, on surveying the state of the Union, has met with a more pleasing prospect than that which appears at the present time.'[2] He had overseen an expanding economy based on easy access to consumer loans for housing, its citizens buying vast numbers of new automobiles on credit instalment plans. The vehicles, once a luxury, were now commonplace and seemingly affordable; there was even a fear that the car would create an amoral society as young couples were now out of sight of their parents. That great barometer of America's health, the stock market indices, were not merely soaring on the back of the credit bubble; they went through the roof. The Dow Jones Industrial Average quadrupled between 1924 and 1929. America appeared to be on the brink of economic greatness.

Led by New York, the modern cities of the USA were a
bustling hive of theatre, movies, arts, food and sober fun. Based
on its global leadership in technological innovation, mass production and consumerism, America had overtaken the British Empire
as the pre-eminent economic power in the world. When Herbert
Hoover campaigned for the presidency in 1928, he assured the
country it could expect ever greater economic prosperity. In a
campaign speech, he said: 'We in America today are nearer to
the final triumph over poverty than ever before in the history
of any land. We shall soon, with the help of God, be in sight of
the day when poverty will be banished from this nation.'[3]

Hoover would later quip that he was the first man in history
to have a depression named after him. For all these dreams came
crashing down in just a few days in 1929, and for the next decade,
even the Big Apple became a sombre city of hopeless, desperate
people. The stock market crash began on 24 October and ended
on the 29th. In a matter of four days, America saw $30 billion
of its wealth wiped out for ever. Within months New Yorkers
were starving to death. Large crowds of bewildered investors,
bank workers and concerned citizens wandered around Wall
Street in a daze during the crash. In an attempt to exercise some
control the police began making arrests. After the initial panic,
worse was to follow.

The administration estimated that any recession resulting from
the crash would be shallow, like the one the United States had
experienced after the Great War. Despite the high drama, the
conservative President Hoover believed that 'anything can make
or break a market . . . from the failure of a bank to the rumor
that your second cousin's grandmother has a cold'.[4] He and his
laissez-faire economist advisors thought it was just a small setback

and the market would soon bounce back. It didn't. Publicly, Hoover continually downplayed the nation's agony, retreating into his dogmatic shell and refusing to act. At this most difficult time, he offered his wounded people no leadership. In the face of the suffering and bewilderment, the White House appeared distant and unmoving.

Throughout the crisis, Hoover would display terrible judgement. One of his most passionate causes was to deny combat veterans an increase in their benefits. When it came to providing depression relief, he insisted that private charity, not state aid, funnelled through the Red Cross was sufficient. He went further, expressing the belief that charity was the sole answer to the enormous and growing needs of America's army of unemployed and starving. He kept up this line even when nature added to the misery, a severe drought creating a dust bowl in the Great Plains region. In a White House press interview Hoover displayed shocking callousness towards his fellow citizens. 'Nobody is starving,' the President blithely asserted. 'The hoboes are better fed than they ever were before.'[5] New York City alone reported ninety-five cases of death by starvation that year.

Describing the start of the Great Depression as merely public hysteria, Hoover declared that 'what the country needs is a real big laugh. If someone could get off a good joke every ten days, I think our troubles would be over in two months.'[6] Far from being gripped by laughter, waves of bank runs began in New York City and spread panic around the country. In fear customers flooded into their banks to take out their savings. The banks didn't have any cash; no one did. By 1931 it became evident that many banks were going out of business. In December, the Bank of the United States in New York collapsed, having at one stage held more than $210 million in customer deposits. It was a tipping point, and within the next month 300 other banks failed. By April 1932, more than 750,000 people in New York alone were on some form of welfare and a further 160,000 were on the waiting list. In desperation, crowds of unemployed men took to wandering the streets wearing signs showcasing their skills in an attempt to find work.

• • •

Klivans gave a series of detailed, teasing interviews to the newspapers about some of her experiences during her ten months teaching English in Russia. Amid the chaos, she sat on an upholstered chair in her parents' elegant drawing room wearing an evening gown for the first time since she had left Youngstown society life to venture into the heart of the Soviet Union. One journalist asked the burning question:

it's raining outside; you are alone in the house, lonely. At the door stand two young men, one Russian, a senior of Moscow University; the other is a Harvard senior. Which would you prefer as company for the evening?' Klivans replied, 'I'd prefer the Russian because he is more mature, more intelligent, not so flippant and doesn't neck. Necking is not a national pastime in Russia. Sex is delegated to secondary importance. Work comes first, then sex. What is immoral in America is moral in Russia.'[7]

A mildly irritated Klivans knew the exact lines to prick the journalist's interest: 'Russians can't understand America's exploitation of sex.' While in Moscow she had shared with her class pictures from American periodicals of bathing beauties in tooth-paste and mouthwash adverts. The reaction was merely raised Russian eyebrows and quizzical smiles. She announced that Soviet society had developed very progressive answers to America's fixations with sex, drinking, divorce and religion. None of the curses of American life existed in the Soviet Union, she believed, and unlike America, there was practically no graft in government. She had found there to be few courts to speak of, no instalment credit plans and few automobiles. Divorce rates had soared in the US during the economic crisis as the strain of unemployment took a vicious toll on relationships, and the busy divorce lawyers were reviled; in the Soviet Union, she believed, divorce and other lawyers were unknown. Klivans spoke of the very different ideas towards love and marriage found in the Soviet Union, where it was now the case that 'whether registered or not the marriage is legal, and the parties can separate permanently without any more ado about it. No five day waiting is required when a Russian wants to get married. He just goes ahead and gets married. If he likes, he can register the marriage, and this means that if he leaves her their property will be equally distributed.'[8]

Some American scaremongers peddled the myth that Communism was synonymous with an amoral society. In Klivans's view, it was American society, whose members had sex in cars, which was promiscuous, and not the atheist Russians. Cars in Russia were few in number and used exclusively for work. It was freedom-loving Americans, she continued, who had to be deprived of alcohol by their own government's prohibition laws. America's deprived drinkers would be jealous of the Russians, who took their daily drinking quite seriously. And yet, despite the ready availability of alcohol, there were in her experience few real drunkards in evidence on the streets of Moscow or Leningrad. Wine and beer were the favoured tipples. Seemingly Russians could be trusted to behave themselves responsibly with alcohol, whereas Americans could not. Moreover, she believed that religion was not prohibited in Russia, although as a result of pressure brought to bear on those who attended worship most Russians did not attend church. Overall she challenged the alarmist conservative view that a lack of religious training in Russia had lowered the moral standard of the country.

Painting a picture of a society with difficult economic problems but one that had embarked on an exciting journey to a much better future, she confirmed to readers that despite the advantages of some aspects of the Communist system, there were extreme shortages of the basics in the Soviet Union. 'One cannot buy the most trivial thing in Russia such as knives, scissors, screwdrivers, thumb tacks and the thousand and one other things that are so common in our five and ten cent store. An American five and ten cent store transplanted to Russia would probably give the Russians the impression that the millennium had arrived.'[9] But Klivans was a convert, as she had found living in Russia had given her a tremendous feeling of stimulation at being part of an energetic society where everyone worked for a definite purpose. She would get her wish to go back to what she described as 'the most exciting place on the globe'. She was not alone. Many fellow left-leaning US thinkers had already made similar pilgrimages to Moscow.

A highly perceptive observer, Klivans could have been an excellent US intelligence asset. She certainly was an important Soviet one, through her work passing on to her charges her observations on American life. She had learned during her stay exactly what was going on in the USSR. Her close friendships with her students had given her invaluable information. Her sources were impeccable, as her engineering students were at the heart of every aspect of the first Five-Year Plan. And her analysis of the state of Soviet economic development was correct. She told America the unvarnished truth that in the mind of the Russians Henry Ford was the greatest American and that they were trying to model Soviet industry on his methods. It was her view, however, that using the Ford method without Ford himself to direct them might not lead to success. She explained the importance of the mission in America her charges were about to be sent on:

> The development in Russia has been so rapid that usually even after new industries have been established the training of the Russian labour has been so inadequate that they cannot run them. A tractor factory that was supposed to have turned out 100,000 tractors per year has turned out not over 2,000 in six months, and none of these would run more than 4 or 5 days without falling apart, solely because of the lack of training on the part of the workers.[10]

Earnestly Klivans explained that the Soviet Union was still very much a work in progress, not the finished article. Her students were now on the way to America in order to learn the skills to train Russian workers to drive the industrialisation programme. In Russia, she exclaimed, engineers were rated highest among the professional men, the value placed on them three times greater than that of a doctor. She adroitly turned the reporters' dumbest questions to her advantage to explain the sacrifices required from the Russian people today for a brighter tomorrow: 'There are no sleepless nights for Russian families, for no coffee is served. Food of the type familiar to us is impossible to obtain. Most of it is shipped to foreign countries, and the proceeds go towards purchasing machinery for the Soviet factories. Wheat, fish and the like are extensively imported, however, as are fine wines.'[11] And the Russians, Miss Klivans declared, actually liked work. But few in the US cared to listen.

The readers of the newspapers were evidently hungry for news about the mysterious Soviet Union, a society with an answer to the world's problems. No doubt they were confused by the conflicting accounts trickling out of Moscow. Jack Hayward, another correspondent, reported, perhaps untruthfully, in the same edition of the newspaper that when a Russian went shopping in Moscow, he was likely to find that his cheese purchase was made of wood; delicious. Klivans confirmed to readers that despite the ongoing effects of the Great Depression, standards of living were still higher for the majority in the United States than in Russia. But the gap was closing. The Ulanovskys, two 'illegal' Military Intelligence agents already embedded in New York at the time, agreed. They had witnessed first hand the conditions of the unemployed, homeless families in the shanty towns known as 'Hoovervilles' set up on the Great Lawn at Central Park and Riverside Park at 72nd Street in New York City. These Russian patriots arrived knowing that America was the classic country of capitalism,

the most disgusting in the world, and we sought to see all the evils of capitalism first hand quickly, and we found a lot of it unattractive . . . We saw the unemployed in line for soup, which was distributed by the Salvation Army. But the unemployed in the queue in 1931, during the Depression, were dressed better than my Moscow friends. We went looking in vain for a slum.[12]

•   •   •

But why was there such an intense American interest in news from the first Communist state? The answer lay in the grim, fatalistic mood of the US at the time. Trapped in the midst of the Great Depression, perhaps they were witnessing the death of the American dream itself. Like many of her generation, Gertrude Klivans had, through her travels, come to question the very future and purpose of liberal democracy and capitalism. She had discovered a 'Soviet atmosphere, an atmosphere strangely free from the tradition of that brand of democracy to be found in the West'.[13]

The Communist state's giant socialist experiment polarised US public opinion. Most US visitors to the Soviet Union returned home with their views reinforced. Those who had come seeking alternatives to the raging social crisis in depression-hit America found hope in the socialist experiment; others who sought it found deprivation, oppression and a rising red menace. Enthusiasm in liberal and left-leaning circles for Communism tracked the ups and downs of the US economic cycle. Initially, the Russian Revolution had been greeted with wild enthusiasm, although US banks lost billions on the default of Tsarist debt. 'I have seen the future, and it works,'[14] proclaimed American journalist Lincoln Steffens, who was targeted by Soviet Military Intelligence in 1931 for possible recruitment as an 'agent of influence'. The Soviets approached many leading left-leaning cultural figures in this period to play an active role as advocates for socialism. Most rebuffed the approaches. Some did not. Steffens refused to join up, but as an ideologically sympathetic fellow traveller, he promised to help the Soviet Union when the interests of the US and the USSR coincided.

In the 1920s, as the US economy prospered in the post-war recovery, the Soviet Union had been roundly criticised by visiting international socialists for its failings. Despite thousands of invitations to sympathetic left-leaning artists, writers and politicians to visit, the Russians could garner few friends. Some criticised the Soviets for insufficient radicalism, as they wanted a world revolution. Many found issue with the Communists' belief that 'the end justifies the means'. The Communists in power were too brutal for their taste. Lincoln Steffens on the other hand found convenient excuses for the bloody excesses of the 'Red Terror'. He concluded that the Soviets were not evil per se but that dire circumstances had forced evil on them. 'Soviet Russia was a revolutionary government with an evolutionary plan enduring a temporary condition of evil, which is made tolerable by hope and a plan.'[15]

In bohemian circles, there was still much praise for Moscow's artistic freedom, avant-garde theatre, movies and poetry. As the US economy boomed in the 1920s, intellectual socialists were out of touch with the day-to-day issues of the working class. It was only during the crisis of the 1930s that the Soviet Union and Communism started to enjoy broader US support and clandestine help. The crisis of capitalism and the rise of fascism (seen by the left as capitalism with murder) proved to be the catalyst for the growth of the US radical left. Marx's theory of historical determinism was in vogue.

• • •

The closing of all American banks on 4 March 1933 marked the nadir for capitalism as the entire nation went into a state of traumatic shock. The illusion of permanent prosperity that had captivated and motivated everyone during the boom evaporated. The deepening economic crisis caught intellectuals such as novelist Theodore Dreiser and socialist writer Upton Sinclair unawares, but they soon recovered to take the lead in asserting that American capitalism was undeserving of support or survival. From 1930 onwards there had begun a quest that took many on a journey leading far from their social, political and philosophical starting points. Along the way some fell into the waiting arms of Soviet intelligence. This was the era when Communists joined the US government, not just to gather useful information for their Soviet controllers but also to influence government policy for Communist ends. Dozens of agents such as Nathan Silvermaster, Lachlan Currie and Harry Dexter White found careers in government service, in particular in the Treasury and the Labor Department.

The battering of the Great Depression dispelled political apathy. No one could remain indifferent to the capitalist system that was creating havoc and misery. Liberalism was the first political casualty of this political awakening. Its spokesmen had failed to foresee the catastrophe and, the radicals believed, were unable to explain its causes, cope effectively with its consequences or offer answers. In their search for a solution many turned their eyes abroad. If the Russians were achieving full employment and economic growth with their backward technology, surely the Americans could do far better with their advanced facilities? In the US, the factories were built but now lay idle, so the priority was a plan for the economy to put America back to work. The leftward move, coupled with the feebleness of right-wing opinion at the time, made the Communist movement the unchallenged attraction. The starry-eyed saw a promised paradise in the land of the Five-Year Plans, while the more grounded were impressed by the achievements of a planned economy operated on the foundation of nationalised property. A Soviet-style economic policy might provide the means of propelling the US economy forward, eliminating the scourge of mass unemployment.

· · ·

Blamed for causing the Depression, Hoover won only 39.7 per cent of the popular vote in the 1932 presidential election, a dismal result, and in 1933 Franklin Delano Roosevelt replaced him as President. Roosevelt's reforms derailed the leftward political momentum in the US. A stream of radicals were hired into the federal government to enact depression relief measures adopted from their leftist agenda. Faith in the vitality of American capitalism revived with the economic upturn. Roosevelt's New Deal aimed to provide support for the millions of unemployed, to grow the economy and to enact reform to prevent a repeat of the financial crisis. It was attractive for some Communists who, as members of the Democratic administration, could be anti-fascist fighters, defend the cause of labour and promote the aims of the Communist Party and the Soviet Union while pursuing a government career with a good salary. It was no wonder at the time that Soviet spy rings flourished unhindered at the heart of the American government. But New Deal reform did not extend much beyond the end of the recession in 1937, when urgent plans for war displaced domestic concerns. And as the vision of an imminent proletarian revolution was eclipsed by the war shadows, the slow journey back to a belief in democracy quickened into a stampede. Patriotic fervour swamped the radicalism of the thirties. Conservatives still depict the Red Decade as an ugly spectacle of rampant subversion in America.

One clear demonstration of the broad appeal of the radical message at the time, but not of the socialist name, was given by the writer and politician Upton Sinclair. Having founded EPIC (End Poverty In California) to pursue a solution more radical than Roosevelt's New Deal, Sinclair came close to becoming Governor of California in 1934. He wrote after his defeat that 'the American People will take Socialism, but they won't take the label. I certainly proved it in the case of EPIC. Running on the Socialist ticket, I got 60,000 votes and running on the slogan to "End Poverty in California" I got 879,000. I think we simply have to recognize the fact that our enemies have succeeded in spreading the Big Lie. There is no use attacking it by a frontal attack; it is much better to out-flank them.'[16]

Sinclair was a lifelong Socialist who had become frustrated with the New Deal's inability to end the Depression at a stroke. Rather than putting the unemployed on relief, Sinclair proposed, via EPIC, to put them to work within a state-organised 'production-for-use' economy distinct from the capitalist marketplace. Under his scheme, the state would take over idle farms and factories, allowing the jobless to grow their own food or produce clothing and other goods. Any surplus could be traded, through a system of barter, only for other goods produced within the system. Considered the front-runner in the election, Sinclair was subjected to intense attacks from both Republicans and Democrats as 'a communistic wolf in the dried skin of the Democratic donkey'.[17]

• • •

The Soviet students tripping down the gangplank in the summer of 1931 arrived with fixed expectations and preconceived ideas about America. The views of Shumovsky and his fellow Soviet students were based on their own political ideology, reinforced by selective imported left-wing reading and popular culture including movies. Long before the Revolution, the idea of America had exercised a profound fascination for Russians, and not just for its technological successes. There was a hungry market in Russia for American movies and cheap novels about cowboys and gangsters.[18] An unusual import was the staging of selected American dramas. Several American plays were produced in Moscow, notably *The Front Page* – famously adapted in 1940 for the screen as *His Girl Friday* starring Cary Grant and Rosalind Russell – which was rechristened *Sensations* for a Communist audience. Giving theatre-going Muscovites a further taste of the life and times of the windy city was a staging of *Chicago*, a 'tale of America's foremost big gun and bullet city' depicting the life of Roxie Hart and today more renowned as a musical. Hollywood movie styles inspired domestically produced Soviet films, which often emulated the style and stunts of Harold Lloyd, Buster Keaton and the Keystone Kops in delivering their ideological message. In one popular movie, *The Extraordinary Adventures of Mr. West in the Land of the Bolsheviks*,[19] an American philanthropist, fearful for his own safety having heard lurid tales of bloodthirsty Communists, brings a cowboy to Moscow as a personal bodyguard. The cowboy, played by a Moscow circus clown, is a carbon copy of Keaton, while Moscow's finest do a passable impression of the Keystone Kops. The philanthropist falls victim to conniving White Guards spinning impossible tales such as that the iconic Bolshoi Theatre was dynamited by the Communists. Mr West returns to the US, and the arms of his relieved wife, knowing that tales of bloodthirsty philistines destroying Moscow are untrue. As the students arrived in America, like Klivans they felt the need to tackle prejudices about the new Russia similar to those held by Mr West and many Americans.

Two Russian satirists, Ilf and Petrov, summed up Russian expectations of arriving in depression-hit New York:

> the word 'America' has well-developed grandiose associations for a Soviet person, for whom it refers to a country of skyscrapers, where day and night one hears the unceasing thunder of surface and underground trains, the hellish roar of automobile horns, and the continuous despairing screams of stockbrokers rushing through the skyscrapers waving their ever-falling shares.[20]

They believed they would find a culture of exploitation in America and that 'the rich people not only had all the money' but 'the poor man was down, and he had to stay down'.[21] They had devoured in Moscow the available books on America, mostly those of socialist writers Sinclair and Dreiser about the current state of the US. Without another source of knowledge, they believed them to be the gospel truth. The students expected to find 'a population, low-class and mostly foreign, hanging always on the verge of starvation and dependent for its opportunities of life upon the whim of men every bit as brutal and unscrupulous as the old-time slave drivers; under such circumstances, immorality is exactly as inevitable, and as prevalent, as it is under the system of chattel slavery'.[22]

As devout Communists, they did not expect a warm welcome on American soil but to be confronted with cold shoulders and suspicion. And they soon learned that outside the narrow circles of intellectuals and émigrés they needed to be careful when discussing Communism. On their travels, they discovered that the deeply conservative soul of America was rooted in traditional churchgoing communities that were suspicious of new-fangled foreign ideas.

> Officially, a man will never be forced out of his job for his beliefs. He is free to hold any views, any convictions. He's a free citizen. But let him try to praise communism – and something like this happens, he will just not find work in a small or big town. He will not even notice it happening. People who do it, do not believe in God but go to church because it is indecent not go to church. As for Communism, that is for Mexicans, Slavs, and black people. It is not an American thing.[23]

Russians were not yet an urbanised people, and they knew that the real America was to be discovered in its myriad small towns and villages, not its cities. Soviet visitors loved taking road trips, driving across America's incredible highway system in the freedom of a car. On their journey they discovered in equal measure much to admire and amuse:

Americans don't like to waste time on stupid things, for example, on the torturous process of coming up with names for their towns. And indeed, why strain yourself when so many beautiful names already exist in the world? That's right, an authentic Moscow, just in the state of Ohio, not in the USSR in Moscow province. There's another Moscow in some other state, and yet another Moscow in a third state. On the whole, every state has the absolute right to have its very own Moscow.[24]

Soviet visitors discovered in America a confusing, happy melting pot of nationalities. One remarked that 'a Spaniard and a Pole worked in the barbershop where we got our hair cut. An Italian shined our shoes. A Croat washed our car.' However, they encountered racism and discrimination of a type that their revolution had eliminated:

To a Soviet person, used to the nationality policy of the USSR, all the mistakes of the American government's Indian policy are evident from the first glance. The errors are, of course, intentional. The fact of the matter is that in Indian schools, the class is conducted exclusively in English. There is no written form of any Indian language at all. It's true that every Indian tribe has its own language, but this doesn't change anything. If there were any desire to do so, the many American specialists who have fallen in love with Indian culture could create Indian written languages in a short time. But imperialism remains imperialism.[25]

Russian visitors to the US often found American society shallow: 'If you should attempt to maintain that film is an art in conversation with a cultured, intelligent American, he'll just plain stop talking to you.'[26] American workers were too materialistic, seem-ingly happy with the system of exploitation, easily bought off rather than striking and heading to the barricades. Americans appeared obsessed with their material conditions to the exclusion of culture and the spiritual. The observation of Gertrude Klivans was that to meet demand the Soviets published more books in a year, she estimated, than any other country. However, many of the avid readers had probably had only one square meal in three years. In addition, 'Art rates [are] very high in Moscow and throughout the Soviet states Opera is highly popular, as are the theater and literature. Among the classic authors, Tolstoy reigns supreme. Gorky is the idol of the modernists. But art, in Russian fashion, must interpret the struggle for expression of the masses, the keynote of present day civilization in that country.'[27]

MIT welcomed the arrival of the Russians. The Institute had embarked on an ambitious investment plan at the very moment the Great Depression hit, leading to a dramatic fall in US student numbers. In 1932 and 1933, across the nation some eighty thou-sand youths who in more prosperous times would have attended college were unable to enrol. Universities were thus desperate for the income that the arrival of the Russian students provided and were correspondingly uninterested in asking any awkward questions. America's finest universities were about to start teaching the cream of Russia's leadership how to build an even stronger socialist society. And one university was to show inadvertently how to spy on America and create a chain leading to the greatest espionage achievement of all time: the theft of the secret of the Manhattan Project – how to build an atomic bomb.

4

'AGENT 001'

Throughout the hot summer of 1931, after more than a year of careful planning, seventy-five determined Russians arrived in the US to enrol as students at its elite universities.[1] Disembarking at the Port of New York, shaky after a week at sea, the first of the generation of Soviet 'super spies' set foot in America when Stanislav Shumovsky, one of the final fifty-four, landed in late September. He travelled on the SS *Europa*, arriving just in time for the start of the new academic term. The group included architects, town planners, mining experts, transport gurus, metallurgists, ship designers, aeronautics experts, chemists, electrical and mechanical engineers. A few were professional intelligence officers, the rest willing helpers. They had all been sent by Stalin to find out first hand how America had met and surmounted the engineering challenges of industrialisation.

It would be wrong to say Soviet intelligence invented industrial espionage. As early as June 1810, Francis Cabot Lowell, a Boston businessman and Harvard alumnus, had embarked on an industrial espionage mission for the US. He set off on a two-year visit with his family to Scotland and England as war clouds darkened in North America, using as his cover story 'poor health'. The mill towns of the north of England were not known for their curative delights and Lowell's interests lay in stealing the secrets of Britain's Industrial Revolution. The textile industry based in the growing towns of Lancashire and Scotland was at the heart of that revolution, one fuelled by new water- or steam-powered spinning and weaving machines. The flint-hearted capitalists of Britain were never going to allow anyone – and certainly not an American – to buy drawings or a model of a powered loom. So Lowell secretly studied the machines on his visits to the mills, although their desperate working conditions must surely have played havoc with his failing health. In a quite prodigious feat, Lowell memorised the workings of the British power looms without committing anything to paper.

By the time he departed Britain's shores in 1812, the country was at war with the United States, and Lowell was carefully searched on his departure. Back in Boston, he built his textile factories, funding his enterprises with a pioneering public stock offering, and was awarded the patent for the powered loom, a stolen copy of the British version, in 1815. There was no end to Lowell's claims; he even suggested that the technology was all his original work adapted to local conditions rather than the fruits of industrial espionage. In recognition of his imaginative schemes, he was inducted into the US Business Hall of Fame in 2013.[2]

In 1931 the intelligence mastermind Artur Artuzov, Shumovsky's recruiter, had unleashed a new type of Soviet intelligence operation, one which would do to the Americans what they had done to the British. It was the start of a process of stealing industrial secrets that was to last for almost eighty years. From late 1931 until 2010★ a trail of agents would penetrate the US by enrolling as students in elite universities following the textbook rules written by Shumovsky.

• • •

Some of Shumovsky's travelling companions were enrolled in undergraduate programmes; others, already qualified engineers, were on shorter specialist courses perhaps lasting a year or more to gain valuable experience. Soviet intelligence targeted American universities for two main reasons. First, America's position as the most competitive modern industrialised society was based on its ability to produce from its universities a steady stream of fresh graduate engineers and scientists who could transfer ideas from university-based research centres to America's factory floors and production lines. Such constant innovation maintained the position of the US as the world's leading economy.

Stalin wanted to emulate and surpass the US economy, but he first needed to learn and then adapt this education system to the peculiarities of Soviet conditions. Engineers were to be his new society's leaders. He termed them 'cadres who decide everything'.[3] But such individuals simply did not exist in the numbers or quality required; hence they needed to be mass produced – and in a hurry. Unlike those in Russia, US universities had a significant number of highly qualified and experienced professors. Stalin planned that on their return to the Soviet

---

★ The last recorded arrest of Russian 'illegals' was in 2015. During Operation Ghost Stories in 2010 several illegals had used universities as cover to recruit contacts.

Union the newly trained engineers, including Shumovsky, were to become professors themselves. They were to spend their lives transferring to the many the benefits of what they had learned in their time in the US.

Stalin's second reason for choosing this route is that a university is an unprotected repository of engineering and scientific knowledge. Elsewhere, the same information was either closely guarded in military bases or scattered among dozens of individual factories, and to gather that intelligence the Soviets would have had to deploy hundreds of agents on risky missions. In contrast, the universities happily transmitted that same knowledge by means of their lecture halls, laboratories and libraries – and, in the case of MIT, by factory placements. Each Soviet student, while educating himself to the highest level, would at the same time identify and arrange to have copied every technological treasure he could find. Books, articles, equipment and other material could wend their way back to the Soviet Union as a resource for Stalin's ambitious industrialisation programme.

The Soviet Union had assembled a remarkable group for the task, its brightest and best talent. They appeared, on the face of it, the ideal team to perform the mission assigned to them: Communist Party loyalists, motivated, intelligent and focused, many went on to be leaders in their chosen fields. Some however disgraced themselves. One was to put the entire mission at risk.

The students, including Shumovsky, travelled to America under their real names,[4] but covers were routinely used by Soviet intelligence when the stakes were high. Two years before, Pyotr Baranov, head of the Red air force, the VVS, had travelled incognito to the US with aircraft designer Andrey Tupolev to visit American factories and trade fairs.[5] His cover was blown when his photograph appeared in a book published while he was in America naming him as a leading figure of the Communist Revolution. At the time Russians travelled abroad in fear of attacks both by exiled White Guard organisations and those they saw as heretical Communists; intercepted telegram traffic shows that the NKVD believed the White Guards could replicate the Soviets' own fearsome counter-intelligence capability.*

After their defeat in the Civil War the White exiles had managed a campaign of assassinations and bombings against Soviet targets, but now generally they were men of intemperate words after dinner rather than of deeds. Everyone in the party heading to America was nevertheless warned about avoiding interactions with the White Guards, as well as with 'Trotskyists', now a catch-all description for heretical Communists.

• • •

A strong sense of camaraderie had developed on the long journey from Moscow and Leningrad and the shared months of intensive language training. Shumovsky was an excellent field agent. Now they were approaching New York the time had come for the party to go their separate ways

Some universities had chosen to welcome just one student, or a few at most, but MIT embraced the programme wholeheartedly. In their trawl for America's secrets, the Soviets had spread their

---

* In 1937 the NKVD would conduct 'special operations' under the leadership of the feared Sergey Shpigelglas (codename DOUGLAS) that included murder and kidnaps across Europe, and his hand reached across to strike in the US.

net far and wide: six went to Harvard, ten to Cornell in Ithaca, New York; five to the University of Wisconsin in Madison; five to Purdue University, West Lafayette, Indiana; three to the Colorado School of Mines in Golden, Colorado; one to the Carnegie Institute of Technology in Pittsburgh, Pennsylvania; and one to Lehigh University in Bethlehem, Pennsylvania.*[6] The remaining twenty-five headed for MIT, in Cambridge, Massachusetts. At some universities the new arrivals went unnoticed. At MIT, there would be a fanfare welcome, and this was replicated at some colleges with articles in newspapers welcoming their foreign visitors,

MIT were ecstatic to receive the twenty-five Russian students. The Institute was not at the time financially well endowed. The fees were most welcome for the struggling university, arriving mid-Great Depression and during a time of collapsing student enrolments. Catering as it did, unlike Ivy League schools, largely to middle-class families, MIT's vulnerability to the Depression was due to its dependence for funding on tuition fees rather than endowments or grants. The Russian fees were therefore gratefully received as MIT was drawing down on its savings. So welcoming indeed was the Institute that it would become the Soviet intelligence services' favourite US university.

The manifest of SS *Europa* shows that Alexander (Sasha) Gramp was the first student of that final party to disembark.[7] Throughout the long voyage from Bremen, he had been mad keen to get onto American soil, to be reunited with his bride Gertrude Klivans and meet the in-laws. For the next few years, the Klivans'

---

* The total is incomplete as the source is from US immigration records. On arrival some students did not record a particular university as their destination.

house in Youngstown would become a magnet for visiting students. Having cleared US customs, compulsory medical quarantine and immigration, the arrivals were met at the dock by a welcoming party of officials from their sponsors, AMTORG. They were then driven by bus a short distance across Manhattan to Fifth Avenue, where AMTORG was based.

To the Soviet students, their first view of the modern American city of New York was a vivid demonstration of the yawning gap between the capitalist and socialist worlds. It was the city that some of the Russians would be trained in the US to emulate on their return home. Moscow planned in time to build its own skyscrapers, as befitted the capital of the Communist world. Eventually, sweeping boulevards would be created by dynamiting old buildings and whole districts, but the capital of the worker state in 1931 had nothing but dreams to compete with the reality of the Big Apple.

The students' accommodation for their one day of acclimatisation to onshore life and an initial briefing was in the recently opened Lincoln Hotel on Eighth Avenue, a few blocks from AMTORG's office at 261 Fifth Avenue. It would become the favourite hotel of visiting Soviet parties. Tupolev had stayed there on his first trip in December 1929, spending his time trying to figure out the technical marvel of the heating system.[8] The hotel was a modern wonder. It boasted an incredible 1,300 luxury rooms spread over 27 floors, occupying an entire city block between 44th and 45th Streets. Just like the luxury ocean liner from which the students had disembarked, the hotel was a showcase of the comforts on offer in a capitalist society, shocking to those used to the overcrowded and squalid conditions of the USSR's developing cities.

The arriving students had been briefed to act as ambassadors for their new society. By and large, they behaved as such. They were examples of what socialism had achieved so far and would achieve in the future. They believed passionately in fairness and equality for all workers and peasants and had dedicated their lives to building that dream. Many were military veterans who had experienced brutality and loss on the battlefield in the fight for their beliefs. Perplexed by the rigid class system in evidence on the boat, they had found themselves more at home in third class. They were attracted to the fun and informality as opposed to the regimented stiffness of the first- and second-class decks. America's relaxed social attitudes suited the students. The Soviet government insisted on premium-class tickets as such passengers were treated differently by customs and immigration. Experience had shown that first- and second-class ticket holders would escape hours of questioning on arrival, or worse, internment at Ellis Island.

The party had arrived in the belly of the great capitalist beast. They had been taught that their class enemy, the American elite, feared the inevitable triumph of Communism and was scheming to destroy the Soviet Union, but that ordinary exploited American workers were their brothers, although politically asleep, bought off by consumerist dreams and neglectful of their political destiny. Lacking such a purpose, they were told, American life was empty or shallow. In a future Communist society, each member would contribute according to their ability and receive according to their need.

The students were instructed to describe the Soviet grand project as work in progress, with many problems, challenges and difficult choices. To succeed in their goal entailed making enormous sacrifices for the certainty of a better tomorrow. Having such beliefs separated the Soviets from most Americans, whose lives and aspirations they found materialistic and selfish. It is notable that none of the students decided to defect after their taste of America. Despite Russia's many privations, Soviet society was on the road to an improvement in living standards for the masses over the squalor and hopelessness of Tsarist autocracy. The students knew that there was still a long way to go, but significantly they had fought hard to come a fair distance already. All of them had benefited from the educational opportunities offered them. Denied formal education under Tsarism, under Communism they were now on their way to study at the most elite universities in the world. Their education would be used not to obtain for themselves a bigger salary but for the greater good of all. Despite the current conditions, the ration cards, public canteens and cramped accommodation, their system was moving forward, offering a brighter future, while capitalism was in retreat and could not even provide jobs for a high proportion of its population. They also expected to meet the cowboys and gangsters they had seen in the movies.

At their first hotel, the Soviets found evidence of the very class oppression they had been warned to avoid. To real Communists, tipping porters for carrying their bags or paying for a shoe shine were open symbols of class exploitation. Communists could never adjust to paying others to perform simple everyday tasks that they were accustomed to do themselves. They would carry their own bags. They had already seen the evidence on the city streets, and would later read in newspapers lurid accounts of the awful privations of the Great Depression that affected the many, while themselves tasting the surreal world of luxury liners and hotels enjoyed by the few.

New York was in crisis. There was unprecedented mass unemployment. A plethora of apple sellers could be found on each city street, the unemployed struggling to earn money in order simply to eat. Others wandered the sidewalks wearing placards advertising their skills. All Soviet visitors at the time were consistently surprised at the diversity of immigrants that made up the population, remarking on the large number of countries represented. At this time, close to 7 million lived in the city, with a population density of over 23,000 people per square mile. Moscow was growing fast but still only had a population of 2.8 million.

Even in the midst of depression, however, New York was the definitive twentieth-century city; its wide streets and boulevards made a deep impression on foreign visitors, not least via the symbol of the modern age, the car and heavy traffic. The New York skyline had only recently taken on its impressive modern form, dominated by the three tallest buildings in the world. The arriving Russians were awed by the three buildings, visible from anywhere in Manhattan.

The Empire State Building at 102 storeys had won the friendly competition with the builders of 40 Wall Street and the Chrysler Building to be the world's tallest. Construction had begun on 17 March 1930, and the skyscraper was officially opened a few months before the students arrived, on 1 May 1931. The total cost of the building, including the land, was $40,948,900. An MIT alumnus, Pierre S. du Pont, had partly financed the project. Construction required the use of up to 3,400 workers working 7 million working hours over a period of just one year and forty-five days including Sundays and holidays, a feat worthy of a Soviet Five-Year Plan. The art deco building, wrapped in Indiana limestone and granite, aluminium and chrome nickel steel, was the wonder of the modern age – even if in 1931 it was virtually empty, the victim of an unfashionable location and the Depression. The three skyscrapers had been built in a race to the sky as symbols of America's business confidence that was now shattered.

•   •   •

On the face of it, the students' host, AMTORG, was a legitimate trading company with a valuable monopoly on Soviet trade with the United States. American conservatives suspected AMTORG was the hub of major Soviet espionage activities designed to undermine the government of the United States; in fact it was neither capable nor sufficiently resourced to be anything of the sort. Soviet intelligence in the US at the time of Shumovsky's arrival was in its infancy, small in scale and disorganised. Only in 1933, with the establishment of official diplomatic relations, would the Soviet Consulate take over the leadership role in intelligence from AMTORG and build up resources. The AMTORG office was not the centre of a grand conspiracy to topple capitalism. Soviet espionage sought to strengthen the position of the USSR not to destroy the US system of government. Marxists believed that the collapse of capitalism was inevitable. In 1925 Stalin had adopted a policy of 'Socialism in One Country', abandoning the cause of world revolution, and would finally close down Comintern (The Communist International) in 1943.

Until Shumovsky's mission, spy work had consisted almost exclusively of the gathering and collation of what would be described today as open-source information, supplemented by an occasional one-off operation. Open-source intelligence is information in the public domain in a particular country that has a value for a foreign power. Intelligence is further subdivided between political and science and technology; activity in the latter field was performed by a small team of technicians at AMTORG who would comb through newspapers and periodicals, mainly technical and scientific journals, for information that might be of use to the industrialising Soviet Union. As the technological gap between the countries was so wide, there was a vast amount of useful information available in US publications.

Valuable intelligence was often received on an unsolicited basis. US firms would sometimes include commercially sensitive information in the marketing material they sent to AMTORG, which would forward anything useful on to Moscow; some of it would end up on Stalin's desk. One explosives manufacturer, the Trojan Powder Company of Allentown, Pennsylvania, disclosed the chemical formulae for its solid explosives hoping for a lucrative deal. Stalin personally annotated the document.[9] The company even offered to provide the Soviet Union with an unlimited quantity of poison gas munitions. Soviet experts were unimpressed with the Trojan Company's proposal.

Accurate political intelligence proved harder to acquire than S&T. Without reliable sources, information was either biased or in some cases downright false. An early large-scale NKVD operation in the 1930s, based in New York and Washington, turned out after many years and a detailed investigation to have relied on a completely fake source. An enterprising *New York Post* journalist, Ludwig Lore, had created a family industry producing political information for the NKVD and employing his son and wife in the enterprise. The NKVD were entirely taken in.

Lore claimed that his intelligence reports came directly from a network of well-placed agents in the State Department in Washington, even insisting that the State Department's Head of

Research, David A. Salmon, was his principal agent. In reality, none of Lore's agents existed. He had plucked names from the internal phone directory of the State Department. Lore was nevertheless able to charge the NKVD exorbitantly for several years for the information he provided, which consisted either of old news stories reheated or pure invention.[10] Without checking, the NKVD had already put some of the fake material on Stalin's desk, describing it as 'must read'.[11] Stalin believed he was reading the very words of America's ambassador to Tokyo, Joseph Grew, in private meetings with the Emperor's top officials. It was nothing of the sort; Lore had made up the entire conversation. Shumovsky's operation at a stroke transformed the quality of Soviet intelligence gathering.

America was conflicted in its dealings with Stalin; on the one hand, they wanted his business, but on the other, they feared Communism. Despite the countries' polar opposite ideologies, however, AMTORG officials briefed the student party that the Soviet Union had become the USA's primary export market, uniquely expanding its economy as the rest of the world contracted.

AMTORG's role was to coordinate all commercial visits by Russian experts to the US, and vice versa. It gave each group of students a list of approved contacts in their university city, and letters of introduction.[12] AMTORG maintained an extensive library of information on the major US manufacturing companies and their suppliers that the students would visit or be assigned work at during their stay. Besides his course at MIT, Shumovsky would be working for AMTORG's aviation department, producing reports and articles on the dynamic US aircraft industry. In 1933, he was to write an article published in *American Engineering and Technology* – an AMTORG magazine filled with US advertising sent to 1,700 key Soviet officials – describing the features of a special plane the Americans had built to fly in the harsh conditions of Antarctica.[13]

AMTORG also controlled immigration to the USSR from the USA. With 25 per cent unemployment, the US was suffering a net outflow of migrants. For several years, more people left the country than arrived. In 1931 AMTORG was receiving 12,500 applications per month from Americans to migrate to the land of Lenin.[14] No wonder to the Soviets capitalism appeared to be teetering on the brink.

• • •

In trading with the US, the Soviets were very careful with their money, committing only to buying the very best products on the most advantageous terms. Experts such as Shumovsky would prove to be invaluable in ensuring that those conditions included the transfer to the USSR of all technical knowledge. And, as a planned economy, they had clear goals with their purchases.

The Soviet Union's ultimate goal was to build its military capability. The German and Soviet high commands shared a vision of how to fight a future war. The Russians called the strategy 'deep penetration' but it is better known by the German term *Blitzkrieg*. Through its secret work with the German military, the Red Army had identified three priorities: to build the world's largest mechanised forces, a powerful air force, and a chemical warfare capability. With political tensions rising in Europe and Asia, the Red Army leadership had been speeding up its modern-isation since November 1929. Before Stalin insisted on a purely domestic solution, the Soviets came to shop in America.

Following a Politburo resolution in early 1930, a high-level

Soviet delegation led by the Red Army's head of mechanisation, Innokenty Khalepsky, visited armaments factories in France, the UK and America. They arrived in the US keen to buy an instant solution to their desperate need for a modern tank. They had decided, without seeing it, to purchase the experimental T1, manufactured by Cunningham, a prototype designed for the US Army. Looking for a bargain, Khalepsky dangled in front of the manufacturer the prospect of a large order dwarfing anything the tiny US Army might buy. The commercial terms presented by the Americans in return were unacceptable to the Russians. The product was crazily expensive, and on closer examination, the tank was found to be inferior both in speed and armour to the British Vickers. Worse, the manufacturer insisted on a minimum order of fifty tanks and a down payment in cash of 50 per cent for the unproven product. Cunningham moreover refused to provide any technical assistance or drawings to the Russians, no doubt as the US Army had been involved in the tank's design.[15]

However, in the process of visiting America, the committee met the maverick inventor John Walter Christie. While attempting to create a tank for the US military, Christie had produced more than his fair share of failed designs. His vehicles were too cramped for the crew, shook violently when in motion, were badly built and mechanically unreliable. This time, however, he had come up with a unique chassis design using large springs as shock absorbers. To reduce the space needed to house the springs and retain a streamlined profile, Christie had invented a lever system that turned the damping effect of the springs from vertical to horizontal. He was, moreover, a great salesman. He promised everything the Russians wanted. They could have a small test batch of his tank, full technical specifications including drawings, and he would come personally to Russia to oversee production. He clinched the deal by dropping into conversation with the credulous Russians the terrifying news that their hostile neighbours the Poles were buying hundreds of his fast-moving tanks. On 28 April 1930, Christie's company, the struggling US Wheel Track Layer Corporation, agreed to sell AMTORG two M-1931 Christie-designed tanks at the cost of $60,000, together with spare parts for a further $4,000, the tanks to be delivered not later than four months from the date of signing. A further $100,000 went on acquiring the manufacturing rights and patents allowing the production, sale and use of the tanks inside the borders of the USSR for ten years.

A spy scandal attached itself to the purchase when it was suggested that, as the Soviet Union had no diplomatic relations with the US at the time, it could not officially obtain military equipment. Although little of it was true, the NKVD and AMTORG were alleged to have secured the plans and specifications for the Christie M-1931 tank chassis using a series of deceptions. The two Christie tanks were apparently falsely documented as agricultural farm tractors and sold illegally without seeking the prior approval of the US Army or the Department of State, and then shipped without turrets to the Soviet Union.

Soviet engineers had acquired valuable experience working with captured or purchased armoured vehicles since 1917, and they soon realised Christie had sold them a pup. His tank chassis did make a favourable impression, but over a ten-day field trial the turret-less tank could only cover a distance of ninety-three miles, breaking down many times. It was fast, clocking up an unprecedented road speed of 43 mph, but cooked the crew in the process to an internal temperature of 104 degrees Fahrenheit. Other flaws in the model were evident; the doors, for example, were so small that no full-sized man could climb inside. After the fiasco, Stalin ordered that there would be no more attempts to buy quick solutions from abroad.

The unsuccessful field testing led the Soviets to reject Christie's design and focus on a domestic solution. They adopted his chassis as standard and copied the innovative sloping front armour for their BT series of fast tanks. The BT series would evolve into the most famous Soviet tank, the T-34, Christie's name entering Soviet folklore when the T-34 was referred to by Stalin as a 'Christie'. But the trip had proved that the Russians' perfect tank did not exist, even abroad.

•   •   •

An earlier mission to the US by the spy Abraham Einhorn (codename TARAS) had entirely random goals and was planned without consulting the leaders of the aviation industry. Einhorn's most notable success had been to steal a blueprint for a Packard aircraft engine, saving in his opinion 'a million dollars'.[16] No one in Russia wanted the engine.[17]

•   •   •

The visit to New York had been an eye-opener for the arriving Russians. It was a glimpse into their future. They were completely unused to cities where human-made buildings obscured the sky. As the Boston party boarded the train to leave New York City, they were treated to one last modern miracle, Grand Central Station, the largest railway station in the world. The railway engineers were thrilled by the scale of the design of the immense central concourse and the two separate underground floors of tracks.*

Five hours later, on arrival at Boston South Station, the Harvard party of six and their MIT-bound colleagues boarded a bus to their accommodation in Cambridge. The students had a date with the Dean, Dr Tryon. They could not be late for registration and the grand tour, but first they must make a stop to change their clothes. Shumovsky hurried to put on his new two-piece double-breasted suit in dark grey.[18] A necessary initial step for any Russian visitor to America was to equip yourself unashamedly with all the fashion accoutrements of capitalism. A trip to a men's outfitter was a prerequisite before meeting your first Americans. As an ambassador of a thriving new society, it was important to look the part, and to be taken seriously in business or around the campus one needed to make a good first impression. Contemporary photographs always show Soviet trade delegations wearing new double-breasted suits, bow ties and even on occasions *pince-nez*. A suit and tie were everyday dress even for students; the army of laboratory technicians at the Institute wore overalls and did all the heavy lifting. Only when smelting metals might a student remove his jacket.

After completing individual registration inside the crush of

---

* Today there is a small dark circle in the hall ceiling amid the stars above the image of Pisces. It is an unintentional monument to this trip. For in 1957, in an attempt to counteract feelings of insecurity spawned by the launch of the Soviet satellite Sputnik, a giant American Redstone missile was set up in the main concourse. With no other way to erect the rocket, a hole was cut in the ceiling to allow a cable to be lowered to lift the rocket into place. Members of the student party in 1931 on their way to MIT, including Shumovsky, were later credited with working on Sputnik.

Building 10, the students filed back outside into the calm and introduced themselves to Dr Tryon, who asked politely which course each was studying and dutifully enquired if they understood their class schedule for the following day. Formed into three lines, each man kitted out in his new elegant American suit – the preference overall being for light grey – the students then posed for a commemorative photo on the steps of Building 10, overlooking Killian Court. Builders had engraved the names of notable scientists and philosophers on the friezes of the surrounding limestone-clad buildings. A measure of the significance of the moment for the plans of the young USSR was that the photo appeared in many Soviet newspapers, and copies survive in the Belorussian state archive today.

Shumovsky was in the front row near the Dean, as befitted his status in the party. Like the others, he is clutching his registration pack. Considerably taller than most of the rest of the group at over six foot, and looking like a serious academic in his glasses, he holds his head high. He is gazing into the distance as if reading the names of the famous scientists on the friezes, contemplating the challenges ahead.

To the exhausted, travel-worn Russians MIT was an alien world. At first sight, the campus was an eclectic mixture of classical-style buildings, designed on a grand scale and housing modern laboratories and lecture theatres. Building 10 with its gigantic pillars, iconic dome and vast auditorium epitomised the attempt to impose old world architecture on the new. It was a shock to learn that the site had only been opened fifteen years ago. The campus had the appearance of a giant classical temple dedicated to the advancement of modern technology. The twenty-five Russians learned that they were the second largest contingent of foreigners after the Canadians among the 182 non-American students enrolled in 1931.[19]

After their individual registration and photograph, Dr Tryon took the Russians to a nearby lecture theatre and showed them an hour-long silent movie introducing MIT and the excitement

Arrival at MIT – Russian students with the dean outside Building 10,
(Shumovsky is second left, front row)

of an engineering career. Its familiar message, that 'Engineers harness the great sources of powers in nature for the convenience and use of mankind',[20] was almost socialist in nature and could have come straight from the Five-Year Plan. The movie, one of Tryon's innovations, designed to recruit students to the Institute in the difficult economic climate, illustrated the importance of engineers to society, showcasing suspension bridges, power plants, aircraft, factories and skyscrapers. Captured on film were the main departments of MIT and its latest investments in state-of-the-art research, such as giant Van de Graaff generators. Also featured was Vannevar Bush's early analogue computer, termed 'a thinking machine', for solving differential equations. (A later version proved a failure at cracking Soviet espionage codes.)

After the movie showing, the Dean gave Shumovsky and the other students a short tour of the excellent facilities, lecture halls and laboratories before they split into groups to visit their faculties. As the party fanned out the Russians gained a feeling for the open space and scale of the campus. With numbers in decline, there were only just over 3,100 students enrolled in the Institute. Russian universities, in contrast, were packed to the rafters; Shumovsky's new aeronautics school in Moscow enrolled 5,000–7,000 students.[21] In comparison, Course 16, on which Shumovsky was now enrolled – undergraduate aeronautics, then part of the mechanical engineering department – was limited to just thirty students per year. With an intake deliberately restricted to keep academic standards high, the course was extremely selective, being only for 'specially qualified students who can assimilate in four years the essentials of mechanical engineering and at the same time, the fundamentals of aeronautical science with some introduction to its application'.[22] It was a tough ask for an American student in four years; Shumovsky was given three. On top of the time pressure, he was required not only to complete the course in an unfamiliar language, but to master at the same time a reading knowledge of French and German.

Nevertheless he was in the best possible place. MIT was training the world's finest aeronautical engineers, and the teachers were industry leaders. While the course was kept small, the laboratory resources were state of the art. MIT was proud to be the first and the best in aeronautics, and was determined to remain so.

In addition to the challenges presented by language, Shumovsky had to get used to the different approach to teaching he found at MIT. The institute followed the European polytechnic university model, emphasising laboratory instruction, not mass lectures. Russian university curriculums in contrast were dominated by hours of theoretical lectures for five months of the year, followed by five months of work on the factory floor. There were no tidy university laboratories with teams of assistants to clean up and set up experiments. The goal in the Soviet Union was quantity, not quality. The new factories needed engineers turned out in short order by the thousands. There was no place for an elite university teaching just thirty engineers to this high level. Stalin's much bigger project demanded engineers who could fix an engine or maintain a machine.

Soviet universities were attempting a social experiment of affirmative action in favour of workers and against those with a bourgeois or intellectual background. Student admission had been expanded, but standards were low thanks to the poor literacy that was a legacy of the Tsarist education system. There were no exams, either at entrance or during the course. Instead, students were awarded a pass or fail based on quizzes and a character reference from the professor.

Perhaps the greatest difference between the two systems was the practice of open democracy. In Russia, despite the acute shortage of teachers, students could vote to remove a professor they felt was not up to standard. Many professors had emigrated, and those who had stayed found it hard to thrive in this heightened political atmosphere, which meant that any teacher who dared to ask challenging questions risked being accused of plotting the overthrow of the Soviet state. It was all a different world from MIT's calm neoclassical temple, dedicated to technology and science.

• • •

In the 1930s, just as the Russians arrived, the prominent scientists President Karl Taylor Compton and Vice-President Vannevar Bush took charge of MIT. Compton's reforms introduced a higher standard that allowed 'the Institute to develop leadership in science as well as in engineering'. Technology in the 1930s never stood still: as the aircraft themselves got faster and more sophisticated, so did the pace of innovation.

New planes were fitted with more powerful engines and routinely flew faster than any wind tunnel in existence could test. So MIT kept up to date by working hand in hand with the industry and the military to afford its investment in the latest equipment. Revenue from its research projects and inventions was as important as fees and endowments in this regard.[23] America's unique and dynamic aviation market was dominated by the civilian sector – especially orders for passenger airliners and cargo planes – rather than by its military. In the USSR, the demands of the military took precedence. At the time, the US lagged well behind the world in military air power despite having the leading civil aviation industry. As a result of the weakness of US armed forces Soviet assessments never viewed the US as a major military threat despite the intense ideological hostility.

At no Soviet university could the facilities compare with those on offer at MIT. On his tour, Shumovsky learned that the Institute had been conceived as a 'Conservatory of Art and Science', founded on 10 April 1861 by William Barton Rogers to address rapid scientific and technological advances. This was the same year that, in Russia, many of the party members' grandparents had been freed from serfdom.

The fledgling school had suffered from chronic financial shortages and had only moved from its original cramped Back Bay location in 1916 to this spacious new campus on a mile-long tract along the Cambridge side of the Charles River. Funded primarily by donations from the industrialist George Eastman, founder of Eastman Kodak,* the new site had space for sports pitches and tranquil gardens along the breezy bank. A glider could take off and land in the grounds.

Aside from the superb academic facilities, Shumovsky looked on with open-mouthed astonishment at the decadence of student life, still in full vibrant swing at the start of a new academic year despite the Great Depression and prohibition. As in Russia, military service was still compulsory for MIT students, and the American freshmen they met during those first days had returned exhausted from a weekend under canvas and games in the woods. The military veterans among the Russians offered to give their classmates drilling on the campus a few pointers on the realities of army life. But while the Russians were at MIT to work, not to party, American students enjoyed a full social life of dances and sport. Drinking was the hot topic. With the end of prohibition, low-alcohol beer would reappear on campus in March 1933. The perplexed Shumovsky explained that excessive

---

* He was later a primary target for Soviet intelligence operations. Several agents worked at Kodak film and explosive plants.

drinking at Soviet universities could lead to expulsion and treatment at a sanatorium. Glancing through contemporary editions of *The Tech*, MIT's student newspaper, Shumovsky was mystified by the range of leisure-time activities on offer to his fellow students. Tugs of war and bow-tied banjo bands were perhaps vaguely understandable, but wrestling in oil was completely incomprehensible.

Equally puzzling was American humour. Shumovsky was horrified to read in *The Tech* in 1935 that 'Agent 001' of the NKVD had infiltrated MIT. The paper said that a Russian secret agent had discharged a tear gas grenade in a chemical warfare lecture, after which the talk had descended into chaos. Tear gas is mixed with other poison gas to force a victim exposed to the mixture to remove their gas masks to rub their irritated eyes, allowing the poison gas to do its work. *The Tech* identified the editor of *Voodoo* magazine, a monthly satirical rival on campus, as the Soviet agent responsible.[24] No one believed at the time that a representative of the much-feared Soviet secret service was actually walking the campus.

None of the Soviets joined the myriad of sport or social clubs on offer. None became fraternity members. As a married man with a young family, Shumovsky was less interested than some in a dance with the coeds from Wellesley. He could not risk jeopardising his vital mission with a romantic entanglement. Many, like Shumovsky himself, did however join the societies relating to their academic specialisation, attracted by the range of 'smokers' – as talks and discussion groups with experts were called – on offer.

•   •   •

After an exhausting day the Russians walked back to their boarding houses for their first night as the sun was setting. The MIT students were boarded in two houses close to the campus, 8 Bigelow Street[25] and 294 Harvard Street, Cambridge.[26] Within five minutes' walk of each other and fifteen minutes from campus, the properties were both large, newly built townhouses. The accommodation was luxurious relative to the barracks-style conditions at Soviet universities. The students continued living communally, as was typical of their homeland. All this was arranged by AMTORG.

Now for the first time they had a few moments to unpack personal possessions, photographs and books, and write a letter home after weeks of travelling. All the Russian students were married, and they were due to be away from their young families for a long time. For an unknown reason, one student was however recalled after just a week. Four more left after completing their studies in a year. Only eight would study for three years, and none stayed as long as Shumovsky.[27] The students divided themselves between the two houses in a way that reflected their characters. The dozen in the Harvard Avenue house with Shumovsky contained the serious members of the group, his friends. Like him, they were eager to learn all that MIT could teach them. His closest friend in this group was the mechanical engineer Ivan Trashutin, from Shumovsky's home city of Kharkov.[28] Trashutin had been fiddling with diesel engines since his childhood. One of only two children to survive from the seven produced by his parents, from a young age he had experienced extreme poverty bordering on deprivation after his father marched off with the Red Army and disappeared in the Civil War. Aged just eight, young Ivan went to work in the Kharkov railway factories. He received no formal education for a decade afterwards but possessed a natural ability with engines, and by the time he arrived in Cambridge he was the number-two diesel engine designer in the Soviet Union. The youngest of the party, he was blessed with infectious enthusiasm and a ready smile. Ivan was a joy to teach, rolling his sleeves up to get to work. His proudest moment was achieving his Master's degree, and he treasured his parchment certificate, signed by Karl Compton, for the rest of his illustrious life.

It is doubtful that any alumnus of MIT contributed more individually to the Allied victory in the Second World War than Trashutin. As his professors at MIT found, when it came to engines Ivan had the rare gift of making the complicated simple. Trashutin deservedly won many awards in his lifetime – although, surprisingly, there has so far been no recognition from MIT. Even the Nazis christened him 'Ivan Diesel' in awe of his achievements. He designed the power unit that drove the victorious Red Army's armoured divisions from the gates of Moscow to Berlin. His was the engine inside every Soviet tank from the T-34 to the T-72. The engine was powerful, lightweight and easy to manufacture and maintain, demonstrating the talent for simplicity identified in his years at MIT – and, running as it did on diesel, it was a lifesaver. Thousands of Soviet tank crews, including my own grandfather, owed their lives to the extra moments they had to escape from their wrecked vehicles, as diesel catches fire less easily than petrol. Trashutin learned at MIT how to mass-produce engines the American way.

As the students unwound in the evenings over endless cups of tea and cigarettes, Shumovsky got to know Eugene Bukley and Yefim Medkov, who were studying electrical and transport engineering. As the elected leader of the Communist Party cell formed by the students, Medkov was responsible for organising the monthly Party meetings, communicating the latest bulletins from Moscow – it was his job to pass on the new orthodoxy in a time of great political change and debate in Russia – and maintaining discipline.

Communists were expected to behave properly at all times. Poor personal discipline could lead to the miscreant's expulsion from the Party, a disaster for a person's career. That ultimate sanction was not in Medkov's power, but he could write reports to the Party leader in New York about the progress of the students and report his concerns about ill discipline.[29]

The metallurgist Alexander 'Rosty' Rostarchuk and mechanical engineer Ivan Eremin were to become long-term friends. 'Rosty', like Shumovsky, got on well with Americans, integrating quickly and easily with his classmates. The paths of Eremin, Rostarchuk and Shumovsky would cross again in 1941, in the Soviet Union's hour of need.[30]

Most helpfully for Shumovsky, there was another Russian on Course 16 in his house. Ivan Protzenko was no ordinary aeronautical engineer or student.[31] He was the Director of TsAGI, and ranked as one of the most prominent figures in the Soviet aircraft industry. What was such a senior figure doing spending those years in an American classroom studying for a Master's degree? In his early thirties at the time, Ivan was already an experienced aircraft designer. Yet such was the scale and importance of the Soviet Union's expansion plans that he was sent on a two-year mission to learn, with Shumovsky's help, how to replicate the MIT aeronautics course in Moscow. He had to complete it first.

On his return to Moscow in 1933 Ivan would duly begin teaching a prestigious new Master's course in aviation offered by

TsAGI. It was a clone of what he and Shumovsky had learned in Cambridge. The core curriculum included mathematics. theoretical mechanics and hydro-aerodynamics, and aircraft design. To gain a Master's in aviation at the Soviet 'MIT', a Soviet student was required to defend a thesis to a robust panel that included Andrey Tupolev himself.[32]

Stanislav Shumovsky – MIT 1932 yearbook

From 1935 onwards, for its fifty-year life, thousands of Soviet aviation engineers would enjoy the educational benefits of the elite Course 16 from MIT without ever having to leave home. In what must be one of the most brazen transfers of intellectual property from America in history, the Soviet Union began to enrol hundreds of students each year. Somewhat ironically, MIT continued limiting itself to turn out just thirty students a year. For a few hundred dollars' investment in MIT fees, the Soviet Union would catch up with and overtake America in teaching aviation engineering in just a few years.

• • •

Shumovsky soon settled down into the daily routine of lectures and laboratory work in Building 33, the Daniel Guggenheim Laboratory. Around the facility were clustered several wind tunnels. To ensure it stayed as the top-rated aeronautics department in the country, the department was planning the world's first pressurised wind tunnel. The Guggenheim family's extraordinary philanthropy extended to an interest in promoting aviation. MIT was the best choice of university for the Russians not just because its course was America's oldest – the study of aeronautics had begun at MIT before the Wright brothers' 1903 pioneering flight, when in 1896 mechanical engineering student Albert J. Wells built a thirty-square-inch wind tunnel as part of his thesis – but because it was also the most respected university aeronautics programme.

The department had a tradition of strong scholarship and solving industrial problems. Shumovsky's profile fitted right in with the other students and faculty staff, who were universally enthralled with the challenges of flight. Later alumni have pursued careers that include astronaut, air force secretary, NASA deputy administrators and chief technologist, air force chief scientist, aerospace executive, and corporate founder. Its alumni are described as entrepreneurs, policy-makers, educators and researchers pushing technology's boundaries.[33] Shumovsky's classmates between 1931 and 1936 would make major contributions to the development of aerospace in the fields of transport, communications, exploration and national security, as well as developing innovative educational programmes. As the yearbook boasted in 1933, 'the men whose pictures you see on the pages immediately following are destined to become important to the world in this generation as its builders, its designers, and its administrators.'[34]

Shumovsky derived great satisfaction from the unlimited access he was offered to his teachers, all world-leading specialists. His new professor was one of America's most influential aviation figures.[35] During a long and illustrious career that spanned the entire existence of the aerospace industry, from the very beginnings of aeronautics to the exploration of the solar system, Jerome C. Hunsaker would keep MIT at the forefront and heart of development.[36] The driving force behind the beginning of aeronautics studies at MIT, he worked with everyone from the first flyers, the Wright Brothers, through to Charles Stark Draper, linchpin of the Apollo project. In between he got to know most of the founders and leaders of aeronautics and astronautics. He became an MIT institution, having enrolled in 1909 and never retiring.

The number-one US Naval Academy graduate of his year, Hunsaker, nicknamed the 'Einstein of the Navy', had enrolled in MIT's graduate programme in naval construction, but instead developed a fascination with the growing amount of aeronautical literature in MIT's library. Hunsaker and Shumovsky shared the same hero, Louis Blériot. In 1912 Hunsaker caught the flying bug by watching a Blériot plane flying around Boston harbour.

In 1914, MIT offered the nation's first course in aerodynamics, taught by Hunsaker himself. MIT's Course 16, aeronautics, had first been offered in 1926 under the auspices of the Department of Mechanical Engineering. Proving widely popular and over-subscribed twice over from the start, it was a major coup for Shumovsky to be allowed to enrol.

No doubt Hunsaker and Shumovsky spoke of their admiration for the great French pilot, though equally Shumovsky would not have revealed his NKVD codename. Hunsaker introduced Shumovsky and the other students to his friend Donald Douglas. The pair had built the first structure on MIT's new Cambridge campus, a wind tunnel. Douglas was the founder of Douglas Aircraft, the manufacturer of the iconic DC-3, one of the world's great planes. Although his company was based on the West Coast, he was a regular visitor to MIT, and was a member of the department's advisory committee.

Hunsaker's contribution to the development of the US aviation industry cannot be overestimated. Most publicly, he managed the new institutions needed to deal with the growth of the aeronautics industry, such as the crucial National Advisory Committee for Aeronautics (NACA), the forerunner of NASA. In fact, he initiated and wrote for NACA the first industry-wide research paper. Recognised as the leading innovator in the field of aviation research, its inventions unrivalled, NACA is rightly credited with contributing to winning the air war for the Allies by its work on introducing the superchargers necessary to maintain the performance of high-altitude bomber and fighter engines. The committee's research was so respected that it became the number-one target for Soviet aviation espionage and much in demand elsewhere in the world.

At MIT, Hunsaker was the advocate of the modern engineering approach to aircraft design. His idea was to render obsolete the 'build it, fly it and see' model that had previously prevailed across the industry. The commercial and safety risks entailed in that approach could be eliminated in the laboratory and through calculation. Scale models tested in wind tunnels were cheaper than prototypes. New construction materials would first be stress tested on the work bench.

By the early 1930s, when Hunsaker first met and taught Shumovsky, he was at the pinnacle of the aeronautics industry in the US, holding leadership roles in academia at MIT, in government at NACA, and in industry as president of Goodyear Zeppelin. MIT's aviation programme was fully integrated into industry despite being located away from the main centres of manufacture on the East and West Coasts. In his role as president of Goodyear Zeppelin, Hunsaker brought to the Institute much commercially valuable research work on dirigibles. In recognition of his many achievements, in 1933 he was awarded the prestigious Guggenheim Medal, only the fifth such recipient.

Among Hunsaker's associates was C. Fayette Taylor,[37] professor of mechanical engineering and director of MIT's Sloan Laboratory for Aircraft and Automotive Engines, funded by General Motors.[38] Earlier in his career, Taylor had been the engineer in charge of the US Army's Air Service Laboratory in Dayton, Ohio. While there, he met Orville Wright and before joining MIT he oversaw aircraft engine design at the Wright Aeronautical Corporation. He was heavily involved in developing the air-cooled 'Whirlwind' engine used on Charles Lindbergh's historic transatlantic flight. Through his research and teaching, Taylor developed the scientific framework for engine design and operation that is still in use today, establishing MIT as an internationally renowned centre in the field. He became a firm friend of Shumovsky and even began publishing his seminal works in Russian. In 1935 his work 'Critical Stresses in Aircraft Engine Parts' was released simultaneously in the USA and Moscow by AMTORG.[39] Curtiss-Wright,* Taylor's former employer, was one of only three US companies Stalin allowed to maintain its contracts in the USSR when the hard currency crisis hit in 1931.

In 1939, Aeronautics became a distinct department at MIT. Hunsaker announced that the early try-and-fly days of aviation were indeed over and, as he had foreseen, the era of the engineered aircraft had fully emerged. He underscored the successes of his department by emphasising that 'the total effect of our graduates on the airplane industry cannot be estimated'.[†]

---

* Curtiss-Wright was the largest US aircraft and engine manufacturer at this time. The Soviets adopted the Wright engine as the standard for their own industry. The ties between the company and the USSR were extremely close.

† MIT graduates included the chief engineers or engineering directors of Curtiss-Wright, Glenn L. Martin, Pratt & Whitney, Vought, Hamilton Standard, Lockheed, Stearman and Douglas, as well as the engineer officers of the Naval Aircraft Factory and of Wright Field. The individual at Wright Field was an active source of intelligence for the USSR.

5

'A NICE FELLOW TO TALK TO'

As the weeks passed at MIT, Shumovsky integrated into college life. He became indistinguishable from his American classmates, attending lectures, working in the lab and attending 'smokers'. He began to learn in his conversations more about America and how the system operated, becoming aware of fissures in the capitalist system that he could exploit for his mission.

In these years of the Great Depression, MIT was an oasis of prosperity for most students, but some felt like fish out of water. The full scholarship boys were different from the others. Their families were suffering from the economic downturn. They were smarter and worked harder, but were less privileged than their peers and felt their lack of money excluded them from the social whirl of college life. The Soviet system, Shumovsky told them, had sent guys just like them halfway around the world to an elite university, paying for everything and supporting their families while they studied. There was, he said, a different way.

As the Depression dragged on, students from all backgrounds grew increasingly concerned about their employment prospects after graduation. Some felt that as the elite they would get a job, if perhaps with reduced salary expectations; others were worried. Shumovsky noticed that most students either had disposable income or the potential to achieve it, and advertisers knew it too. He saw *The Tech* and the yearbook plastered on every page with eye-catching commercial advertising.[1]

Advertisers had a lot to teach a talent spotter; they targeted the intellectual cream of society, employing the proven techniques of mass commercialism to create demand for their client's products. Suggesting that a product made the consumer more alluring to the opposite sex was one effective technique – although it mystified the Russians, who had fewer sexual hang-ups and insecurities. Adverts pitched the sexual allure or health-giving qualities of competing brands of cigarettes; those who caught new smokers early had an affluent, loyal customer for life. Shumovsky thought he could successfully pitch a different view of society to the young and naive in a similar way.

As Shumovsky would prove to Moscow Centre, an agent recruited at a young age would be an asset for life. His vision was to realise that a talented MIT graduate aeronautics engineer would most likely go on in his career to achieve a very senior position in industry or a research institute. Such potential sleeper agents were easier to approach and recruit than a person in mid-career with a family to worry about and a position in society to lose if exposed. Targeting the young, idealistic and naive was a lesson honed on Madison Avenue. Applying Freudian-based mass marketing and advertising techniques to the secret world of espionage recruitment was Shumovsky's novel idea.

Another lesson Shumovsky adopted from the world of advertising was the use of the so-called 'halo effect'. A respected figure who endorsed a positive view of the Soviet Union might well influence others to think the same. Shumovsky understood that public opinion needed creating, it could not be left to form on its own. American consumers followed endorsements. So Soviet intelligence identified, and tried to recruit, American opinion shapers to endorse favourable attitudes to the Soviet Union. Movie stars, journalists and writers in the public eye were targets. Those approached included left-leaning writers such as Ernest Hemingway and – as we shall see – Upton Sinclair.

Although this method would in itself achieve little success, at the same time Shumovsky was evolving his own plan, going to work on MIT's top brass. At his suggestion, the Russians hosted a dinner for fifty guests on 8 November 1933 in the Walker Building to celebrate the sixteenth anniversary of the Communist Revolution; it was to be attended by the remaining students and the great and the good of MIT. As president of the Institute, America's leading scientist Karl Compton was the guest of honour.[2] He made a speech, and received in return from the Russian group a gift: an official chart of the many successes achieved through the Five-Year Plan and a book on the organisation of industry in Russia.

For the wider student body, interest in the Soviet event centred on the showing of 'talkies' at MIT for the first time. The Russians had brought from New York some Soviet movies and assumed America's number-one technical university would have the equipment to show them. It did not, but luckily one department was experimenting with amplification equipment, and so the evening was saved.[3]

The films showcased the role of science in the achievements of the Five-Year Plan, and the timing was spot on for Compton. Amid the emergency of the Great Depression he was chairing a presidential committee to report on how science, if federally funded, could contribute to an economic recovery. In December 1934, his committee proposed a major investment programme: a federal appropriation for scientific research of $75 million for five years, justified because new knowledge would lead to new industries, new jobs and a boost to recovery.

When no government money was forthcoming, Compton – understandably deeply disappointed – came to believe through his interactions with Shumovsky and others that other countries had further-sighted policies.[4] Convinced that Russia spent more on scientific research than on any other part of its budget, including defence, he began using every opportunity to promote the Soviet Union as a beacon of scientific research.[5] Science had been elevated to a level of national religion, he told audiences, adding that the Soviet Academy of Sciences had established 200 world-class laboratories with the best equipment in the world. He convinced audiences that, having seen what it had done to raise living standards in America, Russia was centring its entire economic programme on science. In contrast, the US government was doing nothing. He used the example of the sending of the brightest and best Russians to MIT for training to show how committed the Soviets were to scientific development.

Shumovsky would keep in touch with Compton until early 1939. It became his habit to send a Christmas holiday gift of caviar and cigarettes to the president and his wife. Compton would politely write back thanking Shumovsky for the gift and – clearly without realising the implication – wishing him luck in his work.[6] In 1945 MIT suggested that its distinguished alumnus Shumovsky was the ideal person to represent it at the celebration commemorating fifty years of the Russian Academy of Sciences in Moscow. The world's most famous scientist Albert Einstein declined his invitation due to poor health.

• • •

Advising that more agents should be sent, Shumovsky reported to Moscow Centre that campus life was the ideal, gentle introduction for a novice Soviet S&T spy to learn about America and its way of life. At the same time he had begun to talk, think and act, even subconsciously, as a regular American aviation student. Gradually Stanislav, the Slavic officer from the NKVD, was becoming the Americanised Stan from the Class of '34. In just a few weeks from his arrival, he had become a member of a highly elite club.

In this, he was helped enormously by the ethos of MIT. The Institute reinforced the ideal of total loyalty to your class. There was a tradition of hazing, designed to create a spirit of loyalty to the year group. As one student described, 'in undergraduate, you're building a social network based on shared life experiences. Your college buddies are the ones that you tap into for job opportunities for the rest of your life, and you help each other out because you became fast friends at an important time in your life.'[7] The MIT tradition was that the sophomores would abduct freshmen and generally throw them in the river or some nearby lake. Another jape was to wake a victim at 3 a.m. and take him miles from campus in the dead of night, abandoning him at the roadside to make a weary journey home. It was all designed to build esprit de corps. These strong class bonds included Stan.

Of course, Stan was fundamentally different from the other students on his course; there was a greater purpose behind his education than to get a top job. He had reports to prepare for Moscow on the state of the US aviation industry, so his questions were asked for a reason beyond a desire to simply learn. MIT allowed him the opportunity to develop the industry contacts needed to perform his AMTORG job, and the camaraderie of science created the perfect environment in which to network.

As the information they gleaned was so valuable, Moscow Centre was impatient and demanding of its sources. Their men on the ground, acting as go-betweens between head office and cautious sources, felt the pressure for results. A bureaucrat running a desk without knowledge of the realities of field work could never understand that a source needed to be nurtured, not bullied. This tension provoked much criticism from Moscow about unproductive sources.[8]

The most highly valued sources were those who gave information for ideological reasons and required no payment other than expenses. Moscow was not naive about the motives of some of its sources and was prepared to pay for secrets, sometimes by the page. It preferred not to do so, and such mercenaries, paid by the secret, were despised. But there was also always a place for those at MIT who needed money now, or at some stage in their lives. A relatively small capital investment could harvest long-term benefits in the form of valuable intelligence. Shumovsky's work with meticulously selected individuals useful to the S&T effort, known also as the XY line, would be instrumental in Moscow ordering its New York *Rezidentura* head, Pyotr Gutzeit, in August 1934 to abandon the previous policy of mass recruitment in America.[9] The Centre had come to value the quality of intelligence over the quantity of information received; it was taking too much time to separate the wheat from the chaff. The close connection with the end users of S&T intelligence no doubt played a part in forcing through this necessary change. Tupolev was too busy to be deluged with uninteresting reports on irrelevant subjects that someone ignorant of aviation thought significant.

Shumovsky therefore set himself the task of identifying as potential agent recruits the brightest students who had the most empathy for the Soviet cause, sending their details up the line to New York. If the 'talent' he identified was considered worth recruiting, a specialist recruiter would make an approach. This 'cut out' approach protected Stan and his network. No one contacted would know he was the talent spotter.[10]

Stan's list of industry contacts reached outside the campus. Visitors to the faculty included a bevy of leading industry figures each year, such as the Russian émigré Sikorsky and Donald Douglas, who shared freely with the students their insights on the future of the industry.[11] There would be a faculty dinner at which the guest of honour would speak, giving Stan the opportunity to make himself known. He shrewdly joined every national professional association of automobile and aeronautical engineers he could, and obtained the name, address and company of every leading engineer in the US annually. His name appears on the same page in the membership directories as the Russian émigrés and leading aircraft designers Igor Sikorsky and Alexander Prokofiev de Seversky. In his vacations, he would visit factories to inspect the progress and build quality of the giant seaplanes that the Soviet Union had bought. He became familiar with how an American factory assembly line was organised. He would contrast the experience with a Russian one. The US industry was moving from being craft based, where each part for a plane was individually produced by hand in a single factory, to modern mass production techniques where aircraft were assembled from parts built off-site by different manufacturers. Increasingly aircraft makers used a high percentage of standard parts in their planes, manufactured by third parties to increase efficiency and reduce cost. Stan learned how the supply chain functioned and noted the growing use of subcontractors to mass-produce these standard parts.

In their vacations, the students either worked in US factories on assignment from college or helped inspect the quality of machinery destined for export to the USSR. Trashutin spent his summer inspecting equipment for the Chelyabinsk tractor factory, later converted into the Tankograd, or Tank City.[12] This was his first link to the city where he would live for forty years, becoming an honorary citizen with a street named after him.

• • •

Overlooking obvious differences such as his country of origin and ideology, Stan's fellow students had become his friends. With his amiable manner he could put anyone at their ease. He could charm both the president of MIT and the laboratory technicians. In conversation Stan avoided the subject of American politics, talking mostly about his specialised subject, aviation. He would solicit opinions on people around campus, but even if pressed would never comment himself, developing the art of managing not to answer even a direct question.

Ben Smilg, Shumovsky's college friend and his tutor, was his first agent recruit in America. Smilg's family, when they were interrogated by the FBI in the 1950s, described Stan as an open, jovial individual never without a smile on his face. He would talk to them about their interests – chess, music and literature. Equally at ease discussing reminiscences of the old country with Smilg's émigré parents or the Jewish question in Europe with the worried younger members, he was respectful to his elders but always ready with a joke.[13]

Smilg himself was an exception to the 'cut out' recruitment technique. In July 1934 Stan recruited him directly,[14] taking the risk as there were no NKVD specialist recruiters in New York at the time. (The intelligence service was small and suffered from frequent staff shortages, particularly of experienced operatives.) Smilg was the prototype of a new kind of recruit for Soviet intelligence. As a student, he would not produce secrets immediately, but he represented an investment for the future, a long-term asset.

Benjamin Smilg in MIT yearbook, 1932

To get close to lonely Ben, Stan became his buddy. Smilg was low-hanging fruit. Just eighteen, he was a fresh-faced college kid, while Stan was a 29-year-old man of the world, a Russian Civil War veteran. A shy, awkward genius, Ben was acutely conscious of his Jewish background; Stan was tall, confident and outgoing. On the face of it, the two could have had little in common. Ben was like Stan's awkward kid brother. Stan began calling his classmate 'Benny'.[15]

Ben's background was very different from that of most other students at MIT, and he did not fit in. Neither middle class nor a WASP, he made his way in life tutoring less able but wealthier students, making himself their hired help. To escape anti-Semitism his parents, Harry and Rebecca, had emigrated to Boston from Tsarist Russia before the Revolution, arriving around 1912.[16] The family scraped by, living in straitened circumstances in one of the poor Jewish areas of the city. His father Harry worked in a shoe factory as a leather cutter.[17] Ben was the elder of their two brilliant offspring; a mathematical prodigy, he gained a place at MIT on the aeronautics course that Stan joined in its second year. His father claimed somehow to have found the $400 for his son's first year's tuition fees from savings.

The pair probably first met after a lecture or by striking up a conversation in the department building. Under questioning, however, Ben would give conflicting and implausible accounts of their meeting. According to one version he had noticed during an aerodynamics examination in 1931 that Stan had considerable difficulty with the maths. Ben offered to tutor him, and would continue to do so until he left MIT. In another version, Ben claimed that he knew Stan was a Russian student and had once seen him handing in an examination paper written in Russian.

He asked Stan how he expected the professor to grade such a paper, and offered to tutor him. Stan accepted, since 'he didn't want to flunk out of school and go home to Russia in disgrace.' Although Ben didn't realise it, he was the one being recruited.

Stan would come over to Ben's house for lessons several times a week, and it was there he met his mother, father and brother. He made no comment on the family's circumstances, and quickly established himself as a friend, charming them all. Even twenty years later, and after a deal of trouble, they still considered him a great guy, 'a nice fellow to talk to.'[18] Stan even started helping Ben's mother with her persistent enquiries about the health of her relatives and friends who had stayed behind in Russia. But all the time he spent in Ben's house, Stan was 'talent spotting'. He had the ability, natural to intelligence gatherers, of asking questions without ever seeming to offer any information himself. Despite ten years of close friendship, the Smilgs, other than Ben, knew nothing of Shumovsky's life and work – and certainly not that he was a spy.[19]

Smilg noted with some jealousy that Stan was very well looked after by the Soviet government, which paid for everything, even providing him with discounted textbooks. While Smilg himself struggled to get by, still living at home on the other side of Boston, surviving on scholarship funds and what he could earn tutoring his fellow students, Stan was able to live close to the campus with ten others in a luxury boarding house.

Ben was, however, making enough to support his family, tutoring he claimed around six other students from MIT in maths besides Stan. Indeed, Stan was to pay his friend over $2,000 for tuition. This seems an enormous sum. A new car cost $500 at the time, while annual fees at the Institute itself were only around $400. The hourly rates Ben claimed to charge Stan varied between $2 and $5 according to the proximity to exam time. Even at $5 an hour that is a lot of tuition hours to rack up. Stan asked for and kept receipts, as he said he claimed the money back from the Russian government. The receipts came back to haunt Ben. On top of the $2,000, Stan may well have paid some household bills and medical expenses for the struggling Smilg family. It soon became his habit to bring small gifts for each member of the family on every visit.

The NKVD believed they had paid for Smilg to go through college and set him up for life. This became a pattern for their recruits: they wanted them placed under an obligation. Ben began supplying material to Stan which he later described as only classroom notes. He recalled to the FBI that as Stan often travelled away from MIT on business for AMTORG, he needed the notes in order to catch up on the lectures he missed.[20] It is reported in the NKVD files that as early as 1933 they began to receive copies of student theses and much other material from MIT's aeronautical laboratories.[21]

The FBI would long suspect Smilg of engaging in espionage for the Soviets. In fact, they knew it; but, hamstrung by a desire not to reveal a vital intelligence secret, they could not – or rather would not – publicly prove it. So when in 1955 they brought Smilg to a jury trial in Dayton, Ohio, they tried to convict him on a lesser charge of perjury.[22] He was cleared. It was a pivotal moment in the FBI's efforts to prosecute suspected wartime Soviet agents. In fact, very few of the hundreds of Soviet agents were ever charged with any crime, as FBI witnesses were depicted as fickle turncoats by defence attorneys and the real evidence could not be produced.

As part of its investigation of Smilg, the FBI decided to dig into the minutiae of Shumovsky's academic performance at MIT to find out if it was at all conceivable that Ben could have tutored him that much. They reported that Stan's results in maths-based papers were average to below average.[23] Ben noted that Shumovsky seemed to know a lot more about aircraft than he did, even if his maths was weak. But in comparison to Smilg, who was a prodigy, most people's maths was poor.

It emerged later that Smilg was indeed carefully cultivated and recruited by Shumovsky while at MIT. The NKVD file states:

Benjamin Smilg is code name LEVER, a US citizen, Jewish, born in Boston in 1913. Parents emigrated from Russia in 1905 with the assistance of the Jewish committee. Father is a cutter at a shoe factory. Brother works at the National Cash Register Company. The family has a very friendly attitude toward the USSR. Upon graduating from high school, thanks to exceptional abilities he was accepted at the Massachusetts Inst. of Technology for a free education, where he was always one of the most brilliant students. He remained at the Inst. to obtain a doctorate. Starting in 1935 he worked for the Budd and Glen Martin companies. He is currently part of a group at Wright Field for the study and eliminating of vibration in airplanes and engines. LEVER was a student in the same group with BLÉRIOT beginning in 1931 and had a friendship with him. He was recruited by BLÉRIOT in July 1934. He provided materials on a dirigible, calculations on the vibration of bomber tail assemblies, NACA materials, some students' senior theses, etc. In 1937 the materials stopped coming in.[24]

The LEVER case would be taught at Soviet spy school as an example of a perfect recruitment. MIT was a renowned centre for both military and civilian research, much of it at the very least commercially sensitive, and Shumovsky had access to all of it. But the NKVD records show that he took no risk himself, instead using third parties to acquire these secrets: one of those was Smilg.

• • •

During Ben's long recruitment Shumovsky had to report on each meeting and on his overall progress, seeking approval from Moscow Centre at each step along the way. At this stage, despite the obvious drawbacks Moscow kept all their men in the field on a tight leash, micro-managing every aspect of operational work. Given the distances involved, the time messages took to travel back and forth and the difficulties of communication, it was a cumbersome and inefficient approach. No wonder the recruitment took an age. It was hard work for Shumovsky too. From later accounts of Soviet recruitment at American universities, it is evident he would have to prepare and send off a detailed report on each of his meetings with any target, submit this for approval to Moscow, wait to get permission, and if this was granted wait before moving to the next stage.

From a later intercept of Russian intelligence traffic, we know the duties of a talent spotter were honed thanks to Stan's experience. The rules are clearly laid out. The talent spotter

> should make a broad range of acquaintances among the school's students and instructors in order to seek out people whom we could recruit for our work in the future. Under no circumstances should he talk to anyone about our work or try to recruit anyone for our work. Every two months he should put together detailed reports about his progress in his studies, his new acquaintances,

and scientific activities at the university. The reports should be typed on a typewriter and photographed onto film.[25]

The two crucial elements of the plan are the segregation of the talent spotter from the recruitment process and how vital it was that the agent was to work hard and achieve strong academic results. Shumovsky invented both these rules.

Smilg's recruitment had been achieved by means of a deep sense of personal loyalty to and admiration for Shumovsky. Stan stood out as a charismatic figure, a leader, a man committed to a mission, and his ardour was infectious. His life had a greater purpose than some, and he inspired admiration. The pair were friends first and foremost. Shumovsky used Soviet money to help Smilg's family out financially at times, but that always seemed an act of friendship, not a payment for services. Over the years Ben helped Stan in his work but he did not think he was working for the Soviet Union. He was not political; unlike other agents, he was not even paid a monthly stipend to provide information, or on results.

Smilg's first-generation Russian-Jewish background was typical of many who helped the Soviet secret service in this period. In fact, the majority of recruits were first-generation Russian Jews who felt excluded from the American dream. The Smilg family worried obsessively about the rise of anti-Semitism in America. There were increasing demands to exclude Jews from American social, political and economic life. Henry Ford himself was overtly anti-Semitic and published 500,000 copies of *The Protocols of the Elders of Zion*, a fabricated document purporting to contain the minutes of a global Jewish conspiracy.[26] Especially worrying to the Smilgs was the rise of the American pro-Nazi Bund. The German-American Bund held large parades as close as New York

City, featuring supporters in Nazi uniforms waving swastika flags. At its peak, Madison Square Garden hosted 20,000 people to hear speakers term the President 'Frank D. Rosenfeld' and refer to his key policy, the New Deal, as the 'Jew Deal'.[27] The Smilg family had fled one country to escape anti-Semitism and worried they might have to pack their bags again.

Stan would drop into conversation the claim that in contrast to the US, Jews in the Soviet Union were not threatened and that in fact, Jews held disproportionate numbers of key jobs in government and industry. Lazar Kaganovich, a Jew, was the country's second most important leader after Stalin. The Communist Party leadership had consisted almost entirely of Jews at the time of the Revolution.

• • •

Smilg's primary value as an agent of the Soviet Union was that he was the leading expert in the US on 'flutter', the vibration caused by air passing over a plane's wings at a rate that can cause the airframe to fall apart. Detailed calculations had to be made at the design stage as to the strength of the tabs required to keep the wings attached to the fuselage. During his career, Smilg would be a leading research scientist, author and inventor.[28] He patented several scientific inventions and authored books and articles such as 'The Instability of Pitching Oscillations of an Airfoil in Subsonic Incompressible Potential Flow' and 'Application of Three-dimensional Flutter Theory to Aircraft Structures'. After a couple of jobs, MIT helped place him at the top secret Wright Field military research base. NKVD records show that he provided interesting information on aircraft structures, engine design and aerodynamics.[29] But he proved a difficult agent for anyone other than Stan to manage.[30] Despite many difficulties, the pair would remain close friends into the 1940s.[31]

· · ·

It was Shumovsky who most likely talent-spotted another NKVD recruit at MIT. Radio engineer Norman Leslie Haight* (pronounced 'height'; his codename was LONG) was British born but had become a naturalised American. The Soviet interest in Haight was his work with the defence contractor Sperry Gyro-systems.[32] The NKVD even financed his electronics business in order to maintain extensive contacts with Sperry.[33] At the time Sperry was working on two vital projects, bomb sights and autopilots. The Soviet Union wanted the secrets of both, and used Haight to try to acquire them.

It was aviator Wiley Post who, in dramatic style, had brought Sperry's autopilots to the world's attention. Having set a round-the-world record on 23 June 1931 in his aircraft *Winnie Mae*, accompanied by his navigator, two years later he set out to beat his previous record by flying around the world solo. Having equipped *Winnie Mae* with a Sperry gyroscope autopilot and a radio direction finder, he succeeded.

After the atomic bomb, the most expensive investment made by the US during the Second World War, at more than $1.5 billion, would be in bomb sights. The Americans considered an accurate bomb sight an essential weapon if they were to win the war. Only the advent of the nuclear bomb, so powerful that accuracy was irrelevant, caused a temporary halt to the quest for the perfect sight.

The USAAF used Sperry's rival, the Norden bomb sight, in

---

* The FBI have never traced Haight.

its front-line heavy bombers. An early analogue computer, the Norden could be unerringly accurate in ideal weather conditions, when linked to a Sperry autopilot, in delivering a bomb close to its target. Sperry bomb sights were installed in many other wartime bombers. Unknown to the Americans, the Nazis acquired the blueprints although, lacking a strategic bomber, they never used the bomb sight. At the start of the war, the workings of its bomb sights remained America's number-one secret. Downed bomber crews were ordered to destroy the sight at all costs.

Never uncovered before, Haight would remain on the Soviet intelligence payroll for decades; he was considered such a vital potential agent that the NKVD, learning from the Smilg recruitment, paid for his Master's degrees at MIT.[34]

• • •

Stan's priority at MIT was acquiring the first-class education necessary to be able to operate at the highest levels as an S&T spy and aviation expert. His experience would set the benchmark for future S&T spies. In the future, the Soviets would use top scientists as intelligence officers, finishing off their education with a few years at MIT. These men became their best operatives in the US. Stan developed a first-rate knowledge of American aviation and technology, ensuring that the Soviet Union invested its dollars wisely in purchasing only the best planes and equipment.

US salesmen peddling the ordinary as extraordinary often saw the Soviet Union as a soft target; gullible Communists were easy prey to slick sales patter. But purchasing the wrong product in the Soviet Union could have disastrous consequences. Unfortunate investments could lead to charges of treason or sabotage. One individual upgraded the entire Moscow film stage with what he considered to be the most up-to-date film-making equipment available, only for the advent of 'talkies' to render the entire invest-ment pointless within weeks. The man responsible was arrested and charged with 'wrecking'.★ Under these circumstances, those trusted with responsibility for state acquisition programmes were diligent in pursuit of technology which worked. They came increas-ingly to rely on the expert knowledge of the man on the ground.

Stan was assiduous in acquiring copies of student theses. The main library at MIT was located just above the steps of Building 10 where the newly arrived Russian party had posed for their landmark photograph on that first day. It was a treasure trove of technical publications, original research and graduate dissertations. Seventy years of America's industrial innovation and technological discoveries were there for the taking. At a stroke, the Soviets had managed to place Stan and twenty-four other experts at the heart of America's technology powerhouse, with impossible-to-obtain long-term visas.

• • •

Boston's proximity to New York was another bonus for Stan. The main point of transit between the United States and Europe, New York was the centre of Soviet espionage in the US. Before the establishment of diplomatic relations and the associated ability to transport large quantities of material via the diplomatic bag, the main way of transporting material was by careful smuggling. This

---

★ Upton Sinclair wrote to Stalin on behalf of this individual, after which he was freed.

was usually done by sending microfilm messages concealed inside mirrors carried by the seamen – either communist sympathisers or those paid to smuggle information – on transatlantic liners. Soviet illegals describe setting up a mini factory to process the stream of information that made its way across the Atlantic, and on from Bremen and Cherbourg to Moscow Centre. The NKVD Resident in New York organised a network of Americans to support the new operation in Boston, Cambridge and around the country. The students identified documents and publications to be exfiltrated by the agents.[35] The support network did that work. Exfiltration involved borrowing documents, copying them (normally photographing them) and arranging their safe return.[36] In exceptional circumstances, students would be risked in the extraction process. The original organiser of the support system was to have been Military Intelligence officer Ray Bennett. At an early stage of the planning of this mission, Military Intelligence proposed her as the 'dean' of the student party. Her role was to travel around the colleges monitoring the progress of the students and conducting illegal intelligence work.

• • •

An essential skill of most spies is to be unremarkable, but Shumovsky was not one to hide in the shadows. Even on his first day at MIT, he stood close to the dean in the front row, his natural air of authority on full display. The Soviets knew that scientists freely exchanged information with their colleagues without regard to borders. Thanks to his position as a leading expert placed in an academic environment, Shumovsky learned far more than an ordinary agent could hope to. He knew what information was valuable and innovative and what to dismiss as merely run of the mill.

What has not been appreciated before is that there were direct communication channels between Shumovsky, the agent in the field, and his customer in the Soviet Union. Other than his agent reports, Shumovsky's work went directly to the Tupolev Design Bureau, with questions and requests coming by return. The success of Soviet S&T was to a great extent down to this close cooperation between the man in the field and his end customer. The intelligence officer as a trained scientist understood exactly what his customer wanted and could provide speedy answers to specific questions. A dialogue developed via this expert agent between the leading aeronautics experts of the two countries – even if the American side was unaware of it.

Like Hunsaker, Tupolev was fascinated with acquiring as much knowledge as possible via the use of wind tunnels.[37] In an age before computer modelling, an aircraft designer could spend vast amounts of time with scale models and complicated mathematical algorithms calculated by hand, juggling power, weight and strength to build a plane that could fly faster, higher and further than before. Building a prototype became the culmination of a long process. Tupolev's obsession with wind tunnels eventually got him into hot water,[38] but it did bring him to MIT on his final visit to the USA before he was imprisoned. MIT possessed a state-of-the-art wind tunnel, allowing its students to experiment with scale models to enhance aerodynamics, lift and structure. To complete his mission, Shumovsky needed more than the knowledge that was already on paper. He planned to recruit the brains. But, with rare exceptions, American engineers do not hold left-leaning political views. They tend to be too grounded or practical to be interested in politics. Luckily for the USSR the dire straits of the US economy came to his rescue.

Graduates in the early 1930s, even from top schools such as MIT, faced the worst job prospects for a generation. Graduates from the elite aviation course were in demand by employers even in the depth of the Depression as the MIT President's Report recorded that they could all find jobs in the industry. It was not the same for students on other courses. Chemistry major Edwin Blaisdell said that only one out of his graduating class of twenty-four had been able to find a job in 1932, and that was through a family connection. He decided, perhaps having read Stan's articles in *The Tech*, to enrol in Moscow University's summer school.[39] When the course was cancelled, he spent a few months travelling around the USSR. Impressed with what he saw, on his return to Boston he found the address of the Communist Party in the phone book and joined.[40]

A survey of Columbia's prestigious engineering school conducted at the time shows that graduates' salary expectations were depressed.[41] As the economic crisis dragged on, many graduates were forced to consider different options. An alternative that appealed to some was the possibility of working on a lucrative contract in the USSR. As the US closed factories and pulled back from capital infrastructure projects, the USSR threw vast resources into its development. Stan was besieged with enquiries. The interest led him to his first successful experiment with public relations. There were so many questions about the mysterious USSR that it made sense to reach out to the entire student body. To gain approval for his plan he could not ignore the official leader of the student group, Party loyalist Yefim Medkov, a prickly character very protective of his authority. He roped Medkov into co-authoring a series of articles for *The Tech*, but it is evident from the prose style that they were written by Stan.[42]

Through his articles, Stan sold the MIT student body a vision of student life in the Soviet Union that was attractive and compelling. Under the headline 'Students in USSR Maintained by Government, Families Supported Too', he explained that Soviet students, unlike Americans, were immune from economic worries. There was no need to work your way through a Soviet college or win a scholarship. There were no student loans as there were no fees. The generosity of the state went further; stipends were offered to students and their families. University places were open to any age group, including those with families. Education was open to every worker irrespective of age or gender. Truthfully Stan confirmed that the Russian school system was receiving a massive boost, unlike that in America which was in decline. In Stalin's Russia, for the first time, every child now received ten years' formal education and the opportunity to attend university. No child worked in a factory, as had been the case before the Revolution. Workers could leave work to study full or part time. There were no formal academic entry standards, as this would exclude many who, like Trashutin, had been employed from childhood and had been unable to attend school.[43] To enrol at the university, he explained, students joined the appropriate union for their course, be it engineering or music. The union then paid for all teaching, living expenses and family stipends. Extraordinarily for the time, Shumovsky revealed that 12 per cent of the overall student body was female and that there were no professions that women could not enter. In contrast, only four women studied aviation in his four years at MIT.[44]

Shumovsky talked excitedly about the scale of his alma mater, the Moscow Aeronautics Institute (MAI), which he said had an enrolment of 5,000–7,000 students. To cope with the demand, there were three intakes a year of new students, each roughly 600 strong. Students spent their first year working on the factory floor at the various aircraft factories around Moscow. The Institute was fully integrated with industry and focused on mass-producing engineers for the growing Red air force and Soviet civilian airline. Stan pointed out that MAI was already double the size of MIT but specialised in a single academic field, aviation. The institute was in its infancy and just before coming to the US, Stan had helped construct its first buildings. It was to grow into Russia's most prestigious technical university, providing the backbone for the design bureaus of Sukhoy, MIG, Ilyushin, Tupolev and Yakovlev.[45]

• • •

Being around the MIT campus had some unexpected benefits. On a visit to MIT, the FBI invited all comers to a presentation and demonstration of their latest crime-fighting technology.[46] This was the only time representatives of the Bureau appeared on campus while Stan was at MIT; but in truth, although they did not know it at the time, he and his fellow agents had nothing to fear either from US counter-intelligence or the FBI. The US security agencies had neither the interest nor the budget to look too closely at Soviet espionage activities in the US. The Soviets were just one of a handful of espionage threats and were never a priority, while political pressure focused anti-communist energies against the domestic US Communist Party (CPUSA). Many 1930s Soviet intelligence operations were abandoned prematurely or unnecessarily because of the assumed threat of discovery by US counterintelligence.[47] Russians were very accomplished at counter-intelligence themselves and because of this believed their rivals equally so. They were not. The US was unguarded.

Stan's experience at MIT proved to Soviet intelligence that the right individual could break into and become a member of America's elite science club. Artur Artuzov would ensure that Shumovsky's mission became part of the syllabus at Moscow Central spy training school. A decade after the events, trainers would still repeat the details of how and why he had been able to recruit American students as agents. The intelligence officers who sat in those classes would follow him to MIT, contributing to the Soviets' greatest espionage successes.

The United States was not only unprepared to counter the Soviet espionage efforts in the 1930s but uninterested in doing so. There were higher political considerations, and low commercial ones as well. The FBI's lecture at MIT in December 1935 had demonstrated the Bureau's relative innocence at this time. E. P. Coffey, the deputy director in charge of the Bureau's technical laboratory, had made his invitation to the students oblivious to the presence of Soviet intelligence personnel in the audience. Incredibly they were all invited to visit the lab and inspect the polygraph, a lie detector which was then under development and was later to become a primary tool in counter-espionage.[48]

Furthermore, stealing the design of, for instance, the latest fighter plane was classified at the time as a commercial patent theft, not a state secret. The FBI's investigations into Soviet espionage between the 1930s and 1950s caught few spies and put even fewer on trial. Despite the fact that between 1936 and 1952, its budget ballooned from $5 million to $90 million, and its staff grew from 1,580 employees to 14,657, the Bureau devoted few resources to counter-espionage, preferring to focus on other priorities. Prohibition had created the opportunity for organised crime to thrive, which kept the forces of law and order at full stretch. The newly formed FBI based its counter-espionage methods (such as they were) on its experience of solving common crimes, and these proved inadequate when it came to grappling with battle-hardened Soviet revolutionaries. Nonetheless, the Russians would continue to overestimate the FBI, believing them far more capable and competent than they were. One reason was that the FBI under its leader J. Edgar Hoover was a master of public relations, exaggerating its successes and when necessary the threats to America.

6

'IS THIS REALLY MY MOTHERLAND?'

Among the residents of the Russian student house in Bigelow Street was one of Soviet Military Intelligence's leading officers. His teachers and classmates knew him only by the pseudonym Mikhail Ivanov; the name was a cover, the Russian equivalent of 'John Doe'. The Russian students knew better than to ask his real identity, but they quickly formed their suspicions. In fact Ivanov was Mikhail Cherniavsky, a talented and determined Military Intelligence officer (the Fourth Department, later known as the GRU, was the smaller of the two best-known Soviet intelligence agencies. The other, the NKVD, became the KGB) who arrived ahead of the main party hidden within a small group of nondescript engineers.[1] The organisers of his mission felt that, given his seniority in the GRU, Cherniavsky needed a cover story in order to enrol as an undergraduate at MIT. It was believed that he was at risk following the defection of leading chemist Vladimir Ipatiev to the US.

The students had no idea of his colourful past and his future plans. His Russian colleagues had dark suspicions about this man. He dropped hints to them that he was on a 'special mission'.[2]

They were also somewhat fearful of him. And Mikhail Ivanov – or Cherniavsky, to give him his proper name – was, it would transpire, a dangerous man to know.

Cherniavsky led a party from Bigelow to eat their meals every day in the Russian quarter of the West End of Boston. Perhaps homesick, and finding it hard to adjust to American life, some students had taken to frequenting the Russian kitchen run by Ms Starr, an émigrée and recent widow whose late husband had been a radical socialist.[3] Local Communists gathered in her noisy dining room to discuss politics over borsch, pelmeni and tea. Some regulars went for the food, others for the local women. Several students began affairs and even started living with the wives of the radicals. One relationship grew so intense that the American woman pursued her man to Moscow after his graduation.[4] The recently returned Russian already had a wife back home who was far from amused to meet a rival. Another student became inebriated at an émigré's house. During prohibition, he had to be rescued and smuggled back to college by taxi.[5]

Such gatherings soon began to attract the very people the students had been told back home so many times to avoid: local revolutionary Russian émigrés who had sought asylum in the US. Most disturbingly of all, the students started to receive at their college addresses Trotskyist literature calling for the overthrow of the Soviet leadership.[6] It was Cherniavsky who had sought out the Trotskyists and had begun plotting with them. When the gossip and scandals reached the students' Communist Party cell leader, Yefim Medkov, he was presented with many disciplinary headaches.[7]

Cherniavsky's behaviour around campus was becoming

increasingly troublesome. Although a serving intelligence officer, he was apparently making every effort to reveal himself and was just one step from being exposed to the US authorities, thus putting at risk not just the student exchange plan, Shumovsky's vital mission, but Stalin's grand schemes. Already suspected by his housemates of being an NKVD secret policeman sent to keep an eye on them,* Cherniavsky was irresponsible, unsociable and odd. Worse, he was a political fanatic. No one knows exactly what he told the Trotskyists about his mission, but he certainly told them he worked for military intelligence.[8] His moods were fuelled by a growing sense of frustration and impatience at the political situation back in Russia. His politics was rooted in the soil and in the fortunes of the peasant. Cherniavsky harboured anarchist tendencies, believing that violent action was the way to replace Russia's leadership. Remarkably for an intelligence officer on a secret mission, he gladly included in his political discussions those who did not share his extremist views.

Medkov recognised Cherniavsky as a troublemaker, but what he knew was the tip of the iceberg.[9] At some stage during his studies at MIT, Cherniavsky had fallen in with a leading American Trotskyist whom he called Riaskin.† Riaskin was a friend of Ludwig Lore, who was leading the NKVD a merry dance with his fake intelligence reports. Lore and Riaskin had split from the American Communist Party in the late 1920s – Lore was expelled for political heresy – and Riaskin had worked for AMTORG

---

* Confusingly the Soviet Union operated two foreign intelligence services, one political and a smaller military one. They often had identical missions.
† I have been unable to trace Riaskin so far. Bennett knew him as a leading member of the CPUSA.

at some time. The pair had long political discussions, and at some point, Cherniavsky was recruited to the Trotskyist underground movement. Riaskin convinced Cherniavsky he was receiving direct orders from Trotsky.[10]

At the monthly Party meetings, Cherniavsky would create disputes by making deliberately provocative statements.[11] By temperament he was close to Trotsky's ideal of a permanent revolutionary, he also intermittently embroiled himself in the political infighting of the US Communist Party and in the controversies in Russia provoked by collectivisation and the first Five-Year Plan. Cherniavsky was aghast at the devastation produced in the Russian countryside by the brutality and speed with which collectivisation had been implemented, his conviction that the process had failed horribly becoming part of a broader loss of faith in the Soviet system. He became increasingly disenchanted when he realised that Stalin and his Politburo had abandoned the Soviet Union's commitment to fomenting world revolution, while his time at MIT convinced him that Stalin's planned economy could not catch up and compete with American capitalism. By 1934 he had come to believe that 'Trotskyism' alone could rescue Russia from what he considered to be the dead end of the Stalinist bureaucracy. For Russia to find a way forward and be able to compete with the West, 'the only solution was to overthrow Stalin'.[12]

Convinced by Riaskin that his orders were coming direct from his hero Trotsky, Cherniavsky was persuaded to form a group back in Moscow to work to topple the Soviet leader.[13] He recruited senior members of the Kremlin guard into his group to gain access to Stalin. They resolved to break into the Palace and either execute or arrest the leadership. Riaskin supplied the phone number of the underground liaison person in Moscow who coordinated contacts between the domestic Trotskyist opposition and the exiles. That person was Raisa Bennett.[14]

• • •

So how was such an unstable figure sent to MIT? At the time he undertook his mission to the United States, Cherniavsky ranked number three in the Soviet chemical weapons hierarchy.[15] There was no deep pool of Soviet talent with the experience to analyse poison gases or gas masks, and the mission was considered vital.

Born within a few months of each other, Stan and Mikhail's lives had followed similar paths, leading them to intersect at Boston, but had it not been for the Communist Revolution it is unlikely they would have met, except perhaps in the army. However, Cherniavsky made choices in Boston that ensured that the two men's lives ended very differently.[16]

Cherniavsky was nearing thirty when he arrived at MIT. He like Shumovsky had already led a full and eventful life.[17] He came from Misupt, a small village in the Myadzel in the Tsarist Vilnius province, which today is in Belarus. Cherniavsky had been active in extreme radical peasant politics as a teenager, only turning to Communism in March 1920. In 1917, he was a member of the extreme Left Socialist-Revolutionaries (Left SR), a radical peasant party, and an active member of its terrorist wing. The Left SRs were at one stage coalition partners of the Communists and openly espoused a policy of political assassination to achieve their goals. On joining the Left SRs, Cherniavsky met his lifelong mentor Yakov Fishman, a senior figure in the movement, learning from him all about the methods of assassinating political leaders.[18] The pair were members of a committee violently opposed to the peace signed with imperial Germany at Brest-Litovsk and to the presence of the Kaiser's troops occupying Ukraine. The Left SR movement unleashed a campaign of violence designed to restart the war on the Eastern Front by assassinating world leaders, including President Woodrow Wilson. The campaign began with the murder of the Kaiser's ambassador, Count Mierbach, in Moscow in July 1918. Fishman made the bombs and organised the murder.

'Death to Germans!' Left SRs in Ukraine, 1918. Yakov Fishman (extreme right, front row) and Mikhail Cherniavsky (centre, back row)

Cherniavsky hid from the subsequent round-up by enlisting in the Red Army, and served in the military continuously until his arrest in June 1935. He received his formal education in the army, graduating from the 1st Soviet Command Course in 1920, the Higher Military Chemical School for Commanders Course in 1921–3, and an advanced class for the Chemical Corps of the Red Army in 1924–5.[19]

Like Shumovsky, Cherniavsky fought with distinction in the Civil War in battles against the Whites and the Poles. He served in the 17th Infantry Division from May 1919 to March 1920, operating in Lithuania, Ukraine and Belorussia. Promoted to platoon commander, he was then transferred as a company commander to the 15th *Syvash* Division, serving with them from November 1920 until September 1921. In November 1920, the division fought its way into the Crimea across Lake Syvash, an enormous natural obstacle of stinking mud, and fought in the mopping-up operation against Baron Wrangel's forces. Later he was made head of chemical defence of the 37th Division in Novocherkassk as the unit was readied for an attack on the White holdouts in Siberia.[20]

His collaborator, Yakov Fishman, was nothing if not a survivor and a savvy political operator. Despite murdering the German ambassador, he was now the rising star of the Red Army's Chemical Warfare Division. Dr Fishman was a devotee of US General Amos Fries, head of the US Chemical Warfare Service. Fries helpfully published in 1921 a detailed book expounding every aspect of chemical warfare, including formulae and dozens of pictures.[21] Fishman used the book as his indispensable guide when in 1925 he began organising the Soviet chemical weapons capability. Describing the plan as the 'American model', he focused on four elements: developing the supply of chemical weapons to the army, testing the gases for combat use, acquiring protective equipment, and pyrotechnics.[22]

In 1926, and in need of a trusted colleague to work with the German army specialists now testing poison gases in a secret base outside Moscow, Fishman remembered his old friend.[23] He made Mikhail head of his military laboratory as well as assistant chief of the secret chemical weapons test site. In Dr Fishman's lab, Cherniavsky worked on biological as well as chemical weapons, including tests on the effects of live anthrax spores on animals. Dr Fishman had gained a PhD at Naples University. For the next five years Cherniavsky also spied on German technicians at work in Russia, first for Fishman and then for Military Intelligence. The highly secret and illegal chemical testing project jointly carried out by the Soviets and the Germans was codenamed 'Tomka', and as the work expanded it was moved from Moscow to a larger base at Shikhany, near Volsk in the Volga area. The new site was large enough to test-spray powdered poison gas from aircraft. The results were described to Stalin as 'promising'. It was while working with the Germans that Cherniavsky first demonstrated the skill with languages that would lead to his appointment on missions to the USA.[24]

Mikhail joined Military Intelligence officially in February 1927, becoming chief of the chemical sector of the 3rd (information-statistical) Department.[25] He spent his time reporting on the work of the German specialists in Russia. It had become apparent that the relationship between the Soviets and the Germans was less one of close cooperation than of mutual suspicion. The Soviets believed the Germans were failing to share their latest technology, while the Germans were nervous of being caught openly breaching the Versailles Treaty, and suspicious of the Soviets as they supported the German Communists.

Cherniavsky's military record goes on to show that from June 1931 until January 1935 he went abroad on a series of what are described as 'business trips'.[26] These were his missions to the USA. In his 1934 self-appraisal he explained what he had done in America:'I studied the chemical capabilities of foreign armies.'[27]

His final role was as head of the 3rd branch of the 3rd (military equipment) Department of Military Intelligence between January and June 1935.[28]

Unlike Shumovsky, who arrived as a student, Cherniavsky used the cover of a genuine business trip to New York sponsored by AMTORG to secretly enter America. After disembarking, he quickly disappeared from view; probably he spent his time visiting factories up and down the East Coast as part of a purchasing commission, gathering intelligence. When the opportunity arose to enrol on a course at an elite university, allowing him to extend his visa, he grabbed it. But Cherniavsky was not interested in gaining an education; he already had the practical experience to teach the chemistry course, given his recent assignment working with the Germans. In fact, he never finished the chemistry course, vanishing from campus one day in 1934.[29] His sole goal at MIT had been to collect the valuable intelligence on chemical warfare and high explosives demanded by his mentor Dr Yakov Fishman in line with his American plan.

Fishman is known as the father of the Red Army's biological weapons capability. He was called by Vladimir Ipatiev, an ex-colleague and a defector to the US who formed an intense dislike for him, 'a miniature chemical Napoleon'. As far as Ipatiev was concerned, Fishman was a fanatical plodder, a political animal hand in glove with the security service.[30]

Having been a spy himself, Fishman loved undercover work. In the mid-1920s he had been posted to Berlin as the military attaché as cover for his spying. His letters from the time survive in the Russian archives. He had a double reporting line, writing with news of his discoveries directly to Mikhail Frunze, then head of the Red Army, but also to Yan Berzin, head of Military Intelligence.[31]

His interests were widespread, ranging from chemical warfare and aircraft to politics; among the results of his espionage was the discovery that a gas mask offered to the Soviets by the Germans for mass production was obsolete, and that the German army was introducing a more advanced model. No doubt Fishman would have trained his pupil Cherniavsky in the dark arts of acquiring information.

Germany, the most scientifically innovative country after the US, was viewed as a key target, and secret military cooperation, including on chemical weapons, between Germany and the Soviet Union in the interwar period is well documented. Less is known about the parallel collaboration between Italy and the Soviet Union. As Italy had used gas extensively in its colonial war in Ethiopia, it had experience in its use. Dr Fishman headed a Soviet mission to meet Benito Mussolini, seeking to buy Italy's expertise in chemical weapons. They were an unlikely pair to share toasts – a fascist dictator and a committed Communist.

It was a combination of the publication of Fries' book *Chemical Warfare* and an official visit to the United States by the head of the German army that brought Cherniavsky to the US. Unwisely, in his attempt to lobby Congress for budget dollars to fund his programme, Fries had given away to his Soviet readers vital secrets of chemical warfare. Ironically, as events turned out, this Dr Strangelove figure, fanatical about using gas in war, was a fierce anti-Communist, believing that attempts to disarm the US were an evil plot. He went as far as building up his own intelligence network to infiltrate groups that he considered his opponents. His passionate belief in using gas in war went against the 1925 Geneva Protocol, a treaty signed by thirty-eight countries, including the USA, which made the use of such weapons illegal.

Fries taught the Soviets a persuasive and horrifying story about future gas warfare. The next war, he envisaged, would involve the mass release of powdered mustard gas – now called Yperite, after Ypres where it was first used – from aircraft adapted to spray chemicals over civilian areas such as factories or farmland. With the help of the Germans, the Soviets learned how to spray Yperite gas. The Americans had hosted a long trip for the head of the German Army High Command, General Wilhelm Heye, in 1927. Heye was a close friend of Hans von Seeckt, the driving force behind cooperation with the Soviets. Heye's observations on his trip to every US military facility, including the headquarters of the US Chemical Weapons Service, were passed in their entirety to the Soviets.[32] Based on the trip, Cherniavsky was sent to America to learn from the US experience how to industrialise the production of chemicals and explosives.[33]

Like Shumovsky, Mikhail sourced his information from the works in the university library, from lecture rooms, from working in the chemical laboratories, and most importantly from MIT's connections such as Edgewood Arsenal, the HQ of US Chemical Weapon Services. But their methods were very different. Mikhail went about his work in an extraordinarily brazen manner. He was described by the Russian students as running between libraries in search of chemistry material and behaving in the oddest way. There was no finesse to his work and certainly no attempt to leave the pond undisturbed.

Mikhail was not at MIT to recruit agents but to obtain as quickly as possible much of the knowledge that America had gained since the publication of Fries's book in 1921. His mission was a smash-and-grab raid on MIT. Conveniently, the head of MIT's Department of Chemistry at the time, Professor Frederick

G. Keyes, had served in the US Chemical Warfare Service during the First World War and had established a laboratory for the American Expeditionary Force in France.[34] In February 1918, he had organised a complete laboratory for research and testing in chemistry, physics and bacteriology, and oversaw the shipping of that laboratory to France. General Pershing cited Keyes for outstanding service, and he received the Purple Heart. His specialisations included the thermodynamic properties of gases and experimenting at low temperatures. While studying in the Chemistry Department at MIT, Cherniavsky was able to take 'military science' courses on 'Defense against Chemical Warfare', which gave him the opportunity to examine first hand US gas masks and other technology, as well as to copy recent research.

The main issue with chemical weapons, then as now, is how to make them effective on the battlefield. The First World War's static warfare was ideal for the release of poison gas from storage tanks, and later from shells, but its effectiveness was reduced by changes in wind direction or a drop in temperature. The Germans had first attempted to use tear gas against the Russians at the Battle of Bolimov on 31 January 1915, fired in liquid form contained in 18,000 15 cm howitzer shells. This first experiment proved unsuccessful, with the tear-gas liquid failing to vaporise in the freezing temperatures prevalent in Russia. Mustard gas replaced chlorine and phosgene as the 'king of the battlefield' by 1917. The Russians suffered the largest number of gas casualties, and of those a much higher proportion of fatalities, than any of the other combatants in the First World War. The reasons are twofold: first, the prevailing wind direction was towards their lines, making the use of gas more frequent; and second, they lacked effective countermeasures.

America had a key secret the Soviets wanted. In 1903 a young American priest, Father Julius Arthur Nieuwland, working on his doctoral degree at the Catholic University of America in Washington, DC, created a new substance. This would prove to be America's significant contribution to chemical warfare. While he was mixing compounds during an experiment, his flask turned black, and the mixture formed a black, gummy mass with a penetrating odour. The gas released caused the priest to become seriously ill. Later, in 1918, Winford Lee Lewis, an associate professor of chemistry at Northwestern University, was given the task of developing and producing novel gases. He recreated the priest's compound, with the result that it 'took on a nauseating odor and [caused] marked irritation effect to the mucous surfaces. A headache resulting persists several hours and the material seems to be quite toxic.'[35] The perfected product was named Lewisite after him.

The inventors Lewis and Nieuwland believed in gas warfare. They thought the use of poison gas would make wars more humane by shortening them and avoiding the suffering of innocent civilians. General Amos Fries named Lewisite the 'dew of death' in his book and revealed there had been plans in the First World War to spray it over the enemy from aircraft in order to end the fighting. The gas was thought to be so deadly that ten planes armed with it could eliminate every trace of life in Berlin. Many newspaper articles sensationalised the effects of Lewisite; one reported that it was seventy-two times more potent than mustard gas, a single drop on the back of a hand a fatal dose. Another stated that Lewisite was capable of sterilising the ground so that 'nothing will grow upon it for at least two years and perhaps longer', and that one drop of it on living flesh caused 'mortification'.[36]

The news fascinated Fishman. Lewisite was an ideal gas for Russian conditions as it was believed to be most damaging in dry conditions of low temperature and low humidity. The gas could be fatal in as little as ten minutes when inhaled in high concentrations. It had other benefits too: it was persistent, lasting up to six to eight hours in sunny weather, and even longer in cold, dry climates. The poison vapour was about seven times heavier than air and would therefore hover along the ground and enter caves, trenches and sewers. Having mastered the production of Yperite, Fishman now wished to learn how to mass-produce Lewisite.

US mass production of Lewisite took place at Edgewood Arsenal. In 1921, two British scientists, Stanley Green and Thomas Price, published the formula for Lewisite in *The Journal of the Chemical Society*. Cherniavsky was ordered to find out how to manufacture the gas on a grand scale. His efforts at Edgewood Arsenal and its partner MIT were successful, and following his mission the Soviet Union began producing massive quantities of the material, eventually disposing of approximately twenty thousand tons of it in the Arctic Ocean during the late 1940s and '50s. Churchill offered Stalin thousands of tons of British poison gas in 1941 to repel the German invasion.[37] Thanks to Soviet espionage efforts, Stalin, who had his own vast stocks, could decline the offer.

By the early 1930s, Fishman's and Cherniavsky's work had come to Japanese attention. The Japanese army saw conflict as inevitable and were planning for a grand land war against Russia. It is unclear whether their information about chemical weapons came from espionage; it may have been revealed when the Soviets used mustard gas sprayed from an aircraft in western China. The

Japanese responded by building in Ping Fan, a small village near the city of Harbin, the largest biological and chemical warfare laboratory known to exist at the time. It was known as Unit 731, a vast complex covering six square kilometres and consisting of more than 150 buildings, with living quarters and amenities for up to 3,000 Japanese staff members, 300–500 of whom were medical doctors and scientists.

The prospect of chemical warfare was not mere paranoia; it was a serious threat. During the fourteen years of the Sino-Japanese War (1931–45), Japan used poison gases more than 2,000 times in direct violation of the 1925 Geneva Protocol, to which they had been a signatory. Japanese attacks killed tens of thousands of Chinese, including many civilians. There were reports, moreover, during the Second World War of isolated incidents of the use of biological weapons on the Eastern Front.

Chemical weapons were stored just behind the front by all sides, but the mobility of the war, rather than ethical qualms, made them hard to use. The US deployed 400 chemical battalions consisting of 60,000 men in the Second World War. British Prime Minister Winston Churchill urged the use of poison gas to break the stalemate in Normandy and to bomb industrial sites. In 1944 an air raid on Allied shipping in Bari harbour, southern Italy, caused the accidental release of Allied mustard gas, killing an unknown number of Italian civilians and eighty-three servicemen.

• • •

As soon as he arrived at MIT, Cherniavsky began to scour the libraries for publications and research papers on chemical warfare. In an era before the invention of the photocopier, this involved many hours making handwritten notes. Military Intelligence did not provide him with a secure communication network to transmit his information back to Moscow. Instead, he gave it directly to Military Intelligence's top man in New York, the Rezident, to forward to Moscow. Interrogated a dozen times in 1935 by the NKVD, Cherniavsky revealed that he regarded his espionage mission to MIT as a failure. He put the blame for the failure of his work to narrow the technology gap between the USSR and the rest of the world on his former boss at the Lyublino chemical warfare research centre, located in a Moscow suburb. Cherniavsky denounced Vladimir Rokhinson, number two behind Fishman as a cynical, bureaucratic time-server (the comparison with the supportive, productive relationship Shumovsky enjoyed with Tupolev is notable). Cherniavsky had hoped that the intelligence he collected at MIT would undermine Rokhinson's attempts to conceal from the Soviet leadership the backwardness of his research centre. Although the revelations would cost him his life, his whistleblowing was effective. Rokhinson was removed.[38]

Cherniavsky claimed that Rokhinson had been given samples of the US Army mortars he had acquired. The US models had superior range, rate of fire and accuracy. They easily 'outclassed' those in use by Red Army Chemical Units. But Rokhinson had made no attempt to imitate them. Instead, to satisfy his superiors, he had exaggerated in his reports the performance of the Soviet mortars, whose range and rate of fire was only a third of what he claimed. The troops on the ground were kept ignorant of the fact that their equipment was inferior while the leadership was deliberately misled.

It was the same story with Soviet gas masks. Through his

espionage activities, Cherniavsky had acquired the most advanced model. He had worked with the Reichswehr, secretly testing chemical weapons in Russia. The German gas mask was years ahead of the primitive and outmoded Soviet version. The German model offered protection against the latest generation of gases, which the Red Army and the civilian population were likely to encounter in the next war. Yet, to his frustration, Rokhinson refused even to examine the German gas mask, let alone commission improvements to the Soviet one. The best espionage network had hit a roadblock. Cherniavsky came to blame the entire system.

• • •

Cherniavsky was later arrested for his part in the 'Kremlin Affair', his plot to kill Stalin on 21 June 1935. Dismissed from the Red Army, on 27 July 1935 he was sentenced at a closed court session to be shot.[39] Having been executed on the personal orders of Stalin, the only one of the hundred or so arrested to receive a death sentence, he was rehabilitated in 1958.

Cherniavsky could have enjoyed the same kind of successful espionage career as his more pragmatic colleague Shumovsky, but instead, his life ended in tragedy and disappointment. His life story is preserved in stunning detail in the NKVD files that record Cherniavsky's interrogation at their hands. Notably, Cherniavsky's responses to his interrogators show the immense pressure each of the agents was under, and the difficulty some of them had in reconciling their expectations of a socialist utopia with the great suffering and failures that seemed to characterise the country's attempts to catch up with the rest of the world.

He exclaimed his despair at the state of the USSR relative to the modern USA by saying, 'Is this really my Motherland?'[40]

For many, Cherniavsky was a ghost that could not be laid to rest. The whole Politburo discussed his case at length, believing him to be a terrorist and themselves a target. Stalin explained in a speech what it felt like to be threatened by assassin's bullets because of his policies. Cherniavsky was pilloried nationally as a notorious example of evil in the league of John Wilkes Booth. His fate caused deep ripples in the Soviet intelligence community and resulted in the defection of two wavering agents. It was an uncomfortable time for the MIT party, several of whom were called in for interrogation by the NKVD. For Shumovsky, Mikhail remained a problem. There were awkward questions to be answered in the future.

7

'QUESTIONABLE FROM CONCEPTION'[1]

J oy Bennett was just two years old when she arrived for the first and last time in what should have been her home country, the United States. She had sailed across the Pacific to Los Angeles, California in late 1932 with her mother Raisa, universally known as Ray.[2] The pair then disappeared for several months, only breaking cover when they made a desperate dash to the local hospital, where Joy's mother hoped to have a last meeting with her dying, estranged father. Although – or rather because – she was an American, Ray was Soviet Military Intelligence's primary agent on the West Coast. Two-year-old Joy was her cover.

Ray arrived too late to see her father, but some eight decades later in Moscow, 86-year-old Joy can still recall a few details of the months she spent in the US, playing on the beach and meeting relatives. Joy was later robbed of her mother forever as a result of Mikhail Cherniavsky's confessions. Ray Bennett was arrested and jailed by the Soviets in 1935, but Joy only learned the reasons why in 2017. Ray's story provides the earliest contem-porary evidence of the involvement of some of the leading figures of US-based Soviet spy rings and is one of the few accurate, unvarnished first-hand accounts of working for Military Intelligence.

Ray Epstein Bennett, as she styled herself, was one of a unique generation of Russian-Jewish socialists, a firebrand in search of a cause. Like many of her generation, she found that cause in Communism. In search of a better life, the parents of young people like her had crowded into the tenements of Brooklyn and other cities to take low-paid jobs, often in the garment industry. But in America, their children came to believe as they grew up that the game of life was stacked unfairly against them because they were Jews. The majority accepted their lot and got on with their lives quietly. Some chose to join unions fighting for better pay and conditions. But several thousand joined the radical political parties of the left. Finding themselves at the bottom of the social pile, the Jews felt they had least to lose and most to gain from seeking social change. Among this generation, Soviet intelligence found dozens of volunteers who, like Ray, wanted to make a difference. Without them, Soviet espionage would not have been able to function in the US in the 1930s and 1940s.

Ray was born with a fierce independent streak. Her family understood she was different, and that with her fiery character she was destined to be trouble. As she grew up, she would openly challenge the established order, convinced that unfairness must be confronted, society changed and injustice beaten. The family remembers Ray as a strong-willed, round-faced girl with bright blue eyes who was always laughing. After her disappearance – her family lost all contact with her without explanation. It was not a time to ask too many questions – her brother recalled, 'nobody cried when they spoke of Ray, there would just be a far-away look, a sigh filled with regret or envy, sometimes a resigned shrug of the shoulders.'[3] She had found her cause in life, and she followed it.

Soviet sources record that Ray was born in April 1899 in Petrozavodsk in Karelia Russia, later the site of a famous UFO sighting. Following the premature death of her mother, an actress, her father Solomon Epstein emigrated alone to America in 1907. The three motherless children, Ray and her two brothers, went to Slutsk, a famous rabbinical centre in Belorussia, to live with their grandmother. Following her brothers, in November 1913, at the age of just fourteen, Ray sailed aboard SS *Kursk* from Libau in Latvia for New York to rejoin her demanding father. She barely knew him. Solomon, as the family recalled, 'was a hellion, a man so involved in himself that he didn't realize that he had children to look after. So they looked after themselves, forming a kind of co-op, with the boys looking after their fiery sister.'[4]

Ray joined the large Russian Jewish community in Brooklyn. She came from a family of printers, and her father was a linotype compositor. Almost immediately, she began to challenge her father's traditional views that she should devote her life to looking after him, her elder twin brothers Jacob (Jack) and Julius and her father's new family. One emotional argument culminated in the daughter throwing a loaf of bread at her father.

Ray adjusted quickly to life in America, mastering English in just three years. She terrified her family, when making the vale-dictory speech at her graduation in 1917 from Eastern District High School in Brooklyn, by proclaiming her view that it was immoral to buy Liberty Bonds in support of America's partici-pation in the Great War. Ray saw the conflict as evil and imperialist, and was happy to share her opinion even during the wave of popular patriotic fervour that followed the entry of the US into the war. The family feared that her school might cancel her graduation; instead, the rebel was merely banned from the rest of the celebrations.

The brightest of her family, Ray was the only one who pursued her education, graduating from Hunter College New York in 1921 as a teacher. She taught English as a foreign language and instructed new immigrants about the American way of life. These were skills that would prove useful for her espionage career. She paid her way through college by working as a courier for a publisher, a candy seller for the Soft Candy Store in Brooklyn and a bookseller on Fifth Avenue in Manhattan at the National Education Association store. She married Nisson Neikrug, a remote relative, in 1919 before graduating. She had met her future husband through her brothers Jack and Julius and their union activity. Neikrug had studied engineering at nights at the Cooper Union but could find no work as an engineer and instead became a linotype operator. He had fled Russia to escape military service in the Tsar's army in 1914, and then dodged the US draft in 1917 on the grounds that he was not a US citizen. At some point, in a vain effort to escape the anti-Jewish prejudice that he believed prevented him from pursuing his vocation to be an engineer, he changed his name to Julius (Jules) Bennett.

News of the twin revolutions in 1917 gripped the Russian émigré community in New York with much excitement. Few were more enthusiastic than Ray. She and Jules became immersed in underground activities for the Jewish section of the Communist Party. Ray was a junior Party leader and educator of new recruits.

The family recall that Ray and Jules would have people over most evenings for political meetings at their home and songs sung in Russian could be heard from behind closed doors. Once she found her cause there was no stopping her: there were no limits to her anger at the exploitation of human beings, at the injustice meted out to women and at the brutal way the city and national authorities would seek to control and break the growing labour unions. She joined the CPUSA in 1922, a year after her husband.[5]

Ray was one of many eager volunteers who wanted to go to the USSR immediately, but with no relevant skills to match her enthusiasm she had to be content, like many hundreds of others, with helping the Revolution from afar. To maintain her interest, the Party told her that she was a valued active worker of its New York organisation and that, due to a 'lack of activist cadres', her departure to the Soviet Union had been refused by the Central Committee. She was too valuable to be sent away. Few would remain so persistent in wanting to travel to the land of Lenin.

Eventually, her lobbying to go to Moscow bore fruit. In 1923, she gained permission from the Central Committee of the American Communist Party for a short trip to the Soviet Union. She could finally be spared from her activist duties in New York. She earnestly hoped that if she were to get a job in the Soviet Union, then she would be able to remain and petition for a transfer to the Soviet Communist Party. Her loyalty to the cause was so great that she was prepared to leave her family and her adopted country.[6] Family records suggest that Ray may have taken the trip to recover from the loss of her first child, a daughter, in infancy.[7] She later told the NKVD that the child had been named Stalin.[8]

Ray journeyed to Europe under a false name, as the wife of a doctor. She had first obtained US naturalisation papers and a passport, stating to the authorities that she was travelling to Latvia via Germany as a trade representative of her relatives' leather and fur company. The relatives had no idea she was using their business name in this way.

When Ray finally made it to the Soviet Union she spent months there as a tourist, living in Moscow and visiting her grandmother in Slutsk. Before her departure from New York, she had agreed with her husband Jules that if she were to find a job in the Soviet Union she would remain there permanently and he would come over and join her. In fact, Jules could not travel, as he had lost the right to a US passport and re-entry thanks to his refusal of the draft in 1917, when he had stated he was not a US citizen and had no desire to be so. If he left the US, he would be unable to return.

As it turned out, Ray was unable to find a job in the Soviet Union and so returned to the US. Still waiting for any opportunity to serve the Revolution in the USSR, she worked thereafter at AMTORG's offices promoting Soviet cinema and for a Russian-language newspaper published by the Communist Party in New York. Telling her family that she and her husband had saved enough money to make their dream of living in the USSR a reality, she travelled back to the USSR, this time with Jules, in 1927. They boarded a ship and went to the Soviet Union via Germany. This time she thought she was going back to the land of her birth for good, to a place she believed held new promise, and where the future worked. However, before their departure from America Jules had encountered some serious difficulties in his workplace. Caught by the management of

AMTORG trying to break into the desk of a colleague, Jules explained his actions by saying he had believed the fellow employee was involved in various 'unlawful purchasing operations'– in other words taking bribes.[9] To confirm his suspicions, Jules had decided to examine the documents stored in the desk. Unsurprisingly AMTORG's management did not believe him, and he was fired for attempted theft.

After arriving in the USSR, Jules transferred his membership from the CPUSA to the All-Union Communist Party, eventually becoming deputy head of the RUDA (Iron Ore) Trust in Pivdennorudnyi, Ukraine. He was finally an engineer.

To no one's surprise, the Bennetts divorced shortly after arriving in the Soviet Union. Jules was softly spoken, a gentle soul, while his wife was a force of nature. Ray found herself a job in Moscow teaching English and the American way of life at the Frunze Red Army Military Academy Eastern Division. She began an affair and soon married one of her pupils, Joseph Ovadis, a senior member of the Intelligence Directorate and a man of action. She taught every agent heading to the Far East English, getting to know as friends most of the military intelligence community. She officially joined Soviet military intelligence under what she described as 'rather random circumstances'. In 1928, while staying with a pupil from the Intelligence Directorate in the spa town of Kislovodsk – the hometown of the writer Alexander Solzhenitsyn – at a newly opened sanatorium resort named after the ten-year anniversary of the October Revolution, she met of all people Yan Berzin, head of the Directorate, who by chance was holidaying there. After an introduction from her companion, she struck up a conversation with Berzin; when he discovered she spoke English and held an

American passport, he suggested she should start working for the Directorate. Ray had finally found the opportunity to serve the cause that she had spent her whole life looking for.

Upon her return to Moscow, Berzin enrolled Ray in the central intelligence apparatus of the Red Army, although her background was completely unknown to the Intelligence Directorate. She became a deputy section head. Later on, during her interrogations, the NKVD would express surprise at the lack of any vetting by their fellow espionage agency.[10]

After a few months of training in field craft and radio work, Ray was dispatched on her first overseas mission, to China in July 1929, when she was appointed assistant to the Shanghai-based resident, the head of Military Intelligence in the city. Uprooting herself from Moscow using her now former American nationality, Ray spent twelve days on the Trans-Siberian Railway to Vladivostok, travelling in the luxurious but dangerous international first-class compartment. The route was notorious for the presence of foreign counter-intelligence officers posing as passengers, looking out for Russian agents on their way to China. In order to maintain their cover story, Soviet agents were told never to speak Russian in conversation with their fellow passengers from the moment they boarded the train, and even if possible while asleep. Ray had another important task on the journey: she would have to remember a cipher of thirty-two random numbers, each corresponding to a letter of the Russian alphabet. For security reasons, the cipher could never be written down.

After the train journey, there was a further two-day trip by boat to reach Shanghai. On her arrival in China, she made no mention of a Russian husband and her new nationality when registering with the local authorities. Before her departure, she had renewed her American passport at the consulate in Riga, Latvia. The new passport contained no clues such as inconvenient stamps revealing her long stay in Moscow that would arouse suspicion. She rented an apartment on rue La Fayette in the stylish French concession, near the 50,000-seat greyhound racing track. The premier residential and luxury retail district of Shanghai, the French concession was popular with foreigners and wealthy Chinese alike. At the time Shanghai was the entertainment centre of Asia and a playground for the rich and famous. Foreigners and Chinese flocked to Shanghai to get rich quick and indulge in the pleasures on offer, which included brothels, gambling houses and drug dens. The infamous Triad gangs controlled much of the city, the most notorious being the Green Gang headed by Du Yue-sheng ('Big Eared Du'), a staunch and murderous ally of the Chinese leader Chiang Kai-shek.

To blend into the cultural melting pot, Ray was required to live a double life. At the same time as being an agent codenamed 'Josephine', or 'Joe' in honour of her husband,[11] she had outwardly to maintain the life of a single American English language teacher living in the most vibrant city on the planet. Crucially, Ray still had her American wardrobe, not the shabby, ill-fitting, functional clothes of Muscovites that would give her away. She was required to frequent the spectacular jazz cabarets, nightclubs and restaurants while spending the balance of her nights waiting to decode top secret transmissions from Moscow. The city's nightlife was immortalised by Busby Berkeley in Jimmy Cagney's 1933 movie *Footlight Parade*, in the iconic song and dance routine 'Shanghai Lil'. The film was popular in Moscow, many of the set pieces being adopted for Soviet parades.

It is ironic that Ray's lifelong crusade to end exploitation required her to play the part of a capitalist exploiter.

Shanghai was a divided city. There were various concessions, each policed by a foreign power, and alongside them the Chinese districts were booming. Shanghai was the espionage capital of Asia at the time, a hotbed of international intrigue and a playground for agents of the great powers playing cat and mouse with the local police. Foreign intelligence services and their agents operated without restraint, attempting to gather information on the latest machinations of Chiang Kai-shek and the feuding warlords who ran China. It was a difficult place to find anyone to trust.

In 1927 the Kuomintang leader Chiang Kai-shek had fallen out spectacularly with his Communist allies, massacring many of them in cities across China, and especially in Shanghai. His formerly close relations with Moscow came to an abrupt end, causing the dismantlement of the Soviet intelligence network and leaving Moscow blind. In the summer of 1929, further tensions arose over the controversial ownership of the Chinese Eastern Railway linking Vladivostok to Chita. This was a single-track spur of the Trans-Siberian Railway that crossed Manchuria, cutting thousands of miles from the route to Vladivostok. The argument over the railway had spilled over into open fighting between the Chinese army and the USSR. The Chinese struck first, seizing the railway. To everyone's surprise, the Red Army fought back successfully, routing the Chinese. The Soviets now needed to keep tabs on both the Chinese and the bellicose Japanese, whose territorial ambitions extended to the Soviet Far East, and in 1929 Shanghai suddenly became the pivotal foreign espionage station for the service.

The station was run at the time by Alexander Gurvich, who operated under the codenames JIM and 'Willi Lehman'. Gurvich had learned the espionage trade working for the Soviets in New York, where he had been taught by the Radio Corporation of America (RCA) to operate long-range transmitters.[12] He had only arrived in China in late 1928, travelling via America to divert any suspicion about his real purpose for being in the city.

Gurvich had to build his espionage network from scratch. It was a torrid time for the resident, who was desperate for recruits while short of money and under pressure for results. He used a German trading company financed by the Intelligence Directorate as a front for his illegal operations. Newly arrived illegals for his rebuilt station were preferably non-Russians, whose foreign passports meant there was no need to waste time creating a cover story. One key member of the team was a German named Max Clausen, who installed relay wireless radio stations linking Shanghai with the USSR, but Ray was the more trusted assistant, one of the very few taught in strict confidence the difficult skill of how to code and decode messages. The Soviets used a secret one-time pad system of ciphers that was theoretically unbreakable, sounding like gibberish if intercepted. For extra security, the radio operator was not trusted with the secret of how the codes worked, and would broadcast lists of numbers never knowing what information he was transmitting or receiving. Clausen cooperated closely with Ray. When later captured by the feared Japanese secret police, the Kenpeitai, on his last mission in 1941, he told the entire story of his life, recalling Ray as 'beautiful, despite a big nose'.[13]

Over her first summer in Shanghai, the hot and very wet

climate and the intensity of the work adversely affected Ray's health. Working at night, as this was when messages were transmitted and received, she spent long, arduous hours alone in a hot, airless room deciphering coded documents from memory. This necessitated recalling the latest cipher, while subtracting the number from the right one-time pad in order to retrieve each letter of a message. The sweat would drip off her. It was so humid in Shanghai that one had to bathe at least twice a day, but the mere act of drying oneself would raise a fresh sweat. By day Ray had to run her language school with legitimate clients as a front. It was an exhausting routine.[14]

Both Clausen and Bennett moved on to work with Richard Sorge when he arrived in China to head the ring. A legendary spy described by the French newspaper *Le Figaro* as 'Stalin's James Bond' and by Ian Fleming, Bond's creator, as 'the man whom I regard as the most formidable spy in history',[15] Sorge was tall with dark brown hair; with his broad, wrinkled intelligent face he looked older than his thirty-three years. He had been wounded in the Great War and walked with a limp. To maintain cover, he would only speak to Ray in English. Sorge was the established authority on having a good time in Shanghai, participating enthusiastically in the 'High Life' that expressed the colonial mores of expat Europeans rather than puritanical Communists. He had a notorious reputation with women, especially radicals, and enjoyed numerous affairs. He accompanied Ray to the best shops to ensure she was kitted out for the Shanghai social scene. Fastidious about her appearance, Ray enjoyed wearing clothes in Shanghai custom made from the finest silk.

Soviet intelligence had sent Sorge to China using his favourite cover, that of a German journalist. (Later in 1933, Clausen and

Sorge would use the same cover when they became part of a five-man team on an epic mission to Japan.) Ray was a senior and trusted member of the resident's staff. To be put in charge of cipher communications, correspondence with the junior residents and sending classified agent reports to Moscow were tasks worthy of a resident. She fulfilled some 'special assignments' – in other words, spy activity – which included running two agents in the city. When the resident was absent, she acted as his deputy.[16]

In mid-February 1930 Ray returned from Shanghai to Moscow, again via Siberia. She had missed her new husband and was exhausted by the demands placed on her. It had been agreed that Ovadis would join her in Shanghai, but Ray's health had become too poor for her to stay. Her replacement was Nadezhda Ulanovskaya, a woman who recalls in her memoirs being trained to operate a radio by Ray in Moscow.[17] Ray bequeathed Nadezhda the basics of an appropriate wardrobe for Shanghai, a stylish American leather coat and a knitted dress unobtainable in Moscow. Later Ulanovskaya went on to work with Whittaker Chambers, a Soviet agent and early defector in the US; she features in his memoirs, *Witness*. Her husband was the New York resident from 1931 to 1933, where the couple spent their time crating up Cherniavsky's material to smuggle back to Moscow.

•   •   •

On her return to Moscow Ray quickly became pregnant, and she gave birth to her daughter Joy on 29 December. Soon afterwards, in the spring of 1931, the Intelligence Directorate sent

Joy and Raisa Bennett, 1933

Ray on a second mission. This time she was to join her husband undercover in Kabul, Afghanistan, where he had been working since May 1930 as the correspondent for TASS, the official Soviet news agency. Baby Joy, who was just a few months old, went too. Afghanistan was the pawn in the so-called 'great game' between Russia and the British Empire. The Soviets were trying but failing to install a government friendly to them.[18]

On her return from Kabul, the Intelligence Directorate involved Ray as their core – and possibly only – American asset in their biggest project in its history to date. This was the audacious operation to place up to eighty agents simultaneously in ten elite US universities. Its ultimate success was to a great extent down to Bennett's preparatory work. The scale and importance of the operation to Soviet intelligence cannot be overestimated. It was a vast enterprise in comparison to the limited resources available. The budget had been provided centrally, but the logistics would place a strain on the organisation. The agency only had around eighty-five members in place around the entire world, so to establish a further eighty sources in a key target country was a major operation.

Ray was part of every detail of that operation, from completing each student's initial application to getting the right student to the best university. The most important task was training the team to fit into modern American society. Since other English language teachers in Moscow were Russians and had atrocious accents, it was Ray who had recruited fellow American Gertrude Klivans to give conversational English lessons and an introduction to America.

Although both Russian Jews, Klivans and Bennett were chalk and cheese. Klivans's family had made a success of their immigration. Klivans was frivolous whereas Ray was driven. Klivans had an extremely wealthy, supportive family who sent her regular parcels of otherwise unobtainable items. She was having fun in Moscow and if she ever felt like it could leave at any time to rejoin the family on vacation in Florida. There was no Great Depression for the wealthy Klivans family. In contrast, Ray was a committed Communist, an intelligence officer and had become a citizen of the Soviet Union. She was a member of the inner sanctum, trusted with the secrets of the intelligence service. With their very different backgrounds, Gertrude and Ray did not become friends. Gertrude commented to her parents that Ray was too serious a Communist for her taste.

Initially, the teachers worked with six engineers for just two hours a day, but as departure drew closer, they worked with the group non-stop. After the first challenge of preparing any Russian used to queues and shortages for the shock of America, a second, more difficult task was to knock the rough edges off Communist engineers straight from the factory floor and teach them how to behave at an elite US university such as Harvard. Ray was responsible for an enormous 'Pygmalion' project transforming nearly eighty ex-peasant soldiers and radical Marxists into suave, besuited Ivy Leaguers. There was a lot to explain to the students, from the basics, such as personal hygiene, to instructing them not to chew and spit sunflower seeds. They had to be taught not to scratch, a Moscow habit caused by infestations of bed bugs. Ray had to explain about the use of toilet paper, which was unobtainable in Russia, the liberal use of soap and the importance of ironing shirts. A thorny topic was how to hold a conversation with an American without falling into Marxist rhetoric, for example calling a professor 'Comrade'. Some of the raw material Ray had to work with were, like Shumovsky, genteel by Soviet standards, with a grounding in manners and etiquette, but the majority had no understanding at all.

From her time at AMTORG and her long membership of the CPUSA, Ray had an encyclopedic knowledge of US Communists. She was able to identify some of those who could be relied upon to welcome the students into their communities and help them adjust. In Boston, she selected Professors Cheskis and Halphin, as well as a local businessman named Stephenson, who was a regular visitor to Moscow and friendly to the Soviet Union.[19]

In her role as prospective dean she met each student when

the party, including Shumovsky, assembled in Moscow. She spent weeks briefing them on the do's and don'ts of life in America. Her goal was to keep the party away from any inadvertent brushes with the authorities. In particular, she had to explain to the hard-drinking Russians the rules of prohibition. The lessons in integrating into American society that she had first taught new immigrants in the 1920s were dusted off and put to use teaching agents and students to blend seamlessly into university life.

With her structured English language teaching experience, Bennett was ideally suited to raise the engineers' English, both spoken and written, to a very high standard. The engineers were expected to be completing term papers at Harvard in a second language within weeks. They all had to pass an exacting English proficiency exam. Ray worked closely with Klivans, each teaching part of the group in Moscow.

Ray had one exceptional pupil. In preparation for her trip to the US, she carefully taught her daughter Joy to speak only English, despite living in Moscow. She could not take the risk that while in America her young daughter would suddenly start speaking Russian and break her cover. Sadly, today Joy remembers not a word of the English her mother taught her.

• • •

Once the student operation was launched, Ray was to travel to the US with the party as their official dean and leader. The mission would involve her in a great deal of travel around the universities to arrange the exfiltration of information. At the same time, she was to carry out other unspecified 'illegal' operations such as the recruitment of agents. It is likely that MIT was not the only university to admit as students a quota of intelligence officers.

But the plan to send Ray to the US was overtaken by an unforeseen event and abandoned at the last minute. Just as Ray and Joy were packed and ready to sail. Catching the world by surprise, on 18 September 1931 the Japanese had invaded and annexed the Chinese territory of Manchuria following the Mukden incident, a staged terrorist attack by them on a strategic railway. After this act of military aggression, the Soviet Union expected the large Japanese army based on its border in Manchuria to launch an attack on its territory at any moment. Unprepared militarily to confront Japan at this point, they needed as much warning as possible of any imminent invasion. So Ray was given a new, vital task. She was indeed to go to America on a mission, but not to chaperone engineers. She was to settle down on the West Coast, establish a new residency and organise work in America against Japan. The Soviets knew that Japan lacked many vital war materials. It imported metals and oil for its armaments industry from the USA. By monitoring cargoes that crossed the Pacific to Japan, the Soviets would have advance warning of any planned attack. Ray's new network was to ascertain from Japanese sailors what their cargoes were and how frequently shipments were made.[20] She later described to the NKVD one of the goals of her mission: 'I was supposed to prepare a radio operator and the resident for work in Japan. It was planned that for the role of resident we could use one of the journalists that have connections in Japan. For a cover, it was expected to open a Chinese restaurant in Japan.'

The proposed resident was Richard Sorge, the German journalist with connections to Japan and the German embassy in

Tokyo. In preparation Ray's former boss was recalled to Moscow from Shanghai in 1932. But there was one big problem: he spoke no Japanese. At the very least he needed a Japanese assistant who was fluent in English and committed to Soviet ideals. The search for such an individual led the Intelligence Directorate to the US, then to California and finally to a painter–cum–activist named Yotoku Miyagi, who supported himself as an artist by running a restaurant called the Fukuro or Owl – the Japanese venerate the owl as a symbol to ward off misfortune and hardship – in the crowded Little Tokyo district of West Los Angeles. Moscow's request to Miyagi, channelled through the CPUSA in the autumn of 1932, was that he should return to Japan as a spy. His niece later commented that 'he refused, he had no experience in spying, and he asked them to find someone more suitable.'[21] But in the end Miyagi reluctantly agreed to go, if only until a more appropriate replacement was found. Ray was likely sent to California in late 1932 to vet and train the reluctant Japanese recruit.

Miyagi returned to Japan in 1933 to recruit a network of agents. The least well-known member of the five-man Sorge cell, he would work successfully until the network's arrest in 1941. By that time the cell had provided intelligence of immense value, much of it from unlikely sources developed by Miyagi. They are credited with confirming that Japan would not attack the USSR in 1941, allowing thousands of troops to be transferred to save Moscow from the approaching Nazis. It was however Miyagi's past links to the CPUSA that would eventually contribute to the downfall of Sorge's network in Japan.

Yet Ray's wider mission soon unravelled. In California, she grew disenchanted with the prospects for success as she was 'not given a concrete task or [told] precisely how I was meant to fulfill the task'. Unlike Shumovsky, who acted independently and could adapt to changing circumstances, Ray needed and craved constant hand-holding and detailed instructions. She was better suited to a subordinate's role, to being given a task to perform and instructions on how to do it. This was never going to be possible working alone thousands of miles from Moscow. In hindsight, Ray was too inexperienced to be given such respon-sibility. She would have been perfect as the dean of the student party, but as events in California spiralled out of control she would make extraordinary errors of judgement.

To Ray 'this whole enterprise was questionable in its concep-tion due to the extreme difficulty of conditions around establishing intelligence work on the West Coast of America'.[22] She was nevertheless given a salary of $250 a month and sent off to America for an indefinite period with a list of friendly contacts.

• • •

After an absence of five years, when she stepped ashore in California in 1932 Ray Bennett became the first independent female Soviet Military Intelligence operative in the USA. Along with George Koval, she is one of the very few Americans to serve in the Red Army on US soil. At two years of age Ray's daughter Joy, after her mother's work in Afghanistan, was already an unwitting veteran of two undercover espionage operations, although she never realised that her time playing on the beach or with her American relatives in the Bronx was part of an intelligence mission. Such precious moments were captured in photographs and sent to her father Ovadis in Moscow. In one photo Joy is pictured in a goat cart, looking frightened by the goat, and Ray recommends on the back that they should get her a pet. (After her arrest in 1935, the NKVD interrogators were bemused at the details of her operation and its execution, which seemed distinctly amateurish even to them.)

Bennett's was not the first Military Intelligence operation in the United States. German Communist Felix Wolf had undertaken a similar mission just a few years earlier, and his fate is demonstrative of the stress that agents like Ray felt themselves under. Having enrolled for a short time at Columbia University in New York as a graduate student, he found, like Ray, working as a spy alone so far from home without a support network extremely stressful, and he cracked. After travelling undercover along the East Coast and as far afield as Chicago in a fruitless search for industrial secrets, he abandoned his mission and fled back to Moscow fearing arrest. But there was no threat to him except the one he imagined. There are no US records of his presence, even at Columbia University.

Ray had one special mission to fulfil, and for this she sought the assistance of the Intelligence Directorate resident. To complete the task, she needed to make contact with a trusted representative from the US Communist Party. Having been put in touch with a former church minister with Communist sympathies, she revealed at their meeting that she came from the Soviet Union and was carrying out an illegal mission. She needed urgently to contact Upton Sinclair, the socialist writer; it was hoped that the minister could make an introduction.

Sinclair had written a letter to Stalin in October requesting the pardoning of a Russian from a death sentence. He had also financed a disastrous film made in Hollywood by the Soviet film director Sergey Eisenstein. Provisionally entitled

'Que Viva Mexico', it was a plotless travelogue and in its original version is unwatchable. Eisenstein shot some fifty hours of film before even deciding he was making a six-part social history of Mexico. Having advanced $25,000, Sinclair wanted to dig himself out of the deepening financial hole. Eisenstein's stock had fallen in Moscow following his extended absence from the USSR, and with the advent of talkies his avant-garde style was considered old-fashioned. As it was, the contract he had signed ensured that the USSR would have the finished film for free.

Stalin wrote back promptly, having gained the impression that as a prominent, popular socialist Sinclair could help the Soviet Union in their Manchurian crisis, perhaps by speaking out on their behalf. Showing his close personal involvement in the mission, Ray was under orders directly from Stalin to contact the writer. Stalin even went so far as to underline Sinclair's address in Pasadena so Ray could find him.[23]

Through the good offices of the minister, Ray managed to arrange a meeting with the author, but it was a disaster. Sinclair had a strong belief in the paranormal and the power of psychic prediction, but he was unprepared for what happened next. After introductions and pleasantries, the small, round-faced woman, rather than offer financial support for his film, suddenly announced to Sinclair that she was in America on an illegal spying mission for the Soviet Union and expected him to help her. Sinclair was completely shocked. In panic, and fearing a setup, he started demanding bona fides and a recommendation from the CPUSA. Ray was unable to produce any such assurances and fled.

After the debacle, Ray moved quickly on to San Francisco.

She next met with Kipper, the first wife of Morris Childs, a senior member of the CPUSA. In Moscow at the time, studying at the Lenin School and training to become an NKVD agent himself, Childs would later become the FBI's greatest double agent and was awarded the Presidential Medal of Freedom. Ray and Kipper would become friends, working together to get Joy an American passport.*[24]

The resident at the Consulate had given Ray the most valuable introduction possible, to none other than the General Secretary of the CPUSA, Earl Browder. Ray knew Browder in California, and spoke about him later to the NKVD using his codename FATHER. Through FATHER she made contact with two other leading lights of the Party, Irving Kaplan and Nathan Silvermaster; the three would later be exposed as the leading figures in the Soviet wartime spy rings.

All these meetings were unproductive. Ray had access to the top American Communists, but despite all the help she was receiving, establishing a cell on the West Coast was proving impossible. Lack of money for safe houses or recruiting agents was one issue. She found, like Gurvich, her boss in Shanghai, before her, that Moscow Centre underestimated the expense and difficulties of working in the field. In her opinion, there was too little support on offer for her to succeed. Nor was she the first to find that cooperation with the members of the CPUSA was difficult, as the Upton Sinclair debacle showed. The US Communist Party could and should have given her its white

---

* They tried first to get a fake birth certificate for the two-year-old. Kipper understood that a birth certificate was needed to obtain an American passport through unlawful means.

signed ribbon, identifying her to Sinclair as a person to trust. But the interests of Moscow and the CPUSA were already pulling in different directions. Following its newly adopted 'Socialism in One Country' policy, the USSR energetically sought information from America that was for the benefit of Soviet security alone, while CPUSA members were focused on the prospects for their domestic revolution. Earl Browder, their leader, was revealed by the defector Elizabeth Bentley to be intent less on intelligence gathering for the benefit of the USSR than on finding the details of industrial unrest for his own purposes.

• • •

Given the difficulties she was experiencing, Ray wanted out. She was keen to get home to Moscow and avoid a posting to Japan but suspected that permission would not be forthcoming, so she invented a pretext. She described to the NKVD how she became 'exposed'. She and her contact, named Odner, made a plan to use a White officer for an intelligence operation:

Upon my orders, Odner had some meetings with this White to work on him. Once Odner reported to me that the White informed him that he was interrogated by a Major from American Counter Intelligence who was also interested in Odner. The Major was also interested in a woman who visited Odner at his flat, and the description matched that of myself. It became apparent to me that the police came to know of my relationship with Odner. Because of this, I was forced to abandon San Francisco and travel to New York.[25]

US counter-intelligence may have been interested in Odner, but they were in fact unaware of Ray at that time. The FBI's interest and an urgent investigation started only much later.

Ray fled to New York, staying with a friend from her college days until October 1933 and meeting with her family, old friends and various political contacts. She refused to discuss her life in Moscow with her brothers, and the family knew better than to ask, although they gained the impression she was now married to a Soviet general and was possibly being pursued by the FBI. They were aware she had been in China but did not press her on what she had got up to there. Testing the political temperature, Ray made contact with members of the Trotskyist groups in Boston that were working actively to recruit Mikhail Cherniavsky. Her faith in Communism was as strong as ever, but the official Party line was now at odds with the views she had held since the early 1920s. She opposed the one-country approach to socialism and harboured doubts about the leadership. So she volunteered her services for the dangerous role as a coordinator of the Trotskyist centres abroad with those in Moscow. Her role as a Military Intelligence officer gave her a reason to be in touch with the US, while she passed her contact details in Moscow to the Trotskyist network.

On her return to Moscow, Ray was initially disciplined for abandoning her operation without permission. Suspended from the intelligence service, she was sent to a factory. But her language skills were needed too much. She might not have proved herself as an agent in the field, but Berzin appointed her head of foreign languages at the Intelligence Directorate.

One day in April 1935, Ray's daughter came to her mother's bedroom, as was her habit in the morning when they did exercises together. That morning the room was a mess, and there was no sign of her mother. Ray was gone, arrested by the NKVD over the Kremlin Affair. Her relationship with the 'terrorist' Cherniavsky – they met a few times in Moscow and discussed sedition – had proved her undoing.

After her arrest, Ray gave wholesale denunciations of her friends and colleagues, although much of what she said about their views seemed innocuous enough, had they not been serving intelligence officers. She also accused her ex-husband Jules of making jokes about Stalin and Molotov, reporting to her interrogators without realising the irony of his belief that it was prudent to watch what you said or the next step was a meeting with the NKVD.

Bennett was initially given a light sentence of five years in a labour camp, from where she was able to send secret letters to Joy at her kindergarten:

My little Joy, my Love!

I got your good letter and, you know, I immediately recognized the sunflower and quickly realized that the girl is doing gymnastics, as I did with you in the mornings. Remember how we put pads on the floor and did the bicycle exercise?

Here, two cows gave birth to small calves, one calf is all white with a black mark on the muzzle, and as soon as he was born, he immediately wanted to stand on his feet, and three of us had to hold him while he was bathed.

Then there is a black fox that sits on his tail in front of the cooperative, he is not afraid of people at all and asks for bread from everyone who leaves the store. He is a silver-black fox with a white tip on his tail. You and I have not seen a fox like him in the zoo. Are you now going to the zoo with your Daddy?

Anyuta writes that you are a good girl. You must dress yourself and tidy up all your toys neatly and obey Elena Semenovna and Daddy.

Little Joy, your mother loves you so much and always thinks about you and misses you very, very much. If you are a good girl and study well at the kindergarten, then I will be back with you by the time you go to school. You will already be big then. But do not forget me and know that I always love you and very much want to be with you.

Please give Aunt Anyuta your photograph, choose a good one with dimples, and she will send it to me. And can you draw me pictures and dictate letters to me, and getting them will be such fun for me. Learn to write and write me letters. Give a kiss from me to Elena Semyonovna and Lidochka. I kiss your eyes and dimples. You're my favourite.

Your Mother.[26]

Ray's husband returned from a mission in China a month after her arrest. He had a much better idea which way the wind was blowing and cut Ray out from all family pictures, refusing to discuss her again with his daughter. Ray was to disappear in the madness of the Great Purges. The details of her new crime, most probably a fresh denunciation, are lost for ever.

8

'THE WILY ARMENIAN'

I n the summer of 1933, the next in the line of Soviet super-spies walked down the gangplank and straight into the fray in New York. The small and somewhat overweight man had a medium-dark complexion with dark brown hair and blue eyes. As he planned to be in America for a while, he was accompanied by his attractive wife, Vera, and their small daughter, Eugenia.[1] Despite speaking somewhat broken English, at least according to the FBI, Gaik Ovakimian, codenamed GENNADY, was rapidly to become the nemesis of US counter-intelligence. The Bureau believed he ran hundreds of agents, and he earned the grudging admiration of his FBI tails for his skills in deception. They nicknamed him 'the wily Armenian' despite his cover being so effective that they were not even sure that was his place of origin.[2] There is, however, no longer any doubt about Ovakimian's ethnicity. The intelligence service of the twenty-first-century Armenian Republic still celebrates his successes during the Soviet era. They record with pride specifically his role in acquiring the atomic bomb and the plans for the B-29 Superfortress. Ovakimian was to earn another nickname during his life for his work as 'the puppet master', organising Operation ENORMOZ, which targeted the Manhattan Project. He is a true legend of Soviet espionage.

Posted to New York to take over as Stan Shumovsky's supervisor, Ovakimian and his colleague would energetically transform the scale and intensity of Soviet S&T intelligence operations in the US. With their shared scientific backgrounds, the pair had so much in common that they became a great team. They were excellent planners and schemers. Having inherited a small 'illegal' programme with no formal structure, capable of staging only random pinprick missions, they created in its place a vast information harvesting machine employing several hundred American sub-agents run by a small number of intelligence officers.

Ovakimian's first task had been to put the structures in place to support the new 'legal' networks operating out of the embassy, the consulates and AMTORG. As the results prove, he was successful. In 1939, a difficult year when information gathering was slow, his NKVD operation in the United States would obtain 18,000 pages of technical documents, 487 sets of designs and 54 samples of new technology.[3]

• • •

Gaik Ovakimian was born on 1 August 1898 in the small village of Dhzagrii, close to the Armenian capital of Erevan, then part of the Tsarist Empire.[4] The city is overshadowed by nearby Mount Ararat, a dormant volcano and the traditional resting place of Noah's Ark. He was one of five children of a clerk and, as a railway worker, was among the first to join the Communist Party in June 1917 as an eighteen-year-old. In May 1920, he was imprisoned after an unsuccessful Communist-led rising in Armenia's second city, Alexandropol. At the end of that year, Sergey Kirov's 11th Red Army, including the young Stanislav Shumovsky, marched in to found, 'by the will of the toiling masses of Armenia', a Soviet republic. Ovakimian was freed from prison and appointed a senior member of the small and newly established Armenian security service, the Cheka, before taking a high position in the government.

At the end of 1924, Ovakimian began studying chemistry at the Bauman Moscow Higher Technical School; after a year of study, he went to work at the Economic Directorate of NKVD, which was fighting financial crime. The NKVD was a domestic and international security organisation, but it also had responsibility for border guards and even tax collecting. Resuming his academic studies in January 1925, Ovakimian graduated in December 1929. He moved on to postgraduate work at the Mendeleev Institute (now University) of Chemical Technology, which was renowned for its analytical and chemical engineering laboratories, receiving his first doctorate in 1931, one of the few awarded in the Soviet Union.

• • •

On graduation, and at the suggestion of the local Communist Party, Ovakimian was invited to the Lubyanka for the same friendly chat with Artur Artuzov that Shumovsky had enjoyed the previous year. Having studied metallurgy, Artuzov was the only member of the NKVD leadership with any higher technical education, and he realised the need to recruit outside the service if he was to find suitable XY line (S&T) officers. The Communist

Party network at the universities was alerted to look out for scientists with strong language skills as potential intelligence recruits. In his Lubyanka office at the old insurance company building, now the headquarters of NKVD, the goatee-bearded son of an Italian-Swiss cheese maker, Artuzov – whose real name was Fraucci – sat behind a desk piled with personnel files. The opera singer manqué read Ovakimian's biographical details, noticing he had studied briefly abroad, before asking a few questions about the current political situation. He then explained INO's foreign intelligence role within the Five-Year Plan and offered Ovakimian a position in his newly formed XY department. Ovakimian immediately accepted. He was delighted to serve his motherland. His initial posting was not to America but to Berlin as an XY line officer based at the NKVD legal residency at the Soviet trade mission. Just before leaving Moscow on his first assignment he expressed to Artuzov some doubts about his ability, but was reassured with the words:

> I am convinced that you will be a success in this role. To begin with, you are a scientist. With your education, high intelligence, knowledge of English and German languages you will be able to build friendships with people just like yourself. And not only that, you have a way about you that will persuade them to work with us. You will be able to use these friendships to recruit agents and acquire useful material for us. I have seen that when you are dealing with people, you have qualities of patience, flexibility, politeness and composure. These are vital in our business.[5]

Ovakimian learned his remarkable agent recruitment skills on the job in Germany. Artuzov was correct in his assessment of Ovakimian's winning personality, which soon led to his agents genuinely liking him. It was on this mission that Ovakimian had his introduction to espionage in the field of nuclear physics. His greatest success during his first year was to recruit, at a Berlin laboratory engaged in building high-energy accelerators, a German chemical engineer codenamed ROTHMAN. The summary of Ovakimian's career in the SVR's official history describes the intelligence he obtained from ROTHMAN as including valuable new methods of creating synthetic benzine and the agricultural fertiliser and explosive ammonium nitrate. Both the Red Army General Staff and the Research Institute of the People's Commissariat of the Chemical Industry gave his first intelligence reports an 'exceptionally high score'.[6]

In the United States, there were high expectations for this new German method of making benzine, even if these were misplaced. According to an article published in the US monthly magazine *Popular Mechanics* in May 1929, chemists had developed a process for making synthetic benzine. With the limited German supply of crude oil unable to meet the increasing demand for motor fuel, it was estimated that German synthetic production could reach up to 250,000 tons a year, approximately a quarter of the country's entire fuel consumption.*

Apart from ROTHMAN, Ovakimian's most productive recruit in Berlin was Hans-Heinrich Kummerow (codenamed FILTER), who provided documents on advanced optical instruments, echo

---

* Benzine later became a key blending agent in high-octane fuel. The Soviet chemical industry found it hard to introduce advanced Western production processes because of the state of their old-fashioned equipment. The CIA reported as late as the early Cold War that benzine still remained 'in short supply in the USSR even for the priority chemical and explosive industries, and cannot be counted on to augment the supply of high-octane gasoline.'

sounders and gas masks. Kummerow would remain a Soviet agent for twelve years, becoming a member of the celebrated Red Orchestra espionage ring during the Second World War. He was eventually caught by the Gestapo in 1942 and executed in February 1944. In 1969, the Supreme Soviet posthumously awarded him the Order of the Red Banner. Ovakimian also recruited STRONG, the head engineer at the German company Auergesellschaft,* and LUDWIG, a scientist at the famous Zeiss works.

In August 1932 Ovakimian returned to Moscow to study chemical warfare at the Red Army Military Chemical Academy, Cherniavsky's alma mater. In June 1933, at a meeting with Artuzov to discuss his next foreign assignment, he was told that in the new climate following Hitler's rise to power, the top priority for the XY line (S&T) operations was no longer Germany but the United States, as 'America has a unique position about questions of politics, economy, and technology.' Specifically, he was informed, 'nowhere is technology as advanced in every sphere of industry as in America. The most important thing about the procurement of technical materials for our industry is that the scale of production in America has the closest correspondence to our scale of production. This makes technical intelligence in the USA the main focus of work.'

• • •

But it was the situation with Japan, which had taken a dramatic turn for the worse, that was the pressing problem. There was unrelenting pressure from the Kremlin on intelligence officers in

---

* Auer was the main contractor in the Nazi atomic programme.

the field to provide information. Not for the first time, the Soviet Union was on a war footing. Stalin believed that Japanese policy in China could only be so brazen if they had secretly agreed on a division of its territory with other capitalist powers. His concern was that Japan's next step after swallowing a chunk of China was to attack the Soviet Union. Despite Shumovsky's heroic work, the armed forces of the USSR were not ready for them. Stalin had written to Kliment Voroshilov, Commissar for the Army and Navy, late in November 1931 that 'Japan plans to seize not only Manchuria but also Beijing. It's not impossible and even likely that they will try to capture the Soviet Far East and even Mongolia to soothe the feelings of the Chinese clients with land captured at our expense. It is not likely to attack this winter, but it might try next year.'[7]

Stalin had reason to believe the threat was imminent. He was receiving direct intelligence.[8] So concerned did he remain at the threat of Japanese attack on the Soviet Far East and Eastern Siberia that in March 1932 he took the unprecedented step of ordering the NKVD to publish in the newspaper *Izvestia* extracts from intercepted top-secret Japanese documents, obtained both by breaking Japanese ciphers and from an unidentified NKVD agent working in the office of Lieutenant-Colonel Yukio Kasahara, the Japanese military attaché in Moscow. Though not identifying him by name, *Izvestia* quoted Kasahara as reporting to Tokyo:

It will be [Japan's] unavoidable destiny to clash with the USSR sooner or later . . . The sooner the Soviet–Japanese war comes, the better for us. We must realise that with every day the situation develops more favourably for the USSR. In short, I hope the authorities will make up their minds for a speedy war with the Soviet Union and initiate policies accordingly.[9]

The Japanese ambassador in Moscow, Koki Hirota, also not identified by name, was quoted as saying to a visiting Japanese general, 'On the question of whether to start a war between Japan and the Soviet Union or not, I consider it necessary that Japan takes the path of a firm policy against the Soviet Union. The fundamental goal of this war should be not so much in the prevention of Japan adopting communism but in the appropri-ation of the Soviet Far East and Eastern Siberia.'[10]

On reading *Izvestia*, Kasahara immediately identified himself as the author of the report claiming that war with the Soviet Union was Japan's unavoidable destiny. NKVD codebreakers decrypted a telegram he sent to the Chief Intelligence Directorate of the Tokyo General Staff seeking to deflect the blame for the leak by calling for more secure methods to be devised in Tokyo for secret communications with its representatives in Moscow. The copy of Kasahara's report in Stalin's files, however, does not make it clear whether it had been intercepted en route to Tokyo (as Kasahara believed) or obtained by an agent recruited by the NKVD in his office (of whom he was unaware).

However the information was obtained, the publication of the *Izvestia* article on 4 March 1932 led, on the following day, to a fraught and confused meeting between Lev Karakhan, Soviet Deputy Commissar for Foreign Affairs, and the Japanese ambas-sador Hirota. The ambassador could not openly admit that he had written one of the confidential reports quoted in *Izvestia*, and Karakhan could not acknowledge that Hirota's communi-cations with Tokyo had been decrypted by the NKVD. Hirota thus confined himself to complaining of the damage done by the article to already tense Japanese–Soviet relations, while Karakhan put the blame instead on aggressive actions by Japanese troops and bellicose statements by 'very responsible' Japanese officials.★

In the autumn of 1933, the combative Hirota was appointed foreign minister in Tokyo in place of the relatively moderate Yasuya Uchida. On 26 November, the NKVD provided Stalin with a decrypted dispatch sent by the US ambassador to Japan, Joseph Grew, to the State Department ten weeks earlier. Grew emphasised the influence of General Sadao Araki, nicknamed the 'Tiger' of Japan, the prime mover in the conquest of Manchuria and a self-confessed 'great enemy' of Russia. In the decrypt, which he placed in his personal archive, Stalin underlined the sentence, 'Hirota is a fervent supporter of the policy of General Araki . . .' The dispatch concluded: 'Nothing stands in the way of the Japanese control of China even by next spring. The next step will be a war with Russia.'[11]

• • •

Meanwhile, Ovakimian's new assignment entailed promotion to deputy head of intelligence and head of XY at the legal residency in New York, which was due to be set up as soon as diplomatic relations were established with the United States. His orders left him in no doubt that immediate and dramatic results were expected. And so successful would he be that in sweeping up

---

★ Though it would have seemed unbelievable in 1933, the careers of both Karakhan and Hirota were to end in execution. At the height of the Terror in 1937, Karakhan was shot after being found guilty of charges of espionage and terrorism, though he was later posthumously rehabilitated. A decade later, Hirota became the only Japanese civilian official to be hanged for war crimes by the International Military Tribunal for the Far East.

after him, the FBI believed mistakenly that he was the head of all Soviet intelligence in the US.[12]

Gaik Ovakimian and wife

Ovakimian was an incredibly talented chemist. He had published seventeen scientific papers in the USSR before becoming a spy. His love for chemistry was so strong that he would even take time out from being a spymaster to enrol part time at New York University to work in the labs and eventually to earn a second PhD. Even with what the FBI described as his 'broken English', in 1940 he would publish jointly with Martin

Kuna and Phoebus A. Levene a research paper based on his PhD subject, snappily entitled 'The Correlation of the Configurations of Aminophenylacetic Acid and of Alanine'. Levene, a pioneer in the study of DNA, was head of the laboratories of the Rockefeller Institute for Medical Research, New York, where Ovakimian would study; Kuna's subsequent career in chemical research would include a spell as a chemist at the National Laboratories, Oak Ridge, part of the Manhattan Project.

• • •

With the arrival of Ovakimian in New York, Shumovsky's life changed pace. Ovakimian was charged with establishing the infra-structure for a new 'legal' network. Broadly, a 'legal' had an official reason to be in America by virtue of his cover job; an 'illegal' did not, instead working under a false American identity. Until the arrival of his Armenian colleague, Stan had been working through small-scale 'illegal' networks, operating from the only safe houses, microfilm studios and couriers available. The two networks – legal and illegal – would continue to operate in parallel, but Shumovsky was transferred to the legal side once the infrastruc-ture was in place around the middle of 1934. He was too valuable to be caught up in the high-risk world of the illegals.

Early in his time at MIT, Shumovsky had reported periodically to three different heads of the illegal line, the last being the alcoholic philanderer Valentin Markin, the man responsible for the Ludwig Lore fiasco. Stan explained to Ovakimian that he had previously worked with the illegal CHARLIE, Leon Minster, who was in New York from 1928 to 1934. CHARLIE was a post box operating from a photographic shop in Brooklyn.[13] He collected information from engineers such as the technical sales-people of commercial companies, sending information to Moscow about lifesaving devices for submarines and two types of tanks. Shumovsky supplied to CHARLIE from MIT data on aircraft engines, the characteristics of a bombsight and details of the construction of seaplanes, providing drawings, formulae and manuals so that Soviet engineers could recreate the mechanisms and copy the production processes. One of the best such finds microfilmed and couriered to Moscow was a report written by Robert Goddard, the pioneer of modern rocketry, entitled 'The Results of the Work to Create a Liquid-Fuelled Rocket Engine'. CHARLIE sent to Moscow Centre further open-source material such as technical patents and descriptions of US Army tactics.

The illegal residents were involved in high-risk work as they were the conduit for stolen documents. Having become fully acclimatised to life in America, Shumovsky had now been activated as a full-time agent, operating not just within MIT but across the nation. The legal line established far stronger communications with Moscow Centre. Radio and coded telegram contact replaced the couriers sent to France, Germany and Scandinavia. Diplomatic mail was another possibility, but it was soon discovered that the regular volume of traffic was too low to conceal the amount of espionage material that needed to be sent. The regular mail was found to be reliable but took twelve days to reach Russia. To avoid suspicion, false postal addresses were set up across the Soviet Union that were covers for Moscow Centre. Shumovsky had by now learned to operate with a high level of proficiency in English, and the first tantalising fragments of his handiwork work start to appear in NKVD records in the summer of 1934, when the centre was sent the MIT dissertations acquired by Smilg.[14]

One immediate problem for the pair was with the Curtiss-Wright aircraft engines contract. Just ahead of the Depression, Curtiss – which under its owner Glenn Curtiss had long been the largest manufacturer of aircraft in the US – had merged with the Wright Corporation to form the Curtiss-Wright Corporation. Wilbur and Orville Wright had been the first to fly a powered aircraft, the Kitty Hawk, in Dayton, Ohio. The goal of the merger was to create the General Motors of the sky; in effect a vertically integrated aviation company. The business built and operated aircraft as well as running flight schools under one holding company.

Stalin's immediate priority after the establishment of diplomatic relations with the USA was to get hold of the R-1820 Cyclone 9 radial engine that had been ordered for the Red air force. He complained by telegram dated 17 February 1934 to the newly appointed Soviet ambassador in Washington, Alexander A. Troyanovsky, that Curtiss-Wright was unnecessarily dragging out contract negotiations to license the production of the Cyclone 9 in the Soviet Union and provide technical assistance.[15] Moscow urgently needed the ready-made engines, and feared that the company might even have decided not to conclude this important deal. Influenced by alarmist political intelligence reports from New York, Stalin blamed Curtiss-Wright's obstructionism on 'the influence of Japanese agents' in the United States.

Following a promise made by Stalin to William Bullitt, the US ambassador to Moscow, to give direct access, President Roosevelt had made a similar promise to Troyanovsky. Hoping to make use of Roosevelt's assurances, Stalin instructed Troyanovsky to see the President about the issue as soon as possible: 'We attach a lot of importance to this case. Every day is crucial.' In the event, the contract with Curtiss-Wright was successfully concluded, probably without the intervention of Roosevelt. If the importance of their work had not been clear already, now that Stalin was overseeing aviation activities in America it was more than apparent to both Shumovsky and Ovakimian. Curtiss-Wright was to become Shumovsky's number-one priority.

Based largely on his experiences on the ground in Germany, Ovakimian would create a new Soviet model for S&T espionage gathering in America (a system that would be rolled out across the world when he became global head of S&T in 1941).[16] But as he had no prior knowledge or experience of the US, he relied for initial advice on Shumovsky, who already had three years of first-hand operational experience to pass on. Stan explained the daunting nature of their task. The American scientific community was vast and geographically spread out: in his field of aviation there were pockets of manufacturing concentrated around New York and Los Angeles as well as clusters of activity in the Midwest. Based in New York and with limited resources, the Soviets could only scratch the surface. However, as Shumovsky had learned at MIT, the science community acted as a club; once you were on the inside it was easy to build a network, you just needed the right introductions. Given US conditions, the pair had no choice but to adapt the established Soviet way of conducting intelligence operations. The only public record of foreign intelligence activity, the 'Mitrokhin Archive',[17] details how time and again the Soviet Union returned to their playbook.

To join the chemistry club Ovakimian enrolled at New York University and began recruiting fellow scientists. By the end of 1933 he was running four agents, codenamed BEAM, TALENT, IDEALIST and SINGER.[18] BEAM was Grigory Rabinovich, a

Soviet intelligence officer using the cover of a medical doctor working at the Red Cross. He lasted a year in the USA. Ovakimian's first serious science recruit was TALENT, William Malisoff, a chemistry professor at Brooklyn College at the time of his recruitment. He later worked for several chemical companies before creating his own business, United Laboratories, during the Second World War. Ovakimian wrote of Malisoff: 'He is one of the few chemistry professors with a grounding in Marxism to be found among all our friends, who are willing to do anything for us, and for whom the interests of our homeland and the worldwide revolution are the principal ideals of his life.'[19]

Like many agent recruits at the time, Malisoff was easy to approach. Born in Russia, he had emigrated to the US as a child. He was a believer in the inevitability of the triumph of Marxism and had worked productively over many years for love of the Soviet cause. Like so many agents recruited by Ovakimian, Malisoff developed a close friendship with his controller. Later, Ovakimian recalls his admiration for the scientists who had given him information despite the risk of exposure. He sympathised with their situation but felt the risk worth taking for the cause.

Although Malisoff's own scientific research was highly valued by Moscow Centre and appreciated by Soviet scientists, his greatest contribution was as a recruiter of his own network and freelance information seeker. For the most significant innovation that Ovakimian (with Shumovsky's help) introduced in 1933 was the idea of an agent group leader. The change was based on the underground revolutionary cells developed in Tsarist Russia to confuse the Okhranka. The best description of how these cells operated appears in Fyodor Dostoevsky's masterpiece *The Devils*. The cell structure was designed to ensure the best security for its members. Each member knew little or nothing about his network, possibly only the leader. Only the leader knew all the members. The members communicated with the head via a 'cut out' courier, who would pass orders and collect material from each source without knowing the agent's real name or personal details. The member might never meet the courier as they would use a so-called 'dead letter' box.

The couriers were not supposed to know anything about the material they were couriering. When two American couriers, Harry Gold and Elizabeth Bentley, broke the rules, Bentley's defection from Communism in 1945 to become an informer for the US was among the events that caused the virtual collapse of all Soviet espionage activity in America immediately after the war.

Ovakimian decided a few trusted agents would be allowed to recruit friends and contacts as sub-agents in his group. The process transformed the pace of intelligence gathering. Whole networks of cells across America would be established and operate remotely from Moscow Centre. The idea was contrary to the widespread perception of how Soviet operations worked, as it was completely decentralised. TALENT was perhaps the first agent to be given such latitude.

Previously, the recruitment of agents such as Ben Smilg had taken months or years, with every step run through Moscow Centre. TALENT was able to move much faster. The rise of the Nazis in Germany and the roll-out of their anti-Semitic policies acted moreover as a spur for recruitment. Privately many US citizens were aghast at their government's inaction and in the face of overwhelming evidence of evil were prepared, with a clear conscience, to help the Soviet Union as a counter to Nazism. Given new freedom of action, the size of Ovakimian's agent networks multiplied. TALENT was an ideal agent group leader as he had lived and worked in academic circles up and down the university cities of the East Coast. He was a far more efficient talent spotter in his specialised field than any recruiter the Soviets could bring in from Moscow. The innovation led ultimately to the forming of cells like that of Julius Rosenberg with his wife as a courier, which was built initially around Communist college friends. The process was not without risk and would go disastrously wrong with the next recruit, Jacob Golos (codenamed SOUND). Russian sources suggest that an agent codenamed DAVIS, identified as MIT graduate Norman Leslie Haight, was another group leader, but no evidence has emerged of his activities.[20]

Malisoff was a big early win for Ovakimian and his methods. To the delight of Moscow Centre, TALENT seemingly sought no financial rewards for his work, simply appreciation. In 1939 or 1940, however, he 'discovered that some of the personal processes he had developed and given to us had been used by our chemists and published in Sov[iet] publications as their discoveries'.[21] He complained, claiming that Ovakimian had assured him there would be no further plagiarism. But in 1943, two years after Ovakimian's return to Moscow, Malisoff complained again to the New York legal residency that, despite this assurance, a recent winner of a Stalin prize for chemistry had plagiarised his work. He added that he was not seeking payment from the residency but only wanted his work to be recognised in Russia.

Though the available evidence on the S&T supplied by Malisoff is very fragmentary, it is clear that it covered a remarkably wide range of subjects. Among the more unusual were commercial secrets of the US perfume industry; these appear to have been highly valued by Premier Molotov's wife, Polina Zhemchuzhina, director of the Soviet National Cosmetics trust from 1932 to 1936. Initiatives in the mid-1930s to improve living conditions in the USSR had led to an emphasis on producing consumer goods. There was only one place to go for help, and that was the home of consumerism. The New York legal *Rezidentura* reported to the Centre in January 1937, soon after a visit by Zhemchuzhina:

> During Cde. Zhemchuzhina's stay in the USA, she received from us various samples of perfume and cosmetic products from the American company 'Alco', which were obtained by the source TALENT. Now the source has also received formulas for these 23 products from the 'Alco' Company, which we are sending you. The recipes were obtained free of charge. We request that as soon as you receive the package, you give these recipes to Cde. Zhemchuzhina.[22]

It was Shumovsky who was given the job of aiding Zhemchuzhina in acquiring the perfume secrets. He became personal friends with the Molotovs. Some of the stolen perfumes are still manufactured and on sale in Moscow today.

Aside from his work in perfumery, Malisoff recruited other S&T agents and sources. Among the most important in the mid-1930s was his friend Earl W. Flosdorf, codenamed OUTPOST, a biochemist (and later head of the department) at the University of Pennsylvania who worked as one of the NKVD's best-paid American agents. The NKVD's money seems to have gone to add to Flosdorf's impressive collection of vintage cars; his 1895 Hurtu–Benz roadster was believed to be America's oldest running petrol-powered automobile. Flosdorf was particularly valued by the Centre for his expertise in bacteriological warfare. He was the inventor of the first freeze-drying process for human blood serum and plasma which, as well as making possible blood transfusions, could also be used for what the Centre called 'germ warfare'. There was also a violent side to Flosdorf's character: in 1968, he shot his wife dead as she was leaving home, then committed suicide with the same gun. According to the local newspaper, their twelve-year-old son 'ran screaming from the house'.[23]

•   •   •

The catalyst for the increased pace of activity was political. In November 1933, the United States had become the last significant power officially to establish diplomatic relations with the Soviet Union. Franklin D. Roosevelt's willingness to do so, apparent almost from the moment he entered the White House in March, was prompted both by the hope of increasing trade with Russia during the Great Depression and by the belief that the two powers had a common strategic interest in limiting Japanese territorial expansion in Asia. Stalin shared these goals. Unlike the Americans, however, he believed that diplomatic relations would create the opportunity to boost S&T operations in the United States by making it possible to set up 'legal' intelligence residencies whose staff could operate with impunity protected by diplomatic or official cover. His plan to modernise the economy would receive a significant boost.

Stalin's fear of the Japanese attack forecast by the US ambassador to Tokyo, Joseph Grew, for the spring of 1934 helps to explain the unprecedented number of red carpets rolled out in Moscow to welcome the first US ambassador, William C. Bullitt,

Jr., in December 1933. The dinner in his honour at the Kremlin, personally hosted by Stalin, was, Bullitt reported, 'an amicable one with continual toasts'. The first toast, proposed by Stalin himself, mocked America's most committed anti-Communist Congressman, Hamilton Fish III, founder of the Fish Committee, which specialised in rooting out Communist subversion. In a jovial mood, Stalin raised his glass to 'President Roosevelt who, in spite of the mute growls of the Fishes, dared to recognize the Soviet Union.' After dinner, Bullitt had a 'long talk', extending into the early hours, with Stalin, who told him a Japanese attack in the spring was 'certain'. Stalin believed that the coming war with Japan made the covert Soviet collection of military S&T from the United States even more urgent than before. Though he did not tell Bullitt, he did appeal to him for immediate help in gaining approval for imports of US equipment, which would help Soviet preparations for war: 'There is one thing that I want to ask you. The second line of our railroad to Vladivostok is not completed. To complete it quickly, we need 250,000 tons of steel rails at once. They need not be new rails. Your rails are so much heavier than ours that the tracks you discard will be good enough for us . . . Without the rails, we shall beat the Japanese, but if we have the rails, it will be easier.'[24]

To help out, Bullitt promised to facilitate the rapid sale of US steel rails to the Soviet Union. The importance that Stalin attached to US technological assistance – both overt and covert – to defeat Japan was reflected in his response. His manner became more effusive than it had ever been before when he was talking to a Western diplomat. He told Bullitt: 'I want you to understand that, if you want to see me at any time, day or night, you have only to let me know, and I will see you at once.' As Bullitt informed the State Department: 'This was a somewhat extraordinary gesture since he has hitherto refused to see any Ambassador at any time.' Bullitt held out his hand to shake Stalin's. But, as the astonished ambassador wrote privately to Roosevelt, Stalin brushed his ambassador's hand aside, and instead took Bullitt's head in his hands and kissed it. 'I swallowed my astonishment,' said Bullitt, 'and when he turned up his face for a return kiss, I delivered it.'[25]

Bullitt planned to build on the Lenin Hills a grand embassy in the style of Thomas Jefferson's Virginian mansion at Monticello. Over the entrance, to please his Soviet hosts, he thought of inscribing Jefferson's dictum, 'God forbid that we should live for twenty years without a revolution.' He even obtained an appropriation of $1.2 million to build this new Russian Monticello from a reluctant Congress, which was led to expect 'Red trade offers' in return. It never occurred to either Congress or Bullitt that Stalin confidently expected the new embassy to become a primary source of Soviet intelligence. An extraordinary haemorrhage of classified documents from the US embassy in Moscow would continue for the next thirty years.

When the embassy opened, it had virtually no security and initially no ciphers either. The future US ambassador in Moscow, George Kennan, one of the original members of Bullitt's staff, later recalled, 'Communications with our government went through the regular telegraphic office and lay on the table for the Soviet government to see.' Stalin must have found it difficult to believe his luck. The US Marines supposed to guard the embassy were quickly provided with attentive girlfriends (some of them ballerinas) by the NKVD. 'Chip' Bohlen, a future ambassador, was sitting in the lobby of the Savoy Hotel one day when a heavily made-up Russian woman walked up to the reception desk and said she wished to go up to Marine Sergeant O'Dean's room. 'I,' she announced, 'am his Russian teacher.'[26] With the assistance of other 'Russian teachers', at least one of the first group of cipher clerks posted to the embassy, Tyler Kent, was recruited as a Soviet agent.

The FBI made no attempt to penetrate the new Soviet Embassy on 16th Street in Washington, a few blocks from the White House. In Moscow, by contrast, Bullitt's closest Russian friend, though he failed to realise it, was an NKVD undercover agent codenamed BALKANSKY.[27] Head of the NKVD Genrikh Yagoda sent Stalin a report from BALKANSKY dated 8 March 1934, describing a visit to Bullitt's new personal residence. At the time, the ambassador's residence was also used as the diplomatic chancery while negotiations on a new US embassy continued:

> Upon getting out of his railway carriage, Bullitt noticed me first and greeted me warmly, before greeting other representatives of the Embassy who were meeting him. After a short conversation, he invited me to go to his house for breakfast. Over breakfast, he introduced me to his top employees, and he told everyone that I was his best friend in Moscow and that they can contact me with all their requests and be assured that I will do everything possible to help them in their work.[28]

As soon as they were alone, Bullitt told BALKANSKY: 'I can assure you in the Soviet Union that you are worrying in vain about a possible war with Japan. There will be no war. From the US side, we have been doing everything possible to prevent it.' Roosevelt had agreed 'every last word' of speeches Bullitt made on relations with Japan. Though Stalin and his advisors believed that the threat from Japan remained, the Japanese attack, which Stalin had told Bullitt would take place in the spring of 1934, never came.[29]

Bullitt was at his most reassuring when he briefed BALKANSKY about US embassy personnel:

The President gave me carte blanche in choosing staff for the Embassy. I have been guided only by the interests of our countries and accepted people unconditionally and openly sympathetic to the Soviet Union and to what is happening here. For example, the military attaché [Philip R.] Faymonville, at the time of the [US] intervention in Siberia [during the Civil War] was openly on the side of the Reds and was repeatedly subjected to attacks by the [US] War Department and the press for this. My advisor John Wiley for many years was the special observer from Berlin and Warsaw of the situation in the USSR and, as you know, his chief informant was [the pro-Soviet *New York Times* correspondent] Walter Duranty, with whom he is intimate friends . . . You have to help me personally on how to see the country and familiarize me with the new life and construction, as well as introduce me to Soviet public opinion, leaders, etc.[30]

Stalin's annotations on Bullitt's intercepted telegrams to Washington show that he read them attentively, keeping some in his personal archive. Among the passages he underlined in red in a telegram of 18 September 1934 was a complaint by Bullitt about Russian failure to respect US patents: 'I personally know of some American inventions in the field of machinery, machine parts and so on, which are being used by Soviet industry.' So far as is known, the State Department took no action. Despite the poor 1934 harvest in some parts of the Soviet Union, Bullitt was relatively optimistic about Soviet food supply. Stalin underlined Bullitt's comment that 'Reports of widespread hunger are greatly exaggerated . . . We can say that the starvation of the population, under normal conditions, is already a thing of the past,' and the claim that 'Many [Communist] party members are dissatisfied that the Soviet government has gone too far regarding concessions to the capitalist countries.' He cannot have been pleased to read in another of Bullitt's intercepted telegrams in 1934 the disparaging comments by the Japanese ambassador to Bullitt on the inferior quality of Russian spies sent to Japan – who, it was reported, 'become careless once they have achieved their goal. They drink and womanize, and we have been able to detain them before they have had time to leave.'[31] Stalin marked this passage, and, no doubt, demanded prompt action from the NKVD.

• • •

Back in the US, Ovakimian's skills as an agent recruiter were well illustrated in his handling of the eccentric pro-Communist industrial chemist Thomas 'Tasso' Black, rather obviously codenamed CHERNY ('black' in Russian). According to acquaintances of Black who were belatedly interviewed by the FBI in 1950, he was 'very shabby in appearance and dress, carefree and good-hearted but very eccentric'. The menagerie of pets he kept at home included a crow, rats, mice and snakes; in 1938, he spent twenty weeks in hospital after inadvertently causing an ether explosion at his laboratory. Black first approached Ovakimian at AMTORG, probably soon after his arrival in New York, unaware that he was an intelligence officer as well as an engineer, in the hope of obtaining a job as a chemist in Russia. Ovakimian began by asking Black to get the latest information on the US manufacture of various industrial chemicals, which he pretended would strengthen his chances of employment in the Soviet Union. Having been persuaded to steal information from his current employer, Black was gradually converted by Ovakimian into a 'full-fledged industrial spy'.[32]

Black also worked as courier, recruiter and agent-handler. His best-known recruit was Harry Gold (initially codenamed GOOSE), an industrial chemist born of Russian parents, who later became the courier for the British atom spy Klaus Fuchs after he moved to the United States in 1944.[33] Gold was involved in attempts to run Shumovsky's recruit Ben Smilg. It was Gold who brought Shumovsky to the attention of the FBI in 1949.

By the middle of 1934, having discovered the lie of the land in America, Ovakimian began dividing up the workload. The number-one priority was a task for Shumovsky, aircraft construction at Curtiss-Wright, followed by the production of aircraft armament. Stan's recruit DAVIS would be utilised to acquire 'special military technology' from Sperry Corporation, while GENNADY would focus on chemistry from DuPont. Another role was organising the acquisition of American passports for use as cover by illegals in Europe.

Reinforcements were required on the illegal line following the mysterious death of its head, Valentin Markin, in a New York bar. The new head, Akhmerov, arrived in January 1934 on an illegal passport acquired by GENNADY and was immediately enrolled in courses at Columbia University to improve his English. He described in detail the experience of becoming Americanised at university:

The transition from being a foreign student to being an American in a large city like NY, with its population of millions, was not particularly challenging, as it turned out. At Columbia University, I was known well only to the English language instructor and nine or ten students – most of them foreigners – almost all of whom intended to return to their countries after graduation. It was also unlikely that I would be remembered from university registration, which was typically done by thousands of people. Therefore, the only people who could have known me well were one of the instructors and the landlord at whose apartment I was then living, a Jew by nationality. Thus, there was no particular risk involved. If I had subsequently run into these people by chance, we could have done little more than saying 'hello' and 'goodbye' to each other. I, therefore, thought that I was not risking much by switching to new identity papers. Because I knew that I would have to change to new identity papers, I had made a point of not expanding my circle of acquaintances, and when I began living under American identity papers, I did not restrict myself when establishing connections. After adopting local identity papers, I kept my previous cover for a period of time: I attended classes, where lectures were given on economic, cultural, and socio-political sciences. I was not involved in any other work and therefore had free time at my disposal to learn the language well, study up on socio-political sciences, read magazines, go to libraries, etc.[34]

By the end of 1934 the infrastructure was in place for the greatest successes of Stalin's intelligence service. From 1935 the Soviets began to acquire what one American described as his country's secret weapon – its production know-how.[35]

9

WHISTLE STOP INSPECTIONS

A unique black and white photograph dating from the summer of 1935 captures a party of Russian tourists standing by a white picket fence at the side of an American road.[1] The picture, which could have been taken anywhere in middle America, shows a smartly dressed four-strong party, a husband and wife and their companions. The couple is the aircraft designer Andrey Tupolev and his wife, Julia. Tupolev stands with his deputy, the high-speed bomber designer Alexander Arkhangelsky; the fourth man, their guide, is the unmistakable figure of Stanislav Shumovsky, Tupolev's star pupil.

No mere tour guide, Shumovsky was not only the NKVD's aviation expert in the US, but was now TsAGI's main contact in America. The MIT student was a senior and influential figure on the way up in both TsAGI and the NKVD. Having already spent three productive years at MIT, not only had he assimilated himself into the American way of life, gaining an excellent degree on the way, but he had also helped close the gap in aircraft design between the fledgling USSR and the world leaders, the US. He had fed back to TsAGI every item of information that came into his hands on modern methods of aircraft design. Moreover, he had contributed to the annual report compiled on the state of US aviation that was used as a benchmark for Soviet industry, a copy of which was placed on Stalin's desk to be covered in notes.[2] The Soviets wanted to fly their own planes as fast, as far and as high as the best in the world:

> The victories in aviation, achieved by the Soviet Union, are of fundamental importance. They are the result of practicing the Leninist policy of industrialization which ensures that the USSR will be technically and economically independent of the capitalist world. They demonstrated the preponderance of the socialist economic system, its ability to liquidate the technical backward-ness within the shortest possible time. They convincingly showed the sweep of the scientific and cultural revolution in the Soviet Union. They are a testimony to the incessant care by the Party and the nation to strengthen the defense potential of the country.[3]

Shumovsky now had a new challenge, providing a solution to the USSR's yawning technology gap. He was one of the few let into the secret that Soviet factories were incapable of mass-producing planes that measured up to the world standard for quality and reliability. On the trip, Tupolev had met with Henry Ford, the guru of mass production and an unlikely Soviet hero. It was clear that the 'Ford solution' was not open to Tupolev because the Soviet Union required more than one type of aeroplane. The Soviets needed fighters, bombers, transport and passenger planes, so buying one model factory was out of the question. However, he wanted to adopt the assembly line approach.

The photograph was taken as the party rested after a long

drive to an aviation factory for a tour, one of many organised for their trip. While travelling in America previously, the restless scientist Tupolev had taken to driving fast around bends to test the car's handling and occasionally sliding off the road. Unimpressed by her husband's love of speed and reckless cornering, Julia had insisted others drive. The three-month, 10,000-mile odyssey took in manufacturing centres on both the East and West Coasts, with a few stops in the middle. The party crisscrossed the country from New York to Seattle, down to California and back. Tupolev is pictured clutching in his right hand one of his array of movie cameras. He had a collection for different purposes including one for filming aircraft in flight. On his previous trip, he had used the camera to shoot attractive women, but with his wife in tow, this time was restricted to

Shumovsky and Tupolev (holding camera) on the road in US, 1935

recording the conditions inside each factory. His goal during this latest journey was to discover the secrets of mass-producing high-quality aircraft. Later he would use his extensive home movie collection to illustrate and try to enforce the same standards and methods in the factories of the Soviet Union.

Tupolev knew that the Soviet Union needed thousands of aircraft to deter an enemy attack. By 1935 the rearming Germans had already built 10,000 modern planes and would soon be all set to challenge the Russians for control of the skies. Tupolev himself had announced, 'Comrades, very much has been done, but all that has been done is far from all that is possible. We already have military aircraft, but I declare that we in the Soviet Union can create planes that will far outstrip all that the capitalists have. We will do this because the Soviet country needs powerful aviation, we need such a strong aviation so that no one dares to approach our borders.'[4] The air force was integral to the plan of making the Soviet Union an impregnable fortress.

The golden-toothed Tupolev was at the top of his game in 1935. During his career, he would design or oversee the design of more than a hundred types of aircraft, setting seventy-eight world records. In recognition of his work he was even made, late in life, an honorary member of the American Institute of Aeronautics and Astronautics. Tupolev was the leading light of TsAGI, which was the base for his Central Design Office, or TsKB, producing bombers and airliners. In 1925, he had designed an all-metal twin-engined monoplane, the TB-1, which was the most advanced of the period. One of this model, *Land of Soviets*, had flown via Siberia to New York – a journey taking over a month – in November 1929, showing America the technology the Soviet Union was capable of building.

Tupolev was already far more than an aircraft designer. On 4 December 1935, following his report on this latest trip to the US, he was made deputy head of GUAP, the controlling body of the entire Soviet Union's aviation industry. He had played a pivotal and occasionally divisive role in the evolution of the Soviet air force; so that it was no longer relying on a few outmoded foreign aircraft. By 1935, on paper at least, it was the most powerful in the world, with a fleet designed and built entirely domestically. The Red air force had commissioned from the Tupolev bureau unprecedented numbers of designs for both fast tactical and heavy strategic bombers. To achieve the extraordinary feat of building so many planes of his design, Tupolev had been given an unlimited budget. In the Soviet Union, his talent had propelled him to the very pinnacle of society. He and his wife, to whom he was devoted, could travel outside its borders with complete freedom. He could argue on budget issues with the notoriously parsimonious Stalin and win when seeking support for the development of the aviation industry. Stalin now wanted to see results.

• • •

By 1934 it had become evident to the Soviet leadership that, despite displaying to the world a positive image of its power, the aviation industry was on course for a crisis caused by its own success. The fact was that the industry had conflicting priorities. Each year the goal was to increase production while building a product that matched world-class standards and incorporated the latest technical innovation. But a serious gap had developed between the high quality of Soviet aircraft design in prototype and the poor finished product. In theory, the Soviet Union deployed vast numbers of world-beating planes, but the build quality was so low it was causing serious reliability issues. At best a large percentage of air force planes were always under repair, at worst pilots were killed in avoidable accidents.

The 1929 plan for the air force had set as a goal 'a rapid improvement of its quality to the level of the most advanced bourgeois countries . . . every effort must be made to plant the seeds, cultivate and develop our own, Soviet scientific and design cadres, especially in engine construction.'[5] With new help from the US, both purchased and acquired through intelligence, the hope was that within a decade Soviet industry would complete the journey from craft manufacturer of a few hundred biplanes made from wood and canvas to mass-producing each year 10,000 planes, including all-metal modern fighters and bombers. The starting point had been very low and the aircraft industry had to be built from the beginning. By 1931 onwards, fed by information from abroad that included the latest technological innovations, supplied by Shumovsky in America, Soviet aviation design had evolved to a world-leading standard. But on the production line, the factories' management were isolated from the most recent international developments in materials, methods and techniques. Relative to the best in the world, the US, in even the newest Soviet factories there was a lack of mechanisation, modern materials and labour efficiency. The managers and workforce could not keep up with the demands placed on them for more and better aircraft.

The problems encountered along the way were challenging. Imported technology and ideas helped, but the most obvious difficulty the Soviet Union faced was the absence of a deep pool of skilled workers, especially in factories outside Moscow. Given the extent and significance of the issues developing at home, and in answer to the urgings of Shumovsky to come and see the latest US developments, in 1935 Tupolev and a large entourage of technical experts travelled to America. The party filled seven cars in total.[6] They knew in advance from the painstaking reports sent by Shumovsky in the last two years that they were going to see factories employing modern methods and American efficiency, but had no idea how far the Soviet Union was behind the pace. The Soviet decision-making system was cumbersome, functioning as it did by means of endless commissions and reports, so Tupolev had to make the long journey to see everything for himself. He brought with him not only hand-picked members of his design team but, crucially, the country's leading experts on aviation metals and production methods.[7] He even brought two representatives of his customer, the air force. They were there to rubber-stamp any orders for aircraft, for which Tupolev had been given a generous budget of $600,000 to spend.

As ever, Tupolev was thorough. His demanding travel schedule was to include revisiting every aircraft factory that he had last seen in 1930. The only one of the party to have made that previous trip, he could appreciate the advances. Shumovsky was working to an agenda, driving home to the party how dynamic and efficient American industry had become in adapting to the harsh times of the Depression. He was keen to demonstrate how the removal of the airmail postal subsidy from the airlines had forced efficiency and cost saving into manufacturing. Airlines and plane makers struggled for profitability in the Depression. Many firms had gone bankrupt. The surviving plane manufacturers now produced, efficiently and cheaply, large numbers of high quality, reliable planes for their customers in the civil aviation industry. The simplicity of design and the manufacturing process helped reduce costs, as did using as many high-quality parts as possible. On top of this, mechanisation of the factory floor raised productivity levels. Factories in the US were becoming assembly centres where interchangeable parts sourced from a supply chain were rapidly put together. Curtiss-Wright assembled engines from parts sourced from ten separate suppliers. The airlines received fast, reliable planes with long ranges, allowing them to turn a profit in the growing and competitive transport industry. Travellers could always choose to use the train or drive if they had concerns about cost, safety or punctuality. But for speed, nothing could beat the plane if you wanted lunch in Chicago and dinner in New York.[8]

Air travel was pitched as glamorous and luxurious. An American Airlines infomercial movie of the era profiles its growing customer base. The company's passengers were those who could afford the sky-high fares: glamorous showbiz stars, powerful politicians and successful business executives, the US elite. True mass civil air travel was only to take off after the Second World War, when a surplus of planes and trained pilots hit the market. But even by 1935, the US had built a network of new airports that linked the great cities of the continent, with planes guided by 'the beam', a system of nationwide radio direction finders. Passengers were steered away from bumps and turbulence by an efficient meteorological service that would use radio to keep their journey safe and comfortable.

Tupolev recounted first hand how impressed he was with American transport infrastructure. In one incident, following a road accident outside the then small town of Las Vegas, the party was waiting at the airport for an official to fly in from New York to deal with the issues. The plane was delayed owing to bad weather en route:

In less than five minutes, the head of the airfield at Las Vegas radioed all the intermediate airports and gave us an accurate update: the passenger Braillo and his companion the Doctor are 1600 km away. They could not fly because the airfield is snowbound. Your comrades have decided to continue their journey to you by express train. Here is an area in which we are still far behind America. We still need to work very hard to achieve the heights of American technology in the organization of the flight business.[9]

Fantastic service!

The detailed planning for Tupolev's long trip had taken Shumovsky and his colleagues at AMTORG many months of hard work. The visit was scheduled to last more than three months, and there were many meetings to arrange with manufacturers, suppliers, research facilities and government agencies. Shumovsky had stayed on at MIT as information on new aviation developments flowed through the faculty. The aviation industry was so new that many companies shared common parentage. The founders of Grumman were, for example, all former employees of Curtiss-Wright, as were those of Pratt & Whitney. On the West Coast Northrup had grown out of Douglas. In a country that required letters of introduction, the MIT letterhead was a great door opener.

Much knowledge could be gleaned from the many American magazines that kept the legion of aviation enthusiasts abreast of the latest developments. Unlike today America was a very open market and the aircraft manufacturers had learned from the automobile industry the importance of annually refreshing their model line by adding a few new bells and whistles with a publicity blitz. New model launches were a splash news event. Manufacturers provided their planes to famous pilots such as Amelia Earhart, relying on them to achieve headlines with their feats of daring. The plethora of magazines paid for by advertising spread news of innovations and discussed future developments. US manufacturers would even advertise their wares in magazines published in the Soviet Union. However, there was nothing to beat a face-to-face discussion with Donald Douglas on his visits to MIT for gaining access to cutting-edge thought. Stan's college taught its engineers the theory and application of manufacturing efficiency as part of its course, equipping its graduates with the skills to make a difference on the factory floor.

Each of the travelling Soviet experts required in advance an extensive briefing pack on the companies they were to visit and their latest products. The experts wanted to delve deep. Meetings would not last hours but days, each group involving separate discussions between those interested in different issues.[10] The Soviets were as keen to learn about anti-corrosive paint coatings as the type of aluminium alloy used in the construction of a plane. At the highest level Tupolev wanted to discuss with the top designers aerodynamic theory and his particular passion, wind tunnels. After a factory visit the party would assemble for dinner each evening to debrief on their findings. Tupolev would stay in with his wife unless there was an official dinner, while the balance of the party, away for months from their wives and responsibilities, headed out on the town in search of trouble.

• • •

Stan meanwhile was looking for recruits. The US was becoming cagier and more secretive about the flow of information as war clouds darkened around the world. The Russians were complaining that performance data on aircraft was becoming harder to obtain, and from 1935 the balance of his work began to shift from collecting open-source material to see what could be gained from agents.

To tempt their American hosts to open their doors, Shumovsky's strategy was first to gain official endorsements. On the East Coast he stoked interest by organising gala events in New York and Washington. In New York the presidents and vice presidents of East Coast manufacturers and suppliers were invited to a business breakfast at which several senior State Department officials gave the Soviets endorsements. Tupolev gave exclusive newspaper interviews telling America he had come to buy technology. The State Department 'halo effect' worked wonders in opening doors.[11]

In Washington, the big diplomatic guns were deployed. At a function held at the Soviet embassy, both Soviet ambassador Alexander Troyanovsky and US ambassador to Moscow William Bullitt talked up the commercial opportunities and growing friendship between the two nations. They were even able to gain the endorsement of Henry L. Roosevelt, the Assistant Naval Secretary, who attended the event, as well as the prize of a meeting with NACA.

The second plank of Shumovsky's plan was to give the impression that the Soviets had an open cheque book. Over the years the Americans had grown wise to the fact that the visiting Russian parties were discerning customers. Tupolev bought only two planes immediately on his trip, spending little of the $600,000 he had been allocated,[12] although he committed to several more military aircraft the export of which was subject to State Department approval.

The buying process was slow. Tupolev would identify a key plane to buy, after which AMTORG and others would negotiate the fine detail with the manufacturer. As well as a delay while the plane was built, negotiations over the provision of metric blueprints, access for Soviet engineers to the US factory, technical assistance in Moscow and finally delivery times would drag on. A further delay was guaranteed if a US government export licence was required. It might take up to two years from ordering for a plane to reach Moscow, rendering it obsolete on arrival.

• • •

Stan had greeted his friends and colleagues off the boat in New York, whereafter they decamped to the Lincoln Hotel, the usual Soviet hangout. He did his best to answer the myriad of questions they asked about the plans for the next three and a half months. The party had read up on the wonders of the US and their excitement had been whetted by Tupolev's tales of his previous trip. Many ventured out to see New York at night. They marvelled at the skyscrapers and the shaking of the sidewalks caused by the subway. Like all visitors to the city, they were struck by the pace of New York. Everyone seemed to run, rather than saunter as they did in Moscow. They headed off to see the glittering lights of Broadway. Unusually it was a telescope on the street that intrigued them the most. They had initially thought New Yorkers missed seeing the sky as it was blocked by the tall buildings, until they realised it was trained on the observation deck of the Empire State building. They were shocked to be charged for taking a look.

Early the next morning, fitted out in their best business suits, the sixteen-strong commission and their translators boarded a bus for the short journey across the Hudson for their first day of meetings. The real work began with factory tours around the New York area, including a reunion with their friends Curtiss-Wright at the company's giant engine plant in Paterson, New Jersey. The Russians' suits would become noticeably tighter as the trip went on and they grew used to the liberal availability of food. The haute cuisine meals on the boat had been too delicate for engineers used to a simple diet, but everyday American food was more to their taste. The travellers were amazed to find T-bone steaks available for breakfast at roadside diners. The jovial Tupolev, who had a sharp tongue to match his mind, greeted each passenger boarding the bus with early-morning wisecracks, reminding everyone that he was the expert on America. But he noticed the changes that had taken place: 'The last time I was in America was five years ago. Since then enough time has passed for the technology, especially in aviation, to develop dramatically. Particularly striking is the fact that American aircraft manufacturers are now only making monoplanes.'[13]

There were several days of meetings with Curtiss-Wright ahead, and the Russians also had separate meetings with the ten subcontractors who supplied components. They were immediately struck by the quiet efficiency of the Curtiss-Wright factory floor. Soviet production quality suffered from a practice known as 'storming', a problem which had its source in the way workers were paid. They would meet their monthly production targets, but all the work was done at a frenetic pace in the last few days to maximise overtime and bonuses. The effect on quality was noticeable. Russians were used to seeing workers frantically running around their factories. Outside the 'storming' days workers would be caught asleep at their machines – especially after pay day, when drunkenness was rife. At Curtiss-Wright there were none of the endless smoking breaks that puzzled visitors to Soviet factories. The plant was kept clean and tidy, with no food stored around the machines as in Russia.

By 1932, the Wright engine operation in Paterson, New Jersey was already the largest of its kind in the world, and it would remain so until eclipsed by the company's factory in the USSR. Over 2,400 workers were employed in the plant, which produced the air-cooled Whirlwind engine and the more powerful Cyclone. In its engine development of the 1930s, Curtiss-Wright had pioneered innovations such as forged aluminium pistons, a dynamic damper which absorbed crankshaft vibration, finned cylinder heads for cooling, and nitrided cylinder barrels, a metallurgical process which gave the parts vastly improved life and better resistance to wear. The Cyclone engine powered the new Douglas DC-2/3 transports, which the Soviets were eager to see. In 1934, moreover, Curtiss-Wright had been chosen to build nine-cylinder radial engines for the four-engined Boeing B-17 Flying Fortress bomber commissioned by the US Army and Navy. Aero engines were the Achilles heel of the Soviet industry. Metallurgy was poor with only low-grade steel available for the engine blocks. Curtiss-Wright's propeller division was also in New Jersey, and the Soviets were keen to learn about the variable pitch version that aided higher-altitude flying.

The company headquarters and aircraft assembly plants were a longer journey away in Buffalo. Curtiss were in ebullient mood as they put the finishing touches to their hope for the largest peacetime contract for a fighter from the US military.

• • •

Long Island was known as the 'cradle of aviation', being the base for two dozen companies that built military and civilian aircraft. More aircraft manufacture was concentrated on the island than anywhere else in the country. Grumman, Republic and Sperry Gyroscope were all located there, as was Seversky, a business owned by a one-legged former Tsarist pilot often described as 'flamboyant' and a 'showman'. Alexander Nikolaievich Prokofiev de Seversky was as aristocratic as his name implies. A genius inventor, having patented air-to-air refuelling and the gyroscopic bomb sight, he was however a poor businessman and none too choosy as to whom he sold his aircraft. According to some reports he agreed to sell a fighter to Tupolev, a contract that would have political repercussions both in the US and USSR. While he secretly sold advanced planes to the Japanese in 1938, he had second thoughts about dealing with Communists, writing a letter to the State Department trying to get his fighter sale banned on the grounds the technology was too advanced to be exported. He had, however, staffed his enterprise with Russian émigrés who later proved a happy hunting ground for Shumovsky's recruitment.

• • •

The Soviet party remained in New York for several weeks before boarding their seven newly purchased cars to set out. By that time, they had acquired New Jersey driving licences. The experience of travelling with Tupolev, a ball of energy whose mind and body were always active, was exhausting. The schedule was equally punishing, with many visits to factories, airfields and research institutes crammed in, and stops along the way to take in natural wonders such as Niagara Falls and the Grand Canyon.

The party rose each day at 5 a.m. with a plan to be on the road by 5.45. It was impossible to keep to the schedule, as Tupolev would stop his car without warning and take out his camera to examine anything that caught his fancy along the way, technological and natural marvels alike. At each hotel, he would become fascinated with the workings of the heating or the cooling systems. Colleagues complained they had to sleep with the windows open as Tupolev experimented with how hot he could make their room.

Ever the visionary, the trip inspired Tupolev to embark upon a new round of innovation for the Soviet aviation industry. He reported in the Soviet magazine *Industrialization* that 'our trip abroad gave a lot of valuable information. Particularly useful was getting to see American aviation.'[14] In fact there was much they had not been allowed to see, but Shumovsky was planning the means to get Tupolev what the Americans would not openly sell. While the Soviet party drove a hard bargain over the purchase of a few examples of key planes, Shumovsky had begun creating an agent network on the West Coast to gather intelligence for the Tupolev Design Bureau.

* * *

Since 1934 Shumovsky had been expanding his intelligence-gathering activities beyond MIT to encompass as much of the East Coast of the United States as lay within reach of Boston. It was an easy drive from Boston to Long Island to visit factories and Ovakimian in New York. The West Coast though was new to him, so he was helped by the entire party and local Communists to identify recruits. In 1953 the FBI noted that 'engineers, technicians or others designated to visit a country to buy military or naval equipment were handed over to the intelligence departments for a short course of instructions on the particular secret mission to be carried out during their visit. They were also instructed to find contacts working in factories they entered through whom the Soviets could continue to obtain information.'[15]

Despite Tupolev's $600,000 budget, the Soviets had not come with an open cheque book. The Russians were careful shoppers, buying only the best equipment, in small numbers and on fine terms. They were demanding, insisting on having their people installed in US factories to learn every element of the production process. There were specific problems. The two countries used different measurement systems: America worked in feet and inches whereas the Soviet Union used the metric system, so all its manufacturing capability and machinery was calibrated in millimetres and centimetres. Each tool in an American factory was precisely calibrated for the imperial system. The Russians laboriously calculated tolerances for the conversion to the metric system, but there was never an exact solution, so the Soviet copies of American planes were notorious for rattling. The noise was not only caused by poor build quality but by the difficulty of converting imperial blueprints to metric standards.

Just like the British capitalists of the great age of cotton weaving, the Americans knew when they had a technical edge and demanded extraordinary prices for their innovation. Shumovsky had learned at MIT about the introduction of aluminium alloys to replace wood. The American Aluminum Company had built itself a near monopoly position as the supplier to aircraft manufacturers of finished parts and sheets. The Soviets cast envious eyes at the quality and consistency of ALCO's output, but when they enquired about the cost of a turnkey plant in the USSR they were quoted a take-it-or-leave-it price of $100 million. The Soviets could see when they were being overcharged. Later they bought enough equipment themselves to outfit two plants and a factory blueprint for a fraction of the price.

•   •   •

Shumovsky had completed his undergraduate studies on 5 June 1934, obtaining a bachelor's degree in Aeronautical Science. He received his degree at a ceremony conducted on the ornamental square in front of Building 10, but he was far from finished with MIT. A commemorative photograph was taken to record the end of the students' first chapter. The guest speaker at 'Commencement' was Howard Blakeslee, the first full-time science correspondent of the Associated Press, and later to be one of the few journalists to witness the first secret atomic tests in the deserts of New Mexico. Now able to use the cover of a graduate student working on a thesis at the cutting edge of aviation research, Shumovsky would arouse no comment while gathering intelligence. If he were at AMTORG, he would be dogged by the FBI in doing the same work. So his strategy continued, using the MIT letterhead to contact the leading experts in his field, who fell over themselves to be of use. Shumovsky joined all the national professional societies linking the acknowledged experts in aerospace and was given access to their directories, a Who's Who of the leading practitioners. His name appears on the same pages as Igor Sikorsky and Alexander de Seversky, Russian exiles putting all their efforts into building weapons for their adopted country.

Having finished his course, Shumovsky now had the time and flexibility to begin running agents. From the limited public records disclosed by the KGB, NSA and FBI, it appears that he became active in July 1934. The records finally confirm that Ben Smilg, who had left MIT to work at the Budd Company in Philadelphia, an aviation parts supplier whose greatest innovation was the spot welding of metal sheets, joined up. Meanwhile Shumovsky immediately embarked on the research for his Master's degree. He remains the only graduate student to have the subject of his thesis selected by an intelligence agency.

As recorded in the KGB files, Shumovsky began two years' work gathering information on 'high altitude flying',[16] presenting his results to MIT in a thesis entitled 'The Effectiveness of the Vertical Tail of the Aircraft for Various Combinations of Wing and Fuselage'. He spent hours working with MIT's pressurised wind tunnel to perfect the models.

High-altitude flying was believed to be the best way forward for the slow long-range heavy bomber, which until the advent of radar would be undetectable by the enemy at high altitude. Moreover, the lack of oxygen at altitude meant that a pressurised-cabin bomber such as the B-29 Superfortress was invulnerable to fighters whose pilots could not reach the same cruising height, given that it was impossible to pressurise the small cabin of a fighter with the available technology. The same research also pointed the way forward for civil aviation. Air travel was smoother above the clouds and engine fuel efficiency increased, creating a greater potential range. However, in 1935 all this was theoretical; Boeing only began work on pressurised long-range bombers in 1938 in response to a military request. Shumovsky was at the cutting edge of the research. His Master's thesis worked out the most efficient angles for wings to fly at high altitude.

The visits Shumovsky organised for Tupolev in 1935 included not only factories but the research facilities at MIT, the California Institute of Technology (CalTech) in Pasadena and NACA at Langley Field and Wright Field. Thanks to the largesse of the Guggenheims, CalTech had recently completed a ten-foot wind tunnel around which their aeronautics faculty was built. They attracted to the faculty as professor the jet engine pioneer Theodore von Kármán, as well as Douglas Aircraft's chief designer Arthur Louis 'Maj' Klein. Von Kármán has been quoted as saying: 'I can never pass up the opportunity to dominate the conversation for an entire hour'; given Tupolev's reputation, theirs must have been an interesting meeting. Auzan, an engineer in the party, commented that

Research work on aerodynamics in America is well placed not only in research institutes but even in educational institutions. An example is the California Technological Institute in Pasadena. The Aerodynamic Laboratory of the Institute is led by the world-famous professor of aerodynamics Von Karman. A German by birth, he worked until 1926 in Tokyo. Then he moved to America. Previously, Karman visited our country (in 1927) and got acquainted with the wind tunnel at TsAGI. Showing us the wind tunnel in the institute, Karman said among other things 'Here you are. You will recognise the TsAGI pipe pattern?' This visit to the CalTech in Pasadena showed us that the pupil Von Karman was ahead of his teacher.[17]

Douglas would use CalTech's facilities more than five hundred times to perfect the aerodynamics of a single aircraft, a level of dedication to testing that impressed the visitors. Von Kármán made another visit to TsAGI in 1937, an indication of how scientists ignored frontiers and politics.

With his interest in building a series of new wind tunnels, Tupolev had already visited NACA at Langley earlier in the trip. This was the largest facility of its kind, capable of testing full-sized aircraft. The Langley facility was based on the pioneering work of a friend from Tupolev's Tsarist student days: the nomadic Vladimir Margolis, a fellow pupil of the founder of aeronautics in Russia, Nikolay Zhukovsky. Margolis was now living in exile and had sold his pioneering work to the Americans, publishing a much sought-after NACA research note, and had also helped the French and the Japanese.

The key reason for leaving Shumovsky in place at MIT was explained by Auzan in *For Industrialisation* magazine in 1935:

What accounts for the high level of American aviation technology? Why are Americans so quickly and confidently breaking the accepted technical principles? How can they boldly introduce on a large scale all kinds of innovations? They are all good questions and deserve a detailed answer. The whole secret lies in the excellent organization of scientific research and experimental work with the results deployed quickly through mass production. I state upfront that the Americans have no rivals in this field. The Soviet Union must take special care to examine the American experience of research in aviation and apply it to the science of socialist planning.[18]

• • •

At the end of the trip it was the time they spent in California that proved most rewarding for the Russians, both in terms of purchasing and espionage. Tupolev found at the Douglas factory the model to export to Russia. The DC-2 exemplified American manufacture – simplicity in design and execution – and the Russian visitors were struck by the innovations in design and construction methods. The company had incorporated into its design process 'lofting' and the use of full-sized plywood templates. It was a method of creating three-dimensional templates from two-dimensional drawings. Lofting had evolved from shipbuilding and derives its name from the tradition of drawing offices being in the eaves above factory floors. Applying geometrical principles and using mathematical tables, draughtsmen were able to create curves in streamlined objects such as a wing or fuselage. The Russians learned that standardisation of parts was a byword and new designs incorporated as many machine-made components as possible, to speed production and reduce cost.

The trip to California was highly successful and Shumovsky later made a second trip. He continued his West Coast recruitment campaign, after his masters in Moscow ordered him to interact with the workers and designers in the aviation plants. These trips involved significant time away from college and he was able to use his thesis as a cover story. Douglas and Boeing, the two companies actively researching high-altitude flight, were based on the West Coast, and Stan's work had a commercial value to both. His mathematical models, based on hundreds of observations in the wind tunnel at MIT, eliminated some of the cost of developing high-altitude prototypes, so he went armed with the preliminary results of his work.

Monitoring the manufacture of aircraft bought by Tupolev

gave him the new cover to return to California so soon after the summer visit. There was extreme urgency to his second trip. In late September, a small party of Soviet engineers arrived in Los Angeles for the official handover of the two planes ordered by Tupolev back in the summer: one the DC-2 destined for testing at TsAGI, the other a Northrop 2ED-C, a dual civilian and military use plane. It was a long process: the Russians had to understand every feature of each plane, as well as label each lever and knob in Cyrillic once they understood what it did. To speed the US government export process to Russia the Northrop was designated a civilian version, designed to deliver mail and fitted with no weapons or bomb racks, although a Soviet photograph of the aircraft taken while testing shows that it was in fact a different design with the cockpit set further down the fuselage. Once in the Soviet Union, pilot Mikhail Gromov, one of 'Stalin's Falcons', tested it as a dive bomber and concluded that it was an excellent aircraft but lacked sufficient punch in this role. The Northrop included a cockpit heating system which was much admired and the suggestion was that it should be copied and made standard on Soviet bombers. It would have been a welcome addition to Russian bomber crews but, pilot comfort not being a priority, it was not installed widely. However, the instinctive cockpit control panel layout and easy-to-read instrumentation made it a valuable addition to the Soviet fleet. Tupolev spent only $179,000 of his $600,000 budget on acquiring the two planes.

While working on the handover in the Northrop factory at El Secundo, one of the Russian engineers fell into a 'meaning of life conversation' with Jones Orin York, a designer in the plant. There was a deal of unhappiness in the labour force at Northrop, which would lead ultimately to Donald Douglas dissolving the joint venture and his co-founder, Jack Northrop, moving on. York was unhappy with his rate of pay and had a profound feeling that his talent was underappreciated by the management. The Russian inspector, Belyaev, was alive to an opportunity to recruit an intelligence source. Unable to make an approach himself, he contacted Gaik Ovakimian at AMTORG.[19] The plan behind the recruitment was that the Soviets would have the chance to see cutting designs at the planning stage, rather than years down the road when the plane might be available for sale. If intelligence could land York as a source, they would move at a stroke from saving money by acquiring obsolete designs, to providing vital information on technology even before it went into production. Tupolev argued that the Soviet Union needed to move away from buying foreign planes for military use unless the plane was a new class. (The Northrop was a dive bomber or 'stormer', a type of aircraft the Soviets did not yet have in their fleet.) Moreover, by the time the Soviets got a foreign fighter into mass production and deployed it into front-line service, it would be obsolete. A plane that was slower, less manoeuvrable or could not climb fast enough would cost a pilot his life in combat. The whole industry was moving forward so quickly that a lead time of years was too long. If his information allowed the Soviets to get ahead of the curve, York and others like him might be the answer. If there was any chance of landing him as a source, it was worth taking the risk.

Hurried arrangements needed to be made for a recruiter to meet urgently with York in Los Angeles. A date was set. The Russian aircraft inspectors had arranged a celebratory dinner to commemorate the handover of planes, and York was invited.

The plan was to infiltrate an intelligence recruiter into the party without arousing undue suspicion. The ideal candidate had to have a reason to be at a Northrop celebration. Shumovsky was the designated recruiter. If anyone asked him why he was at the dinner, he would be able to explain that he was there on legitimate business as he had been a member of Tupolev's purchasing team a few months ago. NKVD records show that Shumovsky spent from 5 to 15 November away from his studies at MIT in California with the specific goal 'of the cultivation and recruitment of workers in the Douglas and Northrop aircraft factories'.[20] In advance of the trip Ovakimian had given Shumovsky extensive training in how to land new agents and how to conduct the all-important first meetings. Recruitment was a question of trust, not just money. A potential source, especially one motivated by money, might be more unreliable than a true believer like TALENT. Shumovsky was instructed in the methods of putting a source at ease. The primary concern of any potential source was to avoid getting caught if the information he disclosed was traced back to him. The greatest point of risk for source and controller alike was being observed, perhaps by accident, at a meeting where the information exchange was to take place and having no cover story.

Shumovsky sat next to York at the celebratory dinner and listened attentively to his tale of woe.[21] York needed money in a hurry and could not see how he was ever going to earn it working at Northrop. Shumovsky learned that York in his own opinion was a brilliant designer but was not appreciated by his managers. He needed finance to set up his own business. Currently assigned to designing weaponry, he had created a new aero engine but no one at Northrop would look at it. Shumovsky suggested sending the design to Moscow to get the opinion of Tupolev and his people, who worked on engines. In comparison to the sacrifices of Soviet workers, to Shumovsky York's problems were small beer.

York styled himself as a frustrated entrepreneur who needed capital. Shumovsky presented his suggestion of sending the design to Moscow as a spur-of-the-moment idea to help York with his current financial difficulties, not as a long-planned recruitment. Unsurprisingly, York initially resisted the idea of risking his career for a few hundred dollars per secret, but he did not reject a follow-up meeting. Instead he agreed to bring along a few examples of his work, which as an expert Shumovsky could evaluate on the spot. He explained that if Northrop was selling all the secrets of a dive bomber, dressed up as a postal plane, to the Soviets for $80,000, what was wrong with York profiting from his own hard work?[22]

The second meeting was the peak danger time for Stan. Having had time to reflect on their discussions, York might do anything at this point. He might alert company security, or worse, US counter-intelligence. The next meeting could easily be a set-up. Shumovsky would thoroughly check the rendezvous location for signs of FBI presence or use his trade craft to lose anyone tailing him, but his future was in York's hands.

As a former soldier dedicated to his cause, Shumovsky dispassionately weighed up the cost and benefit of the mission. The potential gain from recruiting York far outweighed any personal risk to himself. He knew he was in danger of exposure just as he was starting his work on the West Coast. But nothing ventured, nothing gained. If caught, he had a cover story that he was performing legitimate work. Unlike Ray Bennett, who had approached her mission in California believing she would fail, Shumovsky set to his task believing he would succeed. This was the confidence of a man who rode his luck and had been wounded three times fighting for a cause that he believed was the future.

Having reflected on the offer, York had dropped all his former resistance. He brought with him as a sign of good faith plans for 'a mechanism for dropping bombs and a reloading mechanism for machine guns',[23] two vital items of technology missing from the plane that had just been delivered to the Russians. York would work productively for his controller Shumovsky for many years. He developed a friendship based on trust and was a diligent and productive source, even asking in advance for vacation time. York was assigned an American 'cut out' courier, initially Emanuel Locke, as it became increasingly difficult to meet with Russians without arousing suspicion. But he still met Shumovsky from time to time for a catch-up.

It was not until 1950 that York was formally identified as a Soviet source by the FBI.[24] American counter-intelligence had kept a copy of every coded telegram sent by the Soviets since the 1930s, photographing them secretly at the telegraph office. These were the famous 'black chambers' – secret rooms in this case at the telegraph office but normally in post offices for the perlustration or interception of mail. But Americans did nothing with the copies until 1943, when a small team began to catalogue and sort them. Codebreaking attempts started late in the war and continued until 1980. The NSA operation, known as Venona, succeeded in breaking only a small percentage of the codes, but those that were broken revealed some teasing details of Soviet operations. The appearance of York's name was a shock to the FBI. Up to this point the Bureau had believed that all Americans who were Soviet agents were Communist Party members, because it was only this type of agent that they had caught. York, though, was not motivated by political beliefs. He was in it for the money.* Fifteen years too late, American counter-intelligence began to gain a glimpse into the genius of Shumovsky's plans.

• • •

The NKVD files record that Shumovsky developed several other contacts around Los Angeles. Each was assigned a codename and they were probably arranged through the local Communist Party cell. He first met with a contact in aviation research with the codename TIKHON, 'who kept on his guard'.[25] Stan's MIT thesis was the subject of their discussion. Unhelpfully 'shortly before the meeting, a number of Los Angeles newspapers had published an interview with the chief of police [James Davis], about how the series of accidents involving experimental military airplanes (4 planes in 2 months) was the work of an international organization, whose goal is to sabotage the aviation industry.'[26]

---

* York told the FBI that Shumovsky was his recruiter and that he had worked for the Russians passing technological secrets for some fifteen years. Belatedly, the FBI found Stan's codename BLÉRIOT and could now begin tracing his footsteps. In their 1951 report, the FBI stated that 'Stanislaus Shumovsky came to the United States in September 1931, as an exchange student. In June 1936, he received his Master's degree from the Massachusetts Institute of Technology. According to the statements of his classmate, Ben Smilg, his paid tutor, Shumovsky was frequently away on trips to the West Coast or Texas with no explanation except that arrangements had been made at AMTORG. Subsequent assignments and contacts support the belief that Shumovsky was an active agent of the Soviet Government.'

Shumovsky also had a potentially fruitful meeting with a source whose codename, GAPON, was a most unusual one. Father Gapon had been a Russian Orthodox priest and a popular workers' leader in the prelude to the 1905 Revolution and the massacre of Bloody Sunday. He was discovered to be a police informant and murdered. This source was a Douglas Company employee, and the discussion with Shumovsky was again about high-altitude flight. He revealed that Douglas was conducting secret tests overseen by a friend of his, who luckily was sympathetic toward the USSR. Shumovsky arranged a follow-up meeting with the pair of them. The friend was outgoing and forthcoming, telling him a good deal about the company's secret tests and giving an update on its progress. He even showed Shumovsky documents, although he would not hand them over.

Disaster struck when GAPON suggested from left field that Shumovsky should appeal officially for further information from the company. The follow-up report sent from New York to Moscow Centre was very critical of GAPON, recording that, 'such conduct on GAPON's part attests to the insincerity of his constant declarations of friendship towards the Soviet Union, his Communist attitudes, etc.'[27] The door was rapidly shut on this particular avenue of information.

The final meeting in California ended better. FALCON was a draughtsman at Douglas who had joined the company from the Sperry Corporation in New York at the end of September. 'FALCON strikes one as having a serious view of the Soviet Union and an interest in strengthening the latter.' The first meeting led quickly to a second. FALCON told Shumovsky, 'I'm still new to the factory, and my duties here are limited, but as soon as I get the hang of things and make acquaintances, we will find much that will be of interest.' To illustrate the difficulties of operating in the US, Shumovsky sent Moscow a clipping from the *Los Angeles Evening Herald and Express* entitled 'Red sabotage suspected in air tragedies'. Following the trip, the NKVD ordered him not only to 'recruit FALCON' but, in the same instruction, to 'develop relations with NEEDLE', a new potential agent.[28] Stan had started to build a roster of agents on the West Coast.

• • •

But before he could devote himself to his studies and aviation espionage, the distraction of the ghost of Cherniavsky arose for the first time. Shumovsky was ordered to investigate what was happening in Boston with the Trotskyists. Moscow had become convinced that the Cherniavsky coup attempt had been organised in Boston on the direct orders of Trotsky himself. Shumovsky was asked to identify any of the other students at Harvard or MIT who might be an undiscovered assassin and to find out what the local Trotskyist cell was planning. In early September 1935 he reported back to Moscow Centre that he had launched a plan to infiltrate the Boston Trotskyists with his undercover agent. This entry is one of only two sections of the files disclosed after the collapse of the Soviet Union about their operations in the USA deemed so important by the NKVD that they underlined them.

The secret service placed enormous emphasis on uncovering the plot to topple Stalin involving Cherniavsky and Bennett. Shumovsky heard about an open meeting in the US organised by birth control activist and long-term socialist Antoinette Konikow to hear James A. Cannon, the editor of the magazine *The Militant*, speak on the future of Trotskyism. Cannon had been expelled from the CPUSA for his nonconformist views and became a prominent activist in favour of Trotskyism. As he could not attend the meeting himself without arousing suspicion, Shumovsky recruited an undercover agent from his contacts in the Boston émigré community to participate in the meeting and report back to him. Shifra Tarr, a widow in her sixties who had been married to a Jewish Communist, had no obvious political affiliation herself. She moonlighted from her work as a hairdresser earning a meagre 50 to 70 dollars a month to infiltrate the revolutionary underground movement that had ordered a hit on Stalin. At the meeting:

> Cannon further reported that although the Trotskyite movement had not embraced the masses broadly enough, it was nevertheless growing and gaining strength. The Trotskyite organization has groups in many countries around the world, and in particular, there is an underground Trotskyite organization in the Soviet Union that connects with foreign Trotskyites.[29]

With these words, Cannon confirmed the whole Cherniavsky and Bennett conspiracy. He had inadvertently closed the loop as far as the NKVD were concerned, confirming to an American audience that Trotsky, from exile, was using his underground movement in the Soviet Union to order from abroad the murder of his political rival, Stalin. By providing fresh evidence that an underground opposition organisation existed ready to stage another revolution, he had inadvertently condemned many old Communists to show trials, and put his own leader Trotsky in the sights of the NKVD execution squads.

The 1917 Revolution had seen a tiny violent minority seize

power in the name of the masses and execute the former leader. As an old seminary student, Stalin knew all about the philosophy of an eye for an eye. He ordered his underground networks to kill Trotsky as an act of revenge and self-protection. The operation took years to complete. Stalin told an audience in a speech in 1935 that he had faced down the opposition bullets to follow the right path. To continue surveillance, the hairdresser 'Tarr' was ordered to 'gradually' infiltrate the Trotskyists in Boston. It was not the last time that Shumovsky would have to deal with the consequences of Cherniavsky's ill-fated mission to Boston.

10

GLORY TO STALIN'S FALCONS

On 14 July 1937, a Soviet long-range experimental aircraft, the Tupolev ANT-25 RD – bearing the initials of its lead designer, Andrey Nikolaevich Tupolev – landed at San Jacinto, California after a record-breaking non-stop flight. The plane, which had taken off from a specially extended runway at Shchelkovo air base in Moscow sixty-two hours and seventeen minutes previously, came down in a cow field outside San Diego. None of the three exhausted airmen on board either spoke or understood a single word of English. They carried three cards, to show people on arrival, bearing the words 'bath', 'eat' and 'sleep'.[1]

On arrival in the United States, the two pilots, Mikhail Gromov and Andrey Yumashev, and navigator Sergey Danilin, met the waiting and smiling Stan Shumovsky, who had arranged for them to receive a heroes' welcome across America. His friend Tupolev's aircraft had got the crew to America; Stan's plan was to get them to the Oval Office and to the attention of the world.

Close to the site of the landing in California today is a commemorative plaque. It reads:

Shumovsky on the sound stage of the Hollywood blockbuster
In Old Chicago with Shirley Temple, 1937

Three miles west of this site, on July 14, 1937, three Soviet aviators completed a transpolar flight from Moscow in 62 hours, 17 minutes, establishing a new world's nonstop distance record of 6,305 miles. The single-engined ANT-25 military reconnaissance monoplane was dismantled and shipped back to the Soviet Union to take its place in a museum. Aircraft Commander Gromov, co-pilot Yumashev and navigator Danilin would all become air force generals in the Second World War.

The 1930s were the golden age of flying heroes, their daring deeds followed as closely as those of the astronauts and cosmonauts in the 1960s space race. Their names were as famous at the time as those of Neil Armstrong or Yuri Gagarin, the first man in space. Nations competed to fly faster, further or higher. Americans cheered Charles Lindbergh and Amelia Earhart; the Soviet Union celebrated 'Stalin's Falcons'. In 1937 Shumovsky turned these Soviet heroes into international celebrities. In nearby Hollywood, he organised for them to be received by the world's undisputed number-one movie star, the twentieth century's most famous child actress, nine-year-old Shirley Temple. She invited the party onto a movie sound stage and later tap-danced at a party at her home. In her later years, she recalled that they were among the best-looking men she ever met.

At each city where the Russians afterwards stopped on their

The Soviet airmen with Shirley Temple

celebratory tours – San Diego, San Francisco, Washington, and New York – he ensured there was a gala presentation hosted by the mayor, and ticker-tape parades. Crowds came out in their thousands to cheer the brave aviators, some running alongside their open-topped car. At small-town railway stops, newspapers reported, the airmen's carriage was mobbed. Stanislav Shumovsky, whose flair for public relations matched his gifts as a spy, had organised it all. In plain sight, he orchestrated the whole show. He was captured on newsreels and gave numerous newspaper interviews. The essential stopping-off points on the celebratory journey were the West Coast aircraft factories. And all the newspaper stories, the meetings with the President and Shirley Temple, were superb door openers that Stan used to 'talent-spot' recruits for Soviet intelligence among America's aviation experts. The mass of information he gleaned in his discussions at factory parties, receptions and dinners was reported back to Moscow.

It was entirely appropriate that the Soviet aviators' record-breaking flight was also an intelligence triumph. Their aircraft, with its 34-metre wingspan, could not have made that flight without technology secretly obtained by Shumovsky. Having seen the plane at the technical design stage on Pavel Sukhoy's desk at TsAGI back in 1931, he was proud to have contributed intelligence that found its way into the final design. The aircraft's enormous range and fuel efficiency were derived from its innovative wings, housing large fuel tanks that gave the rigidity required for take-off, and its massive wingspan. Thanks to the expertise of Stan's MIT agent Benjamin Smilg, the designers had defeated the dangerous phenomenon known as flutter; the plane's structure was robust enough to withstand stress, but not so bulky as to impact its overall performance. It is in no small part thanks to Shumovsky's work between 1933 and 1938 that the USSR broke no fewer than sixty-two world flying records.*

1937 poster celebrating transpolar flights

---

* Ilyushin, Tupolev, Sukhoy and the MiG design team (Mikoyan and Gurevich) incorporated the best of American know-how into their end products. It has been forgotten that in the 1930s most of these Russians visited US factories escorted on their tours by their man on the ground, Shumovsky.

• • •

Planning for Soviet transpolar flights had begun back in 1931, as part of the Politburo's massive investment in developing its aircraft industry. The People's Commissar for Military and Naval Affairs, Kliment Voroshilov, had suggested building the long-range reconnaissance aircraft which became the ANT-25. Adopting the method favoured by Tsar Nicholas, much of the money for the expansion was raised by public subscription and a lottery. In a remarkable letter held in Stalin's archive, some Young Communist members asked if their general secretary was contributing the same percentage of his wages to the cause as they were. Stalin wrote back to confirm that he was.[2]

Support for the expansion of the air force was widespread. To fly the new planes turned out by the factories, the Soviet Union needed to train more pilots. To this end, the air force reserves and the gliding club organisation Osoaviakhim recruited 13 million members in a decade. Even Stalin's second son Vasily became a pilot.

Although not appreciated at the time, Soviet efforts in developing aviation dwarfed those of every other country in terms of the number and type of planes built. Intelligence reports in Stalin's archive detail the numbers and types of aircraft possessed by each foreign nation and their factories' wartime production capacity. Shumovsky was responsible for information on the US, which included detailed and accurate analysis of the strengths and weaknesses of the American air effort. In terms of aircraft production, the Soviet Union outstripped every rival nation.

The plane manufactures required vast numbers of engines. By 1937 the Curtiss-Wright aero-engine plant in the USSR alone employed 30,000 workers and was 'set up on the best American principles', according to Lieutenant Colonel (later Brigadier General) Martin F. Scanlon, American air attaché in London during the late 1930s. Curtiss-Wright only developed a plant on a similar scale in the United States during the Second World War.

• • •

While in London in 1938, Scanlon uncovered some of the contributions of Shumovsky's espionage when he interviewed an American aeronautical engineer who had helped set up a Soviet factory to produce, under licence, US-designed Vultee dive bombers. The engineer estimated that the factory where he was based, Moscow Aircraft Factory Number 1, would be capable when completed of producing an unprecedented 1,500 dive bombers a year, many times the capacity of the US. The Vultee production line in Russia was discontinued in 1938 but even-tually evolved to manufacture the famous Il-2 Shturmovik, a ground attack plane produced in greater quantities than any other single model.★ The engineer told Scanlon he had evidence that 'the Russian espionage system in America has apparently been very much underrated . . . The Russian government has agents in practically all American [aircraft] factories.' He had seen evidence of Shumovsky's work first hand 'as Soviet aircraft designers were using blueprints that could only have been

---

★ The incorporation of the best Vultee design features into the Il-2 goes some way to explain the striking similarities between the two planes. The Vultee business survived to manufacture a range of trainers, dive bombers and fighters for the Allied armed forces in the Second World War. Its planes made an enormous contribution to winning the war in the Pacific.

acquired by espionage'. Working in the USSR and in fear of losing his job, the anonymous Vultee employee explained that his concerns must remain anonymous and under no circumstances be passed on to the army. His concerns stemmed from commercial imperatives. Given that his company had no orders for planes from the US armed forces, Mr Vultee did not wish to hear complaints about the behaviour of his Russian customers. The company was being kept afloat by orders from the Communists and from warring South American countries.

Scanlon informed Washington that this was not an isolated report, as 'other Americans associated with the Russian aviation industry have told me of similar cases'.[3] No one in Washington paid any attention. Despite the warnings, official inaction meant the spying continued unchecked.

• • •

In the 1930s, America was among the most pacifist and isolationist of nations. It was official policy to allow the US military to be run down. There was a widespread and popular belief that the United States' involvement in the Great War had been for the profit of the few – arms manufacturers and bankers – but paid for by the sacrifice of the many. As a result, many joined the Pacifist League, believing that it was in the interests of the US to stay out of others' conflicts. Even if the money were available, there was no desire to divert scarce state resources to building up the US military beyond a minimum level. The State Department had no intention of antagonising any foreign power except imperial Japan, who were a threat to their sovereignty over the Philippines. Even then their involvement was limited to arranging large loans for the Nationalist Chinese government to buy US-made arms, including warplanes, to hit back at the invading Japanese.

Soviet industrial espionage was meanwhile spreading beyond aviation. In 1934, the authorities again ignored reports that visiting Soviet engineers, sitting in a US factory, had been brazenly drawing the design for a brand-new naval anti-aircraft gun. The reality was that, despite the steeply rising war tensions in Asia and Europe, the US armaments industry received little government support and was dependent on foreign orders to keep the factories open, the skilled workers employed and their product up to date.

Airframes at the time were designed around a single-engine model. Motors wore out faster than frames, which led to constant demand for engines. A flow of individual parts manufactured in America to be assembled in Russia soon followed the first complete engines delivered by Curtiss, while the Russians developed their own variant around their Curtiss engine – the only difference between the Soviet M-25 variant and the equivalent US version being the use of entirely metric components. Over 13,888 M-25 engines were eventually built, with performance equal to a Wright motor. The M-25 was developed into the ASh-73, the engine that would power the Tupolev Tu-4 into the sky at Tushino in 1947.

• • •

By this point a great deal of information was flowing to the US authorities about the extent of Soviet espionage in their factories. At another manufacturer, Douglas in California, a cat-and-mouse game developed between the company's private security guards and visiting Russian engineers. The Russians enjoyed the game. They had bought licences to manufacture the DC-3 and the rights to some information, but were intent on taking far more. In particular, they wanted to reproduce every detail of the Douglas design room back home but in metres rather than feet. They wanted the exact dimensions. When a direct request was refused, they took to pacing it out while on smoking breaks, dogged by American security guards trying to protect the company secrets.

Officially, the US authorities took the view that the USSR was simply too far away to be a military problem. Several US diplomats in Moscow including Loy Henderson and George Kennan, on the other hand, were fiercely anti-Soviet. They wrote back to Washington warning about the dangers of arming Moscow with the latest weapons and insisted that only obsolete technology should be sold. The unintended consequence of such letters (which were intercepted and read by the Russians) was to intensify the pace of intelligence gathering in the US. But there was no political will to deal with the reports of Russian spies in the US, especially during the Depression. Ingrained arrogance and complacency were typical of the attitude of the US military and government at the time. Senior US officers believed in the innate superiority of their own forces over any perceived enemies. Soviets flyers were inferior pilots, peasants in the sky lacking the skills to operate modern equipment. As a result, US intelligence-gathering efforts in the USSR were inadequate. The State Department solicited the views of Charles Lindbergh on his visit to the Soviet Union; otherwise, they relied on third parties such as the Baltic states to provide assessments or the travel experiences of embassy staff. They did not believe in the Soviet air myth, and found reports of Soviet air strength and capabilities to be widely exaggerated. Flying around the USSR was described as a far worse experience than anything that could be had on any American airline. There were observations of inadequately trained mechanics and a lack of spare parts. This is the perennial problem of intelligence. It is easy for an agent to find what they set out to look for and ignore the inconvenient truth of Soviet aviation development. The US failed to spot the direction of travel until it was too late.

American entrepreneurs meanwhile saw Soviet efforts at economic expansion as a source of enormous profit. Curtiss-Wright, the world's largest aircraft engine manufacturer, earned Soviet money throughout this period, which allowed it to continue developing its powerful radial engine designs at a time when the US military was actively cancelling its orders. Pratt & Whitney was its only competitor in the engine market, and the precision needed to produce engines was a barrier to other companies entering the market. Nevertheless, during the Depression, sales had dropped, and Curtiss-Wright was forced to close many of its satellite plants. The corporation posted losses for several years even while it remained the country's largest aircraft firm. Undoubtedly, it was saved by export sales from its engine division, Wright Aeronautical, which during the first half of the 1930s provided more than 50 per cent of the company's revenues from China and the USSR.

In the capitalist model, private corporations risk their own capital on prototypes to compete for limited government contracts. To stay ahead in the air race required constant innovation and investment. Sometimes change stemmed from disaster: on 31 March 1931, a wooden-winged Fokker airliner serving the route from Kansas City to Los Angeles crashed in the Kansas prairie, killing sports hero Knute Rockne, 'without question, American football's most-renowned coach', who had been on his way to consult on the movie *The Spirit of Notre Dame*. A wooden wing failed on his aircraft because water had seeped between the layers of laminate and dissolved the glue holding it together. The accident led the Aeronautics Branch of the US Department of Commerce to introduce new restrictions on wooden wings. The result was the development of all-metal aircraft.

There was cut-throat competition even in the fast-developing commercial aviation sector. In a 1935 article, Donald Douglas stated that a single model of the first prototype DC-1 had cost him $325,000 to design and build, while each DC-2 – the sample plane sold to the Russians, at a price of $130,000 – cost $80,000 to manufacture. He sold the licence to produce the DC-3 to the Russians for $207,500. So the profit on each aircraft was thin. Douglas worked out that he would need an order of at least 100 planes to turn a profit on a model; such large orders were non-existent in Depression-hit America. Foreign contracts became the bread and butter of US industry. But this meant sharing or giving away secrets.

In just a few years, meanwhile, the Russians had progressed from buying completed planes abroad to assembling kits and then to building entirely under licence. They were one of the few nations able to do so. In comparison, the DC-2 licence was sold to the Dutch firm Fokker, but they could not build the planes themselves. Fokker's European customers, KLM, LOT, Swissair, CLS (Czech) and LAPE (Iberia), purchased the extraordinary plane via Fokker in the Netherlands. But the aircraft were manufactured in the US and shipped to Europe.

The Japanese aircraft company Nakajima wrestled with the complexities, but only managed to construct one plane before turning to assembling kits. Of the countries who bought the DC-3, the USSR was the only one to be successful. Russian aircraft designers had cut their teeth on reverse engineering;

Tupolev's first project had been to deconstruct and rebuild a Blériot plane. Engineers would take a sample-imported plane to pieces and reassemble it. They might then copy it as far as possible from local materials. Otherwise, they would adopt the best features of several models to build their own. In this way the Soviets developed the skills to be able to produce 22,000 of their DC-3 variant, the Li-2. Boris Pavlovich Lisunov, a member of Shumovsky's 1935 team, was the plane's designer. The plane was built from components sourced in Russia, the Li-2 was a shining example of how Stalin's plan to make Russia self-sufficient in aviation might be fulfilled. Soviet-built planes were cheaper than imports, used local resources, created jobs and ensured the safety of the Soviet Union. There would be no repeat of the Tsar's dependence on foreign arms suppliers.

• • •

Russia and the United States share a border divided by a hostile terrain: the Arctic. In 1936 Stalin devised a plan to symbolically narrow the gap between the two countries by sending aircraft on non-stop flights to the US. The warming of relations between the USA and the USSR could never happen quickly enough for the Soviet leadership with their strategic concerns. Stalin was surrounded by the expanding forces of Nazism in the West and imperial Japan in the East, both aggressively rearming. The Soviet Union's richest natural resources deposits lay within easy striking distance of these expansionary powers: the Soviet breadbasket of the Ukraine and Don was uncomfortably close to Germany, as were the prize oil fields of the Caucasus. Japan eyed Siberia as a potential colony, while the imperial Japanese army had been reluctant to abandon the territories captured during their intervention in the Russian Civil War.

Both Germany and Japan believed that they were peoples with an unfulfilled destiny, trapped within their current borders. Both saw colonies in the territory of the USSR as their right. On the face of it, Fascism and Communism were locked in an ideological battle, but underlying the struggle was a naked plan of conquest and extermination. While the destiny of Germany was to rule, the peoples of the USSR faced annihilation. Stalin understood that he was in a long fight for survival. In a February 1931 speech to industrial leaders he said prophetically:

> One feature of the history of old Russia was the continual beatings she suffered because of her backwardness. She was beaten by the Mongol Khans. She was beaten by the Turkish beys. She was beaten by the Swedish feudal lords. She was beaten by the Polish and Lithuanian gentry. She was beaten by the British and French capitalists. She was beaten by the Japanese barons. All beat her because of her backwardness, military backwardness, cultural backwardness, political backwardness, industrial backwardness, agricultural backwardness. We are fifty or a hundred years behind the advanced countries. We must make good this distance in ten years. Either we do it, or we shall be crushed.[4]

By 1937 few doubted that an armed clash between the forces of Fascism and Communism was inevitable and imminent. Stalin was already in a fight with Japan. The low-level proxy war along the Manchurian border in China started in 1931 and spilled over into set-piece battles. From July 1936, the Spanish Civil War pitted the new generation of Soviet arms against the developing technologies of Germany and Italy. Stalin broke the League of Nations arms embargo to supply the Republican government in Madrid with weapons including his best tanks and aircraft. Thousands of Red Army troops served on the Republican front line alongside other international volunteers. On the battlefield and in the skies of Spain, Russian tanks and planes held their own against all but very latest German fighters, bombers and anti-tank guns. The reason for the defeat of the Republicans was down to their amateur army being unable to resist professional soldiers and the greater level of support given to the rebels by Germany and Italy, rather than to the inferiority of Soviet arms. The experience of the fighting in Spain was somehow lost on Hitler, as would be evidenced by the disaster of Operation Barbarossa when Soviet military equipment proved a match for everything but the best.

The key message for Stalin from the Spanish Civil War had been that the League of Nations and the Western powers were toothless in the face of Fascist aggression. His country needed more and better weapons to defend itself. Internationally, moreover, Stalin needed friends, and so he began to approach his enemies' enemies. America was the block to Japan's expansion in the Pacific, the same development that threatened the USSR. Following the German Kondor Legion's mass air raids on Guernica, Madrid and Barcelona, it was clear that the next war would involve a strategy of bombing raids on civilian population centres. As a deterrent to imperial Japan and Nazi Germany, the Soviets intended to build a strategic bombing capability. To lead the design effort, Stalin chose Tupolev, a designer with an enduring interest in building long-range aircraft.

After the terrible experiences of the Spanish Civil War, the strategic bombing of civilian centres was prohibited by the League of Nations. Many countries focused away from heavy to build medium or fast bombers. The exception was the United States, where a fierce battle over how best to defend the long US coastline would rage for a decade between the traditionalist forces in the US Navy Department and the proponents of air power. A squadron of long-range bombers cost a thousandth of a battleship. But were they as effective? The visionary US Army general Billy Mitchell, 'Father of the Air Force', was a fierce proponent of the ideas of air power theorist General Giulio Douhet that the fundamental principle of strategic bombing was offensive, and that the only defence against carpet-bombing and poison gas attacks was to meet them with equal offensive sorties. For this reason Stalin armed the USSR with nuclear weapons following Douhet's philosophy to meet an attack with an attack.

The US became the leader in bomber design. In August 1934, in response to a rare tender from the War Department for a new plane, Boeing began at its own expense a programme to build a prototype four-engine bomber. Although it took five years for the plane to enter military service, the process would culminate in the development of the heavily armed B-17 Flying Fortress and later the Superfortress. The idea was to rely on heavy defensive armament and giant payload, rather than speed, to be effective. Shumovsky was very interested in gathering information on this innovative plane.

In 1935 the Russians had concluded publicly at the end of Tupolev's US visit that there was little America could teach them about the development of large aircraft. In private, however, they saw the potential in the DC-2 and its successor the DC-3. Enormous efforts went into replicating the Douglas factories, products and methods in the USSR.

The *Maxim Gorky* flies over Red Square

Tupolev built the famous *Maxim Gorky*, at the time the world's largest aircraft. This monster of a plane was so vast that it included a printing press and a cinema as well as a crew of twenty-five.* The plane had little practical value; it was underpowered, the engines straining to lift the vast bulk of the fuselage off the ground, so it could never carry any sizeable cargo. Furthermore, it was so slow that it was vulnerable to even an old fighter. Rumours reached Moscow from Shumovsky's network of the progress made by Boeing and others in heavy bomber design.

---

* The plane crashed over Moscow in 1935.

Developments included new, more powerful engines, the use of durable, lightweight construction materials (mainly aluminium) and finally the development of rotating machine-gun turrets providing the aircraft with an effective all-round defence. The US believed it was possible for a large formation of bombers to defend itself against any number of attacking fighters if it flew in a close enough formation with interlocking machine guns. The development of motorised rotating turrets placed at weak points including the rear and the nose made the design of the new generation of US bombers the most innovative in the world. All this was information that the Russians badly needed.

• • •

It was in this climate that the plan came together in 1937 to establish a new world record for a non-stop flight. If successful, it would combine a dramatic publicity coup with a chance to cement relations between the US and the Soviet people. The stated goal of the programme was the eventual establishment of non-stop commercial passenger flights between Moscow and the United States. But behind the open message of friendship was a more sinister covert message aimed directly at Tokyo and Berlin; if we can fly a plane to America, your capital cities and population centres are within range of a bombing fleet too.

Planning this world record attempt required overcoming significant challenges. First, at the time, pilots flying over remote areas without wireless location beacons relied on a magnetic compass to determine their position. The only practical route between Russian and US territory was over the magnetic pole, but pilots attempting the feat discovered that their key navigational instruments were useless. The Soviet solution was to establish a radio station close to the pole. This required an expedition led by Arctic explorer Otto Schmidt, who built a permanently occupied drifting base that broadcast a location signal to the small number of aircraft flying above.

The next stage was to find an aircraft that could cover this vast distance non-stop. The ANT-25, an experimental prototype, had the range. Once in the air, its engine was incredibly fuel-efficient. However, the ANT-25 could cover the distance only at a very low speed, essential to keep fuel usage to a minimum so that the plane could carry enough supplies to reach its intended destination. This meant that any flight to the United States would last a very long time, testing the mettle of the crew. A second difficulty was that the plane required an enormous runway in order to generate sufficient speed from its single engine to take off.

In the summer of 1937, the elite of 'Stalin's Falcons', a group of his most daring and intrepid pilots, began preparations for more record-breaking flights. The most famous of these, Sigismund Levanevsky, had already denounced Tupolev as a 'wrecker' in an ill-tempered meeting at the Kremlin, having suffered a dangerous oil leak in one of the single-engine aircraft. He refused to fly a Tupolev plane.

Two pilots and their crews were however prepared to undertake the pioneering journey. Legend has manufactured competition between the two, Valery Chkalov and Mikhail Gromov. Chkalov, with an unparalleled reputation for derring-do, was Stalin's favourite pilot. His most famous feat was flying under a bridge in Leningrad against direct orders. With his background and skills, Chkalov epitomised the Soviet pilot. Ruggedly handsome with wide-open peasant features, he was the embodiment of what an

Stalin and Chkalov embrace

ordinary Russian could achieve given the opportunity. He enjoyed a close personal friendship with Stalin and was celebrated as a national hero. He was a fighter test pilot, a hazardous job given the primitive state of aircraft testing in the 1930s. However, his expertise was not in long-distance endurance flights.

His rival, as legend now has it, was Mikhail Gromov, Chkalov's opposite in every way. While Chkalov was daring and flamboyant, Gromov was dull and thorough. Gromov looked every inch a nobleman, even if despite his background he had embraced Communism. But he and his crew were the Soviet's leading experts with large aircraft. Gromov was a vastly experienced pilot responsible for the initial test flights of the ANT-25 and had already set distance records in the plane, flying large loops around Moscow.

San Francisco was the goal, on a route named after Stalin himself. Chkalov was Stalin's personal choice to be given the first opportunity. For his trip, the 35-metre plane was packed with every conceivable piece of equipment. Every emergency had been considered, and the aircraft was equipped with tents, rifles, and food supplies for thirty days. All this weight, it transpired, significantly reduced the plane's range. But it was an experimental flight, and no one knew how much fuel would be used combating the winds over the pole.

Only after twenty-four hours had passed into Chkalov's flight and the plane was well on its way into the polar region had the attempt been announced in Moscow. The United States Army radio communication facilities all the way from San Francisco to the far north, Point Barrow, had been marshalled under a secrecy blanket to aid the daring undertaking. A message from the Royal Canadian Signal Corps station in the remote northwest broke the silence that the flight was under way. Then there was more silence for several hours until the first words from the Russians reached San Francisco at about 12 p.m. on Friday. The crew sent word that the mission was proceeding normally but did not give their position.

The plane had flown almost due north from Moscow for nearly 1,000 miles overland to the Kola Peninsula, the northeasternmost tip of European Russia, and thence over the Arctic Ocean to Franz Joseph Land, 1,750 miles from its starting point. The course changed slightly and they headed towards the actual pole, 700 miles further on, passing it at 12.10 a.m. on Saturday. The report came: 'Everything is all right'.

The next report came at 3.20 a.m., when they were 320 miles south of the pole on the North American side and beginning their downward journey. For the next twelve hours, there was not a word, and during that period the pilot passed close to the magnetic pole, the obscure spot in the far north Canadian islands to which magnetic compasses point. The route also took them

279

through one of the Arctic's two great blind spots. Amid growing fears over the safety of the flight, the pilots finally reported themselves 100 miles south of Fort Norman, in the Canadian Northwest Territory, by 3.25 p.m They were then almost 4,280 miles from Moscow.

Veering west across the Canadian Rockies, they headed down the coast to British Columbia, giving a few brief reports of progress throughout the night. At 1.11 a.m. they announced they would land. After a long tiring flight, the engine had generated an oil leak, and the plane touched down at Pearson Field, a US airbase in Vancouver, Washington State. Chkalov had been successful in crossing the pole but had failed in his mission to fly non-stop to San Francisco. Conquering the pole was a fantastic achievement but set no world distance record.

The exhausted aviators tumbled from their plane dressed in turtleneck sweaters and big army boots. They wore skins fur side out over their legs and feet, giving an effect rather like that of cowboy chaps. Contemporary photographs show them looking stereotypically Russian. The Americans were impressed with their first sight of the ANT-25, describing it as a 'huge, sleek ship with a silver gray body and red wings'.[5] It was impossible not to notice the enormous wingspan compared with the length of the fuselage. The base commander, General George Marshall (later to become Chief of Staff of the United States Army), allowed them the use of his house to wash and clean up and to receive a square meal. They were loaned money to buy clothes. The sudden arrival of the plane had been a complete surprise as no advance warning was given to the Americans that it might suddenly appear at one of their military bases.

The significance of the flight for Russia was demonstrated by

ANT-25 in California, 1937 (note wingspan)

the elaborate preparations. Shumovsky had been intimately involved with the planning on the American side. The Soviet ambassador, Alexander Troyanovsky, had been on standby in a chartered plane to meet the flyers wherever they touched down, while President Roosevelt and Secretary Hull were ready with congratulatory telegrams. Roosevelt was gripped by the news of the safe arrival of the first Russians to cross the Arctic non-stop; his telegram read, 'The skill and daring of the three Soviet airmen who have so brilliantly carried out this historic feat commands the highest praise. The President is pleased to convey to them my warmest congratulations.'[6] After fifty-five hours without sleep, Troyanovsky was so exhausted he slept aboard the plane throughout the flight to Portland. It was left to Shumovsky to handle the American side of the press arrangements for the trip.

Shumovsky carefully positioned the story in the US news-papers. In a masterstroke of public relations, he invited only William McMeremin of the United Press agency aboard the chartered plane carrying the Russian official party to Vancouver to greet the flyers.[7] United Press would have the exclusive and would syndicate his messages. 'Engineer insists flyers scientists, not heroes' was his chosen headline. He was the official spokesman and 'on hand' expert, hailing the achievement as a demonstration of 'the world's greatest attempt to build long-range planes'.[8] In an interview given at Portland, Oregon on 20 June 1937, he described himself in fluent English not as a spy but as a Soviet aeronautical expert. He praised the three Soviet polar flyers led by Chkalov as 'scientists doing a job in the development of aviation'.[9] Such low-key statements were very much in the Soviet style.

Maintaining the appropriate sombre tone, he announced, 'Soviet pilots are not glory seekers, but scientists doing a matter-of-fact job in the world's greatest attempt to build planes for long-range flying.' Pointing out that the airmen had made two previous long-distance flights of over 6,000 miles – although these were Gromov's achievements, not Chkalov's – he explained that 'the trio had completed first a triangular Moscow back to Moscow flight in December 1935. The second flight was from Moscow to the eastern coast of Siberia near Alaska in January 1937. The flight from Moscow to the United States over the pole was the next logical step.'

He took the journalist into his confidence by divulging tech-nical details about the plane and its miraculous engine: 'In making their long hop, the flyers revolutionised the theory that an air cooled motor is best for long-distance flights.'[10] The low-wing monoplane used in the polar flight, he said, was equipped with only one water-cooled engine capable of 125 miles per hour. Use of a water-cooled motor allowed the plane to make the flight using much less fuel than would have been required by an air-cooled engine, leaving space for more equipment.[11] The plane, Shumovsky said, was only one of many types being developed in Russia, adding that the USSR had made much more progress in aviation than was generally believed. He told the press that the plane had been designed in 1932 and built in 1935 particularly for long-range flights. Its body was similar to that of a glider, with long narrow wings. It was streamlined to an exceptional degree, cutting down fuel consumption.[12] Foreshadowing Lend-Lease – the US programme that would supply its allies including the Soviet Union with aid and materiel – Stan predicted that a trade route would be established over the pole from Moscow to San Francisco with a stop-off somewhere in Alaska. However, such a project would take a war to develop.

Shumovsky explained to the gaggle of pressmen, eager for news, the background of the chief pilot. The son of a Volga boatman, Chkalov had joined the Communist army in 1919. He was only fifteen at the time. After the Revolution, he entered pilot school, making a special study of army pursuit planes. He also attained the state's highest honour, the Order of Lenin, awarded for heroism as a test pilot.

Shumovsky knew how to sell a story to the press. He wrapped his audience in the mysteries and intrigue of the USSR, informing them that 'the present venture was guarded in secrecy at the outset'.[13] Back in San Francisco, on 23 June 1937, he disclosed further secrets of the remarkably efficient monoplane that had

carried the three Russian aviators over the North Pole; as the
newspapers reported, 'Performance of Russian Motor Amazes Yanks'
and the 'Machine Slower But Has Greater Lifting Power Than US
Ships'.[14] American engineers were astonished by the Soviet plane,
whose take-off weight of 24,000 pounds was as much as a fully
loaded American sleeper such as the DC-3, designed for overnight
use. The low-wing monoplane had one engine developing about
1,000 hp; American sleeper planes produced approximately 2,400
hp with their twin motors. 'The single water-cooled motor which
we have developed in Soviet Russia and used on this polar flight
and other long-distance flights is superior to your American
Motors,' said Shumovsky dramatically:

> It does not develop so much power but is much more reliable.
> The plane can carry a heavy load because it does not go so
> fast as your transport. Its wings are built like those of a glider:
> much longer, narrower and with a different tilt than those of
> American transport ships. This enables the plane to rise with
> a greater load and fly with the use of much less gasoline than
> your American airships but at less speed. Our plane develops
> about a 125 mph top speed. Your American transports develop
> 200 mph.[15]

Shumovsky smiled knowingly when he was asked whether the
aircraft picked up much speed as its fuel load decreased.

The single-engine aircraft was left behind in Vancouver, while
the three men who had flown across the top of the world started
by train for Washington, DC via receptions in Portland, Oakland
and San Francisco. These parties were the forerunners of receptions to be held for them in the nation's largest cities. Shumovsky

and the Soviet ambassador flew immediately to Washington State to showcase the extraordinary feat and parade their heroes. America embraced the brave pilots. Chkalov and his crew enjoyed three weeks of celebrations in various cities, culminating in a visit to the White House to meet the President. The presidential diaries record that only fifteen minutes of FDR's time was allocated to greeting the heroes but in the event, he enjoyed their company so much that with the help of a translator the visit was extended to double the allotted time. Shumovsky was the first serving NKVD officer to be invited into the Oval Office.

The heroic crew were treated to a first-class ticket to Europe on a passenger liner, travelling on the same boat as the actress Marlene Dietrich. The iconic blonde and the Soviet Union's number-one hero began a ship-board romance; they were voted the man and woman of the voyage. Newsreels of the arrival in Europe focus on the pilot, with the screen siren uncharacteristically having to take a back seat.

· · ·

Evaluation of the flight in Moscow showed that the experimental aircraft could fly a lot further if the weight of additional materials was reduced. Mikhail Gromov was given the green light to attempt a second journey. He crammed the plane with fuel, removing such unnecessary items as brakes, food and safety equipment. To ensure that the flight captured the popular imagination, a much larger PR campaign was planned in both the USSR and the USA. The Russians were poised to exploit the publicity and goodwill engendered by such a heroic achievement, and the man in charge was again Shumovsky. In advance of the trip, he chartered a plane to ensure that he would be on the spot when Gromov eventually touched down somewhere on American soil – or perhaps in Mexico. He made ambitious plans to ensure that this tremendous achievement of the Soviet Union would receive maximum publicity and exposure with the US public.

Among Shumovsky's contributions to the success of the publicity blitz was his understanding that the pilots must be presented as good Communists but similar in all other respects to average Americans. Gromov and his crew certainly looked the part. Despite landing in a field, they did not appear in front of the international press in scruffy clothes crumpled after hours of flying. Taking a lesson from his arrival at MIT, Shumovsky realised the importance of smart American-style clothing. He arrived within twenty minutes of the plane, touching down near San Diego with three elegant ready-to-wear outfits in the correct sizes, ensuring the crew looked nothing like the unkempt individuals described in the 1931 letters of Gertrude Klivans. To meet the press the crew emerged from a farm shed in brand new clothes to greet a large crowd of pressmen, looking remarkably relaxed and fresh considering the long journey and the harsh conditions they had endured. Unfortunately, despite being experts in flying they had no English language skills. Luckily a translator and expert in all matters aeronautical was to hand; none other than Stanislav Shumovsky. For an NKVD spy to appear in a newsreel, other than for being arrested, is quite extraordinary. Shumovsky would continue to fulfil his public relations role, making sure he was on hand to answer any questions from newspaper reporters at each venue on the whistle-stop tour of America's cities and aircraft factories; visits to Boeing, McDonnell Douglas and Consolidated were planned.

Shumovsky with Gromov, 1937

After a visit to the army air base at March Field, Shumovsky drove to San Diego with the crew. He allowed unprecedented press access to the Russians, and every detail was reported in the *Santa Ana Register* of 15 July 1937. 'The Russian aviators who flew to San Jacinto California from Moscow were worn out by 63 hours in the air and slept late in a luxurious hotel suite.' It was not until shortly after 10.30 a.m. the party left their rooms to start shopping. The flyers only ordered tea for their breakfast which was served in their suite at the historic US Grant Hotel overlooking San Diego's historic downtown. Shumovsky disclosed that the trio were in need of clothing to attend a civic, army and navy lunch to be held in their honour. Accompanied by a party of Russian consular officials, they arrived dressed in soft shirts and trousers, socks and shoes; they had no jackets and only one of the trio wore a tie.

Following the luncheon, the flyers left San Diego for Los Angeles. The pilots revealed to the press that they had alternated at the controls during their two and a half days in the air and slept 'when we felt like it'. The navigator kept them true to their course in the strange terrain and said he 'didn't sleep a wink'. It was incorrectly reported that American food was no treat after the 'feast of caviar, chicken, tongue, chocolate and unsweetened tea that they took along on the plane'. Officers from the US Department of Agriculture who gave the plane a 'routine inspection' confiscated some leftover fruit. Shumovsky told them the flyers had no further use for a half-eaten lemon the officers had found. This is the closest he ever came to being arrested in the US. Shumovsky, now describing himself as the aviation representative from Washington, DC, disclosed that the flyers had crossed the Mexican border and gone as far as San Cuente, a resort city fifty miles to the south, looking for an opening in the cloud. They had circled for four hours before finally turning back and searching, again unsuccessfully, for March Field, which they missed by twenty miles. The flyers had therefore passed over Russian, Alaskan, Canadian, United States and Mexican territory, shattering the world non-stop record. The actual figures were kept sealed in three devices removed from the plane and sent to Washington for checking.

After dispatching a message directly to Stalin and broadcasting over a radio network to the Russian people, the flyers apparently 'drew back into a shell of modesty, worried by the publicity. Chief pilot Gromov's cheeks glowed, and he seemed inspired as he talked into the microphone telling the Soviet nation of their feat. He hoped it would create better feeling between the United States and the Soviet Union.'The next stop was a visit to the Hollywood motion picture studios and a tour of 'inspection of all airplane factories that they have time for was on the fliers' schedule'.

After the reception, the heroes were taken to the Consolidated Aircraft Corporation plant where many of the US Navy's planes were built. Major Reuben Fleet led them through the facility to inspect a fleet of giant flying boats being built for the Soviet government. Gromov suggested through an interpreter that a spirit of friendly rivalry be encouraged between Soviet and American flyers: 'I wish American pilots would reply with the same kind of a flight and try to beat our record so we would have something to shoot at again.' He revealed that the flight had originally been planned to take place eighteen months earlier but was postponed because there was some doubt of success: 'We were anxious however to make this trip before the plane and the pilot became too old, he said gravely.' But the dour Gromov's attempt at humour was lost on Americans.

The next day the crew were paraded and feted in Los Angeles, a formal reception arranged by Mayor Frank Belshaw following a parade through the downtown streets. From Los Angeles, the plan was to go to Washington before sailing for home from New York.

In the field at San Jacinto, the red-winged ANT-25 had been covered with tarpaulins even before the newsreel companies arrived to capture the success of the flight. It was now guarded by US soldiers to stop souvenir hunters from stripping it. The only damage suffered on landing had been a cracked fuel line. The powerful single engine, which never missed a beat during the long hours flying through a storm, ice, wind and fog, was not even stained with oil.★ Shumovsky used every possible opportunity to explain to American reporters how advanced in aviation the Soviet Union had become. Styling himself as a Soviet aviation expert, he informed the journalists in his many interviews that the engine was a revolutionary Soviet design. (In fact, it was a derivative of an American one.) He nevertheless single-handedly established the Soviet Union as a major innovator in aviation. Soviet designers could now sit at a dinner table with their American colleagues and discuss aircraft design on an equal basis. No American aircraft had been able to cross the pole non-stop to Moscow. The flights were celebrated as a triumph of Soviet ingenuity, courage and socialism. The trip had brought the American people closer to the Soviet Union.

· · ·

Another of Shumovsky's tasks was to protect the crew from the effects of their sudden immersion in capitalist America. The pilots were astonished by the entrepreneurial spirit of the farmer in whose field they had touched down. Having quickly organised ticket sales to view the plane and enlisted the military to guard his franchise after roping off the field, he made a tidy sum from the crowds swarming to see the strange plane. He approached the Soviet pilots and received permission to siphon off the remaining gas, after which he began selling small souvenir bottles of aviation fuel. The onlookers were hungry for other souvenirs.

★ The plane was later moved to March Field, crated and shipped back to Russia.

One of the aviators dropped his glove, only to see it snatched up by an eager member of the crowd. The glove was never seen again. Later the airmen reported the incessant theft of the shoes that they left outside their hotel rooms for cleaning. The co-pilot, Yumashev, in particular, was taken aback by the aggressive attention of American women. He was blessed with rugged good looks and was regularly approached by interested members of the opposite sex looking for a kiss. He even received an offer to remain in the United States and appear in Hollywood movies. He declined.

When the crew did eventually appear in a movie, it was a Soviet film, not a Hollywood blockbuster. The 1939 film, entitled *If War Comes Tomorrow*, was pure propaganda, showing how the Soviet Union would defeat a Nazi invasion. The crew of the historic flight to America were featured as bomber pilots leading the counter-attack on German cities.

The importance placed by the Soviet Union on developing long-distance strategic bombing is reflected in the decision taken after the success of this flight that Stan would focus full-time on the West Coast factories. Some of the agents he recruited would provide vital information to Moscow.[16]

Other newspaper articles showed that Russia had a very different message to deliver to its enemies. In one edition of the *Oakland Tribune*, the front page carried a warning to Japan and Germany. Military chiefs in Moscow had published a statement saying that Japanese and German cities were within the range of Soviet bombers. The slow-moving ANT-25 was, in reality, no threat to Japan, but the Soviet Union had demonstrated its intention. For the Nazis engaged in the Spanish Civil War, this was another warning that the Soviet Union was building the capability to defend itself. If Hitler attempted to deliver on the promise made in *Mein Kampf* to dismember the Soviet Union, the price Germany paid would be heavy. Fleets of Soviet heavy bombers could easily reach every German city in the first wave of retaliation. The nightmare of terror bombing of civilian cities that Hitler had inflicted on Spain would be revisited on Berlin, Hamburg and Frankfurt by the VVS.

• • •

The year was to end in tragedy for Soviet aviation. The first two flights to cross the North Pole to America in 1937 had been successful, but a third ended in disaster. The most famous of all Stalin's pilots, Sigismund Levanevsky, and his crew died in their attempt to fly to America in a four-engined plane. It had been his idea to develop the trans-polar route, but after his failed attempt in 1935, it was his misfortune to be overtaken by others.

In an effort to showcase Soviet dominance in large multi-engined planes and raise the possibility of passenger travel, Shumovsky had flagged Levanevsky's flight to the US press on the day after Gromov's flight successfully touched down. The pilot, a compatriot of Stan's, was introduced to the American public as the Soviet Charles Lindbergh. Because he did not trust single-engined aircraft following a near fatal incident in 1935, when an oil leak had ended his transpolar flight, Levanevsky would attempt the same journey in an untested four-engined plane. With the full attention of the American press, Shumovsky announced that Levanevsky's red-painted DB-a would depart Moscow on 12 August 1937, its destination Fairbanks, Alaska.

With the weather changing for the worse in the Arctic by August, the window for safely attempting a trans-polar flight was closing fast. After fourteen hours thirty-two minutes in the air, the crew sent their last radio message to ground control that one engine had failed, but that they still intended to press on with the flight to Fairbanks. They never arrived. Levanevsky's flight disappeared somewhere in the Arctic, and its final location remains a mystery. Stalin's leading Falcon was dead; for the family of Soviet flyers, it was the equivalent of losing their father figure.

Many rumours have since circulated about the causes of the tragedy; there were allegations that the aircraft's designers had been arrested and accused of sabotaging the flight, although these are untrue. It seems clear that having lost one engine, the unproven experimental plane went off course and crashed in bad weather. Over three hundred streets in the Soviet Union would be named after their lost hero.★

The loss of the Soviet plane cast a dark shadow over an otherwise splendid year for Shumovsky. But worse news was to follow. This was the great year of suspicion in the Soviet Union. No one is certain what precisely triggered the start of 1937's Great Purges, but news from Spain of the collapse of the Republican government due to infighting played a significant role. When Nationalist general Emilio Mola was asked by a journalist which of the four columns of troops that were marching on the key government stronghold of Madrid would take the city first, he

---

★ Such disasters were all too common in the early pioneering days of aviation. Chkalov was the next to die in an accident, pushing an experimental fighter aircraft beyond its limits. As his plane threatened to crash on houses below, he made the ultimate sacrifice to avoid casualties on the ground rather than bail out to save himself. Stalin was a pallbearer at his funeral.

replied famously that the capital would fall to a 'fifth column' already within the walls. A new phrase for traitors entered the popular imagination. There were swirling accusations throughout the Spanish Civil War of treachery and betrayal, adding layers of suspicion to an already murderous environment.

The unthinkable defeat of the workers' movement in Spain by the forces of Fascism despite the full international support of the Communist movement was a seismic shock to the Soviet Union. The obvious message to Stalin was that only a unified country would be strong enough to survive the inevitable Fascist onslaught. It became an imperative to weed out the real and imagined 'fifth column' in place in the Soviet Union, the allies of fascist and other capitalist enemies, before any coming attack. It did not help that the quisling Trotsky, in exile, was working with the Germans to put himself forward as an alternative leader to Stalin in a dismembered USSR.

Under NKVD head Nikolay Yezhov, the Great Purges or Terror began innocently enough with the administrative expulsion of thousands of members who had found their way into the Communist Party. Out went the 'former people', kulaks★ or simply those who had not been entirely truthful in their applications. It was believed that such elements could, as in Spain, act to weaken the whole Communist movement in wartime from within. Background checks showed that many members did not meet the strict criteria of membership and they were expelled. The loss of Party membership was devastating for these individuals, as one's job, housing and benefits such as schooling went too.

Throughout the Soviet Union, a pervasive atmosphere of arrest

---

★ Rich or exploitative peasants.

and accusation spread like wildfire, victims including any individual or national group that might form an opposition or rally to the side of an invader. A leap to mass executions and imprisonment was soon to follow. The enemies of the people included members of the highest echelons of the Communist Party, perceived as the leaders of a hidden Trotskyist underground, former Whites, some ethnic groups, and a clique in the top leadership of the armed forces. The purges widened to exact a price for the many failures in delivering on the current Five-Year Plan, including the aviation industry. As war approached, official patience with failure and incompetence had run out. It was a time for results, not excuses.

Tupolev and many members of his design team were arrested and imprisoned, some receiving sentences of up to ten years. There remain many theories to explain Tupolev's arrest. The official charges include the formulaic offence of espionage and wrecking; the former resulted from his contacts with White émigrés, namely the aircraft designer de Seversky and the wind tunnel expert Margolis. Tupolev's correspondence with his old friend, and a meeting on the French leg of his 1935 trip, had led to the accusation that Tupolev was working for French intelligence.

An audit of the results of Tupolev's expenditure on foreign aircraft, moreover, concluded it had been wasteful. He had been too powerful for too long and had created many enemies and jealousies while he was at the top. The former hero paid the price for the failures in combat of the planes that bore his name and the abandonment of the heavy bomber strategy that had failed in Spain. He was imprisoned with his design team in a 'sharashka' detention camp, where they could concentrate on aircraft design shorn of other responsibilities.

The fallout from the sudden change of atmosphere spread to the intelligence service in America. The main casualty was the head of New York station, Pyotr Gutzeit, who was summoned back to Moscow and eventually shot. Gutzeit had focused his time and considerable amounts of money on infiltrating the fragmentary White Russian opposition movement in exile and American politics,[17] recruiting at great expense a US congressman appropriately codenamed CROOK. Among the other grand schemes he proposed to Moscow was the purchase of an entire US newspaper publishing house to spread pro-Soviet stories as a challenge to Randolph Hearst. He suggested interfering in US elections to secure 'the entry into the Senate and Congress of people capable of directing and influencing US politics'.[18] Gutzeit was an expensive luxury, a dreamer in a service that was becoming increasingly professional and results orientated. His messages to Moscow ran to pages, irritating the recipients who spent hours decoding and then searching for the one nugget of information that could be useful.

The Soviet culture of denunciation and suspicion spread to the intelligence service. Overnight, heroes were denounced as villains, and few were spared criticism. The initial fallout followed the defections to the United States of senior intelligence officers Walter Krivitsky and Alexander Orlov. Despite the many sacrifices he had made for the cause in the last six years, which included being away from his young family, Shumovsky himself faced several rounds of accusations – even if, at least in INO, few of the wilder charges were believed.

Shumovsky had moved to New York on receiving his Master's degree from MIT in June 1936 to take up a position at AMTORG as cover for expanding his espionage activities.[19] Officially, he was now Deputy Plenipotentiary for the Commissariat of Heavy Industry. He travelled around the country when required in his role as a controller of agents, appearing in Chicago to meet Smilg, and on to California to receive from York (who was now working at Lockheed) the plans for either the twin-engined high-speed P-38 Lightning or the Hudson bomber. Despite this hard work, an inspector from Moscow attacked him for lack of productivity and described his material as only being up to the quality of easily available open-source material, not real intelligence.[20]

Worse, the ghost of Cherniavsky returned to haunt Shumovsky. Back in 1935, Moscow had sent a flurry of urgent messages to New York demanding a major effort to get to the bottom of what had happened in Boston, where Shumovsky had been attempting to infiltrate the organisation. Now, in 1937, he was described as one of a group of Trotskyists surrounding the leadership in New York centre. However untrue, it was a tough charge to face.

By August 1938 the NKVD in New York felt the need to write a stern rebuttal of Moscow's wild allegations. They pulled no punches:

> The content of this report, which was supposedly sent by Navy Intelligence on the West Coast to its office in Washington, is utter hogwash and does not reflect a single authentic fact from our work. You no doubt remember the ridiculous story of how the American multi-millionaire Bendix supposedly sends money to local Communists through BLÉRIOT. In reality, BLÉRIOT met Bendix face to face only once in his life, three years ago, in the company of twenty other Soviet engineers. Or take that other

ridiculous story about how BLÉRIOT's son supposedly travels between Moscow and NY, thereby maintaining a connection. Whoever compiled this report does not even have the basic information about such easy-to-establish facts as BLÉRIOT's age, which in fact is only 36, or that of his son, who is not yet 10 years old.[21]

Even Gaik Ovakimian faced an accusation of being in the pay of the FBI. It was alleged that as he had operated for so long in the United States 'brazenly' as a spy and he had not been caught, he had to be a traitor! The suggestion to recall every single intelligence officer in the US and replace every source as they were counter-intelligence plants was, luckily for the Soviet Union, rejected.[22]

But it was becoming increasingly tough to gather intelligence. Shumovsky discovered in his travels across the country that security measures were being stepped up, not just to combat Russian intelligence gathering but because other foreign security services were at work after the same or similar secrets. Moscow Centre was informed about one of Shumovsky's missions. Before the New Year, he had travelled to Chicago to meet Smilg. His contact had moved jobs, securing a plum position in the research division of USAAF at Wright Field. On the face of it this was a major coup for Shumovsky; all Wright Field employees were supplied with plenty of information regarding developments in aviation not only in the USA but from other countries. The network of US military attachés in Europe supplied detailed reports to Wright Field describing the characteristics of aircraft fighting in Spain. But Smilg was nervous. He explained to Stan that because Wright Field was a repository of secrets from various aviation companies, there was a prevailing fear that employees might give one company's secrets to another. He believed that all employees, especially civilians, were kept under constant surveillance.[23] The regulations categorically prohibited Wright Field employees from meeting with representatives from commercial companies, especially outside the walls of the establishment. Smilg explained that the surveillance was set up so well that, no sooner had someone dined with a company representative, than the very next day he was summoned by the boss for questioning and disciplining.

Shumovsky was worried that he might lose a valuable source just when Smilg had reached the heart of US aviation research. He demonstrated his independence of thought and ability to adapt to the change of LEVER's circumstances by suggesting alternative arrangements for the passing of information. As a new employee and a Jew, Smilg felt he would be shadowed even more closely than other employees. He asked that they should not meet for the next three months, at the end of which he would travel to Boston on vacation and hand over the materials he had accumulated. Moscow was told:

Despite BLÉRIOT's best efforts to convince him that it would be preferable to meet earlier and set up a regular connection, LEVER held his ground, asserting that it would be better to lose 3 months and afterward begin regular work than to get exposed from the start. Considering the complexity of the situation and the fact that we agree with some of LEVER's arguments, we will not meet with him until April. By that time, we will have developed a system for contacting LEVER that would allow us to receive materials from him with ease while minimizing the risk. Because BLÉRIOT is a Soviet engineer, he will not meet with LEVER after April to avoid compromising the latter.[24]

The system Shumovsky devised as a less suspicious means of maintaining contact with sources of such valuable information was the use of American couriers. It was now too risky for Russians to be seen meeting American workers in the defence industries. And the new system worked well, until Ovakimian suggested Harry Gold as LEVER's courier. Luckily for the Bureau, Gold had a hoarding disorder and never threw anything away. His apartment was a treasure trove of ticket stubs, itineraries, and maps from every single trip he had taken on behalf of Soviet intelligence. As a result, he was later to betray Smilg and many others to the FBI.[25]

As Shumovsky had found, the Soviets were no longer the only country to have established an active intelligence-gathering presence in the United States. German, Japanese and Italian spies were chasing down the same or similar secrets. In response to the German theft of the top secret Norden bomb sight, it was reported:

Between the 20th and 30th of Sept. '38, LEVER informed BLÉRIOT that in view of the discovery of a German spy ring working, in part, at Mitchell Field [the eastern base of the USAAF] and at Seversky's factory, which filled orders for fighters, the US War Department is taking special precautions to check up on its staff and increase vigilance. At Wright Field, all the locks on doors, closets, desks, etc., have been changed. Tables are searched more frequently. We have information that all workers are being shadowed by detectives.[26]

The team had built an extensive network of sources but were feeling the strain of constantly operating under the threat of surveillance and arrest. Each source required careful nurturing: they brought their problems, financial and marital, to their controllers, who also had to cope with the frustrations of missed rendezvous and the alarm engendered by unexplained absences. While the sources were becoming more conscious of the risks involved, their controllers were caught in the middle, faced with the increasing demands of their bosses in Moscow for more and better information.

• • •

The authoritative American Aerospace Industries Association had been disparaging about the Soviet aviation capability, but by 1937 it was forced to revisit its assessment in the light of the success of Russian fighters and bombers in Spain. The US embassy thought it could account for the unexplained triumph of Soviet aviation, as reported in the association's yearbook:

Russian planes produced in 1937 were vastly improved over former models. They were much cleaner in design, and this was reflected in better performance. Russia's flying personnel, like Italy's, had extensive practical experience in Spain, where Russian planes flying for the Republican cause had been matched with both Italian and German machines operating under the banner of the Insurgents. Both the German and Russian equipment proved capable, and Italy had been forced to send in her latest machines to prevent being hammered out of the air.[27]

The secret, they thought, was not the impact of Tupolev's 1935 trip and the tremendous level of investment, but that

> Russian women had demonstrated that they could perform much more effectively than men in nearly every branch of aircraft manufacture. They learned their trade more quickly. They were more adept with precision work, and they were more adaptable to the rigorous discipline and care required in airplane construction. The result was that Russian factories were able to increase their output and at the same time train numerous women aircraft mechanics. Insofar as her air power was concerned, Russia was bound to prove a formidable foe. Russia had an air force peculiarly adapted to Russian needs, whether for a campaign with neighbors in the West or the East. The Russian air force was trained and equipped for any possible conflict with either Germany or Japan.[28]

The report was the closest that American intelligence would come to eating humble pie, it could moreover be seen as a backhanded compliment to Shumovsky's secret work.

11

BACK IN THE USSR

In January 1938, the grand old lady SS *Berengaria* set sail from Southampton via Cherbourg in France en route for New York. It was almost the final voyage of the Cunard liner that had started life as a German luxury vessel bearing the appropriate name for a ship of spies, *The Impersonator*. There was no concealing the age of the ship, which had developed a propensity to catch fire owing to her faulty electric wiring. (A final fire in March 1938 would condemn her to a one-way trip to the scrap yard.) Joining the vessel in Cherbourg after a long train journey from Moscow via Warsaw, Berlin and Paris were four NKVD officers travelling under cover as Russian engineering students. One of them was accompanied by his wife Ekaterina and young child Marianna.[1]

There was no pretence at concealment among a large group of students this time. The whole party was made up of spies and their families, new recruits for the roster of dedicated Soviet S&T spies in America. They had one destination, Massachusetts Avenue in Cambridge and the campus of MIT. One of the students, 26-year-old Semyon Semyonov, later commented that when enrolling in MIT, the 'education was not regarded as an end in itself but as a means of preparing for doing intelligence work, studying the country, the language, and broadening my overall range of technical interests'. By the time they left the USA, Semyonov and his companions, thirty-year-old Nikolai Yershov, Fyodor Novikov, thirty-four, and thirty-one-year-old Vasily Markov (in the US, he called himself Mironov) – their NKVD codenames were TWAIN, GLAN, LAUREL and KURT[2] – had written new chapters in the history of Soviet espionage in the US.

Semyonov would be instrumental in stealing atomic secrets; Mironov wrote a letter in Russian to the head of the FBI, J. Edgar Hoover in 1943, revealing the details of the extensive Soviet spying operation in the US. In the most extraordinary passage of his letter, the five foot six inch MIT alumnus confessed to participating in an act of mass murder.

Semyon Semyonov

Shumovsky had gone to considerable trouble to arrange for the four spies to be enrolled at his American alma mater. These were family men with wives and young children who planned to settle down in the US for the long term. They were professional intelligence officers who had all served for some time in the NKVD before being assigned abroad. Stan travelled back to Boston from New York, where he was now based, to personally vouch for the new students and sign them in on their first day at MIT. On a previous trip to Boston, he had arranged their rented accommodation, cars and schooling for the children. Yershov, and probably the others as well, lived in an apartment near the campus at 888 Massachusetts Avenue, paying $45 a month in rent.[3]

On arrival in New York, the four met their new boss Ovakimian at his office at AMTORG, where he explained that they had two goals at MIT. The first and most pressing need was to master a higher standard of English. The second was to network as broadly as possible with the scientific community, both students and teaching staff. In the event of war, it was expected that these talented scientists would be mobilised and their work turned to military use. The labs at MIT were already working on the next generation of technology for the US military, such as early stage radar and direction-finding equipment for gun laying. Karl Compton was Roosevelt's favourite scientist and was a reasonable bet to be involved in planning any wartime scientific effort.

By 1938 MIT was being used as a finishing school for 'legal' Soviet S&T spies. Columbia University in New York was the college of choice for 'illegals'. Its city environment was ideal to acclimatise to America and learn English anonymously; a spy would pass unnoticed in the masses of the metropolis. But the MIT spies were in America to get noticed. In the 1941 academic year a fresh batch of Soviet students planned to enrol at MIT, but the war intervened in the scheme. Soviet intelligence provided equal opportunities for Americans when it came to studying at universities. Among those recommended to apply to MIT with their fees covered by the NKVD was Harry Gold;[4] it was believed that if he had a degree he would be more credible with his contacts as a courier. Another was David Greenglass,[5] who was supposed to gather intelligence on MIT's work on nuclear physics while still a student.

Shumovsky had a further job to do for Soviet intelligence in Boston. He was monitoring the progress of yet another MIT student. Soviet intelligence was paying the fees not only for four Russians but also for the American Norman Haight, codename LONG. Haight had returned to MIT at Russia's expense to study for a Master's degree. In the middle of the Great Terror, Haight's report card was being sent to Moscow: 'The source LONG finished his first semester with good or excellent marks. At present, in his second semester, he has set out to complete his other subject requirements, as well as his thesis work. The state of the source's health has worsened significantly in view of his intensified work.'[6]

Ovakimian, himself a talented scientist, believed a first-class education was essential to success in espionage. In talking to his sources, he demonstrated an understanding of their scientific work and wanted his new officers to show the same attitude. To the recently landed newcomers, he stressed the need for hard work and application in their studies.

With the words fresh in their ears, the new party of students, along with Yershov's wife and child, headed up to a chilly Boston in early January escorted by Shumovsky. A small crocodile of Russians followed the tall figure of Stanislav Antonovich, as they knew him, on a personal tour of the city of Boston, neighbouring

Cambridge and the university campus. The tour was interrupted periodically when Stan ran into an old friend or acquaintance and broke into English.

Having spent five years at MIT as a student and spy, there was no one better to explain how the Institute operated and who to cultivate. Shumovsky was able to show them where in Boston to find the best Russian food and friendly émigrés. A second briefing explained the practicalities of combining open academic life with the secret world of espionage. By now, unlike in 1931, an organisation was in place to support the four newcomers. American couriers brought them their occasional secret orders, identifying themselves with passwords – usually an innocuous question and a rehearsed answer. For urgent matters they could communicate by telephone.

That the four were using their time at university for far more than acclimatisation to life in America remained unknown to the Americans. A recently declassified 1970s CIA report, investigating the routes by which foreign agents entered the US, noted that

A former Soviet agent, whose name cannot be mentioned for security reasons, speaking about USSR students who are sent abroad for higher education, stated that all individuals who are allowed to leave the USSR must have a specific reason such as industrial espionage or preparation for future assignments either in the country to which they are sent or to some other country at a later period. He advised that students come within this category. Semyon M. Semyonov entered the United States as a student on January 18, 1938. He attended the Massachusetts Institute of Technology. During the next few years, Semyonov was reported to be operating a network of agents while he moved from one appropriate cover to another.

Yet despite the mounting evidence, even in the 1970s the CIA could not see that an American university could be a target for infiltration. The FBI was even further off the mark. Their chief investigator Robert Lamphere never spotted the link between America's centre of scientific excellence and the Soviet's extensive S&T espionage effort. Even though he knew that five out of the dozen members of the team were MIT alumni, he only noted that the 'KGB paid Smilg's tuition at MIT – where, incidentally, Semyonov himself had studied'.

•   •   •

By January 1938, Ovakimian was well established as the New York station chief on a salary of $450 a month. BLÉRIOT, as benefited his seniority, was now second on the list, receiving $350 a month. The newly arrived students received generous salaries as well: GLAN was paid $300 a month, and TWAIN, KURT and LAUREL received $250 each.[7] This was not the action of an intelligence organisation in crisis, reeling from the effects of the Great Purges. The US-based S&T team were receiving a significant investment both in money and human resources. The organisation was paying five sets of tuition fees, all living expenses for four families and generous monthly salaries. The Soviets had learned from the Shumovsky experience that the key to success in America was a thorough assimilation in the American way of life, excellent language skills, technical expertise – and above all, hard work.

However, the new intake at MIT was cut from very different cloth than Shumovsky. As far as Ovakimian was concerned, they were trouble from the start. He considered them to be lazy and neglectful of their education. It was imperative that to be successful as S&T agents they should be top-notch scientists like himself and Stan. This was a requirement seemingly lost on the new crop of students, who had no fear of repercussions from not studying and personally profiting from their time in the US. Ovakimian was forced to write seeking an answer to a thorny question. He sent a personal letter regarding the students' behaviour to 'Comrade Philip', apparently a senior officer in Moscow Centre:

Comrades LAUREL, KURT, GLAN, and TWAIN were warmly welcomed by us, and despite an overload of work, we (BLÉRIOT and I) gave them the utmost attention, both here and in Boston. We helped them get settled with apartments, furniture, and their studies. We are in regular contact with them. Obviously, I will handle their little circle. As you see, we have grasped the full seriousness of the problem of replacement and change. But I must point out, unfortunately, that you have pampered the guys and haven't quite properly oriented them on certain matters. Most of them don't like to work hard (for now this applies to studies), especially since their academic training has proved to be rather poor. In addition, there is no Bolshevik modesty. But these things can be corrected. These folks, of course, are completely green and they suffer from conceitedness. They gave BLÉRIOT three gold watches to mail to their wives at home, citing a promise from you. I have temporarily held on to the watches. Please let me know what to do with them.[8]

Ovakimian's frustration was understandable. In the midst of a turf war with the illegals who operated in parallel with his team, he had wanted experienced officers assigned to New York, not trainees who required wet nursing. There were sharp disputes over sources with the illegal line and, more fundamentally, criticism of his overall performance. But Ovakimian was not easily intimidated and went toe to toe in a fight with one of the NKVD's trained assassins. Fresh from a failure to kill Trotsky, YUZIK (Iosif Grigulevich) was not a man to cross. He had eliminated dozens of Trotskyists in Spain during the Civil War, sprayed Trotsky's house in Mexico City with a machine gun and later, impersonating a Costa Rican diplomat, tried to kill President Tito of Yugoslavia. In New York, he operated as an illegal with designs on running the whole intelligence operation. Ovakimian demonstrated great personal courage in facing down this dangerous man.[9]

By the summer of 1938, the MIT students had to be pressed into service. The most talented of the new intake, Semyonov, was a Jew from the Black Sea town of Odessa. His family would join him in the United States once his wife had recovered from the birth of their son.* Semyonov was an orphan in a town famous for its clowns and entertainers. Using his innate ability to be charming, tell jokes and entertain, he had survived, despite his small stature, in a harsh world. A ball of energy with a mind that was always scheming, he was not a man who would thrive in a classroom, but he found his ideal job socialising around the campus. With a wife and young baby in tow, the jocular Semyonov became a fixture at MIT parties. No one ever suspected the real reason why, drink by drink, joke by joke, he cultivated America's top physicists, chemistry and engineering experts, but Semyonov

---

* She arrived in Boston a few months later.

got to know everyone, and they all remembered him. If anything important happened in America's scientific community, Semyonov would know who was doing it, or someone who did. Most scientists he approached would help their friend if he asked them, not realising that the information he was asking for was an American secret.

• • •

BLÉRIOT meanwhile was on his way home. Shumovsky had finally been recalled. After more than seven years away from Moscow, except for short vacations, he was set to rejoin his family, and perhaps resume normal life. He returned to a job as one of the Soviet's elite aviation engineers, with better pay than a government minister. His family occupied a new apartment on the widened Leningrad Prospect near his old university.

It was strange at first for Shumovsky to hear his own language spoken on the street and adjust to the sights and sounds of his home country after so long away. He had to relearn to think in Russian. Many of Moscow's old Tsarist street-names had been replaced, causing him confusion. The city was one giant building site. Whole blocks of buildings had been shifted intact to allow for the widening of the main highways and establish ring roads. A magnificent new metro system had opened, its marble opulence the envy of the world. American-designed cars in their hundreds now crowded the newly widened streets, creating similar traffic problems to New York. But much of Moscow was still a quiet old city with its share of horses and carts and open street markets.

Back in his adopted home town, Shumovsky started to relax, seeing an end to his life of furtive meetings and dodging tails.

He could forget his tradecraft and the fear of betrayal and arrest. The constant stress of espionage work abroad burned out even the strongest-willed individual, and Shumovsky was one of the Soviets' longest-serving overseas agents. His family was well on the way to being grown up; his daughter was sixteen and his son ten. After years living a solitary life, he adjusted to a routine of taking his children to school (which was the same as the one I attended) and started a regular office routine. Having lived apart for years, communicating only by letter, there was a long process of adjustment to being a real family man. Although he was prohibited from talking in detail about his activities or acknowledging that he used to work for intelligence, his family was aware of his status and privilege. He was able to spend a month debriefing before the start of his next important job, at the newly created Ministry Of Defence Aviation Department.[10]

There was much to enjoy in Moscow in 1939; in the words of Stalin in a speech, 'life has become better, comrades, life has become more cheerful'. The great rage in Moscow was the cinema, especially a crop of new musical comedies, Hollywood-style movies such as the Busby Berkeley-inspired *Circus* and Stalin's favourite comedy, *Jolly Fellows*. A great fair had opened in Moscow in which stomach-churning rides swung passengers back and forth in aeroplane-shaped gondolas.

However, it was impossible to escape everywhere the signs that a major war was imminent. The regular civil defence drills included air raid and gas attack practices. And the subject of one new film the family had to see was in contrast to the diet of comedy. *If War Comes Tomorrow* summed up the prevailing sombre mood and tension. The movie was directed by Yefim Dzigan and was a work of propaganda. Its theme song, composed by

Vasily Lebedev-Kumach, was played everywhere in the city. *If War Comes Tomorrow* lacks the artistic and dramatic depth of Sergey Eisenstein's movie *Alexander Nevsky*, but it has a similar message – that anyone who attacks Russia with a sword dies by the sword. The film's characters are shown as simple, brave Soviet citizens, but they play a subsidiary role to the massive battle scenes and aircraft that form a significant part of this movie.

Shumovsky was soon able to introduce his son and daughter to some of the film's stars, the Heroes of the Soviet Union Gromov and his crew, as well as their aircraft, at the newly completed Zhukovsky airfield. The family were able to inspect for themselves the current and prototype planes of the expanding air fleet. No doubt they would have been taken on a VIP test flight in an aeroplane incorporating the technology acquired by Shumovsky in the US. Now he was trying to pass on to his young son his own enthusiasm and love of flying, at the age that he himself had discovered the thrill back in Kharkov.

In Moscow there were many more men in military uniform every day. The Red Army was growing dramatically, from 1.3 million in 1937 to close to 5 million by 1941. Shumovsky was soon back in military uniform himself; already a member of the air force reserves, in his new role as deputy chair of the Technical Council of the People's Commissariat for Aviation Industry (Narodny Komissariat Aviatsionnoy Promyshlennosti or NKAP), he became a member of the regular air force. The whole aviation industry had been taken out of government control and placed under the aegis of the military to improve efficiency. Shumovsky was given the newly created rank of lieutenant colonel.[11] He was now receiving intelligence on aircraft developments rather than sourcing it. As the Soviet Union moved onto a war footing, Shumovsky had stepped into a vital role. His new job combined two functions. First, he was responsible for overseeing improvements in the quality and capacity of production by introducing the American techniques and technology that he had spent the last several years acquiring. In 1939 NKAP employed 272,000 workers in 86 factories, manufacturing components and assembling aircraft. Production that year had shifted to focus almost exclusively on combat planes, and in particular on important new models of fighters and ground-attack planes not bombers. Despite expert opinion, none of the Spanish Republican stronghold cities, such as Barcelona and Madrid, had surrendered during the Spanish Civil War because of the intense air raids conducted by Hitler's Condor Legion. Whereas the British and Americans would remain wedded to the strategic bomber, the Soviets changed their aviation strategy in the light of the experience in Spain to focus on developing a tactical air force capability. There was a rush to refit the air force with faster fighters and tactical bombers, although the work would still be incomplete by 1941 when the Germans attacked. Together with Dmitry Golyaev, an engineer and leading aircraft production specialist, Shumovsky oversaw the reconstruction and refitting of every existing factory with the latest equipment. This was a monumental task, for at the same time several large new enterprises were put into operation. In 1939 the industry had seventeen aircraft assembly plants; by 1940 there were twenty-one and by June 1941 the number had reached twenty-four. Fifteen of these factories turned out fighters and nine produced bombers. Both in an effort to spread economic activity evenly around the USSR and also to locate strategic industries away from the country's frontiers, many of these factories were built in the east.

Manufacturers of aircraft engine parts and metal rolling plants enjoyed similar rates of growth. By the beginning of the war, the aviation industry included in its roster more than 100 enterprises employing 466,000 workers. Furthermore, a strategic decision was taken to simplify production by concentrating from the second half of 1940 on the manufacture of only a few models of the best new types of combat aircraft. The fighters chosen were the Yak-1, MiG-3 and LaGG-3 (in the Soviet Union, fighters have an odd-numbered designation while all other aircraft are even). The Pe-2 was the dive bomber of choice and the Il-2 the ground attack aircraft. The transport aircraft was the Li-2, the Douglas DC-3 derivative. While the Sb-2 and Tu-2 bombers were put into mass production, the emphasis on strategic bombing was scaled back.

The result of these decisions was that the aircraft industry of the USSR had a strategic superiority in military aviation production over Germany and its allies. By June 1941 the USSR was producing over fifty aircraft a day, more than Germany and its allies. In all, during the war, the reforms ensured that 142,775 aircraft were delivered to the front lines, of which 118,140 were combat aircraft.[12] By early 1945, the Soviet air force would be eight times the size of the Luftwaffe.

The contribution of the technical committee to this monumental task was immense. The Douglas methods of design and production were introduced across the industry, creating uniformity, simplicity and quality by means of moulding, pressing, the use of profiles and mechanisation. As Douglas himself had predicted, the side that could produce the most would win, and that was the Soviet Union. Douglas would be reminded in 1945 of his prediction and quip, 'here's proof that free men can out-produce slaves.'[13]

The second element of Shumovsky's job was the supervision of new technology, which included research into new means of propulsion. The ambition was to fly faster and higher than a propeller-driven plane would allow. As well as jet engines Shumovsky became involved in the early days of what would become the landmark Soviet space programme. Following the successful ground testing in the summer of 1939 of the RP-318, the prototype rocket plane bearing the name of its designer Sergey Korolyov, a request to fly the craft was made. A committee of the Technical Department of NKAP was appointed to examine the feasibility of the plan based on the test results, with Shumovsky as its deputy chair. The committee gave its approval and the early manned rocket plane flights proved a success.

For Korolyov this was a godsend. From a tough jail where he was serving a sentence for wrecking, he was transferred to Tupolev's stimulating sharashka. He dedicated his undoubted talent to aircraft design, helping with the design of the Tu-2 and Pe-2 bombers as well as inventing the innovative rocket armament for its ground-attack aircraft. After the war, Korolyov would achieve worldwide fame by becoming the father of the Soviet space programme. He was responsible for putting both the first satellite, Sputnik, and the first man into space. Nor would 1939 see Shumovsky's last involvement in the space programme.

• • •

In 1939 Joseph Stalin followed Adolf Hitler, the recipient of the title a year earlier, in being named *Time* magazine's Man of the Year. The treaty which won him the award, the Nazi–Soviet Pact, would prove a deal with the devil and a devastating blow to the

Soviet espionage network in the US. Stalin bought time for the Soviet Union to prepare for war, but as a direct result of his manoeuvrings many of Shumovsky's old contacts in America were put on ice, and others, dismayed by the turn of events, lost for ever.

For 1939 was a year of tectonic change in the political make-up of Europe. As war clouds darkened, Stalin pulled off two masterful coups and suffered one public relations disaster. He spent frustrating months trying to revive the old Great War Entente to form a grand anti-Nazi alliance with Great Britain and France, but grew frustrated at the snail's pace of negotiations. Through its espionage efforts, the USSR had a better appreciation of the potency of the Nazi military threat than the British and French. The Anglo-French team believed they had the military power to defeat Germany without an ally like Stalin. By sending an underpowered negotiating team to Moscow they failed to engage with the Russians, giving every indication to the Kremlin that they were acting without seriousness or urgency. Within a day of the collapse of the talks in Moscow, a Soviet delegation was in Berlin.

Stalin's western coup was the Molotov–Ribbentrop Pact, signed in Moscow on 23 August 1939. The treaty included a secret protocol that divided the territories of Poland, Lithuania, Latvia, Estonia, Finland and Romania into German and Soviet 'spheres of influence' anticipating 'territorial and political rearrangements' of those countries.

As the democracies failed time and again to stand up to him, Hitler had long proved to be one of the best recruitment sergeants for Soviet espionage in the US. Later analysis of agent recruits shows they were generally motivated by a combination of factors, broadly money, ideology, blackmail or ego. The most prized recruits were those driven solely by ideology. Most despised those selling

317

their secrets. Shumovsky proved adept at exploiting recruits' concerns about the Nazis' anti-Semitic policies and territorial grabs, fears which drove many hundreds of recruits into the arms of Soviet intelligence. As his agent Ben Smilg later argued at his court martial, he could see nothing wrong with working with a foreign power to support a greater cause, one that his own government would not get behind. Indeed there were some extraordinary walk-ins at the Soviet consulates and embassy in this period, when packages of classified documents were dropped off anonymously.

Unsurprisingly, a high proportion of the active agents of Soviet intelligence at this time in the US were of Jewish origin. Some recruits wanted recognition for their discoveries or financing for a project; some needed help with medical bills or other expenses. Others just sold secrets for gain. If agents proved reluctant to continue, generally a little coercion would work as a spur. Shumovsky had to shout at one of Gutzeit's failures, Boris Morros, who had claimed to be a major player in Hollywood but was nothing of the sort.

Stalin delivered his second coup of the year in the Far East. As he had predicted after the Japanese occupation of Manchuria in 1931, Japan had now turned its military interests to the Soviet territories bordering the region. The first major Soviet–Japanese border incident, the Battle of Lake Khasan, occurred in 1938. After that, there were frequent clashes between Japanese and Soviet forces along the Manchurian border. But in 1939, the decisive engagements of this undeclared border, the battles of Khalkhyn Gol, resulted in the complete defeat of the Japanese 6th Army. Following this crushing victory, the combatants would remain at peace until August 1945, when the Soviet Union declared war on Japan and invaded Manchukuo.

• • •

In the West, Stalin was trying to improve his country's security; after Germany invaded Poland on 1 September 1939, he had ordered an invasion of Poland on 17 September to protect Soviet interests. But his primary concern was the protection of Leningrad, which was only twenty miles from the Finnish border. It was the Soviet attempt to redefine the border with Finland that would cause the biggest problems, both for the USSR and for Shumovsky. Finland refused to concede territory voluntarily, and so the USSR invaded the country on 30 November 1939, beginning the Winter War. After the League of Nations deemed the attack illegal and expelled the Soviet Union on 14 December 1939, events took a turn for the worse, bringing Stalin to the brink of war with Britain and France, who sided with the Finns. Soviet losses were heavy, and the country's international reputation suffered. America was horrified by the strong bullying the weak; and none more so than the Soviet volunteer agent network.

In this short war, the Soviets committed vastly more soldiers than the Finns, thirty times as many aircraft and a hundred times as many tanks. Yet in the early months, Finland repelled the massed frontal attacks much longer than the Soviets had expected.

With a renewed Soviet offensive, the Red Army finally overcame Finnish defences, after which Finland agreed to cede more territory than originally demanded by the Soviet Union in 1939. The end of the war cancelled a Franco-British plan to send troops to Finland through northern Scandinavia. But Stalin was furious with the initial results of the campaign. The vaunted Red Army, and by extension Stalin himself, had been humiliated.

Its poor performance against Finland's small armed forces had encouraged the German generals to advise Hitler to attack the Soviet Union and reconfirmed the negative Western opinion of the Soviet army.

Colonel Faymonville, the US military attaché in Moscow, was a shrewder judge. One of the few Westerners who noted that the Soviets, expecting a quick and easy victory against Finland, had initially relied upon hastily called-up reserve divisions ill-equipped for winter fighting, he pointed out that the dramatic Soviet victory against the vastly experienced Japanese army at Nomonhan just a few months before, a conflict that had gone virtually unnoticed in the West, was a better reflection of how the Soviets would fight.

On 20 December 1939, led by former President Herbert Hoover, who was chairman of the Finland Committee, and New York Mayor Fiorello La Guardia, a great sympathy rally for the people of Finland was arranged in Madison Square Garden, New York City. Hoover pushed for the recall of the US ambassador from Moscow. Under pressure, Roosevelt extended 'moral sanctions' to the Soviet Union. This voluntary code to stop the export of aircraft and associated aviation materials to countries who bombed civilians was a crippling blow. The Soviet Union was critically short of the aluminium alloys needed to make aircraft and other metals to make armour plate. Worse than the ineffective moral sanction was the disillusionment of many intelligence agents on the ground. Many had joined the Soviet networks seeing them as part of a grand anti-Nazi movement. Stalin's political machinations created much anger and confusion.

• • •

On his return to the USSR, Shumovsky had expected to be working on a stream of intelligence from his contacts in the US and purchases by AMTORG. But in his absence the connections were lost. Instead of getting information from America, however, his division received an unexpected bonus in the form of virtually unlimited access to Germany's aircraft and component factories. After the Nazis came to power, the USA and to an extent France had replaced the Germans as the USSR's main trade partners, at least where the aircraft industry was concerned. But some ties with Germany in the aviation sphere remained intact. The aircraft engine designer Alexander Mikulin and several TsAGI and Air Forces Academy aerodynamics specialists visited Germany in 1936 and 1937. German military aircraft were brought from the battlefields of the Spanish Civil War for testing, although most were so severely damaged that they had to be examined on the ground. A few were restored, test flown and filmed in simulated air combat with Soviet fighters.

The results of the tests, in which the Soviet aircraft bested the German planes, gave the Russians some hope. It proved false. Analysis showed many design advantages in construction and equipment on German aircraft, such as self-sealing fuel tanks, oxygen equipment and crew intercom. The issue was that German aircraft tested in the USSR were outdated. New Luftwaffe aircraft, such as the improved Bf 109E powered by a Daimler-Benz DB 601 engine and the Ju 88 high-speed bomber, had appeared in Spanish skies in 1938. Disastrous combat experience against the new aircraft demonstrated that Germany enjoyed clear superiority over Soviet aircraft. Panic ensued.

Fearing an early war with Germany, and taking every possible step to delay it, Stalin now banked on German know-how to equip the Red Army. The official signing of an economic agreement between the two countries in 1940 was a formality as a new phase of military and economic cooperation had begun immediately after the signing of the Molotov–Ribbentrop non-aggression pact. The Defence Commissariat quickly compiled a preliminary list of German military equipment they hoped to buy for examination. The section on aviation was a long one. The plan was to acquire several examples of each type of aircraft and engine, the total sum allocated for the purchase of German equipment being an astronomical 1 billion German marks.

If the Germans agreed to the sales, it was Shumovsky who would allocate this extraordinary treasure trove. He joined I. F. Tevosyan, a member of the Central Committee and leader of the commission that went to Germany in October 1939 to study the German aircraft industry and select purchases. They were accompanied by factory managers, military specialists, employees of scientific research institutes, and aircraft designers including Nikolay Polikarpov and Alexander Yakovlev. The German Air Ministry showed the Soviet specialists the majority of its aircraft industry. In just over a month, the members travelled all around the country, visiting the key factories.

Just as the Germans hoped, the Soviet aircraft engineers left their trip highly impressed – and misled – by what they had seen. During a 27 December 1939 conference of the Technical Council of the People's Commissariat of the Aviation Industry at Stalin's dacha, Polikarpov said: 'the German aircraft industry had taken a big step forward and emerged in first place in the world.'[14] It was not only the high quality of the German aircraft but rates of production that worried Soviet leaders. They believed the German factories could produce between 2,500 and 3,000 aircraft a month, three times the Soviet capability. In fact the figures were false and had been inflated; during the whole of 1940, the Germans only built 10,826 planes.[15]

Worse was to follow. The Soviet designer told Stalin that high production quality, labour management and top design offices, combined with the work of scientific aviation centres, were among the reasons why Germany had achieved superb results in developing its aircraft industry in such a short time. Yakovlev gushed to Stalin on their return that unlike the Soviet Union, research and development work in Germany was very well organised. German designers had plans that looked forward two years. He pointed out, to Shumovsky's embarrassment, that TsAGI had been asked to resolve and provide guidance on the perennial problem of radiator weight. In liquid-cooled engines radiators are used to control temperature but those in the Soviet aircraft were both too heavy and, thanks to their design, caused too much drag, preventing the production of true high-speed machines. Yakovlev widened his complaints, pointing out that every German designer had at his disposal wind tunnels, and every experimental plant designer had a strength and a vibration laboratory. They had seen that every designer tested aircraft parts, and the aircraft as a whole, in a testing shop at his plant. Above all the Russians were impressed with the exchange of experience between German designers. The work was organised in such a way that every factory built two or three types of designs. The Messerschmitt plant produced the Me 109 and also made wings for other firms' aircraft. This led to a natural exchange of know-how and results in the German aviation industry, rather than to the exposure of a factory that built the machine from start to finish to acts of sabotage or an air raid.[16]

In an extraordinary admission, Polikarpov explained to Stalin the fundamental problem with the Soviet system – that the designers 'work exclusively and there are no incentives for us to familiarize ourselves with what many other designers are doing'. This led to the situation where 'very often we have to decide issues already solved by others and run into mistakes from which other designers have already learned'.[17]

The commission had identified one key espionage target. German designers had 'special technical literature and periodicals. Several scientific journals publish all modern materials. In addition, they have remarkable books – reference books for designers. These are the most valuable works where you find solutions for a series of elementary things over which we rack our brains. We do not have this, which is sad . . .'[18]

Based upon the recommendations of the delegation, an order for German aircraft and equipment for detailed examination in the USSR was arranged through the Commissariat of Foreign Trade in early 1940. It included more than 100 items. What was actually delivered is unclear, but the amount must have been substantial as the Soviet government paid 25 million roubles for some of the equipment supplied by the summer of 1940.[19]

• • •

It was Shumovsky who decided where the German aircraft and other aviation equipment were brought for examination to the Air Forces Scientific Research Institute, Gromov's newly founded Flight Research Institute (LII), his own TsAGI laboratories. The engines were sent to TsIAM (Central Scientific Research Institute for Aircraft Engine Construction) next door. Many specialists came to Moscow to see the German aircraft first hand. Chertok, an engineer from Plant No. 293 in Khimki, later a missile and aerospace designer and one of S. P. Korolyov's closest assistants, provided his impressions:

We carried out the inspection of German equipment in groups, without any haste. I was most interested in the electrical equipment, piloting and navigational instruments, radios, bomb launchers, and the bomb sights. Our first-hand familiarisation with the German aircraft showed that the Soviet Air Force, although among the world's mightiest, was facing a crisis and taking a back seat to the German Luftwaffe.[20]

It seemed on the surface that Germany was being completely open with the Soviets. The leading Russian aviation specialists could examine examples of the Germans' primary combat machines, including aircraft that had only recently entered operational service with the Luftwaffe. But, beneath the mask of German friendliness and openness, there was a well-planned hidden idea to use German military might to misinform and intimidate their eastern neighbour. The Soviet specialists never got to know anything about the existence of experimental jet planes.

•   •   •

Soon after the trip Shumovsky took up a new job as deputy head of TsAGI and head of its Bureau of New Technology (BNT). 'Bolshoi' (big) TsAGI had opened in 1935 with expanded facilities, a brand new state-of-the-art facility at Zhukovsky – 'the Aero-city of the Soviet Union', named after the pioneer of Russian aviation – just outside Moscow. Even the American diplomats who holed themselves up in their embassy learned that TsAGI 'is the heart and soul of Russia's program for air development. It is rapidly being equipped with all the latest facilities for thorough research and experimentation, including wind tunnels, water channels, and engine development equipment. It is responsible for the giant planes produced in recent years.'[21]

TsAGI projects had ranged from prototype aircraft to aero-sleds and from torpedo boats to wind-generated electricity. The Institute's main direction had by now evolved to centre upon aerodynamic research. It had built its first large wind tunnel in 1925, replacing one built by Tupolev before the 1917 Revolution. Two further wind tunnels were completed in 1937, and by 1939 TsAGI had beaten Langley to become the proud owner of the largest wind tunnel in the world, providing the opportunity to study the behaviour of full-scale aircraft. In the following years, TsAGI would found leading aerospace research institutions and design centres such as the Institute of Aerospace Materials, the Institute of Avia Motors, the Tupolev Design Bureau and the Flight Research Institute.[22]

The Soviet Union now concentrated a great deal of its research and development for aviation in this one new city. The facilities at Shumovsky's expanded Bureau of New Technology included everything required to analyse the intelligence gathered on new foreign aircraft and test Soviet prototypes. The department gave the final go-ahead for any new Soviet planes to enter production, publishing to the factories and design bureaux confidential information on international developments in aircraft design. A monthly magazine detailing the latest discoveries was established. The bureau was the hub of the intelligence networks from which information flooded in from Europe, America and Japan. Surviving examples of its work show that downed enemy aircraft and others were dismantled and analysed in detail. Blueprints of every aircraft that fell into the department's hands were produced down to the minutest detail. TsAGI had its own cinema, which was able to show live testing of sample aircraft, often flown by Gromov or one of his team. Mock dogfights between Soviet and foreign aircraft were filmed at an airfield built nearby specifically for the purpose.

In comparison, the United States had no intelligence on its potential rivals. The US did not even know the names of the advanced Japanese planes that swooped out of the sky on Pearl Harbor. It was only in November 1942 that a unit would be established by the Navy to begin this work. The US Army and Navy refused to cooperate with each other and worked independently. Japanese planes were given US names such as the 'Betty bomber' after a buxom nurse who somewhat resembled the shape of the aircraft.

The Zhukovsky site included a model factory that was responsible for producing prototypes of every new Soviet aircraft. With the best imported equipment and a motivated workforce, prototypes were put through their paces before mass production. The secret factory matched the quality of any in the world. Sadly this was not true of the many facilities tasked with the mass production of components and assembly. It was found that the performance of a prototype would dramatically exceed that of the production model. In some cases, the top speed in service of a final production model proved to be substantially below that of the prototype; in one case the rate of climb of a production fighter was less than half that of the prototype. Worse, many models rolling off the production line were death traps.

Stalin placed a high value on the safety of his pilots and demanded to know who was responsible for the many accidents in his growing air force. The man selected for the task was Shumovsky. It was a thankless job. Often the cause of crashes was pilot error; the air force had many inexperienced pilots, unfamiliar with flying powerful machines in challenging weather conditions. However, on a significant number of occasions a component would fail, leading to a fatal accident. Shumovsky and his team had to investigate each crash site in an attempt to identify the cause of the accident and the factor responsible for the failure of the plane. Passing on the news was politically dangerous, and surviving documents show that the circulation of Shumovsky's conclusions was suppressed.[23]

* * *

In the US, Ovakimian was having a tough time. With Shumovsky's departure he had lost his most experienced deputy. In his place, he had three new but green recruits. An audit of his *Rezidentura* revealed that fifteen employees were employed there full time, but only two of them had more than two years' operational experience. For a group operating in America, finding Russians who spoke English proficiently was a major issue. Only Ovakimian and the three recent MIT graduates were rated good; seven were satisfactory, three poor and one spoke no English at all. Aviation intelligence gathering stopped as he had no one to step into BLÉRIOT's shoes.

So the MIT boys were rushed into duty. Semyonov showed the most promise and spent his summer vacation of 1939 recruiting at the Soviet Pavilion at the New York World's Fair.[24] He worked alongside Morris Cohen, who with his wife was later heavily involved in Operation ENORMOZ. The 1939–40 World's Fair covered the 1,216 acres of Flushing Meadows-Corona Park. The Soviet Pavilion was awarded the overall Grand Prize for its life-size copy of the interior of the Moscow metro's showcase Mayakovskaya station.*

For his work at the fair Semyonov was criticised for being 'garrulous', but such was the need that he was handling agents by the autumn. He was allocated two agents on the West Coast and two on the East, among them the long-term source EMULSION, one of several Soviet agents who worked as scientists at Eastman Kodak. It was an extraordinary vacation for an MIT student. It is not clear if Semyonov knew that the company's founder had paid for the establishment of MIT.

• • •

The pressure of work and exhaustion, meanwhile, was making Ovakimian careless. In April 1941 he detected a persistent tail. Reporting to Moscow that he was under close surveillance, he was instructed to prepare to leave for the USSR.[25] On the day of his departure in May, he was arrested by the FBI, having been observed meeting his source OCTANE. He had been

---

* Semyonov might have met the future atomic spy Ted Hall at the fair. Hall decided to become a source for the USSR after visiting the Russian stand as a boy.

betrayed. He was placed in handcuffs and awaited his fate in jail.

Back at the AMTORG office a plan was quickly created to destroy all paperwork relating to espionage. A message was sent to Ovakimian to admit nothing that the FBI did not already know and hang on as the Soviets would get him out.[26] He was released after the German invasion of the USSR. It was not, however, the end of GENNADY's career. On his return to Moscow he would become global head of S&T; his primary target was America.

12

PROJECT 'AIR'

The last day of peace for the Soviet Union ahead of the devastating Nazi onslaught was Saturday, 21 June 1941. It was a beautiful summer's day of clear blue skies. The young flocked to the parks to celebrate their graduation from high school and a few weeks' vacation before most headed to the armed forces or the factories. The increased military draft was planned to put five million soldiers in uniform by the end of the year. Despite the 1939 treaty with the Nazis, the Red Army's strength was growing fast. Stalin rightly did not trust Hitler. Regardless of his suspicion, under the terms of their agreement the last train delivering raw materials to Germany departed the Soviet Union that evening as Stalin honoured his side of the deal. Many of the army's principal officers and pilots were absent from their posts on leave.

On the eve of the German invasion in June 1941, stationed in uncomfortable proximity to their new frontier in former Poland were over a million raw Red Army soldiers, and behind them thousands of aircraft parked neatly in rows on new airfields. But the German attack came at least a year before the USSR was ready. Even after a decade of preparation, front-line military equipment still required updating. Soviet factories were busy producing modern replacements for obsolete tanks, guns and planes, but much work was still needed. The army and air force was still being trained, experienced officers were in short supply and there was a chronic shortage of communication equipment. Further complication was that the military had moved several hundreds of miles from previously well-prepared positions to unprepared defences much further forward in former Polish territory. In the initial days of the attack, the cohesion of the Red Army came apart and defeat stared Russia in the face.

Facing the Red Army across the frontier in similar numbers was the most powerful military force in Europe. The German army was at the peak of confidence, having cut a bloody swathe across the continent in lightning strikes. So far they had suffered minimal casualties along the way. Germany had defeated France, on paper its most powerful opponent, in just six weeks. The Germans had developed a tactic of mass encirclement that they hoped would lead to the rapid destruction of the Red Army and its air force. They aimed to trap the bulk of their new opponent's forces close to the frontier and quickly destroy all resistance. Operation Barbarossa, the codename for the German offensive, was expected to last a few weeks, at most three months. If all went as expected, the plan was to demobilise much of the German armed forces by Christmas. Believing Russia had neither the will nor the capacity to resist, the Germans initially deployed no more force than they had against France the previous summer.

After defeating the Russian military, the next stage of the Nazi plan was to dismember the Soviet Union. The rich, industrialised west, as far as the Urals, would be cleared of its entire Slavic population and resettled with Germanic people. The existing inhabitants would either be deported to the east to starve or worked to death as slaves. It was a plan for extermination. From its very beginning, the war on the Eastern Front was far more terrible than a clash of ideologies; it was a war to determine the survival or total annihilation of the Russian people.

Few plans in war, however, survive much beyond the first contact with the enemy. The Germans had underestimated the Soviet Union's industrial development in the last decade. As they advanced, they occupied what seemed to Hitler to be a country of giant abandoned armaments factories. The war dragged on for weeks and then months, with no slackening in Red Army resistance. New types of tanks and aircraft appeared on the battlefield or in the sky that in performance were the equal of or superior to the German models. A single T-34 tank with a Trashutin-designed engine, arriving on the battlefield for the first time, crushed an anti-tank gun, knocked out two German Panzers and left a nine-mile swathe of destruction in its wake before the Germans were able to finally destroy it. The appearance of even one T-34 terrified the German infantry, who had nothing in their armoury to stop it. Despite massive, catastrophic losses in men and equipment in the first few weeks of the war, the Soviet Union was able to mobilise new armies, equip them and stubbornly fight on. As the Germans advanced, the toll on front-line Wehrmacht troops continually mounted. Cities such as Leningrad and Odessa resisted sieges for weeks and months, tying down Wehrmacht soldiers in the rear. It started to dawn on the Germans that they had begun a war of attrition against an enemy with vastly greater manpower resources and industrial capacity. The further the Germans advanced, chasing the illusion of a victory, the more certain became their eventual defeat.

'Ivan Diesel'

The Soviet Union had an evacuation plan for its key armaments industries, and this was executed without a hitch as the
German armies advanced into Russia. Equipment and workers
were moved from west to east, out of range of German bombers.
Some 1,523 large factories were uprooted and put back into
production by the end of 1941. One of those was the giant
Kharkov tank factory, whose engine department was run by MIT
graduate Ivan 'Diesel' Trashutin. His and his workers' destination
in the evacuation was Chelyabinsk, east of the Urals, a plant built
on the best American principles of mass production. Trashutin
had personally supervised the manufacture of its initial equipment
in the United States during his vacations from MIT. As planned,
the new plant's 24,000 workers absorbed a further 16,000 skilled

evacuees from the Kharkov and Leningrad tank factories and swiftly ramped up output. In this war of production, Trashutin used his American education and manufacturing equipment to build more and better tank engines than the Germans. He powered the Soviet juggernaut as it advanced ever forward from the gates of Moscow to victory in Berlin.[1]

Tankograd, 1942

• • •

Like all Muscovites, Shumovsky and his family heard his friend Molotov announce news of the German invasion over the public loudspeaker system. The crowds were stunned and silent. Chaos and confusion reigned during the next few weeks of the war. TsAGI had accumulated a mass of data on the combat performance and vulnerabilities of German aircraft, but the VVS was initially in no position to make use of it. Against the greater experience of the Germans in combat their tactics were ineffective. Given this lack of know-how, Shumovsky and his team were mobilised for the war effort. On 17 September 1941, Stalin was informed that 'The Bureau of New Technology under TsAGI (the head of which is Shumovsky) is engaged in the study of enemy aircraft. The Bureau has special brigades that, on instructions from the People's Commissar, leave for the crash site and investigate the design of enemy aircraft and issue reports to our designers.'[2]

Such work would involve travelling close to the front, at times under enemy fire, in order to acquire as much information as possible from downed enemy planes. Shumovsky received his first decoration for this work. The intelligence was published in *Express Information*, a TsAGI publication recording in the finest detail every development in German aviation recovered from downed aircraft. Captured examples of planes that were still airworthy were test flown and the performance data recorded. The Bureau highlighted significant innovations with technical drawings. As quickly as possible the team sent out all the information to the design bureaux and the air force. The work was later expanded to include Allied aircraft that came into Soviet hands, as well as all open and some secret intelligence from the UK and US.

Shumovsky's other role was to continue his work to eliminate the design and manufacturing problems with new Soviet planes exposed by combat. On 29 September 1941, he wrote a letter accompanied by a report on 'the elimination of some deficiencies in the design of the LaGG-3, identified in the investigation of accidents and the destruction of riveted seams in the Pe-2'.[3] Both the fighter and the light bomber had just come into production. Work continued up to the last minute even as the battle for Smolensk – a city termed 'the gateway to Moscow' – ended in late September 1941. Following the fall of Smolensk, just 250 miles from the capital, the German army followed Napoleon's route to Moscow, even crossing the battlefield of Borodino. It was only a matter of days before the authorities gave the order to evacuate TsAGI.

But surrender was never on Stalin's agenda. On 7 November 1941, while the Germans edged forward through the mud towards Moscow, he staged as an act of defiance the traditional Red Square military parade. Moscow was now under martial law. Frozen Muscovites read daily of the great battles as the Red Army tried everything to block the advance. The rains that had slowed the German armoured columns in seas of mud had stopped, and the winter freeze started early that year. The tanks had picked up their pace. German air raids on Moscow left the streets deserted as soon as dusk fell. Intrepid souls spent their nights on the rooftops ready to deal with the incendiary bombs that were the Luftwaffe's primary weapon. The city was well defended from air attack with searchlights, barrage balloons and massed batteries of anti-aircraft guns. Squadrons of factory-fresh Soviet fighters dominated the skies during the day, ensuring each Luftwaffe visit was a painful exercise for the Germans. In the general population, a sense of fatalism was commonplace and soon many abandoned even heading to air raid shelters when the alert sounded. Thousands of noncombatants had been mobilised to build three giant lines of earthworks as the last defence line. Meanwhile, the city emptied as essential workers and the foreign embassies were evacuated. Stalin stayed in Moscow.

• • •

Since the start of the war there had been rounds of meetings in the Kremlin lasting almost all day and night as a solution was sought to the problem of getting more tanks and planes to the front. Despite the loss of some factories, armaments production overall had increased as planned. The aviation and tank factories had been saved by moving them to the east, but now the Soviet Union was using up its stockpiles of essential raw materials at an alarming rate. There would soon be no more aluminium alloys left to make new aircraft or molybdenum for armour plate. New supplies were needed, and quickly. The British were the first to offer help, and then the Americans lifted the moral embargo on selling war materials to Russia imposed after the bombing of Helsinki in November 1939. The system was 'take and pay', and so the Soviet Union, having no cash, had to use gold and other minerals to buy planes and aluminium. Under the terms of the US Neutrality Act, the Russians had to pay in advance for their purchases and arrange delivery in their own ships.

In July 1941, using the funds released from their frozen American bank accounts, the Russians bought a few badly needed fighter planes. Next, in early September 1941 the crew of the 1937 transpolar flight were among the first Russians sent into the Oval Office to ask President Roosevelt for help. Major General Mikhail Gromov, following the Russian tradition of never visiting without a gift, and knowing that FDR was a collector, had brought the President a rare postage stamp.[4] In return, he had a favour to ask. He had arrived with a delegation on board two flying boats to test fly all the best American military aircraft, having been promised before setting out on the hazardous journey from Moscow that they could buy the best

America had to offer, the Boeing B-17 Flying Fortress and Lockheed's twin-engined fighter the Lightning.

In an account of his second trip to America, Gromov described his pivotal meeting with the President. In reply to Roosevelt's questions about his journey, he gave his impressions about the stunningly lax levels of security at the unprotected US military bases he had visited. He had been surprised to meet Japanese and German nationals working at the facilities. There were no anti-aircraft guns in position, or signs of enhanced security.

FDR spared plenty of time for the Russians, greeting them like old friends. He was sympathetic to the Soviets' plight and agreed to supply any aircraft they wanted – except those they had been promised. The B-17 was endowed with top secret equipment, namely the Norden bomb sight. Although it was an open secret that the Germans had already acquired the Norden in 1938, the President explained that Congress had forbidden the sale, insisting that the expensive bomb sight must not fall into enemy hands. Based on information from Smilg, Shumovsky had already reported the tightening of security that followed the Norden theft. Gromov had heard the same story throughout his meetings in Washington. He returned angrily to the Soviet Union in November without being able to order either the strategic bomber or the modern fighter he had been promised.[5]

After these twin failures, another approach was needed. On 1 October FDR's special ambassador, Averell Harriman, met with Stalin in Moscow and gave fresh, extravagant assurances of the aid that the Soviet Union could now expect from the United States. The credit financing known as Lend Lease began in mid-October 1941; it lasted until the end of the war. The Soviet

Union would be able to buy on credit whatever they needed to continue the fight.

During the course of the war, the Soviet Union was to suffer over twenty-five million casualties. The US advanced it just under $11 billion in credit, in comparison to the $31 billion sent to Great Britain. Seventeen and a half million tons of supplies were shipped to Russia – including, of vital importance to winning the war, the raw materials to manufacture planes and aviation fuel.

To manage the process, the Soviets turned to those with most experience in dealing with Americans, the MIT alumni. One senior member of the Soviet Purchasing Commission sent to the US in late 1941 was the now Colonel Stanislav Shumovsky.[6] Under the provisions of Lend Lease, Shumovsky's commission bought over 13,000 American-built military aircraft. Of those eventually delivered to the Soviet Union, 4,746 were of just one type, the Bell P-39 Airacobra fighter.

· · ·

Conditions in Moscow were deteriorating fast. In four short months of the war, civil society to the west of the capital had virtually collapsed under the pressure of the German attack. The economy had ceased to function. Regular supplies of food to the city had stopped – as, with winter approaching, had fuel supplies. The invader had conquered a vast swathe of the country including much of the productive agricultural land. An estimated sixteen million refugees displaced from their homes were fleeing east. The massive plan to relocate factories and key workers out of harm's way to the east was in full swing, monopolising the railways. Otherwise, supplies to the armed forces took precedence.

In Moscow, the search for food and fuel occupied the majority of daylight hours, while the nights were sleepless with the incessant crash of exploding bombs and answering anti-aircraft fire. Eventually, in October 1941, TsAGI was evacuated to far-off Kazan, some 500 miles east of Moscow, to continue its work.[7] The evacuees, taking a few possessions, left the city by a slow train and then travelled by boat down the Volga to Tatarstan. Shumovsky's family was evacuated with them, although he himself did not travel on what was termed the 'science train', after the profession of its passengers. He had other orders.

Unsure what the future held, Stan bid tense farewells to his family, including his eleven-year-old son, at Moscow railway station. Much as he might want to, Colonel Shumovsky was too old at the age of forty to return to active military service, even if his earlier crash-related injuries had allowed him to do so. Instead it had been his old friend Gaik Ovakimian, now head of global S&T for Soviet intelligence, who suggested on 15 October that Stan must be sent back to America for further espionage work.

With his family safely departed, Shumovsky left the blacked-out capital city, ready to abandon science once again to return to the invisible front in the service of the motherland. He was about to embark on a long and potentially highly dangerous journey back to the United States.

As a former official of the Air Ministry (People's Commissariat), with a thorough understanding of aircraft mass production as well as being the Soviet expert on American planes and their manufacturers, Shumovsky was essential to the success of the Purchasing Commission. He spoke English like an American, knew the key players and got business done. He was to help organise American support for the Soviet war effort in the air, selecting the type of aircraft and ensuring the timely and smooth delivery of the supplies necessary to keep the Red air force, the VVS, in the fight.

There was no one at AMTORG like Stan, with sufficient aviation expertise and understanding of Americans and American business to oil the wheels. Many of the Russians sent to the US in the early period of panic did not even speak English, let alone understand America. A culture clash had developed between the desperate Russians and American businessmen awash with orders they could not fulfil. Bureaucracy on both sides was causing delay and confusion. Aircraft ordered in America were arriving in Russia without propellers, machine guns or spares. Parts of the same order from America's West Coast factories would come to Vladivostok, while East Coast plants would ship to Murmansk, 8,000 miles away. It was well-intentioned chaos.

Stan had a second mission. Ovakimian wanted to revive and perhaps expand the BLÉRIOT espionage network that had dissipated with neglect since Shumovsky's return to the USSR two years previously. The Purchasing Commission role was his cover. The Commission was known by the appropriate NKVD codename STORE.[8] Ovakimian and the head of intelligence, Fitin, merged the existing S&T effort into STORE to create a vastly bigger intelligence-gathering machine operating in a dozen separate industries. Aviation, under Shumovsky's leadership, would be the largest line in terms of manpower, and the most successful regarding the material gathered. Stan was the brains, the architect. As a top scientist and expert on new technology, he could direct the sub-agents in the factories to the most vital secrets.[9]

Shumovsky's departure was delayed by a major German and

Finnish ground offensive aimed at capturing Murmansk and other nearby ports. The Axis plan was to cut the Soviet Union off from the outside world by controlling these key points. Only after fierce fighting was the attack beaten back so that he and his party were able to board a British cruiser, HMS *Kenya*, which was escorting a joint British and Russian convoy. The ships' destination was Kirkwall in the Orkney Islands of Scotland (although the convoy dispersed after passing Iceland). Honouring Churchill's promise, the British had recently begun running small convoys twice a month to Arkhangelsk, bringing their new and unlikely ally a trickle of much-needed weapons and armaments.[10]

The sea voyage to Scotland was long and fraught, taking the convoy around the entire coast of German-occupied Norway. The only route brought the slow-moving ships directly into the path of German air, submarine and surface forces, and the journey would later become the most dangerous convoy passage in the war. But these early convoys caught the Germans unprepared and Shumovsky's ship slipped through unscathed. In late November 1941, the convoy's primary battle was with the severe winter weather, including storms, fog and drift ice, in near constant darkness. Describing his return to the Soviet Union by the same cruiser that took Stan to Scotland, Gromov reported riding out sixty-foot waves in one storm.[11] When in the midst of a storm the cruiser hit a mine just off Iceland, his party was ordered to prepare to abandon ship for lifeboats. They all knew they would not survive long in a small boat in the freezing sea. Gromov described the experience as the most terrifying of his adventurous life. Luckily the damage was light, and the ship was able to continue its voyage. The fragile nature of life on the wartime convoys was revealed when Gromov watched in horror a British sailor washed overboard to his death by a massive wave. There was no attempt to turn back or start a search; the water was so cold the unfortunate man had no chance of survival.[12]

The first experimental convoys were small but very slow, sailing at only twelve knots. The journey to Scotland took two weeks. QP-3 included four Soviet ships for the return leg to Britain, joining the inbound convoy that had brought British tanks to be used in the counter-offensive around Moscow. Two of the Soviet ships had to turn back with mechanical difficulties, delaying some members of the Commission. After a week at sea, the convoy dispersed and the larger Navy escort vessels sailed off for other duties. The first stage of Stan's journey was over.

The German advance on Moscow stalled in the snow and ice on 2 December 1941, still fifteen miles short of its objective. Three days later, fifty-eight fresh battalions of Soviet troops launched a massive counter-offensive outside the gates of Moscow that cracked the German front apart, driving the invaders back hundreds of miles. Meanwhile a more challenging journey now awaited Shumovsky's party, across the bitter battlefield of the North Atlantic. Because the British team at Bletchley Park had broken the German naval codes earlier in the summer, the British Admiralty could use the intelligence gained to track the location of most U-boats and steer convoys away from them. But the threat of attack remained.

• • •

On 7 December the Japanese attacked Pearl Harbor; on 11 December, Hitler declared war on the USA, and U-boats were deployed to attack unprotected American shipping along the Atlantic coast. With their eyes fixed on the dramatic events in the Pacific, the US Navy had not introduced even the simplest defensive measures after war broke out. There were no organised convoys or escorts; even a coastal blackout for merchant ships had not been enforced. The vast number of easy targets was a magnet for the U-boats away from more challenging targets in the Atlantic convoys. One U-boat operated undisturbed in New York bay for weeks, sinking ships at will.

In Scotland, a large party of Russians prepared to board a small Atlantic convoy gathering in the Firth of Clyde to set sail for Halifax, Nova Scotia. Now that luxury liners no longer plied the route to New York at high speed, Halifax was the main Atlantic coast port where convoys destined for Britain assembled. Ports along the Clyde and their docks had suffered from extensive Luftwaffe attacks, the towns bearing the scars of regular bombing raids. While the docks still functioned, most of the nearby housing had been destroyed; over 500 civilian deaths had been incurred in one attack on Clydebank alone. The famous shipbuilding centre and others like it were the keys to Britain's survival. The U-boat blockade threatened to starve the country into defeat unless Britain built merchant ships more quickly than the Germans could sink them. The visiting Russians commented that Britain showed many visible signs of the two years of bomb attacks. A blackout was rigorously enforced. There were few men to be seen on the streets, and the number of mobilised women in uniform surprised the Russians.

Stan and his party were to sail in a two-vessel convoy with returning Canadian troops. They travelled on an old Norwegian liner SS *Bergensfjord*, which had been in New York when Norway was invaded and had since been converted to carry over a thousand soldiers.[13] For its return voyages to the New World the ship was near empty, sailing westward with a protective escort of just one British armed merchantman. The convoy's greatest security was the awful weather, which kept the U-boats at bay; because they travelled on the surface, German submarines avoided operating in the fierce Atlantic winter storms.

The journey was nothing like the luxury of his trip a decade previously on SS *Europa*. Instead of bright lights and entertainment, limitless food and drink, the *Bergensfjord* travelled in darkness with few comforts. The fear was of a sudden torpedo attack and if lucky an evacuation to the lifeboats. For the Norwegian crew, in exile from their occupied homeland, the second day out from port was Christmas Day, but for all on board there seemed little to celebrate. The grand alliance that would liberate their country was taking shape, but victory seemed as far away as ever. For the Russians, New Year was the great holiday, but that night the party had much to reflect on – their families left behind, the desperate life-and-death struggle across a thousand-mile front and the battles to come.

• • •

Shumovsky and the other Russians cleared US immigration in Halifax on 2 January 1942.[14] In the Purchasing Commission party heading to Washington with him were Colonel (later Major General) Sergey Piskunov, Ivan Kramarenko (the senior technical specialist), Valentin Bakhtin (an aviation instrumentation specialist) and Pyotr Belyaev (the armaments specialist). Piskunov was a much-decorated Civil War hero, a veteran of 'special operations', in other words the ruthless suppression of opponents. A tough, no-nonsense soldier, his role was to knock heads together. Belyaev was an aviation engineer and a long-term source for the BLÉRIOT network, working under the codename MIKHAILOV.[15] He had relevant experience in America, for while he had been employed as an inspector at Lockheed/Douglas, he talent-spotted the key recruit York (NEEDLE) as an agent. Like Shumovsky he was travelling to perform jobs for both the Purchasing Commission and the secret service.

The party was to travel to Washington by train from New York, which they found entirely unchanged by the war. The Broadway lights were still on, as bright as ever, and the city was a wall of noise. The Russians were disorientated by the hubbub of city life, the sounds of trucks and overland railways amplified by the tall buildings. The noise never stopped, day or night. But America's mood had changed since 1938, when Stan had last been there. The news and photos of the Pearl Harbor attack had created a desire for vengeance and a marked upsurge in patriotism. In response to the 2,400 deaths of American servicemen, the President had proposed to Congress the declaration of war on Japan. A nation previously divided over the issue of intervening in a foreign war swung united behind a policy of forcing unconditional surrender on its enemies. Hitler saved Congress the trouble of a debate by declaring war on America.

The Russians and the Americans were now – in theory – friends. But in the short term, America's arrival in the war was an added complication, making the arduous task of acquiring large numbers of aircraft for the Soviet Union near impossible. The country was mobilising and rearming. Every plane that came off the assembly line was needed for America's war in the Pacific and Western Europe. Great Britain was first in the queue for any surplus aircraft. The challenge for Stan's commission was how to gain anyone's attention to get aircraft for the Soviet Union.

There was time for a catch-up meeting in New York with old friend Semyon Semyonov, soon to be the new head of S&T, and Vasily Zarubin, codenamed MAXIM, the new chief of the New York *Rezidentura* following the arrest of Ovakimian.* Many Soviet citizens had been trapped in the US at the outbreak of hostilities and were desperate to return to the Soviet Union.[16] One experienced intelligence officer could not be persuaded to stay in the US and returned to lead a partisan group in occupied Soviet territory. Others seeking to get home on convoys tragically died with their whole families in German attacks. Everyone in the New York *Rezidentura* was desperate for news from home, especially about the counter-offensive at the gates of Moscow. Semyonov's home city, Odessa, had fallen to Axis forces after a long and bitter siege on 16 October 1941 and he was anxious for any news.

The New York *Rezidentura* team told Stan that conditions for espionage had worsened since his departure in early 1939. All operations on the XY line had been deactivated following the arrest of Ovakimian on 5 May 1941 and placed on hold for two months. Since then, as the Russians saw it, conditions of work on the XY line had become much more challenging. The US economy was finally enjoying an upswing with the 'Defense

---

* In 1941 the NKVD introduced a linear organisational structure. S&T was formally separated from political intelligence gathering. It is tempting to consider the NKVD as a highly structured and bureaucratic organisation, but at least in its early days it was not.

Boom'. Improved job security meant fewer recruits for the Soviets. The US had become the 'Arsenal of Democracy', selling arms to the Western Allies and China at the same time as it rearmed. Belatedly the Americans had become security conscious; there were more American intelligence and counter-intelligence operations aimed at foreign agents. FBI teams were camped outside AMTORG. At the time the FBI deployed about fifty agents on surveillance operations against suspected Russian spies in New York; they used methods that later proved effective against the Ku Klux Klan.[17]

With the signing of its pact with Germany in 1939, the Soviets had joined the top tier of foreign powers of extreme interest to the FBI. The outbreak of war in Europe had kick-started a 'spy-mania' which now gripped America's imagination. Stan learned that several of his long-term sources were refusing to cooperate. Ben Smilg would provide no information at all, although fortuitously he had not revealed to the authorities Harry Gold's clumsy attempt to blackmail him as he felt it would be 'detrimental to the whole Jewish race'.[18] Semyonov raged at Smilg's ingratitude, for without Soviet financial support in paying for his education Smilg would be working on the lingerie floor of a department store.[19] York had gone completely off the rails, causing much alarm when he disappeared from his home in 1940. He was now divorced, and his bitter ex-wife suggested he was spending money on his other women.[20] He had appeared at AMTORG to report that he had apparently been interviewed by US Naval Intelligence about his meetings with Stan. It was believed that as York had not been arrested, he should no longer be trusted. Shumovsky's programme of admitting engineers to MIT to carry out espionage had been all set to continue after his departure; on his advice, the Soviet deputy ambassador Andrey Gromyko, a future longest-serving foreign minister, and even head of state, had written personally to Karl Compton to request approval for a further intake of five students to MIT in September 1941.[21] The war forced a temporary postponement of the plan.*

As a telegram from Moscow made clear, Zarubin had one further delicate mission to fulfil. Moscow Centre had telegraphed ahead to say that BLÉRIOT was returning for a short business trip and something should be said to him in the course of a 'friendly conversation' about the dangers of dalliances with women. A sex scandal had rocked the New York *Rezidentura*. In breach of security arrangements, Yershov (GLAN) had begun an affair with an American and had got her pregnant. Moscow Centre wanted all their agents in the field to be on their best behaviour.[22]

. . .

The Soviet party's final destination was Washington, now a crowded city with its population doubling to one million during wartime as workers, mostly women, flocked to the city to take on new jobs in the expanding administration. Politics had overtaken business as the controlling force in America for the duration of the war; business had to perform its civic duty, and the government was now the major customer in town. With only one theatre showcasing touring companies, Washington

---

* In September 1943, the operation to place spies in US universities restarted when twenty-one female students enrolled at Columbia, including Zinaida V. Osipova. A spy herself, she married Alexander Feklisov, one of the major players in Operation ENORMOZ who was already based in New York.

lacked the attractions of New York. It was a quiet, low-rise city with little industry. The visiting Russians were puzzled that the city's excellent museums with expensively acquired art collections were nearly always empty while the cinemas were always packed.

The headquarters of the Purchasing Commission was 1610 Park Road, NW Washington, an address selected to keep its leadership close to the politicians. The first task of the arriving members was to sort out the problems encountered by the previous group and find a new way to unblock the supply log-jam. The angry Russians had met their match when dealing with Washington bureaucracy. They came from a system where if the leader ordered that aircraft should be delivered, it happened. Washington had ways and means of pouring sand into the machine, whatever the President might want. Few in Washington initially shared Roosevelt's belief that the Soviet Union could survive the Nazi onslaught for more than a few weeks or months. Many in the War Department believed America risked losing its secrets to its enemies or dissipating its resources on wasteful aid to an ally that was likely before long to surrender.

The Commission soon realised that to fulfil their mission the direct approach had to change. They were now in a town of influence peddling, compromises, back channels and deals over dinners. Out went the military uniforms, to be replaced with smart suits. Stan coached the career Soviet soldiers in the nuances of American manners and ways of doing business, informing them that America worked on a system of personal relationships and recommendations. General Belyaev, the overall head of the Commission, and Shumovsky spent their evenings swapping hunting stories with bureaucrats and jokes with politicians, finding this a far more effective way of getting business done than banging tables at angry meetings. The Commission leaders' charm offensive gradually secured allies in Congress and the administration. It was never going to be an easy task, but it would get easier once the Red Army became winners on the battlefield.

Initially, the pressure from Moscow was for planes, and any American planes would do. Some simply had to be delivered as a symbol that Russia was not fighting alone. The decision was taken to buy what could be delivered immediately. This turned out to be the ineffective Curtiss-Wright Kittyhawk, of which the US and Britain had a large surplus stock. The plane had been designed by a committee to be a multi-purpose aircraft and in combat was soon found not to be particularly good at anything. The main issues were its light armament and poor manoeuvrability. As the Soviets faced the renewed German spring and summer offensive into southern Russia in 1942, every available aircraft was desperately needed at the front.

The goal of the German offensive was to capture the Caucasus oilfields and knock Russia out of the war. Over the dinner tables of Washington, a different offensive was being fought to win a broad coalition of support to supply more and better planes. Many American armchair generals were quick to offer opinions that the Soviet Union was doomed. The frustration of these conversations and the resulting painfully slow progress contrasted with the action on the ground, where two of Russia's greatest cities – Leningrad and Stalingrad – were now under siege. One debate between two American army officers in front of a Russian diplomat demonstrated the ignorance of decision makers about events in Russia: 'When Byrd spoke about the urgent need for medicines given the scale of fighting by the

Red Army in Stalingrad, Colonel Pink said in a retort that our battles in the Solomon Islands are much greater than Stalingrad, and therefore we must first of all take care of our army.' Soviet casualties in the Battle of Stalingrad were 1,129,619, of whom 650,878 were sick or wounded; by comparison total Allied casualties in the Solomon Islands campaign amounted to 10,600 dead. Shumovsky explained to the team it was a long game. The Soviets needed to keep smiling and gradually build a coalition of personal relationships.

The decision was taken on Shumovsky's advice to concentrate future purchases with a few top aircraft manufacturers who had the proven capacity to deliver scores of planes on time, and to eliminate from the debate many small companies. The chosen manufacturers were Bell, Douglas, Curtiss-Wright and Republic. The Commission selected just a few models, deciding to stick wherever possible with those planes for the duration of the war. The Russians would work with the manufacturer to suggest improvements straight from the battlefield, based on combat experience. By concentrating on a few models the challenges presented by logistical supply and ground crew training would be minimised. Aircraft, especially in combat, wear out quickly and require frequent maintenance, and a plane could be rendered moribund if a missing spare part was thousands of miles away when suddenly required on the Eastern Front. There were also the peculiarities of the battle conditions of the Soviet Union – including the extreme cold – which demanded the making of adjustments to planes. Battlefield conditions in Russia were rough. The planes had to be robust. The Russians always found the planes supplied undergunned and underprotected, requiring much further work to modify them on arrival.

The most important changes were to the engines. The Soviet Union had very little high-octane fuel for thirsty aviation motors, and what fuel they did have tended to be dirtier than the American equivalent. Eventually, under Lend Lease the Allies would supply half of the Soviets' need, around 1.5 million tons of clean high-octane fuel.

The air war on the Eastern Front was itself of a different character from that fought in the skies over Western Europe. It was highly tactical, with dogfights at close range and low altitude. Fighters and dive bombers were deployed in support of attacking ground forces rather than acting independently as a strategic bombing force. The advantage in choosing the time and altitude of encounters lay with the attacking side. As the Red Army advanced, thousands of Il-2 Shturmovik ground attack aircraft were deployed as mobile artillery and tank busters. Fighters, including American-supplied Airacobras, were used in vast air armies to protect the ground attack aircraft. Luftwaffe fighters were forced to confront the Soviet air force at a time, place and height of the Russians' choosing in order to protect German troops under attack on the ground. The Soviet goal in combat was not to shoot down enemy fighters per se, but to frighten them off to allow the army and ground attack aircraft to do their work unmolested. Fast bombers attacked targets such as airfields, troop concentrations, and supplies in the enemies' rear. The result was to allow the VVS to achieve superiority in numbers and gain control, first in sectors, then eventually across the whole Eastern Front.

In the skies of Western Europe, the British and Americans were fighting a high-altitude war of round-the-clock strategic bombing, or saturation bombing of industrial towns. In the early days of the war in the East, the Russians found strategic bombing expensive and hence an ineffective use of scarce resources and pilots. The Soviet 1941 propaganda revenge raids on Berlin resulted in little but symbolic damage and high casualties in the crews and planes. Regarding numbers of planes downed, the Luftwaffe was matched and then destroyed on the Eastern Front from mid-1943 onwards. In the battles over the Kuban pocket, the VVS achieved decisive superiority in numbers and in the quality of its planes from late 1943, as the types of planes the Purchasing Commission had envisaged back in early 1942 were delivered in bulk.

To the Soviets, it seemed that the Americans had only committed to supplying Russia with scores of aircraft once it became convinced that victory was inevitable. When the Soviets needed aid, it had not been forthcoming. It was only after the crushing Soviet victory in February 1943 at Stalingrad that suddenly American fighters were being supplied in large numbers. Now, though, with hundreds of newly built planes being flown along the newly constructed air bridge from Alaska via Siberia to Moscow − a journey that took five days − the proportion of American fighters deployed on the front line by the Soviets reached 17 per cent by 1944, a very significant contribution.

To achieve this level of supply, the approach the Commission adopted was to integrate American aviation factories into their established delivery methods. Unlike other buyers of American aircraft, the Soviets were very closely involved during the production process. They insisted on having their own engineers on site in America to supervise every stage of construction. Planes had often failed to meet expectations on arrival and there were no facilities in Russia where faults could be remedied. The

American manufacturers appreciated that the Russians had to achieve an intimate understanding of the aircraft they were putting into combat. They were very welcoming to their Soviet guests – who were, after all, their best customers – and built close friendships.

The Russians in turn provided detailed feedback on the combat performance of the American planes. Several of the Soviet engineers posted to American factories had front-line experience or were test pilots with valuable knowledge to pass on. Learning the benefit of Stan's 1937 public relations exercise, the Russians sent aces from the battle front on extensive tours of American aircraft factories to thank the workers personally for their contribution to victory. It was a means of uniting pilot and factory worker in the struggle against Nazism. Russians insisted on the handover of the planes destined for the Eastern Front at the plant, so 'receiver engineers' were brought in their hundreds from Russia to work in US factories. In the process, these workers learned new skills and manufacturing methods that proved transferable to Soviet factories.

There were three main delivery routes for the planes from America to Russia. The first was the highly risky western route via the convoys across the Atlantic, then on to the Arctic. Losses of ships and their cargoes in the early years of the war were daunting. A second, safer route was built overland to the Caucasus from Iran. Eventually, the most efficient way proved to be the transpolar air bridge from Alaska to Siberia. A series of intermediate airfields were built across Siberia in 1942 and air transport divisions created to fly the planes from Fairbanks in Alaska to the front. A direct route ran from the factories of the US, located as they now were in virtually every state, to a new giant air force base in the remote north-west at Great Falls, Montana. Planes were either assembled at Great Falls or flown there before being loaded with supplies and dispatched on the journey to Fairbanks, and on to the heart of the USSR.

•   •   •

The prospects for Shumovsky's secret mission seemed in worse shape than his work with the Commission. As he discussed with his colleagues in New York, the environment for espionage since his departure in 1939 had toughened. With his aviation espionage network having withered through neglect, his initial efforts to rebuild were driven by extreme urgency. The NKVD's New York office had sent no reports on the state of US aviation for two years. Using the Purchasing Commission as cover, Shumovsky started gathering a vast amount of the technical information that had been so sorely missed. Within two months the flow of publications to Moscow had been re-established.[23] He began by supplying in bulk documents with the lowest level of classification, shipping over 700 confidential and secret items to Moscow by March 1942 via the People's Commissariat (Ministry) of Foreign Trade. These included the Army and Navy Air Force standards for aircraft.[24] By November he had shipped a further large tranche of secret reports, including the SAE (Society of Automotive Engineers) Standards Board specifications for all engineering tools used in aviation manufacture and 'all reports of the air forces on tests of planes, motors, assemblies, and ma-terials. The total of reports is over 600 for the period 1938–1942.' Shumovsky next promised to source all the missing NACA reports from 1938 to 1942. Additionally, he forwarded all the technical specifications he had received from US aircraft assemblers, component suppliers and machine tool makers. There were many advantages to being the third largest customer in town (after the US Army Air Force and the British Empire). Stan reported that between 1941 and 1942, of every one hundred planes built in America, fifteen were Lend-Leased, three sold to allies and eighty-two delivered to the US military. He was the spider at the centre of a vast information web. And the Soviets had one other advantage: Ray Bennett's old contact, Nathan Silvermaster, had gained a position at the US War Production Board and was telling the Russians exactly how many planes were manufactured each month and where they were going. The breadth of intelligence Moscow received on aircraft production was perhaps better even than that supplied to Roosevelt. As they were doing the bulk of the fighting and receiving little of the equipment, Russian resentment grew.

·   ·   ·

While Shumovsky was succeeding, his fellow MIT alumni Semyonov, Novikov and Yershov were finding excuses. Ovakimian, now head of global S&T in Moscow, was very unhappy. As the former head of the New York *Rezidentura* and an indefatigable worker, he knew what could be achieved. He wrote a stinging telegram to MAXIM, the current head of the *Rezidentura*, on 25 June 1942, sparing only Shumovsky from criticism:

Results on the tech. line are unsatisfactory. There should be 3 operatives working – TWAIN, GLAN, and LAUREL. GLAN and LAUREL don't do anything. TWAIN is not functioning at full capacity. Inadequate training and management of sources, departure of agents and decline in activity. For my part, I think that the most important aspects of this work should be transferring active probationers to illegal connections using such group handlers as GOOSE, BLACK et al., seeking out new candidates capable of providing us with materials on defence-related topics, and engaging in political education work with everyone – our comrades as well as probationers. CHARON does not understand his assignments, even though the XY is primary in his area. LINK is not working.[25]

The pressure for results was intense.

With the Americans belatedly becoming security conscious, the FBI had finally installed officers at each key factory, research facility and government office. Workers in sensitive industries were briefed about the dangers of espionage. Large new aircraft factories were even built without windows; there were security checkpoints, and ID was inspected. The Careless Talk campaign launched by the US War Department effectively linked Allied losses with 'loose lips'. In the face of such heightened security, Shumovsky adapted his methods. Arranging to have himself appointed a liaison officer to the USAAF, he was given a letter from the State Department demanding the bearer be given unimpeded access to all areas. The fox was in the hen house.

It was Hollywood and the US government who had unwittingly come to Stan's rescue once again. The administration had launched an effective propaganda campaign to rally support in America for their allies the Russians. In a series of films made by Frank Capra called *Why We Fight*, the episode entitled 'The Battle for Russia' was by far and away the strongest. Any potential political problems were sidestepped, and the word 'communism' was not mentioned. Instead, the film's focus was on the heroism of the ordinary Russian people in their life-and-death struggle with Nazism. The American audience was not spared footage of the victims of Nazi atrocities. In one striking scene, the narrator explained to the public that the burnt bodies on the screen were not animals but massacred Russian children slaughtered by the retreating Germans.

Joseph E. Davies, the former US ambassador to the Soviet Union, sold 700,000 copies of his book on his experiences in Moscow. It was later made by Warner Brothers into a strongly pro-Soviet film entitled *Mission to Moscow*. Fellow film studio RKO's 1943 *The North Star*, featuring top American stars in the role of partisans from a collective farm fighting off the Nazis, was nominated for six Oscars. MGM's 1944 romantic adventure *Song of Russia* was later heavily criticised by the House Un-American Activities Committee (HUAC) for its unrealistic portrayal of the Soviet Union. When a glossy edition of *Life* magazine focused on the sacrifices of the Russian people, Stalin kept a copy in his archive. Surprised to learn that Americans were putting an individual bay leaf in each of the millions of cans of pork exported to feed his armies, he asked the question in the margin 'is this true?' From 1941 onwards, Americans were bombarded with tales of the heroic Russian people's fight on behalf of everyone's freedom, which must be supported at all costs. The message was clear: if Russia goes under we will all be defeated.

• • •

On 29 July 1942, the NKVD in New York, responding to complaints, reported back to Moscow that since the start of the war in Europe, and especially after 7 December 1941 – when America actively joined the war – working conditions on the XY line had undergone a radical change. They noticed that 'feelings of patriotism have grown', which presented a problem not only when cultivating new candidates but when working with long-time agents as well.

A significant factor is a significant rise in activity among counter-intelligence and police agencies. The increase in the average American's vigilance as a result of propaganda in the press, film, and radio against the activities of foreign agents has to do with this same factor. Compared to how it was before the war, there has been a radical change in the methods of storing documents and working drawings. The procedure for gaining access to factories has become significantly more complicated, not only for foreigners but for Americans as well. Workers and managers who are offered jobs at defense plants are carefully vetted by the FBI and counter-intelligence agencies.

The means and opportunities for travel across the country have become significantly more complicated. Surveillance has increased so much that travel without official reasons to cities such as San Diego, Los Angeles, Norfolk, and so forth, is completely unthinkable. Even to go to Boston, Rochester, or Chicago, one must be on official business of some kind that can serve as an entirely logical reason for the trip. When buying a ticket to the West Coast, they write down the name and address, and the conductor does the same thing when he checks the ticket. It is practically impossible to get airplane tickets, especially on the day of the trip, and there is no question that all passengers are carefully checked.[26]

It had become clear that the Purchasing Commission was a better cover for S&T information gathering than AMTORG. Shumovsky had successfully adapted his methods to wartime conditions while others had not. His role as liaison officer with the USAAF allowed him access to all secure facilities, including NACA and the secret air force base at Wright Field. At some point in late 1942, he managed to secure himself a position at Wright Field, becoming more familiar with the goings-on than many Americans stationed there. Under the auspices of the Purchasing Commission, he installed a hand-picked qualified Russian engineer in each of the major aircraft factories supplying Russia as an information conduit and agent gatherer. At least two of these engineers, Raina (known as Shevchenko) at Bell and Belyaev at Douglas, were experienced spies. As supervisor in chief and in possession of the ultimate security pass, Shumovsky could travel anywhere with a driver supplied by the US government. He could even meet with his old agents. As the New York *Rezidentura* informed Moscow Centre, 'BLÉRIOT is meeting with LEVER [Benjamin Smilg] in an attempt to restore the friendly relations that had once existed between them. It is difficult to meet. However, b/c LEVER was drafted into the Armed Forces, and walks around in an officer's uniform.'[27]

Stan rose to the challenge, arranging to bump into Smilg 'by accident' at the air force base. According to Smilg, they met a half dozen times afterwards for dinners with his wife. Stan even attended Smilg's wedding at the airbase in full Soviet uniform. The general commanding the base at the time saw nothing untoward about a scientist working on top secret projects having as a friend a senior officer in the Red air force.[28] Stan also travelled further afield to the Lockheed and Douglas factories in California, informing Moscow of his plans at each step of the way. The purpose of the trip was to establish new channels of communication with the West Coast agents. In the future, American cut-out couriers from the illegal network would do the leg-work.

• • •

In addition to administrating $11 billion of purchases, the Commission was a cover for large-scale espionage activity. But the reach and success of the operation was placing a strain on resources. On 20 October 1943 Moscow Centre ordered a re-organisation 'to form 3 independent stations with centers in NY, Washington, and San Francisco, and one sub-station in LA under the authority of San Francisco. There should be a special assistant on XY in each station.'[29] It was quite a turnaround from the excuses for inactivity offered in July 1942. The scale of the organisation could be glimpsed in a report sent on that date to General Fitin, head of intelligence. It showed that at least twenty-two agents had been sent to America and become active across various branches of industry involved in Lend Lease. Each agent was a qualified engineer or specialist in his given field, able to perform alongside factory workers while acquiring information and identifying potential sources. Each arrived knowing a code phrase, which was normally a question, and had agreed on the answer to allow a controller to activate him.

The Purchasing Commission owed an enormous debt of gratitude to MIT, for the university had now trained two of its most senior managers. Ivan Eremin, one of Stan's former housemates from Boston had arrived with his family in February 1942 to become its deputy head and take charge of the Department of Heavy Industrial Equipment, working alongside Stan. 'Rosty' Rostarchuk, another housemate and now the deputy chairman of AMTORG, was transferred to Washington the same month. It was quite a reunion. Photographs show the Russians, dressed in sharp suits, with their charm to negotiate in English billions of dollars of business deals, with the skills acquired in Boston a decade before. The number of MIT alumni grew when the three spies Semyonov, Novikov and Yershov were transferred into the Commission to join Stan. They were appointed group leaders of agents operating under cover in factories.

On the aviation side, there were two priorities: Project 'AIR' aimed to discover the secrets of jet engines and 'RAINBOW' those of radar. Bell Aviation, the Soviets' primary supplier of fighter aircraft, was responsible for designing and secretly building America's first jet plane, the P-59 Airacomet, powered by twin General Electric versions of the advanced British Whittle engine manufactured in Syracuse. Assigned to work at Bell under the alias of Shevchenko, Stan's deputy Raina built up a network of sources in the aviation factories in Buffalo and nearby Syracuse.

When tested, the first American jet was a disappointment, its performance worse than a propeller-driven plane. One of Raina's sources, Professor Petroff, was head of aerodynamics at Curtiss-Wright, which was also designing jets; he informed the Russians in June 1943 that the British were having much greater success than the Americans:

> Professor PETROV told ARSENY (Raina) that the development of aircraft construction in the ISLAND [UK] in many [4 groups unrecovered] outstripped the COUNTRY [the US]. For this reason, a large group of the COUNTRY's aviation experts, including three from KEEL's [Petroff] firm, was sent to the ISLAND to study the experience.[30]

Ovakimian had transferred Yershov to London to establish a specialist S&T presence. The MIT connection was used to roll out globally the intelligence-gathering model that had worked so well in the US. Raina was taken to Wright Field in 1944 as a guest of Bell to witness a test flight of the top secret jet. Later he was offered the opportunity to purchase the jet planes from Bell just as the US government withdrew its funding for the project.

• • •

Even using cameras and microfilming the vast amount of material gathered was exhausting for the agents. A solution to the problem of shipping intelligence material to Russia finally arrived in November 1942 with the opening of the air bridge. At Great Falls, the planes heading to Russia were loaded with crates of diplomatic cargo. This was 'Super Lend Lease', a defector named Kravchenko was to tell HUAC in 1949.[31] The committee appeared particularly irritated that the Russians had been smuggling out America's pilfered secrets in US-supplied ships and planes. The defector described seeing

> Big books like this, approximately (indicating) which contained many pictures of the aviation industry, the special machines, special details, and so on. There were pictures and blueprints. Three large volumes in the Purchasing Commission Office. This material was signed by General Belyaev, Alexander Rostarchuk. I know General Belyaev took them when he flew to Moscow.[32]

The Russians also raided the US patent office. Russian officials were able to collect many industrial and military inventions simply by buying the patents, an activity carried out in plain sight. Among the patent reprints supplied to Russia, as listed by HUAC, were those for bomb sights, tanks, aircraft, ship controls, bomb-dropping devices, helicopters, minesweepers, ammunition and bullet-resisting armour.

At Gore Field in Great Falls could be found a self-appointed, one-man guardian of American interests. Major George Racey Jordan felt he could not stand idly by and watch the flood of secrets leave his country without doing something. He describes how

> Another 'diplomatic' cargo which arrived at Great Falls was a planeload of films. Colonel Stanislau Shumovsky, the Russian in charge, tried to prevent me from making an inspection by flaunting a letter from the State Department. I told him the letter did not apply to me. It was a letter authorising this Russian to visit any restricted plant and to make motion pictures of intricate machinery and manufacturing processes. I looked over a half dozen of the hundreds of cans of films. That one plane carried a tremendous amount of America's technical know-how to Russia.[33]

By November 1944 the New York *Rezidentura* could report back to Moscow that, thanks to American propaganda and Soviet victories, 'the agent situation for developing work in technical intelligence in America at present is to be considered more favorable than at the start of the war'.[34] An emerging interest in the Soviet Union among American engineering and technical personnel had allowed talent spotters the chance to circulate in the milieu of American experts and to recruit new agents:

Given the wartime labour shortages, progressive elements with a friendly attitude towards the Soviet Union and a wish to provide us with assistance have had more opportunity to get jobs with businesses and institutions that they couldn't get into before the war. The rapid development of US industry during the war had led to the emergence of many new businesses to fulfil military orders. These businesses have little experience in counter intelligence work such as the safekeeping of secret diagrams, specifications, and documents. Crucially, the agent situation in the area of 'Enormous' had become more favourable because 'the range of scientists, engineers, and technicians allowed into this work is expanding more and more with each passing day, thereby making counterintelligence work in this area more difficult.'[35]

By May 1943 Shumovsky was on his way home. He had completed his two missions. Aircraft were now flowing in a steady stream to the front from American factories, and his secret work was going from strength to strength. Unlike in 1939, he left behind a flourishing legacy of agents. At his departure, there was a team of four in aviation to carry on his work. His deputy Raina had recruited a dozen active sources. But Stan was still missed; no one was as good as him. The armaments specialist Belyaev (agent MIKHAILOV), a fellow passenger on the storm-tossed convoys and now working at Douglas in California, complained that 'valuable intelligence was being lost' since Stan had gone. He harked back to the great days of 1942 when the pair had delivered 'first-class intelligence'.[36]

13

ENORMOZ

S tan climbed aboard a Soviet Li-2 military transport at Ladd Army Airfield in Fairbanks, Alaska, bound for Siberia. He turned to take his final look at the country that had been his home for the best part of a decade. America was no longer the peaceful isolationist nation he had found when he first set foot in New York in 1931. The Japanese attack on Pearl Harbor had stirred the beast. The entire industrial and creative power of the world's largest economy had turned itself over to war production. Billions of dollars and thousands of scientists were devoted to creating and deploying state-of-the-art technology to win the war. The small aircraft factories he had visited in the thirties had expanded beyond recognition, commissioning giant new facilities and taking on thousands of workers. Production lines were running twenty-four hours a day, seven days a week, turning out aircraft brimming with high technology that no other nation could match either in quantity or quality.

The evidence of America's manufacturing power was lined up in rows on both sides of the runway, dozens of factory-fresh American-built military aircraft each adorned with the bright red star of the Soviet air force. Newly trained United States ferry pilots had delivered the aircraft from the giant base at Great Falls in Montana to this remote Alaskan airfield, which was an unexpected hive of activity. Ladd Field in May 1942 served as the forward base for the forgotten American military campaign to evict the Japanese army from the Aleutian Islands. Stan's departure coincided with the only battle in the Second World War to take place on the soil of the USA. Each of the many aircraft destined for the Eastern Front was given a final service by USAAF personnel in preparation for handover. The planes had arrived at Ladd Field stripped of all but basic instrumentation and armament. After the team of Russian inspectors permanently living at the US military base accepted the aircraft, the first of five regiments of Soviet ferry pilots took their place in the cockpits to fly them in a series of hops from Fairbanks to the VVS pilot training facilities near Krasnoyarsk in Siberia. With no navigational aids, the Russian pilots took off on the first leg to Galena, Alaska, on the Yukon River. After stopping to refuel, the aircraft went on to Nome for the short hop across the Bering Strait to Siberia.

The four other regiments positioned along the route across Siberia were each assigned to a specific segment, becoming familiar with the tricky navigation and inclement weather. The single-seat Bell P-39 Airacobra, and later the Bell P-63 Kingcobra fighters, flew for safety in groups, accompanied by a pair of multi-engined North American B-25 Mitchell or Douglas A-20 Havoc bombers. The lead bomber navigated for the flight, while the trailing bomber watched for stragglers.

As his plane sped down the runway, the lines of aircraft destined for the battlefields of the Eastern Front were Shumovsky's final sight of the US. He had crossed the Atlantic in the darkest days of the war to arrange a lifeline for his country. It was fitting that after all his work, the culmination of his trip was the imposing sight of the joint effort to defeat Nazism. The air corridor was just one of three supply routes to the front line. Tons of arms and ammunition were arriving in the Caucasus via the Persian Corridor from the ports of Iran and Iraq, along specially built railways and roads. British, Russian and American ships still sailed the dangerous convoy routes across the Arctic waters.

Back in 1935, Shumovsky had seen the first Douglas being manufactured in Santa Monica for export to TsAGI. He had visited many times the teams of Soviet engineers who had meticulously redesigned the Douglas DC-3 at the factory in southern California in 1938. The Li-2 in which he now flew was a mass-produced Russian version of the DC-3, planes built under licence first near Moscow and then in an evacuated factory in Tashkent. Donald Douglas had made several million dollars from the fees the Soviets had paid him to build thousands of his planes, and had told visiting Russians how much he appreciated their business. Now running the fourth largest company in America, with a host of plants manufacturing his planes, Douglas was happy to show his Russian friends what the US War Department did not want them to see. He took one group of Russians on a factory tour of his C-47 Skytrain, pointing out the new design features. A company photographer came along to record the tour, allowing the Russians to pose by the significant features. Douglas even promised to provide the Russians with the radar that was included in his planes.

The route that thousands of planes flew across the North

Pole and the Arctic in May 1943 was the same one that the pilots Chkalov and Gromov had opened with their non-stop flights in 1937. Shumovsky had helped organise the ground-breaking trips. It had been hoped then that the route would be a commercial artery, bringing the countries closer together. No one would have imagined that six years later thousands of military aircraft would be repeating the feat. Somewhere in the icy wastes that he looked down on while flying east, Sigismund Levanevsky's flight had mysteriously disappeared without trace. It had been a terrible month organising the desperate search for the lost airmen.

Stan's business trip of October 1941 had lasted a year and a half. He smiled to himself realising that in the holds of the planes, safely packaged in diplomatic crates, were thousands of documents, films and samples of industrial secrets. A mission that he had begun alone in 1931 now employed dozens, working to ensure that the Soviet Union never again found itself left behind in the technology race. On his five-day journey home, and during the many stops on the way, he broke the tedium by reflecting on the recent past. He had spent the best part of a decade working far from home as a Soviet intelligence officer. Under the intense pressure, few 'super spies' had lasted so long. Stan had always operated in plain sight, and without ever being caught. Along the way he had rubbed shoulders with America's top scientists, businessmen and military officers, a Hollywood star and the US President. Despite being a life-long and dedicated Communist, he had come to respect American scientists and entrepreneurs for their extraordinary achievements in his beloved field of aviation. He had worked in the heart of capitalism and seen the rewards on offer for a successful entrepreneur like Donald Douglas, but was never tempted to defect; he was too aware of the inequalities and injustices of capitalism. All the American technological treasures he acquired were the tools needed to defend his people from a merciless invader.

Shumovsky was remarkable as an intelligence officer because he continually adapted his methods to changing circumstances and used America's strengths and weaknesses to his advantage. He had worked with the disenchanted who felt excluded from the American dream by their ethnic origin, the greedy who sold secrets for cash because they wanted money, and the idealists who believed in the inevitable triumph of Communism. He had always used a legal cover in his operations: first he was a talented student; next he became the representative of a major aviation customer; and finally he was a skilled military advisor. His lasting contribution to Soviet espionage was the development of a new style of intelligence gatherer, the scientist spy. The student programme that he had instigated had brought to MIT spies whose networking into America's scientific community paid dividends in the most unexpected areas. His successors, using his methods, and their contacts in the scientific community and factories brought to the Soviet Union valuable intelligence on America's developments in jets, rockets and the atomic bomb: the weapons of a future war.

• • •

Semyon Semyonov, in particular, was producing extraordinary results. Semyonov learned from Stan to use 'his connections at the Massachusetts Institute of Technology' to discover 'which of the prominent scientists are participating in the so-called Manhattan Project for the creation of an atomic bomb'.[1] He 'managed to establish firm contacts with physicists close to Oppenheimer'. Semyonov employed as a route into the highly secure Los Alamos facility the couriers Morris and Lona Cohen, and as a 'backup' Julius and Ethel Rosenberg. Semyonov's outstanding contribution to the success of Operation ENORMOZ was the creation of channels around the elaborate US security which allowed scientists to give intelligence information on the atomic bomb. The materials he sent back to Moscow described the main nuclear experiments, the reactors, various types of uranium-235 diffusion separation units and the results of atomic bomb tests. Besides nuclear secrets, Semyonov is known to have saved hundreds of lives by acquiring the secrets of the mass manufacture of the drug penicillin.

•   •   •

By the time of Shumovsky's return to his home in Moscow, the tide of war had changed decisively in favour of the Red Army. For the first time the Soviet Union, with its armament factories in full production, was preparing for a massive summer campaign to confront and defeat the German army. The pivotal battle of Kursk, following soon after their humiliating surrender at Stalingrad, was another bloody disaster for the Wehrmacht. Their extensive losses in manpower and equipment blunted German ambitions for the summer of 1943. In its last strategic offensive, the German army's objective was limited to pinching out a giant salient in its front lines. Yet, despite two years of fighting, the German High Command still underestimated Soviet ability to resist. In the summer of 1943 the Red Army met, matched and destroyed the next generation of Hitler's tanks, the Tigers and Panthers, with MIT graduate Ivan Trashutin's upgunned T-34s and thousands of attack aircraft. After this battle, Germany lost the initiative in the war against Russia and could never envisage an offensive on the Eastern Front again. Instead they fought a stubborn retreat, destroying everything, including houses, factories and dams, in the process. The destruction of the Soviet Union was on such a scale that when FDR was taken on a shocking tour of recently liberated Crimea, he had a controversial conversation with Stalin about the possibility of executing 50,000 Prussian officers to eliminate German militarism once and for all.

The long journey home took Stan five days by plane. When he eventually arrived back in Moscow, he discovered TsAGI's research facilities had been repaired. The laboratories had suffered extensive damage during the air raids in late 1941 after the Germans identified the site and the scientists as a target of high military value. At a time of extreme shortages, Stalin had personally authorised the extensive repairs in January 1942.[2] Two hundred and fifty staff were transferred back to Moscow from Kazan and Novosibirsk to repair the damaged wind tunnels and aircraft testing facilities. The rest of the workers returned to Moscow in September. Given the numbers, it was a massive operation involving special trains to bring the hundreds of evacuees and equipment back to Moscow. The Institute was back in full operation by early 1943, another sign that the Soviet Union was gradually returning to some sense of normality.[3]

On his arrival, Shumovsky remarried. The fate of his first

wife and daughter is unclear, but he met his second wife Tamara at the Aviation Ministry, and they had a son, Alexander, in 1945.[4]

After a lengthy debriefing at the NKVD's Lubyanka head-quarters, Shumovsky left espionage behind and returned to his first love, science. He had remained deputy head of TsAGI and head of the Bureau of New Technology throughout, despite being in America for fifteen months. The Soviets were now starting to turn their minds to the future after the war. The BNT was at the forefront of preparations for the next generation of aviation. There was no secret as to the new challenges: jets, missiles and radar. After the British inventor Frank Whittle publicly patented his innovative jet engine in 1930, the rearming German Luftwaffe bought a copy of the design from the UK patent office, although the Royal Air Force had failed to invest in the revolutionary development until 1940.

By 1943 the Red Army had learned after eighteen months of hard fighting how to defeat the Wehrmacht in summer as well as winter. They had grown in strength and confidence, becoming the dominant army in the European theatre. The Soviets could deploy more men, tanks and guns to the battlefield than any opponent or any other army. They were masters of the giant set-piece battle. But in a future war the USSR would have to face an opponent with a radically distinct strategy. The Americans fought a different style of war from the Soviets and Germans. They embraced a philosophy that attempted to minimise their own casualties by committing few ground forces and deploying strategic air power against their opponents on an unprecedented scale. The idea of precision bombing had been replaced by that of enormously destructive area attacks; today we would call such raids carpet or saturation bombing. There was no attempt to limit 'collateral damage'– in fact civilians were the target. The aim of the air war was to destroy the enemy's will to resist. In Europe, the cities of Cologne, Berlin, Hamburg and Dresden were destroyed. In the latter two a deliberate firestorm was created using incendiary bombs to maximise casualties and destruction. However, it was the US attacks from 1944 on the home islands of Japan that show-cased the full destructive power of the US bombing force. Under its leader General Curtis LeMay, the Americans had firebombed sixty-three Japanese cities, killing as many as 400,000 civilians. The B-29s' nightly raids overwhelmed Japan's civil defence, which had no ability to cope with the scale of casualties. The Japanese even stopped their air force from trying to intercept the attackers.

On 8 April 1945, in one of his final acts, President Roosevelt sent Stalin an unusual present. It was a collection of air recon-naissance photographs of German cities before and after USAAF raids.[5] The book contained a warm greeting and expressed the hope that attacks could be made from aircraft based on Soviet territory. Following Roosevelt's death, the Americans sent Stalin a follow-up book of photographs from the devastating B-29 Superfortress firestorm raids on Japan's home island cities. A single attack shattered Tokyo, killing 100,000 civilians, injuring a similar number and leaving a million homeless. The new volume was entitled *Japan On Fire*.[6]

Stalin interpreted the book as a threat. The Soviet Union had no defence against a high-altitude US bombing campaign and was now within its range. Having abandoned its strategic bombing

Bombing of Japan, 1945, from album sent to Stalin

development because of a shortage of resources, the Russians lacked any means of retaliating if such an attack was launched against it. Stalin felt the book demonstrated how prickly the alliance between the two powers was becoming. Relations with the Americans were deteriorating, not least because Stalin was receiving intelligence that the Manhattan Project was nearing completion.

Despite planning the attacks on Hiroshima and Nagasaki for August 1945, the Americans intended to conceal from their ally Stalin the existence of the atomic bomb until the last minute. For unlike their fellow allies the British, the Soviets had been excluded from the nuclear club that was developing the first bombs. It was not until the Potsdam Conference in July 1945, after the end of the war in Europe, that President Truman sidled up to Stalin to tell him obliquely about America's development of a 'new weapon of unusual destructive force'. Truman was puzzled when Stalin did not react to his news and believed Stalin had not understood him. Churchill would later write: 'I was sure that [Stalin] had no idea of the significance of what he was being told.'[7] Churchill could not have been more wrong. The lack of reaction was because Stalin had known for years about his allies' worrying development of an atomic bomb. In fact, thanks to Soviet intelligence, he had found out about the Allied project well before Truman. The incoming president was only trusted with the knowledge when he assumed office on 12 April 1945. For years Roosevelt had kept the secret from his vice president. Stalin returned to Moscow from Potsdam intent on speeding up the USSR's scientific efforts and redoubling intelligence gathering towards making his own bomb. He knew the Soviet Union's only defence against the US's weapon would be to develop its own.

• • •

The race to create an atomic bomb sprang from the peace-time scientific work of the 1930s. From splitting the atom in 1932, scientists had made great strides towards unleashing the energy trapped within. The collective dream of researchers was to unlock the atom's power to create unlimited safe electricity. Before the clouds of war descended, the international community shared all scientific advances, publishing discoveries in magazines and for peer review. But after 17 December 1938, when for the first time German scientists Otto Hahn and Fritz Strassmann split the uranium nucleus, research began shifting to the potential military use of atomic reactions. Hahn and Strassmann had witnessed a new type of nuclear disintegration, one much more powerful than any seen before: a chain reaction. Faced with the horrifying implications of the new discovery being in the hands of the Nazis, other German scientists in exile alerted the international community. Otto Frisch and Lise Meitner published analysis of this worrying development in *Nature* magazine, coining the phrase 'nuclear fission'. The shocked international community realised that the power released in the chain reaction had military potential, with some fearing the Nazis would use an atomic weapon first.

Early in the war a British team developed the design required to create a devastating atomic chain reaction using an enriched-uranium-fuelled device. Scientists at Birmingham University calculated that the critical mass of the uranium-235 isotope required for a workable bomb twenty thousand times as powerful as a conventional weapon was only 10 kg. A bomber could easily carry a weapon of this size. Initially working alone, the British had made faster progress than anyone else and believed that an atomic bomb was within reach. Yet the British government quickly realised that without disrupting all other vital war work, the tremendous cost of developing their own device would be beyond them. On the other side of the Atlantic, at the urging of Albert Einstein, Karl Compton and others, President Roosevelt had in complete secrecy committed vast resources to an American nuclear programme: the Manhattan Project. With their greater investment, the Americans would soon surpass British achievements.

Even before the idea of harnessing the power of nuclear fission for a bomb was first proposed, Stalin and Soviet scientists had been receiving intelligence reports on nuclear projects underway outside the USSR. At the start of the war the Soviets had in place a world-class team of experts and, thanks in part to the stream of intelligence, enough technical knowledge and skills to begin an atomic weapons programme. Yet the Russians assumed such a weapon would not be ready for use in the war and so the state offered no support for an atomic project for military use. In science-obsessed Russia, the ongoing atomic research was aimed at developing energy and was led by the nuclear scientist Igor Kurchatov and the Cambridge University-educated pair Yuliy Khariton and Pyotr Kapitsa. By the standards of the time, their research was well advanced. Kapitsa had spent more than a decade at Cambridge University's Cavendish Laboratory, working as assistant to Ernest Rutherford, the father of nuclear physics. It had been Rutherford's team that first split the atom in 1932. Kapitsa had introduced Khariton to Cavendish, and Khariton gained his doctorate researching the effects of alpha radiation on the human eye.

Thanks in great part to intelligence gathered by Gaik Ovakimian, Soviet scientists were the first to successfully repeat the groundbreaking British experiment to split the lithium atom by neutron bombardment. Ovakimian had successfully recruited Herbert Muraviev, a Russo-German scientist in Berlin who provided much of the intelligence.★ Through information from sources like Muraviev, scientists monitored international developments such as the crucial discovery of nuclear fission in Germany. In 1939 the future Nobel laureate Igor Tamm explained the implication to his students: 'Do you know what this new discovery [fission] means? It means a bomb can be built that will destroy a city out to a radius of maybe ten kilometres.[8] In 1941, Soviet chemist Nikolay Semyonov was the first to define the conditions for establishing a chain reaction.† His mentor Kurchatov submitted the results in a paper published in the US magazine *Physical Review*. Unusually, this important paper elicited no international reaction, causing the Soviets to suspect that nuclear research had become classified. With the German invasion in June 1941, all Soviet research stopped and the scientists were assigned to more immediate tasks or sent to the front.

But in autumn 1941, John Cairncross, an intelligence source at the heart of the British establishment, informed his Soviet controller within days of the British government's decision to move beyond theoretical laboratory work to begin the manufacture of a practical weapon of 'enormous destructive power'. Cairncross was one of the infamous Cambridge Spies, who was then working as private secretary to Lord Hankey, the politician in charge of overseeing the British atomic work, known first as the MAUD Committee and later as the Tube Alloys project or Uranium Committee. The British were aiming to manufacture atomic bombs at the rate of three a month by 1943, for use against

---

★ Codenamed ATOM, Muraviev later travelled to Moscow to work on a secret military project to create an electric 'death ray' powered by atomic energy.
† In 1956 Semyonov was awarded a Nobel Prize for this work.

Germany. The codename of the successful Soviet espionage operation that followed the arrival of the report, ENORMOZ, is
derived from the bomb's destructive power. The espionage would
progress in stages, mirroring the eventual progress of the US and
UK projects. First ENORMOZ aimed to gain an understanding
of the feasibility of the US, UK or Germany creating a device
and to discover the possible defences against such a weapon.

Before President Boris Yeltsin ordered the official release in
1998 of a selection of Soviet-era documents on its atomic project,
historians in the West believed Soviet intelligence's involvement
in the atomic issue started from the date the British commissioned a weapon. This is not the case. Already by early 1939,
when wartime secrecy had made atomic information impossible
to acquire, Soviet intelligence suspected, correctly, that its potential foes had begun working secretly on the feasibility of
developing an atomic bomb. It became imperative to develop
contacts inside the UK and US scientific communities with
knowledge of the work underway. Soviet agents began tracking
scientists they suspected were involved in any early experiments.
They shared the intelligence they gathered with leading Soviet
scientists, as well as the political leadership.[9] In January 1941,
Gaik Ovakimian, the head of the New York *Rezidentura*, had
been alerted by Moscow about the work of US scientists on
what was then known as the uranium problem.[10] He was told:
'Soviet physicists are also very engaged in the study of this
problem and, apparently, the problem is real.' Of particular interest
to Moscow was the work of University of Minnesota professor
Alfred Nier. In February 1940 Nier's scientific breakthrough
had been to use mass spectrometry to isolate a detectable amount
of the uranium-235 isotope.[11] Ovakimian discovered that the

Americans had 'obtained a new substance, possessing enormous energy, exceeding carbon energy several million times, the substance is called u-235'. Thanks to Nier's work, a Columbia University team split the u-235 atom, releasing explosive energy in their cyclotron. Moscow noted that the 'tests yielded positive results and encouraged further efforts in this work'. *Physical Review* even reported the outcome in an article that was picked up by the *North China Daily*, enabling Soviet intelligence to track reports of American scientific developments from as far away as China.

Soon after Cairncross's report reached Moscow in October 1941, the New York *Rezidentura* made their first contribution from contacts in the US scientific community. They reported that a party of eminent American scientists, including the renowned chemistry Professor Harold Urey of Columbia and leading nuclear physicist William Fowler of the California Institute of Technology,[12] had travelled to the UK to study the progress in the development of a uranium-235 isotope-fuelled bomb. The Soviets had been tipped off by a Communist sympathiser, Davrun Wittenberg,[13] who was chief assistant to Urey at Columbia University. Wittenberg had spoken to a Communist friend of his horror that the Western allies were making a bomb so powerful that a single device would be capable of destroying an entire city.

On receipt of this crucial piece of information, Stalin ordered the launch of the first coordinated, multi-continent intelligence-gathering operation in history. Given the amount of money and the quality of scientific resources the British and Americans were allocating, Stalin made the shadowing of his allies' scientific developments a priority. Another mistake of some Western historians' analysis of the Soviet intelligence operation is a failure to understand its goals at the start: these were to assess the feasibility of producing such a weapon and to learn about possible defensive counter-measures to the effects of an atomic explosion. Only later would the operation move on to gather secrets to help build a Soviet device. In 1941 it was still generally believed the Nazis were the most likely to be the first to deploy a bomb and that the Russians would be their target.

In response to the reports received from London in October 1941, the Russians had turned to their expert on the USA and atomic espionage, Gaik Ovakimian. On top of his undoubted scientific knowledge, he had unparalleled understanding of the American system of science and technology. He was the only Russian intelligence officer who knew where and by whom atomic work could be conducted. From mid 1941 onwards Ovakimian had been pulling the strings of all intelligence operations in the UK and US from Moscow. Now he focused increasingly on gathering information on the atomic programme that was the main scientific effort of the Western allies. The problem of u-235 was initially linked to the quest for information on chemical and bacteriological weapons. He later reported in a summary to the head of the KGB, Vsevolod Merkulov, on the first steps of Operation ENORMOZ:

> our agent cultivation of 'E-s' began at the end of 1941 on the basis of agent reports that had come in, stating that England and the USA were pouring their major scientific and material resources into solving the latest scientific problem of utilising the internal energy contained in the nucleus of the uranium atom; specifically, using it for military purposes – to create a uranium bomb of enormous destructive power.

In addition to studying all the field reports, Ovakimian prepared intelligence summaries for his political masters, and from early 1942 targeted the recruitment of potential intelligence assets at secure laboratories across America and the UK. In the US, he masterminded a plan identifying targets to be approached and the individuals to contact them. A telegram sent on 27 March 1942 from Moscow to New York read:

Letter No 7 (XY)

The present situation urgently calls for the mobilisation of all the resources we have for the deployment of intelligence work for the tasks letter No. 4 (1941), and other orders and, especially, on the chemistry of poison gas, protection from poison gas, issue of bacteriological weapons and the problem of uranium–235.

To accomplish this, we consider it necessary to inform you about a number of persons who need to be immediately recruited for our work. Among them will be those already mentioned in our letters of 1941.

III. The problem of uranium–235

In England, Germany and the USA they are working very hard on the problem of obtaining uranium–235 and using it as an explosive for making bombs of tremendous destructive force. Apparently the problem is quite close to being solved. We need to take this issue seriously.[14]

To Ovakimian's frustration, over the course of 1942 cleverly planned approaches to Russian emigrés and other scientists in the US associated with atomic work were rebuffed. But despite the many false starts, after he assigned some of his most experienced operatives to the work in the US and UK, his team's successes began to mount. Early in 1942, he had transferred the experienced Leonid Kvasnikov (ANTON) to New York from Moscow, where Kvasnikov had been head of S&T, and one of the MIT alumni, GLAN, to London from the US.

In April 1942, a telegram sent to Vasily Zarubin, the head of New York *Rezidentura*, shows how close Ovakimian had become to the subject. Moscow had received an alarming report based on information from a source working in the Chicago University Metallurgical Laboratory, an American scientist and Communist, Clarence Hiskey (RAMSAY):

Together with a group of prominent physicists and chemists at Columb. U., he [Hiskey] is urgently working on a radioactive bomb. It is thought that this bomb will have enormous destructive power with a very large blast radius, possibly hundreds of miles long. Those who know about the bomb fear it could annihilate millions of people, which is why a large part of the work has to do with developing means of protection against the bomb. As of yet, no one knows what effect the sudden release of radioactivity will have on solid material such as cement, or how long this effect will last.

So many recent advances in the work have been made that scientists are ready to test the bomb in some vast, desolate area, which will have to be blocked off for hundreds of miles. The Germans are far ahead of the Americans in their work in this field. The Germans already have the ability to use the bombs, but fear that the large affected area will be inaccessible to them.

Within days Ovakimian had replied to Zarubin in detail, pointing out and correcting the exaggeration in Hiskey's alarmist statements, while attaching a list of questions for the scientist to follow up on:

Ovakimyan's decision: To Cde. Kvasnikov. Discuss it with me.
p.34 C/t C – NY dated 5.4.42.

The report, received from Hiskey, on the major work being done by the Americans on uranium-235 is accurate, although in many respects it exaggerates in terms of what has been achieved. They are working on the problem intensively in England, Germany and the USA.

The question of using the energy of uranium for military purposes is of great interest to us. With regard to this question, we need the following information:

1. Isolating the main source of uranium energy – uranium-235 – from uranium. The Americans' achievements in this regard. Laboratory and factory methods of isolation. Industrial equipment for the isolation process.
2. At what stage is the current research on using uranium energy in bombs?
3. Who is working on developing a shell for the uranium bomb, and where?
4. A means of detonating the uranium bomb, i.e. a primer.
5. Means and protective measures against uranium's radioactivity during production.
6. What information is available on the Germans' work on developing a uranium bomb, and in what way does their work have an advantage over that of the Amer-s, as H reports?

7. What information is available on the factory application of
laboratory work on the uran. bomb?

The main customer for Ovakimian's intelligence was Igor
Kurchatov, who was to become the trusted scientist in charge of
the Soviet atomic project. By late 1942 Kurchatov began receiving
a copy of all the available intelligence to ascertain whether it
was scientifically accurate. In parallel Stalin took a decision on
27 September 1942 to restart very limited Soviet atomic research
on determining the feasibility of building a bomb.

Kurchatov responded enthusiastically to a letter from Molotov
in November, praising the quality of material on British and
American scientific breakthroughs. His note was copied to Stalin.
The detailed note testified not only to how deep was the penetration of British laboratories in Cambridge, Birmingham and
Liverpool, as well as the Chicago University Metals Lab, but also
how much had been accomplished over the course of that year.
Already in October, following extensive consultations with Soviet
scientists, Moscow Centre had submitted the first detailed report
on the Anglo-American plans to the Central Committee of the
Communist Party and the State Defence Committee, both of
which were chaired by Stalin. Kurchatov stated to Molotov and
Stalin that Soviet science was behind that of the allies and the
Soviets' proposed plan was inadequate. He had concluded that
'the [intelligence] materials available are not sufficient to determine that the production of uranium bombs is practically feasible
. . . although there is almost no doubt that a definite conclusion
has been made in this direction abroad'. He attached to his own
report a list of technical information for the intelligence services
to acquire from both the UK and the US, naming laboratories

and scientists to target. Ovakimian directed agents to fulfil Kurchatov's demands and in answer to the scientist's detailed questions shared translations of agent material he had received.

The close manner in which this pair were to work over the course of the project was reminiscent of the way that Shumovsky had operated with Tupolev from 1931 to 1937. When Kurchatov's team encountered technical problems, Ovakimian would provide answers from his agent in the field. Crucially, his team would provide the method to produce plutonium for the first Soviet bomb. The Soviets would also later copy the design of Enrico Fermi's reactor at Chicago Met Lab. In March 1943 Kurchatov wrote about a set of documents Ovakimian had gathered that were passed to him:

> My examination of these materials shows them to be of inesti-mable value to our country and Soviet science . . . The documents contain vital markers for our research, allowing us to bypass many highly labour-intensive phases of development and uncover new scientific and technical ways of resolving issues.[15]

Kurchatov attached four pages of further requests. He concluded, 'It should be noted that the entire body of information on the material points to the technical feasibility of solving the entire uranium problem in a much shorter period than our scientists, who are not familiar with the progress of work on this problem abroad.'[16]

Initially Kurchatov and Ovakimian had worked through inter-mediaries, but by July 1943, as the volume of highly technical information increased, the two scientists were communicating directly.

In August that year, after several months of squabbles, Churchill and Roosevelt took the decision at the Quebec Conference to pool UK and US scientific resources on the atomic project, to share information and to move British scientists to the US. Having signed agreements not to share any secrets of the work with third parties, a galaxy of international scientific talent, excluding any Russians, began researching and then building an atomic bomb.

The Allies' joint ultra-secret Manhattan Project had started making progress in earnest from the middle of the year. It had become a huge, international undertaking, and would eventually employ more than 130,000 workers[*] and cost the US government $2 billion. For additional security, the research and eventual production was divided across more than thirty separate sites in the US, the UK and Canada, but at its heart was the Los Alamos laboratory. This remote New Mexico facility would ultimately include twelve Nobel Laureates, a majority still in their twenties, the most remarkable collection of youthful talent ever assembled in a single laboratory. Hardly anyone involved in the ultra-secret work knew the complete process of how to build a nuclear device, yet the Americans failed spectacularly to keep the secrets from their then allies, the Russians.

Just as Shumovsky played a vital role in creating the Soviet strategic bomber, Ovakimian masterminded the intelligence operation that acquired its cargo, the bomb. In support of his efforts, MIT alumni recruited and ran agents on both sides of the Atlantic. After his move to the UK, GLAN (Nikolay Yershov)[17] set up the London end of the S&T operation. In his time in the UK,

---

[*] The majority of the workers were left completely in the dark as to the exact nature of the vital war work they were involved in.

the London *Rezidentura* provided the majority of important atomic intelligence to Moscow, giving details of the far more exciting advances being achieved in the United States as the Americans' massive investment in research paid off. He even tried to recruit Ernest Hemingway as an agent of influence, and developed as a source the UK-based scientist ERIC, identified as Austrian Engelbert Broda, who on 11 August 1943 was credited as 'at pres., the main source of info. on work being done on E., both in England and in the USA'. Based on the papers ERIC supplied, by spring 1943 Ovakimian had concluded that: 'The scale of the work carried out in America is much broader. Hundreds of highly qualified researchers participate in it, and their work has yielded more tangible results, and therefore the results of English works do not deserve much attention'. In August 1943 Ovakimian stressed the urgency of penetrating America by proclaiming that 'cultivating the "E"(normoz) problem should be considered the main priority of station chiefs' assistants working on the XY line in England and the USA in the upcoming period. [In E(ngland). – Glan; in the USA – Anton.]'[18]

When Ovakimian shifted the intelligence focus to the US, Semyon Semyonov (TWAIN*), who was now running S&T in New York, became more important to the success of the operation than Yershov. Semyonov ran at least twenty agents in the US and his name pops up in many later FBI investigations as a

---

* Semyonov had chosen TWAIN as his codename in tribute to his favourite American writer. Mark Twain was an early tourist to Russia in 1867, visiting Semyonov's home town Odessa, publishing a travelogue. Twain was the number-one foreign writer in the USSR, selling 1.5 million books in just three years, and in New York translations were exhibited at the Soviet Pavilion where Semyonov worked.

talent spotter, recruiter and controller of sources. Among his atomic-related activities, he formally recruited Julius Rosenberg on Labor Day 1942[19], ran the key figure of Klaus Fuchs when the scientist moved to America,[20] managed the Cohens (Fuchs' couriers) and from 1940 onwards was Harry Gold's controller. Semyonov worked more methodically and energetically than his peers. His first involvement in ENORMOZ was in the problematic recruitment of the American scientist Boris Podolsky (QUANTUM) in 1943.★ The codename was appropriate as Podolsky had co-authored a seminal paper on quantum mechanics with Albert Einstein. He had approached the Soviets in 1942, claiming he wanted to help them by moving to Russia to work on researching uranium-235. At the time no such work was being conducted in the Soviet Union. In 1943, the plan was for Semyonov to 'persuade [Podolsky] that it would be more useful for him to stay in the USA and become involved in work at one of the places that interests us'. Although Podolsky was never directly involved in the Manhattan Project, at a follow-up meeting in the Russian embassy facilitated by the future foreign minister Andrey Gromyko, Semyonov paid him $300 for material on the top-secret gaseous diffusion method of separating the prized uranium-235 isotope from uranium. QUANTUM was the first source recruited by the US *Rezidentura* to provide any significant information, but after the first transaction Podolsky refused to provide any more intelligence and was quietly dropped.

In late July 1943, in a document he had prepared on the latest intelligence, Ovakimian dismissed the threat of the Germans

---

★ Podolsky was a professor of mathematics at the University of Cincinnati. The university played no part in the Manhattan Project.

developing a nuclear bomb, a concern that had been hanging over the USSR. Ovakimian had learned from the American and British efforts what was required to succeed in developing an atomic weapon, and these clearly showed the task to be beyond the Germans. They lacked the scientific and natural resources to move beyond laboratory work. Up to that time the most vital atomic work had been taking place in the Metals Lab in Chicago University, but getting more Soviet operatives on the inside had proved difficult. Before the Quebec Conference resolved their differences, the British and Americans had stopped sharing information. As the Soviet sources on American achievements were all British, this had been a problem. Ironically, the Americans had stopped sharing secrets with the British because they were concerned their allies were under an obligation to share them with the Russians officially.

Chicago was where Fermi's first nuclear reactor, known as a pile, had been built and where the fissile element atomic weight 94 (later named plutonium) was discovered. Moscow considered sending someone to join source Clarence Hiskey (RAMSAY) at the Met Lab and came up with his friend Zelmond Franklin (CHAP), who seemed a likely candidate. But Moscow feared that Franklin's membership of the CPUSA would mean he would fail the background security check and in turn throw suspicion on Hiskey. As it transpired, Hiskey was later observed meeting Arthur Adams, a Soviet Military Intelligence officer, and would be transferred out of the Manhattan Project, sent by the US military to count warm underwear in a base in Canada.

As the speed of American achievements increased, and following complaints from scientists, the lack of progress in agent recruitment in the US drew criticism from the highest levels of the

Soviet security services. Progress could never be fast enough or the intelligence deep enough. Ovakimian rode his agents hard, even sending reading lists to New York to get them along the curve, especially on 'element 94'. The lists were so secret they had to be destroyed after reading. For the Russians the thaw in UK and US relations following Quebec came as an unexpected boon as it brought some of their established British-based intelligence sources to North America. The most important of these was Klaus Fuchs, a German-born Communist and scientist. He had begun work in Britain on the Tube Alloys atomic project in 1941 before being transferred to Columbia University in 1943 (and in 1944 to Los Alamos). His controller until his departure to New Mexico was Semyon Semyonov and the intermediary was Harry Gold. Described as 'a reserved, serious comrade, and he works with full awareness of the importance of the job he is doing', Fuchs would prove to be one of the most significant sources of information inside Los Alamos.[21] A second Soviet recruit was the prodigy Ted Hall, who had graduated aged just eighteen from Harvard. He joined the Manhattan Project without knowing the nature of the work, and at the first opportunity volunteered to provide secrets to the Russians, giving a detailed description of the 'Fat Man' plutonium bomb and the processes for purifying plutonium. A third Soviet source at the New Mexico laboratory, David Greenglass,★ was at best a minor player.

Semyonov's recruit Julius Rosenberg proved energetic and useful as a group leader. Semyonov described him as 'a skilled agent, commands authority with the group, which he is successfully

---

★ He was Julius Rosenberg's brother-in-law. He later testified against his sister and brother-in-law at their trial.

handling. He is enthusiastic about his work and wants to do as much as possible'.[22] Rosenberg was an electrical engineer who recruited friends working in defence industries – people he had known from his days at City College of New York who were Communist sympathisers – or members of his family to join his group. He was able to persuade one friend, Russell McNutt (FOGEL), to join the design bureau for the construction of facilities at Oak Ridge, a key Manhattan Project site in Tennessee. At one stage McNutt did not realise he was working for the Russians but happily passed on plans and designs to Rosenberg. Another Soviet military intelligence illegal who would become a valuable source at Oak Ridge was George Koval, who had been drafted into the army and fortuitously assigned to the facility.

By 1943 the intelligence gathering was widespread and the Soviet scientist demands so brazen that the US authorities started taking notice. But it was Vasily Mironov (KURT), the fourth MIT alumnus uninvolved in atomic espionage, who, as it transpired, was responsible for the disruption of Ovakimian's spy networks. Unlike the others, KURT worked in the Washington embassy on the political line, not S&T. As a result of schizophrenia he developed a pathological hatred of his boss and in 1943 secretly wrote a letter to the head of the FBI, naming the key Russians working as intelligence officers in the US and Canada:

KVASNIKOV works as an engineer at AMTORG is ZUBILIN's [Zarubin's] assistant for technical intelligence, through SEMYONOV – who also works in AMTORG, is robbing the whole of the war industry of America. SEMYONOV has his agents in all the industrial towns of the USA in all aviation and chemical war factories and in big institutes. He works very brazenly and roughly, it would be very easy to follow him up and catch him red-handed. He would just be glad to be arrested as he long been seeking a reason to remain in the USA, hates the NKVD but is a frightful coward and loves money. He will give all his agents away with pleasure if he is promised an American passport.

The letter exposed the scale and activities of the Soviet espionage ring stretching from New York to Los Angeles. Mironov was insane and accused his boss, the resident Vasily Zarubin, of being both a German and Japanese agent. He later wrote a second letter to Stalin making similar accusations about his colleagues that forced the recall of the linchpins of the Soviet organisation. When the FBI received the first letter they were puzzled by much of the rambling and did the minimum to follow up. They ignored the big fish protected by diplomatic immunity but did gradually increase surveillance on Semyonov.

By July 1944 the surveillance would become so intense on Semyonov that he was unable to perform his activities and returned to Moscow. The Bureau similarly followed BLERIOT's replacement Raina (Shevchenko) at the Bell aviation factories in Buffalo, turning two of his sources.* The Soviets responded by withdrawing the leadership of their espionage network and severing ties with the CPUSA.

Luckily for the Russian spies, as the Manhattan Project moved towards its conclusion several members of the international scientific community grew alarmed at the possibility that a single nation might acquire a monopoly on nuclear power for military purposes.

---

* Raina (Shevchenko) was a professional intelligence officer who later had the responsibility of dealing with the fallout from Klaus Fuchs' confession.

One unidentified source, codenamed KEMP, said to his controller: 'By giving documents to you, I am defending the future that an atomic bomb could destroy if it remained in the hands of the politicians of only one country.' Like KEMP, many scientists had joined the programme expressly to fight Nazism and hoped the secrets of the bomb they were creating would be shared. As a result, even from within the most top-secret facilities information leaked out to the Soviets on the goals, progress and methods of the Allied work. By mid 1944 the flow of technical intelligence on the atomic issue had reached such a level that the relatively small number of trusted scientists it was sent to could no longer process it all. It was proposed that a special bureau be established to deal with the thousands of pages of material. Intelligence officers could now chide scientists for being slow and inefficient. 'In 1944 we handed over 117 items of works, of which 86 conclusions have not yet been received, despite repeated requests from our side,' agent Pavel Fitin recorded in a letter in 1945.

Understandably, given the conditions of wartime Russia, research had remained small-scale in comparison to the vast Manhattan Project, employing perhaps twenty physicists. Despite assessments becomingly increasingly concerning that an atomic bomb would be a reality quicker than anyone in Russia thought, it had also been clear that the large amounts of raw materials, uranium and graphite required exceeded the known reserves in the Soviet Union. So even if its scientists could surmount the technical challenges of building a bomb, the project might be stumped by a lack of raw materials.

However, by 1945 Stalin had enough confidence that Russia could build a bomb to put Lavrenty Beria, deputy prime minister and head of the NKVD, in charge of a project to manufacture the Soviet Union's own weapon, following the path mapped by the US, UK and Canada. In March 1945 Igor Kurchatov decided that a plutonium device would be easier to build if enough uranium could be found.

When the Soviets moved to producing a bomb yet more scientists were given access to intelligence. As they began practical work, they gained a fresh appreciation of how valuable the intelligence was and the pressure to produce results shifted again. Yet Soviet scientists had the luxury of blueprints to work with while following the trail the Americans had unwittingly created. In April 1945 Yuri Khariton, as the designer of the Soviet bomb, was given permission by Ovakimian to access all intelligence material. By 10 July Kurchatov was told the Americans were ready to detonate their first device in the Nevada desert ahead of schedule. He was provided with a complete description of the plutonium device, including the vital firing mechanism. (Later he received the technical specifications of both devices dropped on Japan.) At the start of the year it had been believed the test would not happen before 1946 but this changed when in July Beria handed a copy of the document to an ailing Stalin who was recovering from a heart attack.

Following the Americans' successful 'Trinity' test in the Nevada desert, Soviet intelligence gained the final specifications, material composition and inner workings of the atomic bombs assembled at Los Alamos. At the same time Stalin ordered Tupolev to begin construction of the strategic bomber, the Tu-4, to carry his atomic weapons.

Despite this, at the end of 1945, after a series of defections, further work became impossible given the risk. Intelligence gathering wound down and the majority of experienced Soviet intelligence officers were recalled and their contacts put on ice. With his networks unwound, Ovakimian was exhausted, and left espionage behind him to return to academia. He researched fertilisers and possibly chemical weapons. Semyonov returned to Moscow and conducted a highly successful operation in France, gathering intelligence while operating as a film distribution agent. After being tried for spreading lies, Mironov was treated for his mental condition in a sanatorium. He persisted in trying to contact the Americans and was eventually executed. The MIT alumni awaited the fruits of their long labours to produce a nuclear-armed strategic bomber capability.

Yet Soviet work continued. In December 1946, supported by German scientists, the Soviet team achieved its first nuclear chain reaction using a copy of the original American reactor. By 1948, having finally secured sufficient supplies of uranium and graphite, the Russians commissioned their first plutonium production reactor. Soon after, in 1949, to the astonishment of President Truman who believed the 'Asiatics' (his description) incapable of such a sophisticated task, they achieved the extraordinary feat of detonating an atomic device.* 'First Lightning' was a copy of the American bomb 'Fat Man' that had destroyed Nagasaki. By using detailed intelligence reports on the Manhattan Project's progress, the Soviets' had cut two years or more of research work from their device's development. That the Soviet atomic programme relied so heavily on intelligence had been kept from the majority of Russian scientists working on the project. If their

---

* Truman demanded that each member of the commission investigating evidence of a Soviet atomic test individually sign a letter saying that they believed the Russians had the bomb.

leader Kurchatov arrived with answers to problems, they believed he had obtained them from another Soviet institute working on the same project. When their device was successfully tested on 29 August 1949, the watching scientists cheered, knowing the bright flash and rising mushroom cloud signified the end of the Americans' four-year monopoly of the A-bomb.

In the tense atmosphere of the Cold War the US reacted to the Soviet test with shock, and started an investigation into the 'theft' of their prized nuclear monopoly. The 'Asiatics' could not have built a bomb without significant help. With hindsight it is clear that the only secret behind the bombs lay in their specifi-cations, material composition and inner workings, and that any government with the determination and the resources to develop an atomic weapon could do so given enough time. The FBI quickly found informers, Harry Gold and then David Greenglass. These led them to Ethel and Julius Rosenberg. Under sympa-thetic British interrogation Klaus Fuchs confessed his part, exposing Harry Gold.* The Rosenbergs were executed, Fuchs jailed. The case was closed.

But the FBI investigation knew they had only scratched the surface of the Soviet operation. Harry Gold was to become the

---

* There was no firm evidence against Fuchs that could be used in a court of law. Venona intercepts identified him but the FBI would not allow them to be used. In May 1950 the FBI recognised that 'the fragmentary nature of the messages themselves, the assumptions made by the cryptographers, in breaking the messages themselves, and the questionable interpretations and translations involved, plus the extensive use of cover names for persons and places, make the problem of positive identification extremely difficult'. The NSA intercepts were useful in so far as they confirmed suspicions in already open FBI files.

FBI informer-in-chief, albeit an unreliable one. At times he would prove too eager to please his masters. He talked earnestly in several interrogations about his second Soviet controller, a man he knew as FRED. FRED taught Gold on-the-job fieldcraft like how to check if you were being followed by stopping to tie a shoelace or ducking down an empty street; or that documents should be exchanged concealed in newspapers or brown envelopes. Short and fat, with a waddling gait not unlike that of his codename GOOSE, the distinctive Gold was no master of fieldcraft. Anyone who met him remembered him, a disadvantage for a spy. Under investigation, he had been filmed and photographed with ease by the FBI when a suspect in the Fuchs case. Sources preferred working with individuals who demonstrated some scientific knowledge and FRED had tried to persuade Gold to enrol at MIT to become more effective. Gold's fees would be covered by the NKVD in exactly the same manner as his fellow agent Norman Haight. In the accumulated clutter of Gold's life that the FBI recovered from his apartment were his draft applications to MIT. FRED had given him detailed instructions on how to dispose of incriminating paperwork by screwing it up and scattering small balls over several blocks. Gold had ignored the advice and unwisely retained every scrap of paper, ticket and hotel receipt. He believed that FRED had a close connection with MIT and this persuaded the FBI to focus its investigation on the campus. Leaving no stone unturned in the 1950s, the FBI wended their way to Boston. The Bureau drew up a long list of suspects for FRED, including the entire 1931 student party, the 1938 party and an MIT chemical engineering professor, Edwin R. Gilliland. For a while Stan Shumovsky became the number-one suspect. Eventually it dawned on the investigators that Stan was at least six inches taller than Gold's description of his controller. FRED remains undiscovered, perhaps a figment of Gold's fertile imagination.

When prompted, local Boston residents did try to remember Shumovsky in detail. Eager to please, one described him as driving an array of fast and expensive cars and having a commanding air of authority. Another recalled seeing him hunched over a powerful radio transmitter. Despite these vivid memories from helpful patriotic Bostonians, Shumovsky was living in New York during the period. Nonetheless the investigation cost him a plum job at UNESCO. Tipped off by the FBI, the US State Department objected to his appointment as head of department and instead offered him a subordinate position.

14

MISSION ACCOMPLISHED

The pace of new developments in aviation was always rapid, and never more so than during the last year of the war. The Bureau of New Technology was still publishing 'Express Information' at a frenetic pace; in 1944 it produced forty-three separate reports on topics such as 'USA and Canada Developments in the War Years', 'Tables for the Translation of Anglo-American Measurements into Metric and Metric into Anglo-American Ones' and 'Post-War Aviation', and the forty-eight reports published in 1945 included a special edition on 'Aviation air-jet engines'.[1] The scope of the reports had expanded to include work on Allied aviation tactics and aircraft, and the BNT were still examining German aircraft that were either downed or captured.

The combatants were in a race to develop and deploy new weapons in the hope of changing the outcome of the war. Even before the outbreak of conflict, the Soviet Union had been investigating two key areas of German research, jet aircraft and rockets. Shumovsky had been intimately involved in both projects. Appointed deputy chairman of rocket plane test commissions and chairman of those for the first jet engine, he oversaw the first

Russian test, in which two ramjet engines had been attached to a Polyakov I-15 biplane. The strange craft had flown over the city of Moscow. A ramjet engine has to be ignited in mid-air, and the test pilot described the terrifying experience as flying 'a wall of fire'.[2] The next stage of development was to fit the rocket plane with ramjet engines to create a real beast of speed, but with the outbreak of war the highly ambitious project was cancelled. By the time Shumovsky arrived in the US in early 1942, however, he was one of very few experts on jets and rockets.

After three years of destructive war, the Soviet Union was an impoverished country whose factories to the west of Moscow lay in ruins. Soviet technological developments lagged behind those of the Germans and the British, the leaders in the race to deploy jet-powered aircraft, and there was no investment capital available to compete. The war on the Eastern Front was being fought and won with more conventional weapons. None of the new technology in development, save the atomic bomb, would have a decisive impact on the outcome. Germany was close to completing its pilotless rocket programme, utilising the V1 'Doodlebug' and the V2. By 1944 Allied intelligence sources reported that the Germans were on the brink of using in front-line service the rockets and jet fighters termed by Hitler 'revenge weapons', with which he hoped to rain down destruction on London.

Following the advice of Richard Wilmer Rowan in his book *Spy and Counter Spy*, Stalin used his limited budget on espionage. His intelligence service pierced his allies' veil of secrecy, learning of others' successes and failures. The Soviet Union would later enjoy all the cost and time advantages of being the second mover. Ovakimian had expanded the reach of S&T intelligence gathering to include the UK, mirroring how the British and

Americans conducted their scientific research.* Thus, Operation ENORMOZ gathered intelligence simultaneously on both sides of the Atlantic.

Shumovsky's Project 'AIR' had made it a priority for his intelligence network to monitor American jet developments. In February 1944, the Soviets started afresh their initiative to build jet planes that had come to a halt in 1940. At the newly re-organised Jet Engine Research Bureau, Soviet scientists built a jet engine to their own design. Four leading aircraft design bureaus were given the job of developing a prototype airframe. The planes all flew, with varying degrees of success.

From 1944 onwards German jet aircraft, built with armies of slave labour, began tackling the fleets of US bombers that crowded the skies over the crumbling Reich. But the planes were too few in number and arrived too late to make a difference to the outcome of the war, while a shortage of heat-resistant metal alloys meant that the German engines disintegrated quickly with use. Allied bombing had destroyed German fuel stocks, so many jets were abandoned, unable to fly. As Soviet troops advanced, a large bounty from conquered German territory fell into Soviet laps, halting the need for further tests. The German Messerschmitt Me-163 'Komet' rocket plane could achieve unprecedented speed in level flight. Although fast in combat, it was an ineffective interceptor and more of a risk to its pilots

---

* Ovakimian is still the only intelligence officer to have possessed the talent to run hundreds of agents across the US, Mexico and Canada while at the same time conducting groundbreaking scientific research. With his return to academia at the end of his service, after a distinguished career in which he had reached the rank of major general, he enjoyed equal success, picking up his research where he had left off.

than enemy aircraft, while it had a powered flight of just seven minutes. The Allies had nothing in their armoury to match the speed, but the simple expedient of avoiding flying near rocket planes' bases rendered the Me-163 useless. The Messerschmitt Me-262 jet fighter was more successful. Its introduction into the skies was revolutionary. Given its high acceleration, cruising speed and rate of climb it was a potent heavily armed threat to enemy aircraft. The first operational jet, it could only be tackled by Allied fighters when it was taking off or slowed down for landing. The speed and manoeuvrability of this first jet fighter at altitude was a glimpse into the future of air combat.

All Hitler's vaunted 'wonder weapons', however, failed to alter the outcome of the war, and each fell into Soviet hands. It was not long before the Allies added captured German technology to their own jet programmes. In common with the Western Allies, the Soviet Union organised an extensive technology transfer operation in the German territories they occupied. Fortuitously, the Nazis had based many of the highly dispersed factories in the east, out of easy range of American bombing raids. Specialist Soviet teams followed close behind the front line, securing factories, research laboratories and any examples of rockets, planes and radar equipment they came across before the physical transfer of equipment to the USSR. Within two weeks of the end of hostilities, on 21 May 1945, a commission including Shumovsky had begun the methodical looting of German aviation technology with the stated goal of quickly relocating and rationally distributing the equipment of German research institutes, laboratories and pilot plants, as well as arranging the improved processing of German technical materials, their translation, reproduction and distribution by NKAP, the People's Commissariat for Aviation Industry.[3]

Shumovsky's Bureau of New Technology began translating a vast number of captured documents, analysing the material and producing detailed technical drawings and photographs. Dozens of captured trophy planes that could still fly were taken to the flight testing ground at LII, located next to TsAGI; jet engines went to the specialist Aviation Motor Institute, conveniently located on the same site. It was a monumental task given the scale of material captured from the Germans. Shumovsky and the BNT were also receiving thousands of pages of material from espionage sources in the US about the American analysis of German technology. The US was copying captured Nazi technology at an impressive rate, far quicker than the Russians. The V1 flying bomb was reverse-engineered at high speed in just three months of 1944. Salvaged parts were recovered in southern England only during June; yet by 8 September, the first prototype JB-2 'Loon' had been assembled at Republic Aviation, which with help from Ford was building the device's pulse jet engine. The weapon was tested at Wright Field. (Bizarrely, later in the 1950s, the FBI became concerned that Smilg had passed on the secrets of their reverse-engineered flying bomb to his friend Stan. The investigators interrogated Smilg and a friend of his at Republic about the possibility.)[4] The US built thousands of these early cruise missile weapons to rain down on the Japanese home islands, the potential use of the ineffective German 'wonder weapon' on Japan being made an official US top secret. The Soviets had no significant interest in the pilotless American drone, as the BNT analysis was that it was ineffective. When they wanted to build a V1, they had all the information they needed from captured German documents and equipment, a possibility that escaped the FBI investigators interrogating Smilg. Shumovsky's former deputy Andrey Raina was now in charge of aviation espionage and was providing updates from his source at Republic.[5]

The Russians established factories and laboratories in the Soviet zone of occupied Germany, allowing thousands of German engineers and scientists to carry on their high-technology work. Russian specialists were seconded to work side by side with the German scientists on projects that included a renewal of work on jet engines, long-range rockets and radar. Germans working for the Russians enjoyed better food rations and rates of pay. However, the arrangement would end within a year when the Allied agreement to demilitarise the whole of former German territory required the relocation of the scientists and their families to the USSR. Shumovsky was sent in March 1946 on a second month-long trip to Germany to arrange the export to the enterprises of the People's Commissariat of the Aviation Industry of equipment and materials from the German aviation plants of Hirt in Berlin and Arado in Warnemünde, and its branches in the cities of Malchine, Stavenhagen, Teteren, Tissen, Tutow, Greinzwald and at the Gil station.[6]

Shumovsky relied on the itinerary of his first trip to Germany in 1940 to identify the most useful targets. Among his key goals was the Arado Company, which had designed and manufactured the first operational jet bomber, the AR-234. The last German aircraft to fly over Great Britain during the war, it was so fast it could not be intercepted; the Americans had already taken two captured AR-234s intact to Wright Field. If mass produced it would make a startling addition to the Soviet armoury.

Shumovsky directed the removal of the entire Arado works and its staff to the Soviet Union. Ilyushin then designed a two-engined prototype jet bomber based on the AR-234, which was built in time to make its maiden flight in front of the crowds at the 1947 Tushino air show. As was a common problem, the aircraft's Achilles heel was its underpowered engines. While the Russians were producing variants of German jet engines, the British had stolen a march in terms of the reliability, durability and fuel economy of their engines. The British post-war Labour government gave the Russians their advanced Nene jet engines in 1946. This time the method of acquisition was simple; the Russians merely asked for them. The Russian airframes with their swept wings were already the most advanced in the world, and now the excellence of the design was complemented by a powerful engine. In combat in the skies over Korea, the simple MiG-15 would demonstrate that the Soviets had overtaken America in the field of jet fighter design.

• • •

There remained a thorny problem. The Soviets needed a strategic bomber with the capability to deliver their planned atomic response. On 6 June 1945, Stalin chaired the State Defence Committee and gave Tupolev a tough new assignment.[7] He was to deliver into mass production a Soviet version of the most powerful strategic bomber in the world, America's B-29 Superfortress. In August 1945, two B-29s would fly the missions that dropped the atomic bombs on Nagasaki and Hiroshima. A single plane could now drop one bomb with the destructive power of the load of 2,000 others.

It was a measure of how far Shumovsky and Tupolev had succeeded in modernising Soviet aviation manufacturing techniques that such a project could even be attempted. In 1931 the

Soviet aircraft industry had struggled to produce outmoded biplanes. Now, having survived a major war, the Soviets were confronting the technological challenge of building the most advanced aircraft in the skies. Most daunting of all was that the feat was to be accomplished in just two years. The B-29 was a pressurised high-altitude plane with an enormous range and operational ceiling. As fast as most fighters, it was constructed with alloys unknown to Russian factories and featured a fire control computer allowing a single operator to fire all the weapon turrets.

The Russians did not start at square one. The Soviet intelligence operation in America was reported to have obtained as early as 1943 a partial blueprint of the Superfortress's design, and this had been sent to Stan in Moscow.[8] By June 1945 the completed B-29 was well known to them. The first information on the proposed new high-altitude heavy bomber had come courtesy of the US First World War ace and legend Captain Eddie Rickenbacker, who visited the USSR in 1943. Rickenbacker was shown aircraft factories and front-line military units. In conversation with his English-speaking guide he indiscreetly mentioned the performance characteristics of the new bomber, and the conversation, including the valuable information about the new plane, was reported. The Soviets began the systematic collection of information about the B-29 through official and unofficial channels alike. General Belyaev, head of the Purchasing Commission in the US, asked to buy the B-29 in 1943 and again in 1945 to use against the Japanese. The requests were ignored.

During US operations against Japan in 1944, three damaged but airworthy US B-29s landed in Soviet territory. The aircraft had to be interned as the Soviet Union and Japan were at that stage still at peace. The crews were kept in a comfortable stockade which the Japanese could inspect at any time. The camp was porous, with the airmen 'helped' to escape to rejoin US armed forces based in Iran. The planes could not be returned. Instead the Russians inspected, repaired and test flew them. Soviet scientists and pilots became familiar with the innovative aircraft. American sources suggest that one plane had even landed with some of its operational manuals on board. In 1944 TsAGI published a long article revealing all the details of the world's first modern pressurised high-altitude plane.

One of the American B-29s, nicknamed 'Ramp Tramp', was flown to the Central Airfield in Moscow on 11 July 1945 and squirrelled away in a large hangar. After an initial inspection by Tupolev and his assistants, it was meticulously and painstakingly dismantled.[9] Each of the thousands of separate parts was studied by a team of designers and technologists. Each item was carefully weighed and photographed, and a technical description prepared. The parts were next subjected to spectral analysis to ascertain the construction material. Several tens of thousands of drawings were made. Unsurprisingly, the B-29's technology and structural materials were entirely different from those in use in the domestic aircraft industry. American production standards were also far stricter than in Russia. Each new part would have to be made in a Soviet factory to a near perfect standard.

The initial order was for twenty aircraft. To reach the required manufacturing standards, a leading figure of the aircraft industry announced at a special meeting to discuss progress on the Tu-4 project in December 1945 that 'it will take tremendous work to raise our aviation manufacturing culture to these new, very high levels'.

The Russians sought to accelerate the programme by purchasing in the United States some of the components they could not manufacture. These included the engine starters, the AN/APQ-13 advanced radar, the VS-733 blind landing systems, the wheels, the Hamilton Standard propellers, bearings, cockpit instruments, and the spark plugs for the motors. But it was impossible to purchase such items without arousing suspicion, so every single component had to be made in the USSR, which was ultimately to their advantage as it forced through a leap forward across industries. The NKAP stipulated: 'All orders for the Tu-4 aircraft must considered to be the priority.'[10] Revolutionary new metal alloys were developed from the spectral analysis and the state-of-the-art technology recreated. At the end of the exercise 'Ramp Tramp' was reassembled.

The Tupolev version of the B-29, officially named the Tu-4 and later given the NATO codename 'Bull', was not as is sometimes claimed an exact copy of the B-29. The Tu-4's Russian engines were derived originally from a Curtiss-Wright design. Its sophisticated radar systems and friend-or-foe identifier evolved from captured German equipment, as the US had refused to officially supply the Russians with any radar technology under Lend Lease. When the US manufacturers built radar into their planes, USAAF technicians would take it out before delivery to the Soviets, although substantive intelligence on radar had been provided by William Perl and Alfred Sarant, members of the Rosenberg spy ring, while the US Navy, unaware of the requirement to remove the technology, had supplied some planes with radar. The defensive armament on the plane was considered inadequate, so the machine guns were enhanced with more powerful Nudelman cannons in remodelled turrets. The Tu-4 would have been more difficult to attack than a B-29 if it had ever been involved in combat.

The Tu-4 was designed as a metric aircraft. Each component had to be analysed and converted to a metric equivalent with the help of Shumovsky's calculation tables, meticulously worked out at the BNT. The crucial decision concerned the gauge of the aluminium sheets that covered the plane's vast surface area. There was no metric equivalent to the American ⅛ inch gauge. If the Russians selected a gauge that was too thick or too thin, there might be a dramatic impact on the aircraft's performance. But the complete Tu-4, when assembled, weighed within a few per cent of an American B-29, showing how accurate the calculations had been. The Soviets' main problem was a failure to master the technique of making curved plexiglas without causing distortion. Despite the amount of clear glass all round the cockpit, the distortion meant it was a challenge for the pilot to see out of the first Tu-4s.[11]

• • •

The early August air display gave Tupolev and Shumovsky an unmissable deadline. The traditional 'Aviation Day' flypast in front of holidaying Moscow crowds was to be held for the first time since the end of the war, and everything must be ready and perfect. The launch of the Tu-4 was a direct challenge to America's supremacy in the air. A crucial message was to be delivered that August day: that Stalin and the Soviet Union were challenging America's nuclear monopoly head on.

Even before America dropped 'Little Boy' and 'Fat Man' on Hiroshima and Nagasaki, there had been grave international concern that a single state might have a monopoly on such destructive power. The fear that Nazi Germany would be that state had led the international scientific community to approach President Roosevelt with a proposal to build the first bomb. The US had refused to share its nuclear secrets even with the British, who had contributed so much to the programme. On 8 August 1945, British Prime Minister Clement Attlee sent President Harry Truman a message in which he referred to the pair as 'the heads of the Governments which have control of this great force'. Truman refused to accept the comparison. For the next year Attlee attempted unsuccessfully to persuade Truman to grant the access to the scientific information which the British believed they deserved, given their extensive involvement in the original research. In the meantime, they had restarted their own independent work to build what was now known as a deterrent.

For the all-important Tushino display, Tu-4s with the serial numbers 001 to 003 were manufactured, prepared and test flown by July. Hundreds of factories and thousands of workers had given their all for this day. Thanks to its importance, Tupolev travelled to the distant city of Kazan dressed in his general's cap to supervise the post-factory testing of each plane. One of the Soviets' top test pilots, Mark Gallay, who flew one of the planes in the parade, marvelled at the advance in Soviet bomber design represented by the Tu-4. He well remembered the bad old days of open cockpits and thick flying suits; in contrast, the Tu-4's pressurised environment maintained a comfortable interior temperature in flight. Gallay noted that this remarkable plane flew at the speed of a fighter, at the height of an experimental plane, and had the range of a reconnaissance aircraft.[12] Everything worked perfectly – except that no one was able to locate the button which turned the heating down. Gallay and his crew flew to Moscow in tropical heat.

B-29 Superfortress

Tu-4

Dismantling of B-29 'Ramp Tramp', Moscow, 1945

The Tushino Air Display was an important summer holiday for ordinary Muscovites as well as the great and the good. Tens of thousands flocked out of the city by tram, train and even river boat. It was important to arrive early to secure the best viewing spot.[13] Those watching the display traditionally wore white clothes, necessary to keep cool in the sweltering heat of the summer of 1947.

Stalin arrived in an upbeat mood. Resplendent in his generalissimo's uniform, specially tailored in blue in honour of the air force, he chatted and smiled with the Minister of Defence and the head of the VVS. Standing nearby in civilian clothes was Beria, who was there to see the aircraft purpose-built to drop the atomic bomb that he was close to perfecting. Tupolev was dressed for once in a smart general's uniform decked with medals, including the treasured 'Hero of Socialist Labour', the only medal Stalin himself wore. With all the preparations complete he was confident. He had been informed that the Tu-4s, his special surprise, were airborne.

Shumovsky was there with his family to witness the climax

of his work in America and Germany. The Soviet Union was about to showcase its jet fighters and bombers. The Western diplomats gathered in their enclosure expected the jets, but the Tu-4's entrance was to be a complete shock.

Within the last few days, the head of the air force, Chief Marshal of Aviation Alexander Golovanov, had decided to lead the fly-past himself, piloting the first Tu-4.[14] The many aircraft for the show formed up several miles from Tushino, circling as they awaited their opportunity to make a high-speed pass low over the parade ground. For the pilots of the Tu-4, these were harrowing moments; they had to watch out for a myriad of smaller twin-engined planes in close proximity, while also keeping formation with the inexperienced air marshal. The two test pilots had some hairy moments following their leader. His turns were not long and smooth but hurried and sharp.

At last, it was time for the Tu-4s to open the parade with their grand entrance. Throttles were opened to full as the three planes began their first fast, low pass over the crowd. Everyone was expecting bombers – traditionally it was always the large planes that were the crowd pleasers – but the dots approaching at speed in the distance were not, as expected, obsolete pre-war aircraft. The hum of the approaching engines was loud and distinct. Even from a distance, the sheer scale of the planes was obvious to the naked eye. As the planes closed in on the airfield, each formed into a shape unfamiliar in Soviet aviation. The three Tu-4s passed low over the crowd, the roar of their engines announcing that Stalin had a potent strategic bomber force at his disposal. As it dawned on the assembled foreign observers that America's dominance of the skies was over, Stan Shumovsky allowed himself an inward smile.

POST-SCRIPTUM

The success of Shumovsky's work from 1931 would be epitomised in the manufacture of hundreds of Tu-4s. The Soviet Union had caught up with and overtaken the best America could make. The construction of this first ultra-modern plane and its supporting technology was a fitting conclusion to his mission to modernise the Soviet aviation industry. The Tu-4 was the father of a whole family of Soviet strategic bombers.

When it mattered, during the days between 1941 and 1945, the Soviet factories and their trained workers had won the war of production over Germany. Shumovsky's legacy was to establish an equilibrium in Soviet and American capabilities that lasted the length of the Cold War. Both superpowers were equipped with nuclear weapons and long-range bombers, the ultimate tools of the Douhet strategic bomber philosophy that envisaged aircraft as the ultimate weapon. But soon America and the USSR would deploy fleets of nuclear-armed bombers that neither side could or would use.

Deputy Director Shumovsky left TsAGI shortly after the public flights of the Tu-4 and the first Soviet jet aeroplanes.[1] For his

Professor Shumovsky in 1982,
with his MIT graduation picture in the background

service to the Motherland, he was awarded the Order of the Great Patriotic War Grade I and the Medal for Valiant Labour in the Great Patriotic War. It was time to pass the baton. Tupolev's son was heading the design bureau, Stalin's son was flying Tu-4s, and Shumovsky's elder son Yuri was at work in a secret aircraft factory. Professor Shumovsky started a new career in education, helping to found the Moscow Physical Technical University along similar lines to MIT.[2] He was later the Soviets' choice to be appointed head of UNESCO (the United Nations Organisation for Education, Science and Culture), although he was prevented from taking up the position when, given their belated discovery of his espionage activity, the US objected to his candidature. Nonetheless, he worked for many years in Paris as a deputy director of UNESCO, making a valuable contribution to the improvement of education in the developing world.[3] Shumovsky died on 1 October 1984.

NOTES

Abbreviations

MFTI – Moscow Institute of Physics and Technology
MIT – Massachusetts Institute of Technology
NSA – National Security Agency, USA
RGASPI – Russian State Archive of Socio-Political History, Moscow
RGAVMF – Russian State Archive of the Navy, St Petersburg
TsAGI – Central Aero and Hydrodynamics Institute, Moscow

Preface

1. J. V. Stalin, 'The Tasks of Business Executives. Speech Delivered at the First All-Union Conference of Leading Personnel of Socialist Industry 1, February 4, 1931', www.marxists.org
2. The Mitrokhin Archive, Churchill Archive Centre, Cambridge University, trans. Svetlana Lokhova. The FBI described the Mitrokhin material as the 'most complete and extensive intelligence ever received from any source'.
3. Ibid.
4. Ibid.
5. Ibid.

Introduction

1. Russian Central Studio of Documentary Films. *'The Cold War Superfortress Russian Style': Newsreel Footage of Tushino Airshow 1947.* Moscow: Russian Central Studio of Documentary Films, 2004.

2. Yuliy Abramovich Hight (music), Paul Davidovich Herman (lyrics), 'March of the Pilots'. Moscow, 1923.

3. Communist Party Membership Records of Stanislav Antonovich Shumovsky, RGASPI. Moscow, 1973.

4. Contemporary Soviet newsreels.

5. FBI files on Rosenberg, Gold and others released under FOIA.

6. Federal Bureau of Investigation (FBI), *FBI Records: The Vault.* The files on Harry Gold and the Rosenbergs contain information on Shumovsky. https://vault.fbi.gov/

7. *The Stalin Digital Archive,* RGASPI. This archive contains a selection of documents from Fond 558, which covers Stalin's personal biography, his work in government, and his conduct of foreign affairs. *Opis'* 1: documents written by Stalin in 1889–1952. *Opis'* 2: documents written by Stalin in 1911–1944. *Opis'* 3: over 300 books from Stalin's personal library with his marginal notes. *Opis'* 4: Stalin's biographical materials. *Opis'* 11: Stalin's correspondence and documents. This *opis'* covers a period from 1917 to 1952. http://rgaspi.org/

8. NSA, Cables decrypted by the National Security Agency's Venona Project, transcribed by students of the Mercyhurst College Institute for Intelligence Studies. Arranged by John Earl Haynes, Library of Congress, 2010. www.wilsoncenter.org

9. US Immigration Department Records, passenger manifests from New York and Halifax arrivals, www.ancestry.com.

10. Major George Racey Jordan, 'From Major Jordan's Diaries – The Truth about the US and USSR', www.archive.org

11. *The Massachusetts Institute of Technology Yearbooks 1932–35,* Cambridge, MA: MIT, 1932–5.

12. Alexander Vassiliev, Vassiliev Notebooks, trans. Svetlana Lokhova. www.wilsoncenter.org. A collection of eight notebooks and loose pages kept by Alexander Vassiliev while researching in the KGB archives. In the mid-1990s, Vassiliev researched Soviet espionage in America as part of an SVR-supported book project. His notebooks contain

summaries of documents, transcriptions, and his own notes. Three
versions of each notebook are provided: a scanned copy of the original
notebook, a Russian transcription and an English translation.

13. Ibid.
14. Communist Party Membership Records of Stanislav Antonovich
Shumovsky, RGASPI.
15. 'A Celebration of the Life of Professor Stanislav Shumovsky', MFTI,
The Journal of Applied Mathematics and Technical Physics. Moscow: 2002.
16. Ibid.
17. Ibid.

1 'Son of the Working People'

1. Military Service Record of Stanislav Antonovich Shumovsky,
RGAVMF, trans. Svetlana Lokhova. St Petersburg: 1924. Fond R1108,
Opis 3, File 195.
2. Theodore A. Shumovsky, *Svet s Vostoka* [The Light from the East],
trans. Svetlana Lokhova. St Petersburg: St Petersburg University Press,
2006.
3. 'A Celebration of the Life of Professor Stanislav Shumovsky', MFTI.
4. Wikipedia.org
5. 'A Celebration of the Life of Professor Stanislav Shumovsky', MFTI.
6. Shumovsky, *Svet s Vostoka* [The Light from the East].
7. Military Service Record of Stanislav Antonovich Shumovsky,
RGAVMF.
8. Shumovsky, *Svet s Vostoka* [The Light from the East].
9. Military Service Record of Stanislav Antonovich Shumovsky,
RGAVMF; MIT, *The Massachusetts Institute of Technology Yearbooks
1932–35*; Communist Party Membership Records of Stanislav
Antonovich Shumovsky., RGASPI.
10. Stanislav A. Shumovsky, 'The Planning of Technical Education in
Developing Countries: Lessons from the USSR Lecture – Discussion
Series'. unesdoc.unesco.org. 1969.
11. Wikipedia.org
12. Shumovsky, 'The Planning of Technical Education in Developing
Countries'.

Notes

13. Ivan Trashutin, *Tankovye dizeli* [Diesel Tank Engines], trans. Svetlana Lokhova. Moscow: Voennoe izdatel'stvo ministerstva oboroni, 1959.

14. Wikipedia.org

15. Ibid.

16. Okhranka, Department for Protecting the Public Security and Order, Okhranka Records of the Paris Office, https://digitalcollections. hoover.org; Intelligence reports from agents in the field and the Paris office of the Russian imperial secret police, dispatches, circulars, headquarters studies, correspondence of revolutionaries and photographs relating to activities of Russian revolutionists abroad.

17. Wikipedia.org

18. Ibid.

19. Evgeny Primakov, *Ocherki istorii Rossiiskoy vneshnei razvedki* [Selected History of Russian Foreign Intelligence]. Moscow: Mezhdunarodnye otnoshenia (Foreign Relations), 1996.

20. G. I. Kasabova, *O vremeni, o Noril'ske, o sebe . . .* [Of the Times, Of Norilsk, Of Myself . . .], Moscow: PoliMedia, 2001. English-language versions of Klivans's letters are in Harvard University's Radcliffe College Archives.

21. Bennett and Epstein family records. Documents kindly provided to the author by the family of Ray Bennett.

22. Vladimir Lotta, *GRU i atomnaya bomba* [The GRU and the Atomic Bomb], Moscow: Olma Press, 2002.

23. Allen Hornblum, *The Invisible Harry Gold: The Man Who Gave the Soviets the Atom Bomb*, New Haven and London: Yale University Press, 2010.

24. *FBI Records: The Vault*, https://vault.fbi.gov/

25. NSA, Cables decrypted by the National Security Agency's Venona Project.

26. *Aviatsiya Vtoroy mirovoy* [Aviation of the Second World War], www. airpages.ru

27. Ibid.

28. Ibid.

29. Mikhail Butov, 'When the Tsar Banned Booze', Russia and Beyond, 2014. www.rbth.com

30. Raymond Kevorkian, *The Armenian Genocide: A Complete History*, London: I. B. Tauris, 2011.

31. Arsen Melik-Shakhnazarov, 'Small Caucasian Paris', www.analyticon. com

32. Wikipedia.org

33. Anton Denikin, *The Russian Turmoil: Memoirs Military, Social and Political*, London: Hutchinson, 1922.

34. Sigismund Levanevsky, *Moya stikhiya* [My Element], Rostov on Don, 1935.

35. Kevorkian, *The Armenian Genocide*.

36. Ibid.

37. Wikipedia.org

38. Shumovsky, *Svet s Vostoka* [The Light from the East].

39. Military Service Record of Stanislav Antonovich Shumovsky, RGAVMF.

40. Ibid.

41. Wikipedia.org

42. Military Service Record of Stanislav Antonovich Shumovsky, RGAVMF.

43. N. I. Ivanko, *Konstantin Trunov: Ocherk o zhizni i deyatel'nosti geroya grazhdanskoy voyny na Stavropol'ye* [Konstantin Trunov: Essay on the Life and Activities of the Hero of the Civil War in the Stavropol Area], Stavropol Book Publishing, 1954.

44. Mikkel Thorup, *An Intellectual History of Terror: War, Violence and the State*, London: Routledge, 2010.

45. Ivanko, *Konstantin Trunov*.

46. Ibid.

47. Military Service Record of Stanislav Antonovich Shumovsky, RGAVMF; NSA, Cables decrypted by the National Security Agency's Venona Project.

48. Ivanko, *Konstantin Trunov*.

49. Ibid.; Military Service Record of Stanislav Antonovich Shumovsky, RGAVMF.

50. Military Service Record of Stanislav Antonovich Shumovsky, RGAVMF.

51. Philip White, 'A Leadership Legacy: Happy 138th, Winston, Friday,

December 7, 2012', National Churchill Museum, 2012, www.national churchillmuseum.org

52. Military Service Record of Stanislav Antonovich Shumovsky, RGAVMF.

53. Communist Party Membership Records of Stanislav Antonovich Shumovsky, RGASPI.

54. Military Service Record of Stanislav Antonovich Shumovsky, RGAVMF.

55. Ibid.

56. Communist Party Membership Records of Stanislav Antonovich Shumovsky, RGASPI.

57. Military Service Record of Stanislav Antonovich Shumovsky, RGAVMF.

58. *Aviatsiya Vtoroy mirovoy* [Aviation of the Second World War], www.airpages.ru

59. Ibid.

60. Shumovsky, *Svet s Vostoka* [The Light from the East].

61. Lotta, *The GRU and the Atomic Bomb*.

62. Communist Party Membership Records of Stanislav Antonovich Shumovsky, RGASPI.

63. Shumovsky, *Svet s Vostoka* [The Light from the East].

2 'We Must Catch Up or They Will Crush Us'

1. Communist Party Membership Records of Stanislav Antonovich Shumovsky, RGASPI.

2. Alan M. Ball, *Imagining America: Influence and Images in Twentieth Century Russia*, Rowman & Littlefield, 2003.

3. Svetlana Lokhova, *Stalin, the NKVD and the Investigation of the Kremlin Case: Prelude to the Great Terror*, London: Routledge, 2015.

4. Richard B. Spence, *Wall Street and the Russian Revolution 1905–1925*, Waterville, OR: Trine Day, 2017.

5. Charles E. Sorenson with Samuel T. Williamson, *My Forty Years with Ford*, New York: Norton, 1956.

6. Ball, *Imagining America*.

7. *The Stalin Digital Archive*, RGASPI.

8. Ball, *Imagining America*.

9. Levanevsky, *My Element*.

10. R. W. Davies et al., *The Stalin-Kaganovich Correspondence 1931–6*, New Haven and London: Yale University Press, 1993.

11. Primakov. *Ocherki istorii rossiyskoy vneshney razvedki* [Selected History of the SVR].

12. J. V. Stalin, 'The Tasks of Business Executives. Speech Delivered at the First All-Union Conference of Leading Personnel of Socialist Industry 1 February 4, 1931', www.marxists.org

13. Richard Wilmer Rowan. *Spy and Counterspy: The Development of Modern Espionage*, New York: Viking Press, 1928; babel.hathitrust.org

14. Yu. Dyakov, T. Bushueva, *Fashistky mech kovalsya v SSSR* [The Fascist Sword was Forged in the USSR: A Collection of Documents], Moscow: Sovetskaya Rossiya, 1992.

15. Primakov, *Ocherki istorii rossiyskoy vneshney razvedki* [Selected History of the SVR].

16. Vladimir V. Poznyakov, *Sovetskaya razvedka v Amerike, 1919–1941* [Soviet Intelligence in America, 1919–1941], Moscow: Mezhdunarodnye otnosheniya, 2005.

17. Alexander Feklisov, *The Man Behind the Rosenbergs: Memoirs of the KGB Spymaster Who Also Controlled Klaus Fuchs and Helped Resolve the Cuban Missile Crisis*, New York: Enigma Books, 2001.

18. Mikhail Lyubimov, *Angliya. Gulyaniya s Cheshirskim Kotom* [England. Celebrations with the Cheshire Cat], Moscow: Amfora, 2010.

19. Oleg Kalugin, *Spymaster: My Thirty-two Years in Intelligence and Espionage Against the West*, New York: Basic Books, 2002.

20. Feklisov, *The Man Behind the Rosenbergs*.

21. NKVD Interrogation Protocols of Raisa Bennett, RGASPI, trans. Svetlana Lokhova. Moscow, USSR: 1935, f. 671, op. 1, d. 107–11.

22. Shumovsky, 'The Planning of Technical Education in Developing Countries: Lessons from the USSR Lecture – Discussion Series'; G. A. Tokaty, *Spaceflight Volume X: The Origins of Soviet Cosmonautics*, London: British Interplanetary Society, 1968. A rare mistake allowed Shumovsky's name to be published in the West in connection with the secret acquisition of aeronautics information from abroad.

23. John Reed, *Ten Days that Shook the World*, New York: Boni & Liveright, 1919.

24. Victor Serge, *Memoirs of a Revolutionary*, Oxford: Oxford University Press, 1963.
25. *FBI Records: The Vault*, https://vault.fbi.gov/
26. Ibid.
27. Kasabova, *O vremeni, o Noril'ske, o sebe* . . . [Of the Times, Of Norilsk, Of Myself . . .].
28. Ibid.
29. Ibid.
30. Wikipedia.org
31. Kasabova, *O vremeni, o Noril'ske, o sebe* . . . [Of the Times, Of Norilsk, Of Myself . . .].
32. Ibid.

3 'What the Country Needs Is a Real Big Laugh'

1. *Youngstown Vindicator*, 20 August 1931.
2. Calvin Coolidge, State of the Union Address to Congress 1928, Whitefish: Kessinger Publishing, 2016.
3. Gordon Lloyd, *The Two Faces of Liberalism: How the Hoover–Roosevelt Debate Shapes the 21st Century*, Salem: M&M Scrivener Press, 2006.
4. Theodore Dreiser, *The Financier*, New York: Harper, 1912.
5. President Hoover in a statement to Raymond Clapper, 1931. Quoted in Charles Rappleye, *Herbert Hoover in the White House: The Ordeal of the Presidency*, New York: Simon & Schuster, 2016.
6. Ibid.
7. 'We Break a Lance for Harvard', *Coshocton Tribune*, 22 September 1931.
8. 'It Girl in Russia Is Only Hick in USA', *Casper Star-Tribune*, 2 September 1931.
9. 'Well of All Things Soviets Don't Neck', *Pittsburgh Press*, 23 August 1931.
10. Ibid.
11. *Cleveland Plain Dealer*, 3 September 1931.
12. Maya and Nadezhda Ulanovskaya, *Istoriya Odnoi Semyi* [One Family's Story], Moscow: Chalidze Publications, 1982.
13. 'Interviews with Gertrude Klivans', *Youngstown Telegram*, 1931.

14. Ella Winter, *Red Virtue: Human Relationships in the New Russia*, London: Victor Gollancz, 1933.
15. Lincoln Steffens, *Autobiography*, Volume 2, Boston: Mariner Books, 1968.
16. Upton Sinclair, *The Metropolis,* Lititz: AP Publishing House, 2012. From the biography section quoting a 1951 interview with the author.
17. William E. Leuchtenberg, *Franklin D. Roosevelt and the New Deal*, New York: Harper & Row, 1963.
18. Ball, *Imagining America.*
19. Lev Kuleshov, *Neobychaynye priklyucheniya mistera Vesta v strane bol'shevikov* [The Extraordinary Adventures of Mr West in the Land of the Bolsheviks], Moscow: Goskino, 1924.
20. Ilf and Petrov, *One-storied America or Ilf and Petrov's American Road Trip: The 1935 Travelogue of Two Soviet Writers*, 1936; New York: Princeton Architectural Press, 2006.
21. Upton Sinclair, *The Jungle*, New York: Doubleday Page, 1906.
22. Ibid.
23. Ilf and Petrov, *Ilf and Petrov's American Road Trip.*
24. Ibid.
25. Ibid.
26. Ibid.
27. 'Interviews with Gertrude Klivans', *Youngstown Telegram*, 1931.

4 'Agent 001'

1. US Immigration Department Records, passenger manifests from New York and Halifax arrivals, www.ancestry.com
2. 'Brief Life of American Textile Industry Entrepreneur Francis Cabot Lowell', *Harvard Magazine*, Boston: Harvard, 2009.
3. J. V. Stalin, 'Address to the Graduates from the Red Army Academies. Delivered in the Kremlin, May 4, 1935', London: Red Star Press, 1978.
4. US Immigration Department Records, passenger manifests from New York and Halifax arrivals, www.ancestry.com
5. S. Glukhovsky, *Kogda vyrastali kryl'ya* [When the Wings Grew], Moscow: Military Publishing, 1965.

6. US Immigration Department Records, passenger manifests from New York and Halifax arrivals, www.ancestry.com

7. Ibid.

8. Felix Ivanovich Chuev, *Stechkin*, Moscow: Molodaya gvardiya, 1978.

9. *The Stalin Digital Archive*, RGASPI.

10. Svetlana Chervonnaya, 'Documents Talk: Ludwig Lore', 2010, www.documentstalk.com

11. *The Stalin Digital Archive*, RGASPI.

12. NKVD interview with Yefim Medkov, RGASPI, 1935, f. 671, op. 1, d. 107–11.

13. Stanislav A. Shumovsky, 'Samolet dlya Antarktiki' [Aeroplane for Antarctica]. *Amerikanskaya tekhnika i promyshlennost* [American Engineering and Technology], 1933, No. 10.

14. Tim Tzouliadis, *The Forsaken: An American Tragedy in Stalin's Russia*, New York: Penguin Press, 2008.

15. Alexander Vershinin. 'Christie's Chassis: An American tank for the Soviets', Moscow, 2015, www.rbth.com

16. *The Stalin Digital Archive*, RGASPI.

17. Ibid.

18. Belorussian State Archive, 'Soviet Students Arrive at MIT', World Photo, 1931, www.tut.by

19. Karl Compton, 'MIT President's Report 1931', Boston: MIT, 1932.

20. MIT, 'Technology', The Vault of MIT, 1934, www.youtube.com

21. Stanislav A. Shumovsky, 'Students in USSR Maintained by Government, Families Supported Too', *The Tech*, Cambridge, MA: 19 February 1932.

22. The MIT Archives, Cambridge, MA: www.mit.com

23. Compton, 'MIT President's Report 1931'.

24. 'Student Disclosed as Secret Agent of OGPU; Throws Bomb into Class', *The Tech*, 1935.

25. NKVD Interrogations of Mikhail Cherniavsky, RGASPI, 1935, f. 671, op. 1, d. 107–11, and MIT Yearbook.

26. RGASPI, 1935, f. 671, op. 1, d. 107–11.

27. The MIT Archives.

28. Ivan Trashutin, *Tankovye dizeli* [*Diesel Tank Engines*].

29. RGASPI, 1935, f. 671, op. 1, d. 107–11.
30. Edward Reilly Stettinius, *Lend-lease: Weapon for Victory*, New York: Penguin Books, 1944.
31. The MIT Archives.
32. TsAGI, 'History', www.tsagi.com
33. The MIT Archives.
34. MIT Yearbook 1933. MIT, 1933.
35. Jack L. Kerrebrock, *Biographical Memoirs: Jerome Clarke Hunsaker*, The National Academies Press, 2000.
36. Lauren Clark and Eric Feron, with additional material by William T. G. Litant, 'A Brief History of MIT Aeronautics and Astronautics', Cambridge: MIT.
37. MIT 'Professor C. Fayette Taylor Centenary Celebration', 1994, http://web.mit.edu/hmtl/www/taylor.pdf
38. Taylor obituary, http://web.mit.edu/hmtl/www/taylor.pdf
39. Compton, 'MIT President's Reports 1931–1935'.

5 'A Nice Fellow to Talk To'

1. MIT Yearbook 1933.
2. 'Soviet Students Celebrate 16th Year of Regime', *The Tech*, Cambridge, MA: 17 November 1933.
3. Ibid.
4. Peter J. Kuznick, *Beyond the Laboratory: Scientists as Political Activists in 1930s America*, Chicago: University of Chicago Press, 1987.
5. Ibid.
6. Stanislav A. Shumovsky, 'Letter to Karl Compton', Cambridge, MA: MIT Archive, 1939.
7. Geoff Olynyk, 'Rings: Is It Looked Down Upon For an MIT Graduate Student to Wear the Grad Rat?', 2014. www.quora.com
8. NSA, Cables decrypted by the National Security Agency's Venona Project.
9. Vassiliev, Notebooks.
10. Ibid.
11. Compton, 'MIT President's Reports 1931–1935'.
12. Trashutin, *Diesel Tank Engines*.

13. *FBI Records: The Vault.*
14. Vassiliev, Notebooks.
15. US Immigration Department Records, passenger manifests from New York and Halifax arrivals, www.ancestry.com
16. Ibid.
17. *FBI Records: The Vault.*
18. Ibid.
19. Ibid.
20. Ibid.
21. Vassiliev, Notebooks.
22. Nigel West, *Historical Dictionary of Cold War Counterintelligence*, Lanham, MD: Scarecrow Press, 2007; 'Spy Case Figure Freed; Smilg, Approached by Gold, Acquitted of Perjury', *New York Times*, 1955.
23. *FBI Records: The Vault.*
24. Vassiliev, Notebooks.
25. NSA, Cables decrypted by the National Security Agency's Venona Project.
26. A. James Rudin, *The Dark Legacy of Henry Ford's Anti-Semitism*, Washington: Washington Post, 2014.
27. L. Dinnerstein, 'Jews and the New Deal', *American Jewish History*, Vol. 72, No. 4 (June 1983), pp. 461–76.
28. Benjamin Smilg, 'Application of Three-dimensional Flutter Theory to Aircraft Structures with Corrections for the Effects of Control Surface Aerodynamic Balance and Geared Tabs', Washington: War Department, Air Corps, Materiel Division, 1942; Benjamin Smilg and Frank Louis, 'The Development of a Procedure for Vibrating Loaded Structures', Cambridge, MA: MIT Department of Aeronautical Engineering, 1934.
29. Vassiliev, Notebooks.
30. NSA, Cables decrypted by the National Security Agency's Venona Project.
31. *FBI Records: The Vault.*
32. The MIT Archives.
33. Vassiliev, Notebooks.
34. Ibid.
35. NKVD Interrogations of Mikhail Cherniavsky, RGASPI, 1935, f. 671, op. 1, d. 107–11.

36. Ibid.
37. S. Kanevsky, 'Na aviatsionnykh zavodakh Ameriki, Frantsii, Anglii' [At the Aviation Factories of America, France and England], 6 July 1935, quoted in *Rossiya i SShA: ekonomicheskiye otnosheniya 1933–1941. Sbornik dokumentov* [Russia and USA Economic Relations 1933–1941. A Collection of Documents], Moscow: Nauka, 2001.
38. N. S. Babaev, Yu. S. Ustinov, *Kavalery zolotykh zvezd* [Knights of the Golden Stars], Moscow, Patriot: 2001; 'Andrey Nikolaevich Tupolev', trans. Svetlana Lokhova, SI Vavilov Institute of the History of Natural Science and Technology of the Russian Academy of Sciences (IIET NAS).
39. Testimony to Congress House Investigation into Un-American Activities.
40. Hearings before Committee on Un-American Activities. House of Representatives 83rd Congress 25, 26 and 27 February 1953. Washington: Library of Congress, 1953.
41. Columbia University Archive.
42. Shumovsky, 'Students in USSR Maintained by Government, Families Supported Too', *The Tech*; Babaev and Ustinov, *Knights of the Golden Stars*.
43. Trashutin, *Diesel Tank Engines*.
44. Compton, 'MIT President's Report 1931'.
45. Shumovsky, 'Students in USSR Maintained by Government, Families Supported Too', *The Tech*.
46. 'Tech Union Hears G Men Talk on Crime Detection', *The Tech*, 20 December 1935.
47. John Fox, *The FBI. A Brief History*, www.fbi.com; 'Andrey Nikolaevich Tupolev', trans. Svetlana Lokhova, IIET NAS. Moscow: www.ihst.ru
48. 'Tech Union Hears G Men Talk on Crime Detection', *The Tech*, 20 December 1935.

6 'Is This Really My Motherland?'

1. NKVD Interrogation Protocols of Raisa Bennett, RGASPI, 1935, f. 671, op. 1, d. 107–11.
2. NKVD Interview with Eugene Bukley in ibid.
3. NKVD Interrogations of Mikhail Cherniavsky in ibid.

4. NKVD Interview with Yefim Medkov and NKVD Interview with Eugene Bukley.

5. Ibid.

6. NKVD Interrogations of Mikhail Cherniavsky and NKVD Interview with Yefim Medkov.

7. NKVD Interview with Yefim Medkov.

8. M. A. Alekseev, A. L. Kolpakidi, V. Y. Kochik, *Encyclopedia of Military Intelligence 1918–1945*, Moscow: Kuchkovo Pole, 2012; S. Glukhovsky, *When the Wings Grew*, Moscow: Military Publishing, 1965.

9. NKVD Interview with Yefim Medkov.

10. NKVD Interrogation Protocols of Raisa Bennett.

11. NKVD Interview with Yefim Medkov.

12. NKVD Interrogations of Mikhail Cherniavsky.

13. Ibid.

14. Ibid.; NKVD Interrogation Protocols of Raisa Bennett.

15. Military Service Records of Mikhail Kondratevich Cherniavsky, Red Army, 1935; Alekseev et al., *Encyclopedia of Military Intelligence 1918–1945*, p. 827.

16. Communist Party Membership Records of Mikhail Kondratevich Cherniavsky, RGASPI.

17. Ibid.

18. A. Velidov, *Krasnaya kniga VChK* [Red Book of the All-Union CHEKA]. Photograph of Fishman and Cherniavsky. Moscow: Politizdat, 1989.

19. Military Service Records of Mikhail Kondratevich Cherniavsky.

20. Ibid.

21. Amos Fries, *Chemical Warfare*, New York: McGraw-Hill, 1921.

22. L. A. Fedorov, *Chemical Weapons: War with One's Own People*, Moscow: Lesnaya Strana, 2009.

23. Yu. Dyakov, T. Bushueva, *Fashistky mech kovalsya v SSSR* [The Fascist Sword was Forged in Soviet Union: A Collection of Documents], Moscow: Sovetskaya Rossiya, 1992.

24. NKVD Interrogations of Mikhail Cherniavsky.

25. Military Service Records of Mikhail Kondratevich Cherniavsky.

26. NKVD Interrogations of Mikhail Cherniavsky.

27. Communist Party Membership Records of Mikhail Kondratevich Cherniavsky, RGASPI.

28. Military Service Records of Mikhail Kondratevich Cherniavsky.
29. The MIT Archives.
30. Vladimir Nikolaevich Ipatieff, *The Life of a Chemist: Memoirs of Vladimir N. Ipatieff*, Stanford: Stanford University Press, 1946.
31. Dyakov, 'The Fascist Sword was Forged in Soviet Union: A Collection of Documents'.
32. Ibid.
33. NKVD Interrogations of Mikhail Cherniavsky.
34. John Ross, 'Frederick George Keyes June 24, 1885–April 14, 1976', The National Acadamies, www.nap.edu, 1998.
35. Joel A. Vilensky, *Dew of Death: The Story of Lewisite, America's World War I Weapon of Mass Destruction*, Bloomington: Indiana University Press, 2005.
36. Ibid.
37. *The Stalin Digital Archive*, RGASPI.
38. Ibid.
39. NKVD Interrogations of Mikhail Cherniavsky.
40. Ibid.

7 'Questionable from Conception'

1. NKVD Interrogation Protocols of Raisa Bennett.
2. Bennett and Epstein Family Records, Ray Bennett.
3. Ibid.
4. Ibid.
5. NKVD Interrogation Protocols of Raisa Bennett.
6. Ibid.
7. Bennett and Epstein Family Records.
8. NKVD Interrogation Protocols of Raisa Bennett.
9. Ibid.
10. Ibid.
11. Mikhail Alekseev, *Sovetskaya voennaya razvedka v Kitae* [Soviet Military Intelligence in China], Moscow: Kuchkovo Pole, 2010.
12. Ibid.
13. *FBI Records: The Vault*; Bennett and Epstein Family Records.
14. Bennett and Epstein Family Records.

15. The Spy Museum, Washington, DC, 'The Tokyo Spy Ring', www.spymuseum.com
16. Alekseev, *Soviet Military Intelligence in China*.
17. Maya and Nadezhda Ulanovskaya, *Istoriya odnoy semyi* [One Family's Story], Moscow: Chalidze Publications, 1982.
18. NKVD Interrogation Protocols of Raisa Bennett.
19. Ibid.
20. Ibid.
21. Chalmers Johnson and Edan Corkill, 'Sorge's Spy is Brought in From the Cold: A Soviet-Okinawan Connection', *Asia Pacific Journal*, 2014.
22. NKVD Interview with Eugene Bukley.
23. *The Stalin Digital Archive*, RGASPI.
24. NKVD Interrogation Protocols of Raisa Bennett.
25. Ibid.
26. Bennett and Epstein Family Records.

8 'The Wily Armenian'

1. US Immigration Department Records. Passenger manifests from New York and Halifax arrivals, www.ancestry.com.
2. Robert J. Lamphere and Tom Shachtman, *FBI–KGB War: A Special Agent's Story*, New York: W. H. Allen/Virgin Books, 1987.
3. Alexander Vassiliev, Notebooks, trans. Svetlana Lokhova. wilsoncenter.com
4. SVR, 'Gaik Ovakimian', Moscow: SVR, http://svr.gov.ru/history/ovakimjan.htm
5. Vladimir Chikov, *Nelegaly* [Illegals], 2, Moscow: AST, 1997.
6. SVR, 'Gaik Ovakimian'.
7. *The Stalin Digital Archive*, RGASPI.
8. Ibid.
9. Ibid.
10. Ibid.
11. Ibid.
12. Lamphere and Shachtman, *FBI-KGB War*.
13. Vladimir V. Poznyakov, *Sovetskaya razvedka v Amerike, 1919–1941* [Soviet

Intelligence in America, 1919–1941], Moscow: Mezhdunarodnye otnosheniya. 2005.

14. Vassiliev, Notebooks.
15. *The Stalin Digital Archive*, RGASPI.
16. Vassiliev, Notebooks.
17. Christopher Andrew and Vasili Mitrokhin, *The Mitrokhin Archive: The KGB in Europe and the West*, London: Penguin Books, 1999.
18. Vassiliev, Notebooks.
19. Ibid.
20. Ibid.
21. Ibid.
22. NSA, Cables decrypted by the National Security Agency's Venona Project.
23. John Earl Haynes, Howard Klehr and Alexander Vassiliev, *Spies: The Rise and Fall of the KGB in America*, New Haven: Yale University Press, 2009.
24. William Christian Bullitt, *The Great Globe Itself*, New York: Scribner's, 1946.
25. Ibid.
26. Charles E. Bohlen, *Witness to History, 1929–1969*, New York: Norton, 1973.
27. *The Stalin Digital Archive*, RGASPI.
28. Ibid.
29. Ibid.
30. Ibid.
31. Ibid.
32. Haynes, Klehr and Vassiliev, *Spies.*
33. *FBI Records: The Vault.*
34. Vassiliev, Notebooks.
35. Major George Racey Jordan, 'From Major Jordan's Diaries – The Truth about the US and USSR', www.archive.org

9 Whistle Stop Inspections

1. S. Glukhovsky, *When the Wings Grew*.
2. *The Stalin Digital Archive*, RGASPI.

3. A. S. Yakovlev, *Fifty Years of Aircraft Construction*. Translated from the Russian: Jerusalem: Israel Program from Scientific Translations, 1970.
4. Andrey Tupolev, 'Speech to Seventh Congress of the Soviets', www.monimo.ru
5. Yakovlev, *Fifty Years of Aircraft Construction*.
6. S. Kanevsky and A. N. Tupolev, *At Aviation Factories of America, France and England*, Moscow: For Industrialisation, 1935.
7. A. Auzan, *Aviation of the USA*, Moscow: For Industrialisation, 1935.
8. Kanevsky and Tupolev, *At Aviation Factories of America, France and England*.
9. Ibid.
10. Auzan, *Aviation of the USA*.
11. Kanevsky and Tupolev, *At Aviation Factories of America, France and England*.
12. Aerospace Industries Association, 'Aircraft Year Book – Aerospace Industries Association', 1931 to 1939, www.aia.com
13. Kanevsky and Tupolev, *At Aviation Factories of America, France and England*.
14. Ibid.
15. *FBI Records: The Vault*.
16. Vassiliev, Notebooks.
17. Auzan, *Aviation of the USA*.
18. Ibid.
19. Vassiliev, Notebooks.
20. Ibid.
21. Ibid.
22. Ibid.
23. Ibid.
24. Haynes, Klehr and Vassiliev, *Spies*.
25. NSA, Cables decrypted by the National Security Agency's Venona Project.
26. Haynes, Klehr and Vassiliev, *Spies*.
27. Ibid.
28. Ibid.
29. Ibid.

10 Glory to Stalin's Falcons

1. Mikhail Gromov, *Na zemlei v nebe* [On the Ground and in the Sky], Moscow: Glasnost-AS, 2005.
2. *The Stalin Digital Archive*, RGASPI.
3. Leonard Leshuk, *US Intelligence Perceptions of Soviet Power, 1921–1946*, London: Routledge, 2003; 2018.
4. J. V. Stalin, 'The Tasks of Business Executives. Speech Delivered at the First All-Union Conference of Leading Personnel of Socialist Industry 1, February 4, 1931', www.marxists.org; J. V. Stalin, *Voprosy leninizma* [Problems of Leninism], Moscow: Foreign Languages Publishing House, 1953, pp. 454–8.
5. 'Soviet Air Expert Lauds Successful Flights', *Orlando Sentinel*, 24 June 1937, interview with Shumovsky.
6. 'President Wires Russian Flyers', *Indianapolis Star*, 21 June 1937.
7. 'Soviet Air Expert Lauds Successful Flights', *Orlando Sentinel*, 24 June 1937.
8. Ibid.
9. Ibid.
10. Ibid.
11. 'Soviet Engineer Discloses Some of Secrets of Over-Top-of-World Airplane', *Montana Standard*, 24 June 1937.
12. Ibid.
13. Ibid.
14. Ibid.
15. Ibid
16. Vassiliev, Notebooks.
17. Ibid.
18. Ibid.
19. Communist Party Membership Records of Stanislav Antonovich Shumovsky, RGASPI.
20. Vassiliev, Notebooks.
21. Ibid.
22. Ibid.
23. Ibid.
24. Ibid.
25. Hornblum, *The Invisible Harry Gold*.

26. Vassiliev, Notebooks.
27. Aerospace Industries Association, 'Aircraft Year Book – Aerospace Industries Association', 1931 to 1939.
28. Ibid.

11 Back in the USSR

1. US Immigration Department Records, passenger manifests from New York and Halifax arrivals, www.ancestry.com
2. NSA, Cables decrypted by the National Security Agency's Venona Project; Vassiliev, Notebooks.
3. Vassiliev, Notebooks.
4. Ibid.
5. NSA, Cables decrypted by the National Security Agency's Venona Project.
6. Vassiliev, Notebooks.
7. Ibid.
8. Ibid.
9. Ibid.
10. Communist Party Membership Records of Stanislav Antonovich Shumovsky, RGASPI.
11. Ibid.
12. 'Lessons in the management of domestic aircraft construction: to the 75th anniversary of the creation of the USSR People's Commissariat for Aircraft Industry' in Russian by Viktor Kuznetsov, published 20 December 2013 on aex.ru
13. Dana T. Parker, *Building Victory: Aircraft Manufacturing in the Los Angeles Area in World War II*, Cypress: Dana T. Parker, 2013.
14. *Aviatsiya Vtoroy mirovoy* [Aviation of the Second World War], www. airpages.ru
15. Ibid.
16. Ibid.
17. Ibid.
18. Ibid.
19. Ibid.
20. Ibid.

21. Aerospace Industries Association, 'Aircraft Year Book – Aerospace Industries Association', 1931 to 1939.

22. TsAGI, 'History', www.tsagi.com

23. *The Stalin Digital Archive*, RGASPI.

24. Vassiliev, Notebooks.

25. SVR, 'Gaik Ovakimian'.

26. Vassiliev, Notebooks.

12 Project 'AIR'

1. Trashutin, *Tankovye dizeli* [Diesel Tank Engines].

2. *The Stalin Digital Archive*, RGASPI.

3. Ibid.

4. Gromov, *On the Ground and in the Sky*.

5. Ibid.

6. Communist Party Membership Records of Stanislav Antonovich Shumovsky, RGASPI.

7. TsAGI, 'History'. www.tsagi.com

8. NSA, Cables decrypted by the National Security Agency's Venona Project.

9. Ibid.

10. Convoys to Russia and Halifax, www.convoyweb.org

11. Gromov, *On the Ground and in the Sky*.

12. Ibid.

13. US Immigration Department Records, passenger manifests from New York and Halifax arrivals, www.ancestry.com; Convoys to Russia and Halifax, www.convoyweb.org

14. Convoys to Russia and Halifax, www.convoyweb.org

15. Vassiliev, Notebooks.

16. Andrey Gromyko, *Memoirs*, New York: Doubleday, 1989.

17. Vassiliev, Notebooks.

18. Ibid.

19. Hornblum, *The Invisible Harry Gold*.

20. Vassiliev, Notebooks.

21. The MIT Archives.

22. NSA, Cables decrypted by the National Security Agency's Venona Project.

23. Ibid.
24. Ibid.
25. Ibid.
26. Vassiliev, Notebooks.
27. NSA, Cables decrypted by the National Security Agency's Venona Project.
28. *FBI Records: The Vault.*
29. NSA, Cables decrypted by the National Security Agency's Venona Project.
30. Vassiliev, Notebooks.
31. US Congress, Testimony of Victor A. Kravchenko: Hearings Before the Committee on Un-American Activities, House of Representatives, Eightieth Congress, First Session, on H.R.1884 and H.R.2122, Bills to Curb Or Outlaw the Communist Party of the United States. Public Law 601 (section 121, Subsection Q (2)) July 22, 1947. Washington, DC: US Government Printing Office, 1948.
32. Ibid.
33. Major George Racey Jordan, 'From Major Jordan's Diaries – The Truth about the US and USSR', www. archive.org
34. Vassiliev, Notebooks.
35. Ibid.
36. NSA, Cables decrypted by the National Security Agency's Venona Project.

13 ENORMOZ

1. Pavel Anatoli Sudoplatov, Jerrold L. Schecter, Leona P. Schecter, *Special Tasks: The Memoirs of an Unwanted Witness – A Soviet Spymaster*, Boston: Little, Brown, 1994.
2. TsAGI. 'History'. www.tsagi.com
3. Ibid.
4. Communist Party Membership Records of Stanislav Antonovich Shumovsky, RGASPI.
5. *The Stalin Digital Archive*, RGASPI.
6. Ibid.
7. Michael Neiberg, *Potsdam: The End of World War II and the Remaking of Europe*, New York: Basic Books, 2015.

8. Herbert Frank York, *The Advisors: Oppenheimer, Teller, and the Superbomb*, Redwood City, CA: Stanford University Press, 1989.
9. Kurchatov letters to Molotov, Atomny Proekt SSSR. Dokumenty I Materialy [USSR's Atomic Project Documents and Materials]. Moscow: Naeuka, 1998.
10. Pavel Fitin's letter to Ovamikian, January 1941, in Ibid.
11. History of the University of Minnesota online: https://www.physics.umn.edu/about/history/
12. Vassiliev, Notebooks.
13. Ibid.
14. Ibid.
15. Kurchatov letters to Molotov, USSR's Atomic Project Documents and Materials.
16. Ibid.
17. Yershov had a mixed portfolio of political and S&T intelligence responsibilities.
18. Vassiliev, Notebooks.
19. Feklisov, *The Man Behind the Rosenbergs*.
20. Fuchs started providing valuable information to the Soviets in England before his transfer to the US.
21. Vassiliev, Notebooks.
22. Ibid.

14 Mission Accomplished

1. M. D. Yevtif'ev, *Ognennye Kryl'ya* [Fiery Wings], Moscow: Veche, 2005, p. 144.
2. Ibid.
3. A. S. Stepanov, *Razvitie Sovetskoy aviatsii v predvoennyy period (1938 god – pervaya polovina 1941 goda)* [The Development of Soviet Aviation in the Pre-war Period (1938– Early 1941)], Moscow: Litres, 2017.
4. *FBI Records: The Vault.*
5. NSA, Cables decrypted by the National Security Agency's Venona Project.
6. Stepanov, *The Development of Soviet Aviation.*
7. *The Stalin Digital Archive*, RGASPI.

8. *Aviation of the Second World War*, www.airpages.ru
9. Andrey Tupolev, 'The Dismantling of B29 Superfortress'. www. monimo.ru
10. Stepanov, *The Development of Soviet Aviation*.
11. Mark Gallay, *Ispytano v nebe* [Tested in the Heavens], Moscow: Molodaya gvardiya, 1963.
12. Ibid.
13. *The Cold War Superfortress Russian Style: Newsreel Footage of Tushino Airshow 1947*, Moscow: Russian Central Studio of Documentary Films, 2004.
14. Gallay, *Tested in the Heavens*.

Post-scriptum

1. Communist Party Membership Records of Stanislav Antonovich Shumovsky, RGASPI.
2. 'A Celebration of the Life of Professor Stanislav Shumovsky', MFTI.
3. Shumovsky, 'The Planning of Technical Education in Developing Countries'.

APPENDIX I

Biography of Stanislav Shumovsky

1902	Born in Kharkov.
1918	Graduates after 5 years at Realschule (science school), Shusha.
August 1918	Volunteers for Red Army. Appointed section commander Pyotr Ipatov's detachment.
1919	Appointed Head of machine-gun section of 7th Regiment of the 2nd Stavropol Rifle Division.
April 1920	Appointed Commissar (political instructor) and Field Adjutant of 32nd Rifle Division,11th Army, based in Baku and Dagestan.
July 1920	Appointed Staff Military Commissar of the 281st Rifle Regiment, 32nd Rifle Division.
May 1921	Head of Information, Political Department, 32nd Rifle Division, based in Derbent.
July 1921	Head of Registration and Allocation, and Head of Mobilisation Department, Political Directorate, Samara and the Volga Military District.

December 1922	Head of Organisational Instruct Department and Head of Registration-Mobilisation Unit of Political Department, 33rd Rifle Division, Samara, Zhizdra.
May 1924	Commissar of Engineering Department, 33rd Rifle Division, Mogilev on Dnieper.
September 1924	Senior instructor for special units, Political Department, Smolensk, Western Military District.
December 1924	Trainee pilot-observer, 2nd Independent Reconnaissance Squadron.
September 1925	Executive organiser of the party collective, electro-mining school of the Baltic Fleet, Kronstadt.
1926	Death of Adam Shumovsky.
September 1926	Leaves army.
	Head investigator for military affairs, People's Commissariat for Finance, Moscow.
August 1929	Student at Bauman Moscow Higher Technical School.
October 1930	Student at the Special Courses of the Central Committee of the Communist Party, Leningrad.
September 1931	Student at Massachusetts Institute of Technology, USA.
June 1934	Graduates with a BSc from MIT.
March 1935	Leave of absence from MIT for Tupolev trip.
June 1936	Completes Master's degree at MIT. Thesis on 'The Effectiveness of the Vertical Tail of the Aircraft for Various Combinations of Wing and Fuselage'. Appointed Deputy Plenipotentiary for the Commissariat of Heavy Industry, based at AMTORG in New York.

February 1939   Leaves USA to be appointed Deputy Chair of
                 Technical Council, People's Commissariat for
                 Aviation Industry, Moscow.

June 1940   Deputy Head of Central Aero and Hydrodynamics
                 Institute (TSAGI) and Head of its Bureau of New
                 Technology, Moscow.

October 1941   Secondment to USA to join Soviet Purchasing
                 Commision.

May 1943   Returns to USSR, Head of Bureau of New
                 Technology, TsAGI.

1944   Medal for Defence of Moscow.

1945   Order of the Great Patriotic War Grade I.

1946   Medal for Valiant Labour in the Great Patriotic
                 War.

1947   Medal In Commemoration of 800th Anniversary
                 of Moscow.

September 1951   Head Lecturer, Moscow Aviation Technological
                 Institute.

October 1952   Dean, Moscow Aviation Technological Institute.

March 1953   Acting Deputy Director of Studies, Moscow
                 Aviation Technological Institute.

September 1954   Deputy Director of Studies, Moscow Physical–
                 Technical Institute.

February 1961   Head of Methodological Directorate, Ministry of
                 High and Secondary Special Education of RSFSR,
                 Moscow.

July 1961   Awarded Order of the Badge of Honour for great
                 service in preparing specialists and developing
                 science.

September 1964   Appointed Member of the USSR Commission for UNESCO Affairs.

October 1969   Consultant professor, Moscow Aviation Technological Institute.

October 1975   Awarded the Order of the Badge of Honour, for his work establishing the Council for Security and Cooperation in Europe.

February 1982   Awarded the badge for 50 Years of Membership in the Communist Party.

1 October 1984   Dies in Moscow.

APPENDIX II

NKVD Reports on Stanislav Shumovsky, 1942

From: WASHINGTON

To: MOSCOW

No.: 7238   27 November 1942

To [1 group unidentified][a]

    Your 5023[b]. [1 group unrecovered] aviation standard
of the air forces of the army [and][c] the navy [1 group
unrecovered] we sent through the People's Commissariat of
Foreign Trade [NARKOMVNEShTORG] in March 1942. [1 group
unrecovered] immediately three more renovated [3 groups
unrecovered] standard in the amount of over 700. Moreover
we sent off in November [1 group unrecovered] aviation
specifications of the S.A.E. standard. [1 group unrecovered]
[C% unlimited] [B% copies[d]] of all reports of the air forces
on tests of planes, motors, [1 group unrecovered], assemblies,
and materials. Part of [C% what we] already [C% have gotten]
we are sending off by the next pouch. The total of reports is
over 600 for the period 1938-1942 and includes confidential and
secret. We are taking steps to get [B% copies[d]] of all NACA
works from 1940 to 1942. We sent off in November a large
quantity of descriptions of planes, motors, assemblies, also
a lot of [B% materials] from firms.

                                   ShUMOVSKIJ[i]

T.N.: [a] This name begins with Ch or Sh.

       [b] Not published; addressed to ShUMOVSKIJ. The few
           recovered fragments do not relate to the subject
           of the present telegram.

Appendix II

[c] Added by translator.

[d] The word used for "copies", if correctly recovered,
is KOPII, which should mean "copies taken, made from
an original," not EKZEMPLARY, which means "examples
or representatives of a given production or publication."
Stanislav

Comment: [i] ~~Vladislav~~ ShUMOVSKIJ, believed to be the BLÉRIOT
[BLERIO] of New York ███ traffic.

From: MOSCOW

To: WASHINGTON

No.: 5594   10 December 1942

To BELYaEV, ShUMOVSKIJ[i] 7238[a] -

Comrade ShUMOVSKIJ [8 groups unrecovered]
a considerable quantity of materials on

[13 groups unrecovered, 18 groups unrecoverable, 1 group
unrecovered]

in America. In

[10 groups unrecovered].

Comrade ShUMOVSKIJ [4 groups unrecovered] those confidential
and secret reports which he has gotten for the period 1938-1942.
[1 group unrecovered] Comrade ShUMOVSKIJ must arrange for
[1 group unrecovered] on planes via FAIRBANKS. [5 groups
unrecovered] to FAIRBANKS

[18 groups unrecovered]

to the U.S.S.R by this route,

[32 groups unrecoverable, 16 groups unrecovered,
10 groups unrecoverable]

T.N.: [a] Wash. to Moscow #7238 of 27 November 1942 ███.
Stanislav

Comments: [i] ~~Vladislav~~ ShUMOVSKIJ, believed to be the
BLERIOT [BLERIO] of New York ███ traffic.

Appendix II

FBI Report on Stanislav Shumovsky, 1951

FEDERAL BUREAU OF INVESTIGATION

Form No. 1 THIS CASE ORIGINATED AT LOS ANGELES			FILE No. 65-396	
REPORT MADE AT LOS ANGELES	DATE WHEN MADE 7/21/51	PERIOD FOR WHICH MADE 6,11,14/51	REPORT MADE BY THOMAS E. BRYANT	BAJ
TITLE STANISLAUS SHUMOVSKY, was.			CHARACTER OF CASE ESPIONAGE - R	

SYNOPSIS OF FACTS:

Testimony of BENJAMIN SMILG before the Loyalty-Security Board, Wright-Patterson Air Force Base, Dayton, Ohio on November 9 and 10, 1950 reviewed and information set forth concerning SMILG'S association with subject.

DETAILS:

By letter dated June 2, 1951 the Bureau transmitted a photostatic copy of the testimony given by BENJAMIN SMILG before a Loyalty-Security Hearing Board at the Wright-Patterson Air Force Base, Dayton, Ohio. This transcript is in question and answer form and the following is a summary of the pertinent information concerning SMILG'S association with subject who has been positively identified as a Soviet espionage agent.

SMILG stated that he became acquainted with subject at the Massachusetts Institute of Technology (MIT) in 1931. SMILG stated he recalled that during an examination in a class in aerodynamics, SHUMOVSKY had considerable difficulty and as SMILG sat near SHUMOVSKY he offered to tutor the latter, and did so until SHUMOVSKY left MIT shortly before May of 1935. SMILG stated that SHUMOVSKY would come to SMILG'S home for these lessons, at which time SHUMOVSKY met SMILG'S mother, father and brother. SMILG stated that SHUMOVSKY resided in Cambridge with ten or twelve other Russian students.

SMILG stated that SHUMOVSKY, during this period, never engaged in political discussions and that SHUMOVSKY stated before he came to

455

ACKNOWLEDGEMENTS

This book began its life almost twenty years ago when, upon the urgings of my mentor Professor Christopher Andrew of Corpus Christi College at the University of Cambridge, I visited a Russian archive in Moscow. Newly declassified documents from the personal archive of Nikolay Yezhov, head of Stalin's security service, were made available to me. I bought as many pages as an impoverished student could afford. Hidden in those documents since 1935 were the first clues about this intelligence operation.

I owe an enormous debt to Professor Christopher Andrew for introducing me to the fascinating subject of intelligence history in my undergraduate days at Cambridge. Over the many years it has taken to complete this work, Chris has been unstinting in his support and praise for my work. He has been enormously helpful in providing copious amounts of background from his unrivalled knowledge of this subject.

Espionage books are unusual in that of the people who have helped me, many have asked not to be named or publicly acknowledged. The reader will understand that this reluctance to make themselves known is due to the sensitivities of the roles that they have or hold. I am extremely grateful for their many contributions. They have helped in so many ways to grow my understanding of this subject. I am not a practitioner of either intelligence or counter-intelligence but a historian grateful for their shared insights.

In pursuit of my research over the years, I have been encouraged and supported by my fellow historians. They have kindly shared their own experiences, knowledge and above all given encouragement. Foremost among them I would like to thank Dr John Barber of King's College, Cambridge, for all his time and generosity of support. John first spotted my rough early research efforts and continually encouraged me to believe that they would become a story worth telling. I am indebted to the mentoring at Cambridge of Professor Christopher Clark, Dr Peter Warner and Dr William Foster. I am grateful to Professor Donald Rayfield of Queen Mary's College whom I first met in the Russian archives in the midst of a Moscow winter. Emeritus Professor Robert Davies aided my understanding of the economic history of the Soviet Union, a subject in which he is the unrivalled expert.

Security services historians have helped me develop an understanding of the work and methods of US counter-intelligence in the 1940s. I am grateful to Hayden Peake and to John Fox, official historian of the FBI. Aside from his extraordinarily valuable insights, John has helped me navigate the Freedom of Information minefield in the US.

Among my friends who have shared my journey I must thank Gordon Corera, security correspondent of the BBC, in particular. Gordon was a rock when certain members of the press confused an espionage historian with an actual practitioner. He is a role

Acknowledgements

model for journalists, sadly one of the few. Other friends who have been helpful along the way include John Andrews of the Special Forces Club. I have been encouraged by the reception of my work from the members of the Cambridge Intelligence Seminar.

Without archivists and the extraordinary work they do I could have never completed this work. The huge number of revelations and clarifications were sourced from the files in their trust. It has been my privilege to work with Allen Packwood, director of the Churchill Archive Centre at Churchill College, University of Cambridge. The Mitrokhin Archive in his care is a valuable resource. I thank the teams at various Russian archives, including in Moscow the Russian State Archive of Socio-Political History (RGASPI), the Russian State Army Archive (RGAV) and the Archive of the Ministry of Foreign Affairs of the Russian Federation (MID); the Russian State Archive of the Navy (RGAVMF) in St Petersburg; the Archive of the President of the Russian Federation and the Archive of Alexander Yakovlev.

In North America, I have found helpful material in the archives of the FBI, CIA, Massachusetts Institute of Technology, Harvard University, Columbia University, University of Toronto, Purdue University and the Wilson Center.

I am honoured and humbled to have spoken with the family of Ray Bennett both in Russia and the USA. They have all been extremely generous with their time and in sharing their family's personal papers and photographs. Joy Bennett is the only surviving member of the team deployed by Soviet Intelligence acting as cover for her mother at a very young age.

My team at my publisher HarperCollins have all worked tremendously hard. I thank them for their commitment to and for sharing all their enthusiasm for my book. The striking cover artwork reflects the talent of the designer Jack Smyth. The copy editor Steve Gove did an amazing job making sense of my draft. I owe a debt of gratitude to my unstinting project editor Iain Hunt. Above all I am grateful for all the support of Arabella Pike. She is a wonderful editor, guiding me tirelessly through the tortuous journey of getting my first book across the line. Thank you.

A special thank you to my friends who have helped with researching and editing this book.

Finally, I must mention my immediate family. My father has provided inspiration, given me unstinting support, helped me with everything from historical knowledge and insights on Soviet life to translations to proofreading. My daughter has made a fantastic contribution by giving me so much joy in her first year of life and providing entertainment while I was completing the book.

My partner David has supported me through what was 'the best of times and the worst of times'. His contribution to this book is inestimable.

INDEX

Index

Index

Index

Index

Index

Index

Red Army: advance into German territory (1944-5), 121, 407, 408; and air war on Eastern Front, 354; in Armenia (1920), 203; buys M-1931 tanks, 109–11; Chemical Warfare Division, 161–3, 206; Cherniavsky in, 160–1; and civil war, 35–9, 40, 41, 161; civil war partisans, 31, 32, 33, 33–5; command structure, 37, 43★; commissars' role, 37; 'deep penetration' strategy, 108; defeat of Chinese in Manchuria (1929), 182; delegation to West (1930), 109–10; Eastern Front victories (1943), 355, 374–5, 376; on eve of Barbarossa, 331–2; illiteracy eradicated in, 67; Military Chemical Academy, 206; military discipline introduced (1919), 36–7; oath of loyalty, 11★, 35–6; rapid expansion (from 1937), 313, 331; resistance to Nazi advance, 333, 337, 374–5; seizes Baku's oil wealth, 39, 40; Trotsky's 'blocking troops', 37; winter war with Finland, 319–20

Reed, John, 66

Reilly, Sidney ('Ace of Spies'), 62

Republic aircraft company, 241, 409, 410

revolutionary period (1917-19): Russian revolutions (1917), 26–7, 176, 257–8; in Transcaucasia, 27–30, 40

Riaskin (American Trotskyist), 157–9

Rickenbacker, Eddie, 412

Rockefeller Foundation, 68–9

Rockefeller Institute for Medical Research, New York, 211

rocketry and missiles, 2–3, 112★, 212, 373, 376, 405–6, 407–8, 409, 410–11; JB-2 'Loon' (reverse-engineered V1), 409–10; RP-318 rocket plane, 316

Rockne, Knute, 269–70

Rogers, William Barton, 118

Rokhinson, Vladimir, 170, 171

Roosevelt, Franklin Delano, 87–8, 213–14, 219, 220, 222, 281, 285, 320, 351; and carpet/saturation bombing, 377; and Manhattan Project, 379, 381, 391, 416; meeting with Gromov (September 1941), 338–9; and Pearl Harbor attack, 347; tour of recently liberated Crimea, 375

Roosevelt, Henry L., 237

Rosenberg, Ethel and Julius, 8★, 217, 374, 393, 395★, 395–6, 401

Rostarchuk, Alexander 'Rosty', 122, 363–4, 365

Rowan, Richard Wilmer, *Spy and Counterspy*, 58, *59*, 406

Royal Air Force, 376

Russian Civil War (1917-22), 31–6, 161; and Caucasus region, 39, 40, 41; exiled White Guard organisations, 99, 296; Japanese intervention, 271–2; large-scale battles (1919), 37–9; Western support for Whites, 38–9; 'White Terror', 38

Russian Empire: 1905 Revolution, 17–18, 19; anti-Semitism in, 18–19, 20; and aviation, 11–13, 21–2; and Caucasus, 25, 27–30; emigration to USA from, 19–21, 66, 156, 174–6; February revolution (1917), 26–7, 176; and First World War, 21–7, 57, 166; inequality and social division, 14, 15–17, 18, 19; invasions of, 56–7; Lena Goldfields Massacre (1912), 19; nationalities in, 18–19, 25, 27–30; October revolution (1917), 27, 66–7, 176, 257–8; Okhranka (Tsar's secret police), 17, 18, 215; rapid industrialisation, 15, 16–17; Russification policy, 18–19; and Shumovsky's family, 13–15; Tsarist fear of education, 65–6; violent responses to protest, 16, 17, 18, 19; war with Sweden (1610-17), 57★; WW1 banning of vodka sales, 23–4

Rutherford, Ernest, 68, 381

Sanguszko, Roman Damian (Polish prince), 13–14

Sarant, Alfred, 414

Scanlon, Martin F., 265–6

Schmidt, Otto, 277

Scientific American, the Advocate of Industry and Enterprise (magazine), 47

scientific and technological (S&T) espionage: agent-end customer communications, 149; air bridge from USA to USSR, 365, 366, 369–72; AMTORG's role, 56, 105, 106, 110, 330; annual report on US aviation, 228; and Artuzov, 203–4, 206; becomes an INO objective (1925), 60, 62, 204; Dzerzhinsky's role, 52; ENORMOZ operation, 202, 329, 350★, 374, 383, 384–90, 391–6, 397–9, 400–1; FBI search

262; biographical writings on, 9–10; Blériot as hero of, 11, 125, 126; and Boston émigré circle, 20–1, 257; and Boston Trotskyists, 256–7, 258, 297; in California (November 1935), 251–3; childhood and education, 11–13, 14–15, 18, 23, 24–5, 31; in civil war Red Army, 35–6, 37, 39, 203; as civil war Red Army partisan, 31, 32, *33*, 33–5; civil war wounds, 38, 39, 41; with commission to Germany (October 1939), 322–4; and Compton, 131–2; crash ends flying career, 42–3; and Curtiss-Wright, 214, 225; death of (1 October 1984), 423; expansion beyond MIT (from 1934), 242–3, 248–56, 262; extrovert image, 7, 148; family background, 13–14, 31; family life, 41, 312, 375–6; first flight as pilot (1924), 41–2; as FRED suspect, 5–6, 403; and German aircraft/equipment, 324–5, 336, 407–9, 410–11; and German invasion, 336–7; in Germany (1946), 410; and Great Terror (1937), 296–8; at Harvard Avenue house, 119–20; as head investigator of armaments industry, 45–7, 58; and heavy bomber design, 274, 275–6; industry contacts of, 8, 135; INO recruits as spy, 61, 62–3; and jet aircraft, 2–3, 405–6, 409, 410–11; joins Soviet Communist Party (1920), 40–1; legacy of, 373, 421; lessons from advertising industry, 130–1; as liaison officer to USAAF, 359, 362; at MIT, 2, 6–9, 64, 112–20, *123*, 124–8, 129–35, 136–45, 146–53, 211–12; as MIT graduate student, 244–6, 248, 254; and the Molotovs, 218; moves to West Coast, 291; and Nazi technology, 2–3, 321, 408–9, 410–11; network of contacts and agents in US, 8, 214, 242, 244; and new Soviet recruits at MIT (1938), 305, 306–10; and NKAP, 313–16, 408; and Ovakimian, 202, 211–12, 214; physical appearance, 2; Polish origins of, 13–14; post-1947 career in education, 421–3; Purchasing Commission to USA (late-1941), 340, 341–3, 344, 345–8, 350–4, 355–6, 357, 362, 363–4; radical politics

of, 23, 27, 29–31, 372–3; recalled to Moscow (1938), 311–12; Red Army service after civil war, 41, 43; return to Moscow (May 1943), 367, 369–72, 375; revives (S&T) espionage in USA, 357–8, 362–3, 367; on Russian education, 66; sees plane fly in Kharkov (1910), 11, 12–13; and space programme, 316; spy training, 63–4; success of in USA, 6–7, 9, 121, 227–8, 264, 265–6; *Tech* articles on student life in USSR, 150–2; and tightened US security, 298–301, 339, 359; transferred to legal side (1934), 211, 212; and transpolar flights, 259–60, *260*, 261–2, 281–8, *287*, 290, 292–3, 372; at TsAGI, 325–7, 336–7, 376, 405–6, 409; with Tupolev in USA (1935), 227, 228–30, *229*, 233, 235, 236–7, 238, 242–3, 246; UNESCO post, 403, 423; use of American couriers, 300, 307; and world flying records, 263

Shumovsky, Tamara (second wife), 375–6
Shumovsky, Theodore (brother), 14, 43
Shumovsky, Vera (wife), 41, 375–6
Shumovsky, Yuri (son), 298, 312, 313, 341, 423
Shusha (city in Transcaucasia), 24–5, 27, 28–9, 30
Sikorsky, Igor, 21, 135, 244
Silvermaster, Nathan, 86, 195, 358
Simpson Thacher (US legal firm), 68
Sinclair, Upton, 86, 88–9, 90, 131, 193–4, 195–6
Sino-Japanese War (1931–45), 169, 207, 266–7
Smilg, Benjamin (LEVER), 225, 245, 297, 298–300, 339, 349, 362; family background, 20, 136, 141, 143–4; FBI investigation of, 138, 140–1, 318, 409; and 'flutter', 144, 262; at MIT, 136–41, *137*, 212, 254★, 308
Smolensk, 41–2, 337
Solomon Islands, 353
Solzhenitsyn, Alexander, 179
Song of Russia (MGM film, 1944), 360
Sorensen, Charles, 50
Sorge, Richard, 184–5, 190–1
Soviet Academy of Sciences, 132

Index

62, 83, 84–5, 155–9, 162–4, 170–1, 173–4, 179–87, 190–7; 'Mitrokhin Archive', 214; most highly valued sources, 134; naval operations in USA, 267; New York as US centre of, 147–8, 348; Ovakimian as legend of, 201–2, 407★; political intelligence, 62, 106–7, 348★; post-war collapse of in USA, 216; Primakov's career, 70, 71; Red Orchestra espionage ring, 206; smuggling of information, 147–8; spy training programme, 63–4, 153; SVR (Sluzhba Vneshney Razvedki) [Foreign Intelligence Service], 10, 57, 205; and US embassy in Moscow, 221–2, 223; use of ciphers, 180, 183, 184, 185; see also NKVD (also CHEKA/KGB); scientific and technological (S&T) espionage; Soviet students in USA

St Petersburg, 15, 17, 19

Stalin, Joseph: Anglo-French negotiations (1939), 317; and atomic bomb intelligence, 378, 379, 384, 389, 398–9; Aviation Day (1947), 1–2, 3–4, 418–19; Chkalov as favourite pilot, 277–9, 278, 293★; and Cyclone 9 engine, 213–14; defence of Tsaritsyn, 33, 35; and Dzerzhinsky, 51–3; Five-Year Plans, 53, 54–5, 56–7, 60–1, 62, 65, 67, 76, 82, 131–2; Great Purges/Terror (1937), 71, 199, 209★, 293, 294–8; hosts Bullitt at Kremlin, 220–1; and Japan, 207, 209, 219–20, 222–3, 224, 271, 291; modernisation of defence industry, 56, 57–8; and Nazi Germany, 272, 291–2; Nazi–Soviet Pact (1939), 316–17, 321–5, 331, 349; need for US friendship, 271, 276–7; orders murder of Trotsky, 258; and pilot safety, 328; plot to kill (1935) ('Kremlin Affair'), 158–9, 171, 172, 198, 256, 257, 258; and poison gas stocks, 168; receives *Japan On Fire* from Americans, 377–8; and Upton Sinclair, 193, 194; 'Socialism in One Country' policy, 105, 196; and Spanish Civil War, 272–3, 293, 294, 321; stays in Moscow (late 1941), 337; targeting of American universities, 6–7, 97–8, 99–100, 307–8, 350★; and technology gap, 6, 7–8, 42, 47–51, 57–60, 106, 170, 228–30; and Tupolev, 231; and Rowan's

Spy and Counterspy, 58, *59*, 406; and winter war with Finland, 319–20

Stalingrad, 352–3, 355, 374

Steffens, Lincoln, 84–5

Strassmann, Fritz, 380

submarines, 212

Sukhoy, Pavel, 152, 262, 263★

Sultanov, Khosrov Bey, 28–9

SVR (Sluzhba Vneshney Razvedki) [Foreign Intelligence Service], 10, 57, 205

Sweden, 56–7

Tamm, Igor, 382

Tankograd (Tank City), 136, 334–5, *335*

tanks, 109–11, 121, 212, 334–5, 338, 375; M-1931 Christie tanks, 109–11; T-34 tank, 111, 121, 333, 375; T-72 tank, 121

Tarr, Shifra, 257, 258

Taylor, C. Fayette, 127–8

Temple, Shirley, *261*, 261, 262

Tevosyan, I. F., 322

theatre, 89, 93

Trans-Siberian Railway, 180, 182

Trashutin, Ivan, 17, 120–1, 136, 151, 333, *334*, 334–5, 375

Trojan Powder Company, Pennsylvania, 106

Trotsky, Leon, 20, 37, 48, 256, 257, 258, 294, 310

'Trotskyists', 99, 156, 157–9, 197, 256–8, 297, 310

Troyanovsky, Alexander A., 213, 237, 281, 284–5

Truman, Harry S., 379, 400, 416

TsAGI (Soviet centre of aircraft design), 62, 249, 262, 321, 324; aerodynamic research, 327; Aviation Motor Institute, 326, 409; Bureau of New Technology (BNT), 325–7, 336, 376, 405–6, 409; evacuated to Kazan, 341; Flight Research Institute (LII), 324, 326, 409; and German invasion, 335–7, 341; as hub of intelligence networks, 327; Institute of Aerospace Materials, 326; Master's course in aviation, 122–4; and radiator weight problem, 323; research facilities repaired (1942-3), 375; return to

474

Index

Wilhelm II, Kaiser, 26, 57
wind tunnels, 124, 126, 127, 149, 236, 245, 246, 247, 323, 326, 375
Wisconsin, University of, 100
Wittenberg, Davrun, 384
Wolf, Felix, 193
Wrangel, Baron, 39, 161
Wright brothers, 125, 127, 213
Wright Field military research base, 128†, 141, 144, 246, 298–300, 362, 365, 409, 410

Yagoda, Genrikh, 222
Yakovlev, Alexander, 2†, 152, 322, 323
Yefimov, Mikhail, 12★

Yeltsin, Boris, 383
Yershov, Nikolay (GLAN), 304, 305, 306, 308, 309, 350, 358, 364; sent to London (1943), 365, 387, 391–2
Yezhov, Nikolay, 294
York, Jones Orin (NEEDLE), 249–54, 297, 298, 347, 349
Yumashev, Andrey, 259–60, *260*, *261*, 291
Zarubin, Vasily (MAXIM), 348, 350, 358, 387–8, 396, 397
Zeiss works, 206
Zhemchuzhina, Polina, 217–18
Zhukovsky facility, 313, 326, 327
Zhukovsky, Nikolay, 247